A Regionalism That Travels
Writings on (Mostly) Montana Arts

1975—2022

RICK NEWBY

Other Books & Exhibition Catalogs by Rick Newby

Poetry

A Radiant Map of the World ~ 1981. Montana Arts Council First Book Award.
The Man in the Green Loden Overcoat (with artist Jack Jasper) ~ 1983
Old Friends Walking in the Mountains (etchings by Doug Turman) ~ 1994
The Suburb of Long Suffering ~ 2002
Sketches Begun in My Studio on a Sunday Afternoon and Completed the Following Day Near the Noon Hour on the Lower Slopes of the Rocky Mountains ~ 2008

Cultural History/Visual Arts

Richard Swanson: Material Witness, Sculpture 1994–1998 ~ 1999
A Ceramic Continuum: Fifty Years of the Archie Bray Influence (with Peter Held, Chere Jiusto, Janet Koplos, & Patricia Failing) ~ 2001
The Most Difficult Journey: The Poindexter Collections of American Modernist Painting (with Ben Mitchell & Andrea Pappas) ~ 2002
Intimate Terrain: The Paintings of Michael Haykin ~ 2003
Humor, Irony and Wit: Ceramic Funk from the Sixties and Beyond (with Peter Held & John Natsoulas) ~ 2004
Perforation: Tony Marsh, Jeffrey Mongrain, Mary Roehm, Marit Tingleff, Xavier Toubes ~ 2005
The New Utilitarian: Examining Our Place on the Motherboard of Ceramics (with Dana Plautz) ~ 2006
New Works: Lawson Oyekan: Solstice Lip Series, Minneapolis (with Emily Galusha) ~ 2006
Dale Livezey: Paintings ~ 2007
Stephen Braun: Cause & Effect (with David & Janet Peoples) ~ 2007
Richard Notkin ~ 2008
Long Lines of Dancing Letters: The Japanese Drawings of Patricia Forsberg ~ 2008
Stephen De Staebler ~ 2008
Robert Harrison: The Architecture of Space (with Glen R. Brown) ~ 2009
Barry Hood: Flow ~ 2010
Joseph Baráz: Paintings & Sculpture, 1990–2011 ~ 2011
Persistence in Clay: Contemporary Ceramics in Montana (with Hipólito Rafael Chacón and Stephen Glueckert) ~ 2011
Matter + Spirit: Stephen De Staebler (with Dore Ashton and Timothy Anglin Burgard) ~ 2012
Jazz Icons: Wood Engravings, Woodcuts & Paintings by James Gilbert Todd, Jr. (with James Todd and Yvonne Seng) ~ 2012
West of True: Jane Waggoner Deschner & Gordon McConnell (with Marci

Advance Praise for *A Regionalism That Travels*

"If you want to understand the creative artists of today's Montana, read this book! Rick Newby, one of Montana's most insightful critics, guides us to a deeper understanding of the joys, relationships, challenges, and achievements of contemporary Montana writers, artists, collectors, and arts centers. Drawn from his years of passionate engagement with Montana art and literature, these selected essays illuminate the creative spirits and communities which continue to enliven our state and region."

— **Margaret Kingsland**, Executive Director,
Montana Committee for the Humanities, 1974–1995

"Creativity in all its forms calls to Rick Newby. He revels in original writing and visual arts from his beloved Montana. In the process he uncovers shadow traditions that defy stereotypes about the American West. Whether it's an irreverent surrealist movement, or a gifted poet living on an isolated ranch, or a Chinese American ceramics artist, or a painter combining Modernism with immersion in his home place, Newby asks us to pay attention to makers who live out cosmopolitan regionalism. Through these artful, spirited essays, he discloses a far more uncanny and diverse place than one might at first suppose. At a time when some call for a homogenized culture, Newby reminds us of the exuberance of a dynamic provincialism. I for one would not want to live in a place without the insights and eccentrics of Rick Newby's wonderful book."

— **Ken Egan, Jr.**, author of *Hope and Dread
in Montana Literature* and *Montana 1864*

"Rick Newby . . . is engaging Montanans in eloquent and insightful discussions on the art and artists of our time and region. Nothing is needed more right now for a popular appreciation of contemporary art than such a development of ideas and vocabulary."

— **Daniel Biehl,** Montana printmaker and sculptor

Rae McDade) ~ 2014

Theodore Waddell – My Montana: Paintings & Sculpture, 1959–2016 (with the Hon. Pat Williams, Robyn Peterson, Bob Durden, Donna Forbes, Gordon McConnell, et al) ~ 2017. High Plains Book Award, Art/Photography, 2018.

Provocative Clay (with Lena Vigna, Jo Lauria, Leslie Umberger, Beth Lipman, and Carmen Devine) ~ 2010/2022

Sandra Dal Poggetto: Immersive Landscapes ~ 2022

As Editor

On Flatwillow Creek: The Story of Montana's N Bar Ranch, by Linda Grosskopf ~ 1989

Writing Montana: Literature under the Big Sky (with Suzanne Hunger) ~ 1996

An Ornery Bunch: Tales and Anecdotes Collected by the W.P.A. Montana Writers' Project (with Megan Hiller, Elaine Peterson, & Alexandra Swaney) ~ 1999

A Most Desperate Situation: Frontier Adventures of a Young Scout, 1858–1864, by Walter Cooper; illustrations by Charles M. Russell ~ 2000

The New Montana Story: An Anthology ~ 2003

Crown of the Continent: The Last Great Wilderness of the Rocky Mountains, by Ralph Waldt ~ 2004

The Rocky Mountain Region, Greenwood Encyclopedia of American Regional Cultures ~ 2004

Food of Gods & Starvelings: The Selected Poems of Grace Stone Coates (with Lee Rostad) ~ 2007

Notes for a Novel: The Selected Poems of Frieda Fligelman (with Alexandra Swaney) ~ 2008

In Poetic Silence: The Floral Paintings of Joseph Henry Sharp, by Thomas Minckler ~ 2010

"The Whole Country was . . . 'One Robe'": The Little Shell Tribe's America, by Nicholas C. P. Vrooman ~ 2013

On the Chinese Wall: New & Selected Poems, 1966–2018, by Roger Dunsmore ~ 2018

A Regionalism That Travels
Writings on (Mostly) Montana Arts

1975—2022

RICK NEWBY

Foreword by Melissa Kwasny

DRUMLUMMON INSTITUTE
in association with
BAR R BOOKS
Helena, Montana
2024

A Regionalism that Travels
Writings on (Mostly) Montana Arts
1975–2022

Copyright © 2024 Rick Newby

Published by Drumlummon Institute, Helena, Montana
in association with Bar R Books

Cover design: Eric Heidle
Interior design: Geoffrey Wyatt, Wyatt Design, Helena, Montana

DRUMLUMMON
INSTITUTE

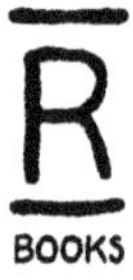

BOOKS

*Drumlummon Institute is a 501(c)(3) nonprofit that seeks to foster a deeper
understanding of the rich culture(s) of Montana and the broader
American West through research, writing, and publishing.*

All rights reserved, including the right to reproduce this book
or parts thereof, in any form, except for the inclusion of
brief quotations in a review.

Manufactured in the United States of America.
10 9 8 7 6 5 4 3 2 1

Correspondence:
Drumlummon Institute
PO Box 914
Helena, MT 59624

ISBN-13: 979-8-218-40509-0

Dedication

I dedicate this book to the memory of nine wonderful friends who have inspired and sustained me and who left this world too soon:

Poet, fiction writer, teacher, and pastor **Lowell Uda** (1938–2014) / attorney, philosopher, jazz impresario, and best friend **Robert F. W. Smith** (1949–1997) / publisher, editor, and mentor **Marnie Hagmann Pavelich** (1955–1997) / journalist and editor **Ric Bourie** (1954–2006) / all–around bookman and sportsman **Jeffrey W. Williams** (1954–2010) / anthropologist, folklorist, jazz composer and pianist **Alexandra Swaney** (1944–2017) / folklorist, historian, and raconteur **Nicholas C. P. Vrooman** (1949–2019) / librarian, archivist, jazz fan, tabla player, blacksmith, and birder **Christian Frazza** (1955–2020) / conservationist, filmmaker, author, and broadcast journalist **Brian Kahn** (1947–2020)

Foreword
Melissa Kwasny

"And in the springtime of the year, the blooms of lilac lend a cold perfume to our musical air," writes Rick Newby in his poem *The Suburb of Long Suffering*. I think of these lines this early June morning in the mountains, the cold rain pouring down, darkening the lilacs outside my window, and of the voice of my friend, the poet, rising above them, omniscient, lyric, yet also ironic, by which I mean at a historical – and sometimes humorous – remove, beginning a mythic story set in an ancient Chinese village, or of Franz Kafka at the Hotel Broadwater, or of a small congeries of artists in a Western provincial city: "Our beloved little suburb – built of brick and wood and stone – welcomes you. Nestled here at the base of this earthquake-shattered mountain, far from the great cities of this world, it strives to be charming, handsome, even cosmopolitan, an oasis in the Great American Desert. And we, its residents, find it so."

I met Rick in 1980, soon after graduating from the University of Montana, where he, too, had studied under the iconic poets Richard Hugo and Madeline DeFrees. He was living in a Victorian apartment on Helena's historic West side, in high-ceilinged rooms lined with hundreds of books: monographs on visual artists, collections of surrealist poets, novels by the European avant-garde, and row after row of first editions of Montana history and literature – not to mention his enormous jazz collection. I learned much later, and from reading his classic essay, "The Montana-Paris Axis, or Unpacking my Grandfather's Library," that many of these books were inherited from his maternal grandfather, a man "unrepentantly bookish," as Rick describes him, quietly yet defiantly challenging, with his "frontier erudition," the stereotype of the illiterate frontiersman. Only two years older than I, Rick was already established in a career and situated amidst passions that would focus the rest of his life, working at the Montana Historical Society as editor and researcher, writing poetry, making friends left and right with artists, writers, philosophers, and musicians, and co-publishing a literary journal called *Scratchgravel Hills*.

Poet. Essayist. Critic. Publisher. An old-fashioned public intellectual in the tradition of John Berger, Guy Davenport, and Rebecca Solnit. If you have been in Montana more than a few years, your knowledge of our arts and culture most likely comes from something Rick wrote, edited, or published, something he said publicly in a lecture or privately in a conversation, from a reading he sponsored or jazz he gave a stage to. For Rick, besides being a writer – the author of five books of poetry, over fifty catalogs, essays, and monographs on visual artists, including *A Ceramic Continuum: Fifty Years of the Archie Bray Influence* and *The Most Difficult Journey: The Poindexter Collections of American Modernist Painting* – is a celebrant, a tireless promoter of the work of others, and a generous sharer of enthusiasms. (Rick called me a poet long before I would ever have thought to do so.)

As co-editor, with Suzanne Hunger, of the game-changing anthology *Writing Montana: Literature Under the Big Sky* and editor of *The New Montana Story*, Rick sought to broaden and analyze assumptions about the state's literary and artistic canon by opening the field to those working in Eastern Montana, on ranches and smaller cities, to the lesser known, the overlooked, the undiscovered. He has championed the work of indigenous, gay, and, in particular, women writers. Bedrock to these endeavors is a philosophy of regionalism developed thoughtfully over many years, what he calls a "new provincialism," defined as the state of living far from urban centers of culture yet being open to, and searching out, new ideas from them, while at the same time paying strenuous attention to what is happening in one's backyard. Eager to move beyond a merely scenic and overromanticized depiction of the West, with its often-underlying anti-intellectualism, Rick re-imagines Montana as a site of diverse perspectives and experiences. Through his many contributions and achievements – he has been awarded both the Governor's Award for the Arts and the Governor's Award for the Humanities – his work complicates, as well as contextualizes, our sense of where we live.

Rick founded the Drumlummon Institute in 2006, and its accompanying online journal, *Drumlummon Views*, as a next step in his lifelong commitment to the intellectual life of his home state. The Institute published long out of print works by legendary Montana writers like Grace Stone Coates, Thomas Savage, and Frieda Fligelman; Nicholas C. P. Vrooman's groundbreaking history of the Little Shell band of the Chippewa, *The Whole Country was . . . "One Robe": The Little Shell Tribe's America;* and the important *Coming*

Home: A Special Issue Devoted to the Historic Built Environment of Butte & Anaconda, Montana, edited by Patty Dean. For those of us who love the arts, yet live far from each other in a state, even now, with no large newspapers or other media with regular coverage of contemporary art, no Harry's Bar or Les Deux Magots café to gather in, *Drumlummon Views*, which featured timely reviews and essays by some of Montana's best-known writers, gave us a place to meet.

A Regionalism That Travels is an apt title for this collection of essays. A regionalism that travels does exactly that, *it travels* – physically and imaginatively, on horseback and planes, through books and time, from international museums to ramshackle studios on ranches and galleries on the outskirts of our small towns. It is a regionalism that is enriched by the innovations of the larger world and, in turn, contributes its fair share of riches to it. "It has been my great pleasure to spend my life among artists: poets, storytellers, and novelists, painters and photographers, printmakers, book artists, and sculptors," Rick Newby writes in the introduction to this valuable archive, one I envision will take its place in courses in Montana studies, and on the shelves of many libraries, civic and personal, for generations to come.

Introduction

Rick Newby

Place for me is the locus of desire.
— Lucy Lippard, *The Lure of the Local*

This gathering of essays, articles, talks, and reviews is a straightforward record of more than four decades of writing about literary and visual artists. As it happens, many of the featured artists are based in my home state of Montana or have strong ties to Big Sky Country. Some of these texts might be called cultural journalism (book reviews, artist profiles, etc.), others are more scholarly explorations of cultural history, and still others are talks, prefaces, or introductions offering context for book projects in which I have had a hand as writer, editor, or publisher. In almost every instance, I have kept them as originally written.

It has been my great pleasure to spend my life among artists: poets, storytellers, and novelists, painters and photographers, printmakers, book artists, and potters, ceramic sculptors and sculptors working in steel, aluminum, glass, baling twine, straw, animal carcasses, cockleburs, and barbed wire. This book is a record of my enthusiasms.

If there is an overriding theme to *A Regionalism That Travels*, it is the notion that I've liked to call *cosmopolitan regionalism*, a term drawn from literary studies, but appropriate to all the arts. Here's how poet and scholar Jim Wayne Miller describes cosmopolitan regionalism: "a regional perspective which does not exclude a knowledge of the wider world, but is concerned with and appreciative of the little traditions within the great traditions of human history, and of ways in which small and great traditions are connected. . . ." In the monograph, *Theodore Waddell – My Montana: Paintings & Sculpture, 1959–2016* (Drumlummon Institute, 2017), I attempted to apply this notion to the works and philosophies of a trio of Montana painters, sculptors, and performance artists – Theodore Waddell, Patrick Zentz, and Dennis Voss – who first achieved notice in the 1980s:

> The Kentucky poet Wendell Berry has written wisely and well about a new sort of regionalism in the arts. In his essay, "The Regional Motive," he argues against a regionalism "based on pride, which behaves like nationalism" and

against a regionalism "based on condescension, which specializes in the quaint and the eccentric and the picturesque, and which behaves in general like an exploitive industry." Instead, Berry writes, "The regionalism that I adhere to could be defined simply as *local life aware of itself*," in which a person can bring to "bear on the life of [his/her] place as much as [he/she] is able to know."

This new regionalism, which might be called cosmopolitan regionalism, is the version practiced by Theodore Waddell and his fellow Montana contemporary artists in consciously countering a Montana art steeped in nostalgia and outdated mythologies. The most authentic representative of the old view was Charles M. Russell, but as historian Dan Flores argues, Russell's heartfelt regret at the loss of "our ancient connection to our life in nature" has since been appropriated and commodified into, in Wendell Berry's terms, an exploitive industry. Now, Flores notes, "the material objects of the Old West – the saddles, camp gear, boots and hats, firearms, the ethnographic detail of Indian life," not to mention paintings and bronzes of a "West That Has Passed" (Russell's term) and the wide-open landscape itself, have become highly marketable.

Instead of dwelling in a haze of nostalgia (and consciously ignoring broader trends in the art world), Montana rancher-artists Theodore Waddell, Patrick Zentz, and Dennis Voss, along with their distinguished modernist predecessors, Isabelle Johnson and Bill Stockton, have brought to bear on the life of their place everything they are able to know: all the skills needed to run a ranch *and* to make cutting-edge art; theories about minimalism, performance art, kinetic sculpture, and abstraction; a profound knowledge of the land and its limits; an abiding curiosity about the wider world *and* a passionate engagement with local history, traditions, and people.

Alongside my passion for a more worldly regionalism, I've long been deeply interested in the rise of modernism in both literature and the visual arts, and as a young poet, I was drawn to all the tradition-shattering innovations of the early modernist movements: Post-Impressionism, Cubism, Constructivism, de Stijl, German Expressionism, Dada, Merz, Surrealism, and all those other contending isms. While my study of modernism engendered in me, as poet, a sense of play and experimentation, I began, as a cultural journalist, to be fascinated by the stories of those who introduced modernist notions and methods to Montana arts. I had to search long and hard to find vestiges of modernism in Montana writing, but I discovered that modernist and postmodernist strategies and techniques abound among Montana's visual artists.

I am not a trained art historian, but because of my friendships and spirited conversations with ceramic artists from all over the world – potters and sculptors – in residence at the Archie Bray Foundation for the Ceramic Arts in my hometown of Helena, I began to write profiles of the artists whose works most intrigued me, for journals in the U.S., Australia, Great Britain, and Greece (see my profiles of "15 Ceramic Artists" in this volume). And then a pair of curators, Peter Held at the Holter Museum of Art, Helena, and Ben Mitchell at the Yellowstone Art Museum, Billings, asked me to write about two of the most important stories in the introduction of modernism within Montana's cultural fabric: the founding of the Archie Bray Foundation (I co-wrote this essay with ceramist and historian Chere Jiusto) and the creation of the Poindexter collections of American modernist painting at both the Montana Historical Society and the Yellowstone Art Museum. From there, I went on to write articles and catalog essays on a number of Montanans who work in non-ceramic art forms, painters, printmakers, photographers, and sculptors.

Although this is a book about "(Mostly) Montana Arts," I have included a group of essays titled "Ceramic Globalism." These essays range over some pretty diverse terrain: the rise of Funk ceramics in California; the individual genius of Berkeley sculptor Stephen De Staebler; the collision of the earthy ceramic arts with the digital world; the role of perforation in contemporary ceramic practice; two iconoclastic clay artists from Philadelphia and the Bay Area; the remarkable Nigerian-British sculptor Lawson Oyekan; and the impact of teaware traditionally made in Yixing, China, on a wide range of contemporary American ceramists.

You may ask, what do any of these subjects have to do with Montana? The truth is that this ceramic globalism – wildly diverse, internationalist, and endlessly innovating – had one of its beginnings in the wilds of Montana in the early 1950s. As I've written elsewhere ("Montana's Archie Bray Foundation for the Ceramic Arts: Origin and Impact," *Persistence in Clay: Contemporary Ceramics in Montana* [Missoula Art Museum, 2011]):

> A place, an idea, a set of experiences shared by hundreds, if not thousands, of ceramists: The Archie Bray Foundation for the Ceramic Arts – affectionately known as the Bray – has had a profound impact on the development of ceramics in Montana, in the United States, and around the world. As pre-eminent ceramics historian Garth Clark has written, "The Bray was without doubt the incubator for . . . the 'new ceramic presence,'" the modernist revolution in ceramic arts that emerged in the 1950s, primarily in the western United States. Montana's own Rudy Autio, one of the founding artists at the Bray (together with Peter Voulkos), once noted that "it all began in Montana," and specifically at the foundation headquartered in an old brickyard in Montana's capital city. . . .

> The Bray influence has been, and continues to be, positively viral, elaborating a vast (and intimate) network. Several past directors have become influential teachers, spreading the Bray spirit: Peter Voulkos (Otis Art Institute and UC Berkeley), Rudy Autio (University of Montana), Ken Ferguson (Kansas City Art Institute), Kurt Weiser (Arizona State University), and Josh DeWeese (Montana State University). . . .

> Former residents have started Bray-like residency programs as far afield as Berlin (Kaja Witt and Thomas Hirschler's Zentrum für Keramik) and Joseph, Oregon (Chris Antemann's LH Project, founded with her husband Jacob Hasslacher); other past resident artists now direct a variety of non-academic ceramics programs, including Wally Bivins (Pottery Northwest, Seattle), Bobby Silverman (the Ceramic Center at New York's 92nd Street Y), and Michio Sugiyama (Shigaraki Ceramic Cultural Park, Japan).

I remember speaking about Montana literature to a class on regionalism hosted by the Honorable Pat Williams and Dr. William Farr at the O'Connor Center for the Rocky Mountain West. The series' previous lecture had been about Montana's ceramic arts traditions, and the students seemed a bit bewildered by the apparent lack of a regional flavor in the work the lecturers had shown them. All I could tell the students was that the Montana ceramic tradition, the Montana Way, as it were, was this immensely sophisticated, vibrant approach that honored the clay works of many cultures, partook of many different aesthetic modalities, and resulted in intensely individual expressions.

I powerfully identify with my home state of Montana. And in the course of my writing life, I've only forged a greater appreciation for the people, the communities, and the natural environment that make this place worthy of love and respect. Given my particular tastes and predilections, what's most important to me are Montana's literary and visual arts traditions, their diversity, their balance between the local and the universal, their sheer beauty and energy, their refusal to give in to the worst kinds of retrograde mythologies.

My mother's family came to the Judith Basin in the early 1880s, settling in the little town of Geyser and starting up a sheep operation and, for a time, partnering up with Paris Gibson, the founder of Great Falls and the first president of the Montana Sheep Growers Association. Meanwhile, in those same years, my wife's family became central players in the Judith Basin Cattle Pool, where Charlie Russell cowboyed and the notion of the open range was made manifest. When I try to visualize their lives, I like to think of Joseph Kinsey Howard's assertion that Montana's "cultural isolation has never been so complete as some Montanans and far too many in other regions thought it was." Provincialism, in its negative, know-nothing sense, he added,

> would have been fatal on the frontier. To survive, the newcomers had not only to adopt some of the aboriginal customs . . . but also to seize eagerly upon anything else, from

anywhere, that would work, or even that might work – they were not afraid to try new things.

While shocks natural and unnatural – the terrible winter of 1886–1887 and the Silver Panic of 1893 among them – derailed our families for a time, they remained resilient, and later generations went on to become small ranchers, educators, businesspeople, artists, and environmentalists. More to the point, they retained that openness to new things Howard speaks of, they believed in progressive ideas, and they opposed, through action and word, the hostility some in Montana have always felt toward ideas, toward other races and religions, toward a culture that cherishes difference rather than tries to eliminate it.

I use the word "bookishness" frequently in this book; it is a quality I cherish because it signifies a fierce openness to all manner of cultural differences, forms of knowledge, and ways of being. At the time of this writing (June 2023), there are powerful forces in Montana that are intent on stamping out our bookishness (censoring what we can read), creating a White Christian Nationalist state (driving out the heretics among us), and stealing away the personal freedoms that make all the art and literature I write about in this book able to flourish. It is my great hope that all Montanans who retain a love for a Montana diverse, creative, and truly free will turn the tide against these dark forces.

A Regionalism That Travels
Writings on (Mostly) Montana Arts

Rick Newby

15 Ceramic Artists

Ceramic Globalism

Literary Matters

Richard Hugo's *Rain Five Days and I Love It*

Originally published in *CutBank* 5 (Missoula, MT), Fall 1975.

Rain Five Days and I Love It
Richard Hugo
Graywolf Press, Port Townsend, Washington, 1975
Poetry, unpaginated

More often than not, a chapbook bespeaks a cohesion (of subject and emotional intensity) rarely found in a full-length collection of poems, and this beautifully produced new chapbook by Richard Hugo is no exception. Comprised of eight poems printed on three colors of heavy stock and in three colors of ink, it draws its cohesiveness from a place – the Port Townsend area – and from Hugo's complex attitude toward that place. As he does so frequently and so well, Hugo grounds us in the richness of local detail, and then allows those details to speak. But through some manner of alchemy, the eloquence of things is not separable from the things themselves; in their very *being*, they cut deep, becoming emblems of the poet's emotional life, moving freely between the imaginative and experiential realms. In "Letter to Wagoner from Port Townsend," Hugo tells his fellow poet, "Here, the grass explodes and trees/ rage black green deep as the distance they rage in."

While Hugo's poetry, almost by definition, bursts with emotionality, these poems are most touching because they celebrate, they affirm that place and the life it holds within its boundaries, that "home between the forest and the sea," as Malcolm Lowry puts it, where "ferryboats would pass, ferrying song upstream." This affirmation finds its center, as it must, in that "crashing source," the sea. The first poem, "Port Townsend, 1974" gives us the seductive call of the sea, that call back to the womb, away from what Beckett calls the "great trouble":

> On this dishonored, this perverted globe
> we go back to the sea and the sea opens for us.
> It spreads a comforting green we knew when children –

❖   ❖   ❖

Aches of what we wanted to be and reluctantly are
play out in the wash, wash up the sand and die
and slip back placid to the crashing source.

But Hugo does not simply present us with the primordial image of sea as great equalizer; he knows we still have our lives to live – "The power/ to make us better is limited even in the democratic sea." These poems recognize the violence inherent in living one's life, the small slights, the bitternesses engendered, but they still seek the untroubled moments and when they find them, no questions are asked – there is "no real/ accounting for calm." Most markedly, this chapbook is filled with the inevitability of hope, the yearning for substance, for value – "Call those high birds hungry and your vision meat." Let Hugo speak his own affirmation, in a language that never hedges and thus rings true:

> Discovery of cancer, a broken back, our inability to pass
> our final exam – I guess the rain is finally getting me down.
> What matter? I plan to spend my life dependent on moon
> and tide and the tide is coming, creeping over the rocks,
> washing the remains of crippled fish back deep to the source,
> renewing the driftwood supply and the promise of all night
> fires on the beach, stars and dreams of girls, and that's
> as rich as I'll ever get. We are called human. C'iao. Dick.

Graywolf Press is to be commended for the publication of this beautiful chapbook. Not only is the level of craftsmanship remarkable, but there is something magical about an editorial staff with the good sense to give us these poems, poems that cohere not only to each other but to our lives as well.

Wally McRae's *It's Just Grass and Water*

Originally published in *Scratchgravel Hills* (Helena, MT), Spring 1979.

It's Just Grass and Water
Wally McRae
Regional Poets Series 1, Billings, Montana, 1979
Poetry, 44 pages.

> *I have been unable to escape the sense that I have been to the top of the mountain, and that I have looked over and seen, not the promised land vouchsafed to a chosen people, but a land of violence and sterility prepared and set aside for the damned.*
>
> – Wendell Berry,
> "The Landscaping of Hell:
> Strip-mine Morality in East Kentucky,"
> *The Long-Legged House*, 1969

In 1976, a McCone County, Montana rancher, Bob Yarger, self-published a record album entitled *Smoke 'n Ash 'n Promises*. Like the many albums of Appalachian folk music, it carries the distinct flavor of a place and of the people who live there: in this case, of an Eastern Montana threatened by uncontrolled coal development and of the ranch and farm folk who stand to lose everything in the wake of that development.

Wally McRae's *It's Just Grass and Water* stands in the same tradition as *Smoke 'n Ash 'n Promises*. An Eastern Montana rancher and Northern Plains Resource Council activist, McRae does not write poetry; he writes what he calls "verse." Reminiscent, at times, of the populist poetry of Robert Service and, at others, of the dramatic monologues of Robert Frost, his verse is filled with end rhymes, archaic and colloquial words, and equal doses of anger and humor. And like Yarger, McRae is committed to a way of life that, unless carefully protected, is destined to vanish.

McRae's verses could be easily broken down into neat categories: verses in celebration of his world ("The Land"); verses full of range wit and wisdom ("Clear and Still"); affectionate tales of the people and animals of the plains ("Jerry Kinzel"); verses describing the difficulties of ranch life ("Seasonal Labor"); and finally, verses of protest and anger ("The Mines, From the Strip Mines"). But such categorization would do violence to the unity of McRae's book. Each verse contributes equally to a picture of life on the edge of disintegration.

Eastern Montana has not yet become the "land of violence and sterility" Wendell Berry saw in East Kentucky, but it is only one step away. Listen to McRae in "Our Communion":

> Our bodies are this fertile land.
> This water is our blood.
> Our plains form our communion.
> Our god's organic mud.
>
> You'd load our bones on somber
> Black, unit funeral trains.
> Or burn them in cremation
> Pyres. Dachaus of the plains.

McRae's title *It's Just Grass and Water* aptly captures the contradictions that presently exist in Eastern Montana. On the one hand, it simply and directly describes the land he has come to love, and on the other, it is an equally simple recipe for *bullshit*. And McRae is determined to fight the stuff wherever he finds it. In "The Crisis," when the coal companies promise:

> Damn pristine air! There's water to spare!
> We'll lower your taxes for you.
> We'll pave all your roads. Help shoulder your loads.
> Their cajoling beats a tattoo.
> We'll build swimming pools and public schools –
> Build an empire upon your Plains .
> Just climb in with us, on our omnibus.
> Eat our truffles and drink our champagnes.

McRae responds:

> *On their shrill voices go. Drifting, sifting like snow.*
> *I resist them with all of my might.*
> *For their cloying, sweet song is grievously wrong.*

Wally McRae is not a great poet, nor does he pretend to be. In the final analysis, that doesn't greatly matter. His book is an important contribution to our discussion of the future of Eastern Montana because it is a *personal* document, a testament to and a defense of a way of life few of us know or understand. While it can be classified as folk art, it is not simply an artifact. It speaks out of a living tradition.

When McRae says, in "The Land":

> You'd ravish her with mindless lust,
> Then curse her for a whore.
> You've never loved her as I have,
> Or you'd respect her more.

we should listen very carefully. *It's Just Grass and Water* should be read by every Montanan who is interested in more than the inhuman "logic" of economic arguments.

In Praise of Provincialism
A Manifesto

Presented in the lecture series, "Written Locations: Views on Western Place," Regional Writers Project, Yellowstone Art Center, Billings, Montana, September 25, 1986.

I'm delighted to be back in my old hometown. And it is a great pleasure for me to speak here at the Yellowstone Art Center, beyond doubt the finest of Montana's art museums and home to the Regional Writers Project, the first such project in the nation and a boon to readers, writers, and small presses of this region.

When I was first asked to participate in the Regional Writers Project lecture series, I immediately began to worry about how I could appropriately address the avowed purpose of the series contained in its title: "Written Locations: Views on Western Place." I do not see myself as a regional writer, concerned primarily with evoking this place where we live, and I don't see the Montana writers I most admire as regional in that sense either. One critic has noted that my work "displays very few of the overt, tell-tale signs of 'Western' writing," and although I often use what might be called "regional" subject matter, I feel very far indeed from the new western realism, with its obsession with Western landscape and images of pickup trucks with loaded gunracks, gum-chewing cowgirls, fly-fishermen flailing snow-fed streams for monster trout, and violent encounters in smoky, dangerous bars.

Some of my favorite Montana writers write poems and stories even more radically dissociated from concerns about place, and yet they are, I believe, as much "Western" writers as those who are steeped in the details of their native region. I quickly realized, in thinking about this talk, that I needed a new term, something akin to "regional," but broader, more inclusive, and I stumbled upon that old word of French derivation, "provincial." Hence the title of my talk tonight: "In Praise of Provincialism."

My dictionary defines "provincialism" as "narrowness of mind, ignorance, or the like, considered as resulting from lack of exposure to cultural or intellectual activity." I don't much like that definition of the term, with its assumption of urban superiority and its contempt for those of us who live out here in the sticks, and so I have redefined provincialism, idiosyncratically to be sure, but in such a way that, I hope, gives at least a partial explanation for what it is that's shared by all of Montana's best writers, whether they write about this place or not. My definition of "provincialism" then: the condition of living far from the centers of established culture, where artists, in relative isolation, must draw upon inner resources rather than received ideas and have the opportunity and the innocence to produce works that are out of the mainstream, eccentric, vital, and alive.

Once I had seized upon provincialism as a signpost and a rallying point, I began looking around for some historical sub-stantiation for my rather reckless claim that a place as isolated and culturally impoverished as Montana sometimes is, can produce artists of substance. I found an essay on the American tradition of provincialism in literature, published in an excellent (and now-de-funct) little Connecticut journal called *Glitch*. The author, Robert Buckeye, writes:

> [T]he great American writers have, for the most part, worked in isolation; established community if that was necessary, even if community was just correspondence; found influence where they could or needed to: Herman Melville in Pittsfield, Massachusetts, Walt Whitman in Brooklyn, Emily Dickinson in Amherst, William Faulkner in Oxford, Mississippi, William Carlos Williams in New Jersey. . . . We have been and are a frontier people and our great writers are no different: every work beginning with the blank page, establishing its own rules in the writing. Our writer is as likely to depend upon experience, formal study, painting, or folk art, as much as he does upon other writers. In short, he brings to his work what is important to it, in terms of what he is and what he needs and wants, no matter how unlikely that might be.
>
> Even in [Montana], then, you can avoid the genteel tradition of secondraters; study the masters (if you can't lis-ten to a poet give a reading, you read his books, write him [or her], visit or if you can't, go to a gallery or a concert,

there are catalogs, records); find community (there is the phone, mail, Greyhound). You look out the window, talk to your neighbors, listen, read. You write.

There are provinces, and then there are provinces, those blessed with a genius of place, a kind of built-in muse. And Montana, today, seems to be one of the latter. In the last ten years, Montana has produced more than its share of fine writers (and painters and ceramists and woodworkers and photographers and jazz musicians). But perhaps most visibly, the Montana writers have attracted the kind of critical attention that all artists yearn for. James Welch's third novel, *Fools Crow*, before the first copies have even hit the bookstores this fall, is being hailed as a masterpiece. William Kittredge has been called the best Western short-story writer working today. James Crumley's beautifully crafted novels about love and alienation disguised as hardboiled detective stories have earned him the title, "heir apparent to Raymond Chandler." Tom McGuane's darkly comic novels are widely admired for their wit and fine prose. And Mary Clearman Blew's *Lambing Out and Other Stories* has been cited for its vivid and humane realism.

At last fall's Montana History Conference, the editor of the *New Mexico Historical Quarterly,* in introducing a panel of Montana writers that included fiction writers William Kittredge, Ralph Beer, and David Long and poet Paul Zarzyski, noted that the West is the hottest literary region going and that, of the western states, Montana and Texas are, by far, the most fertile breeding grounds for quality prose and poetry.

What is it, then, that makes Montana such a uniquely congenial home for writers? For one thing, Montanans have always been avid readers, and good writers need good readers. I work in the Montana Historical Society's publications office, and when we publish books, the University of Washington Press distributes them. We were startled to learn recently that the UW Press considers Montana, in proportion to population, its best market in the Northern Rockies, better than Idaho, Wyoming, or Oregon.

Besides having fellow citizens who are avid readers, Montana's writers are lucky to have a state literary tradition that is, though strong and nurturing, mercifully brief. Montana writers are free to create new worlds, they can write whatever they please, the possibilities are endless and seductive. The modern Montana literary tradition, to give a short and necessarily incomplete history, began in the 1930s when Myron Brinig was publishing his evocative novels about Butte's Jewish community, and Grace Stone Coates, hidden away in Martinsdale, was writing, like a latter-day Emily Dickinson, wry, witty poems about a life seemingly limited, but rich in imagination. In the same decade, H. G. Merriam, with the aid of Joseph Kinsey Howard, Grace Stone Coates, and others, began publishing the works of Montana writers in his acclaimed little magazine, *Frontier and Midland*, based in Missoula. Merriam believed strongly in the possibilities of a home-grown Montana literature, and although many of the writers he published have since faded from view, his vision has been an inspiration for succeeding generations. By the 1940s, A. B. Guthrie, Jr. and Dorothy Johnson were publishing their first works, and by the 1950s, both were acknowledged as masters of a gritty, well-researched, and lasting western realism.

It was during the 1960s, however, that Montana literature really came of age, with the firing-up of the creative writing graduate program at the University of Montana and the arrival of talented teachers and writers Richard Hugo, Madeline DeFrees, and William Kittredge. The writing program provided a training ground for young Montana writers, and Hugo, DeFrees, and Kittredge, by publishing their poems and stories in magazines like the *New Yorker, Atlantic,* and *Poetry Northwest*, began to put Montana on the national literary map. Hugo, above all, with his dark, sonorous, moving poems about the Milltown Union Bar (Laundromat & Cafe), about Indian Graves at Jocko, about that Lady in Kicking Horse Reservoir, made it possible for other writers to draw their themes and material from the Montana they saw around them, creating literature out of the raw materials of their daily lives. Other mature writers, drawn by rumors of a lively literary community in Missoula or by the state's natural beauty and unhurried pace, came to settle in Montana. Today Richard Hugo is gone, but his legacy, and that of Merriam and Coates, Guthrie and Johnson, lives on in a vital Montana literary community that encompasses Roundup and Billings, Helena and Havre, Livingston and Bozeman, Missoula and Kalispell.

Artists, of almost every medium, recognize Montana as a good place to work. There are accomplished painters in nearly every town, and because of the internationally famous Archie Bray Foundation for the Ceramic Arts in Helena and the presence of Rudy Autio at the University of Montana, Montana has an extraordinary number of skilled potters and ceramic sculptors. The Primrose Center, housed in a renovated factory in downtown Missoula, has brought top-flight furniture designers here, and sculptors like Debby Butterfield, Clarice Dreyer, Pat Zentz, and John Buck have ever-growing national reputations. And then there are all those writers. Why do all these artists stay in a place where there are too few collectors for their work, no publishing houses, scarcely any critics, and not enough galleries like the Yellowstone Art Center?

William Kittredge, in a recent interview, attributed it to the fact that Montana is "a humanly comfortable place to live." Other Montana writers, quoted in a *New York Times* article about the Montana writing scene, alluded to the "cheap rent." And *Newsweek* art critic Mark Stevens, in his October 1983 article about contemporary Montana artists, said that artists live and work here because "much of their energy [comes] from the landscape, that incredible 'house of sky' that Montanans use for a museum."

But I think Montana's attractiveness for artists also has to do with its provincial quality, its very distance from the frenzy of urban art scenes, where a new trend is born every minute and artists lack the solitude, the space, and the time to discover their own indisputably individual and eccentric visions. A couple of months ago, I was talking to Sarah Jaeger, a talented young potter at the Archie Bray Foundation, and she told me that she'd had an eye-opening experience on a recent visit to Denver, where she had worked for several years before coming to Helena. She had visited all of the Denver galleries that exhibit ceramics, and she quickly discovered herself becoming very bored: everybody's pots looked the same; they all might have come from the same mold. Sarah noted, too, that her own pots, since her arrival at the Bray, had grown looser, more expressive, more her own. Here I have no peers, she said, each of us at the Bray is pursuing an entirely different direction, we talk shop, but we never concern ourselves about the latest trend, except as something very distant and vaguely curious. Jack Walrath, the superb jazz trumpet player who hails originally from Rapelje, Montana, and who established his reputation as a member of Charles Mingus's last band, once said that he loves coming home to Montana to play with local jazz groups like the Nell/ Roberty/ Edwards Trio because they play so "weird." I think what Walrath means is that these Montanans, blessed with the innocence of provincials, have attained in their isolation a remarkable degree of freedom, irreverence, and originality.

The film critic and painter Manny Farber divides art into two categories: white-elephant art and termite art. White-elephant art, for which Farber has no patience, is that which, however well-crafted, is conventional, safe, and gutless and follows, in Farber's words, "a slow, embalming surface route." Termite art, on the other hand, is what I've been calling provincial art. Says Farber, "The best examples of termite art appear where the spotlight of culture is nowhere in evidence, so that the craftsman can be ornery, wasteful, stubbornly self-involved, doing go-for-broke art and not caring what comes of it." Termite artists take "private runways to the truth."

I want to talk now about two Helena-area writers who are producing termite art, who are quintessentially provincial, and whose work I admire greatly. The first, Ralph Beer, I understand will be speaking in this series sometime in the next two years and I urge you strongly to attend his lecture. Ralph is a fourth-generation Montanan living near Clancy, who divides his time between raising cattle and writing novels. By his own account, Ralph hasn't done that well as a rancher lately, as he's watched his feeder calves drop in price nearly thirty cents a live pound from 1972 to 1984. But this past year has been a very good one, indeed, for Ralph the writer.

He published a thoughtful and provocative essay, "Holding to the Land: A Rancher's Sorrow," in the September 1985 issue of *Harper's Magazine*, and soon thereafter he was named a contributing editor to that magazine. With the appearance of his article in *Harper's*, Ralph came to the attention of the national media generally, and he was interviewed on CBS News and NBC-TV's *American Almanac*. Ralph received national recognition again when he was awarded a $20,000 writer's grant from the National Endowment for the Arts. But Ralph's greatest coup was the publication of his first novel, *The Blind Corral*, released this spring by Viking.

Ralph Beer stands in a grand tradition, that of the Montana rancher who is also an exceptional artist. I am thinking here of such ranchers as the painters Isabelle Johnson of Absarokee and Ted Waddell of Molt, the writer-sculptor-painter Bill Stockton of Grass Range, and the sculptor and performance artist Pat Zentz of Laurel.

Something about ranching – whether it is the rancher's particularly intense and intimate relationship with his land, the long winters, or simply the isolation of rural life – lends itself to artistic production of a high order, and in Ralph's case, at least, to an art of extraordinary precision and quiet, deeply felt beauty.

The Blind Corral has received almost exclusively rave reviews: James Welch called it a "brilliant book"; the *Sewanee Review* declared it the "best first novel of the 1980s"; and James Crumley wrote, "*The Blind Corral* is the best novel I have read in a long, long time." But because *The Blind Corral* is such a provincial novel, it is sometimes misunderstood by those critics who are accustomed to evaluating works that follow "the slow, embalming surface route" characteristic of white-elephant art. Charles Salzberg, in his review of *The Blind Corral* published in the June 22 *New York Times Book Review,* complained that "what little action takes place in this contemporary western is all too predictable," that it is "short on dramatic tension" and is " too often heavily sociological." Pardon me, but Mr. Salzberg is a misguided fool. It is true that Ralph Beer has used the basic form of the contemporary western novel, and if I were to tell you the outlines of *The Blind Corral's* plot, it might sound cliched, but that is not the point.

Ralph has had the courage, derived no doubt from his provincial innocence, to take a conventional structure and subvert it, make it his own. Mr. Salzberg does note that Ralph is a "fine, evocative writer with a knack for the descriptive phrase," and in that only is he right. *The Blind Corral* is a good story, with strongly etched characters, a plot most of us would find sufficiently gripping, and equal parts of humor and drama, but more than that, and this no doubt is what Mr. Salzberg objected to, it steps outside its form to become a kind of love poem to a place and the people who live there. Ralph Beer is a fine, evocative writer who believes, with Mies van der Rohe, that "God is in the details," and *The Blind Corral* is filled with the details of life on a small Montana cattle ranch in the second half of the twentieth century. In crystalline prose, Ralph tells us the contents of the ranch's tack room, about the easy rhythm and hard work of a roundup, what it is like to clear brush and pick rock, and about the enormous, work-coarsened hands of an eighty-year-old man who is dying of emphysema but whose pride and will remain indomitable.

The Blind Corral might seem an anachronism were its world not so freshly seen; its people, contrary to most Americans' experience, are not faceless, alienated ciphers caught in a Kafkaesque nightmare of numbers and suburban ranchettes. Instead, they have lived on the same piece of rocky, beautiful ground for four generations, and in the process, they have developed ties with land and family that are difficult, indeed almost impossible, for most of us to imagine. Read Ralph Beer's book for its rich language, for its complex but ultimately hopeful vision, and above all, for its lovingly evoked landscape and people, and when you turn its last page, I can bet that you will feel, as I did, that you have discovered a new country, a Montana more real than the one in which we live and work every unseeing day. *The Blind Corral* is an important step in the evolution of Montana's literature, and by any standard worthy of the name, it is a magnificent novel. Ralph Beer is currently at work on a novella about Montana's first great woman rodeo rider, Fannie Steele. Let's hope his second book is as resolutely provincial as *The Blind Corral.*

The second provincial writer I want to talk about tonight is Bill Borneman of Helena. Bill, like Ralph Beer, comes from a rural background, having grown up on a farm near the little town of Leaf River, Illinois, but there the similarity ends. Ralph is always fiercely regional in his subject matter, while Bill, when I recently asked him if he thought of himself as a regional writer, said that, on that issue, he took the position of his three-year-old son, Karl. One morning, when Bill told Karl, "You live in the United States of America," Karl replied, "No, I live on the planet."

Like Ralph, Bill writes from what he knows best, but instead of ranch life, Bill draws his inspiration from linguistic philosophy, especially the work of Ludwig Wittgenstein, modernist and post-modernist art practice and theory, jazz and folk music, cutting-edge poetics, overheard conversations, and video. Although he has lived in Montana for the past fifteen years, Bill's wide-ranging curiosity makes him a true citizen of the planet. And yet, because of his provincial status, he brings to all of his work an extraordinary freshness, an innocence approaching silliness, and foremost, a bracing and infectious sense of humor.

To call Bill Borneman a writer is to give you only part of the man. In addition to his poems and stories, Bill produces drawings, collages, and mixed-media agglomerations of varying descriptions, he is an accomplished guitarist and songwriter, he creates sound-text tapes in his home recording studio, he runs Zetesis Books, my bookstore of choice, and for the past few years, he has published, with his collaborator Paul Piper of Missoula, an excellent literary journal that, for its first six issues, changed its name with each issue; it was called, in turn, *Zetesis 1, Popular Poetix 2, African Golfer 3, Wrld Wr 4, 1733 South Fifth West,* and *Multiples 6.* A true librarian's nightmare.

Bill is much more than a writer, and yet all of his multifarious works involve or invoke words. In a recent interview, Bill told me that he hasn't written a poem in years. "I think we can safely say," he said, echoing critic Jed Rasula, "enough has been written." Because he really believes (most of the time) that "enough has been written," Bill has turned more and more to techniques and forms that make use of what has already been written. It is not that he hates the written word (in fact, he is a voracious reader, and he once wrote that "a poem is an inoculation against the innocuous, a vaccine for vacuousness"), but that he seeks in all his activities to shake the word out of its old contexts, to make it shine forth as if newly minted.

He has set many poems to music, including works by e. e. cummings, Kenneth Patchen, William Wordsworth, Sir Thomas Wyatt, Robert Creeley, and Shinkichi Takahashi. He constructs visual poems, using favorite quotations from poets and philosophers arranged on the page as nearly abstract images constructed of typography and white space. And in a press release announcing his show of drawings and collages, "The: Daily Gri(n)d," he noted that many of his grid drawings, which often incorporate words, some for their literal meanings, some for pure texture, are meant to be "read" as much as viewed. "Whether there are words or not," he went on, "I want the viewer to 'read' the pieces. That's part of the strategy of working as small as I can. It forces you right up against the lines."

Bill is notorious for his fascination with the miniature, the tiny. In "The Daily Gri(n)d" press release, he explained, "I once heard someone remark, 'There is more going on of interest in one square inch of a painting by Jackson Pollock than there is in all the paintings in the Western Rendezvous of Art put together.' That got me think-ing. I figured I'd better start with a square inch and work my way up. Then I discovered that I love small squares."

Another of Bill's projects, entitled "Acoustic Disturbances," is made up of two-word units, hundreds of them, handsomely ar-ranged on the page. "Acoustic Disturbances" is introduced by an ep-igram from Walt Whitman: "Two little breaths of words comprising it,/Two words, yet all from first to last comprised in it." "Acoustic Disturbances" reads something like this: "Crystal Palace. Polyester candy. Radio Shack. Licorice schtick. Poetic crapioca. Aqua Velveeta. Hard shell. Soft core. Ad diction. Buy now! Pay Forever! Titillating Adverteasing. Putrid perfumes. Familiarity breeds. Two words! Never more!"

Bill's passion for the small has grown increasingly obsessive, and when I recently offered to edit his journals, which comprise twenty-six volumes of rough sketches, drafts of poems and stories, bits of sentences, and solitary words, he said, "Fine, my only stipu-lation is that you reduce it down to what can fit on a bumper sticker or, at most, a postcard," which led him to enthuse about his latest project, a series of one-of-a-kind postcards he calls Post-Art cards.

Bill is very big on projects, having followed his own advice to "arrange the contexts of your life such that you are always working on a project – whatever you're doing," and my favorite Borneman project is what he calls his "Desk Blotter Series," twelve monthly calendars he decorated over the course of one year with drawings, quotations, orig-inal aphorisms, found images, the odd accidental ink spot, tiny paint-ings, photographic self-portraits, and poems like this one:

> The long white-gloved hand of death
> reaches for the phone,
> dials your number. You are not at home.
> She lets it ring and ring.
> You're coming home, late,
> drunk, stoned, dejected.
> A. You enter and answer.
> B. Death hangs up just as you answer.
> C. Fumbling with the key,
> you mutter, "Damned phone . . Shut up . . ."

As someone wrote of Kurt Schwitters, Bill Borneman's "very eclecticism is that of an outsider, of someone independent of a mainstream taste," and his provincialism has given him "a happy freedom of mobility" and led him to an extreme originality. And like Ralph Beer, Bill has taken established forms and techniques – like the appropriation of images and words, collage, and the standard song – and made them his own by bringing to "his work what is important to it, in terms of what he is and what he needs and wants, no matter how unlikely that might be."

Unfortunately for us, Bill's difficult, irreverent, crude, silly, philosophically rigorous, and oftentimes beautiful termite art is not readily available. He has published only one book, the handsome catalog to his "Daily Gri(n)d" show, limited to an edition of thirty copies. He publishes reviews of records, books, and the performing arts in various difficult-to-obtain specialty journals. And his poems, visual poems, and (now that it has a cassette magazine edition) songs appear in *Exquisite Corpse*, the literary magazine published in Baton Rouge, Louisiana, by expatriate Romanian surrealist, Andrei Codrescu.

But for those of us who value Bill's antic provincial spirit, there is still hope. Last year, Bill received a grant from the Helena Film Society's Grants to Artists program to record and produce a tape of his original musical compositions, and Second Story Verlag, the press that brought out my own, and Jack Jasper's, *The Man in the Green Loden Overcoat,* is considering publishing Bill's "Acoustic Disturbances." Watch for these Borneman projects.

I chose to speak tonight about Bill Borneman and Ralph Beer because their work is an ever-present inspiration to my own. But there are many other distinctive writers within the provincial confines of this state who could have served to illustrate my point as well. I urge you to seek out their books – in your favorite bookstore or here, through the Regional Writers Project. I think I can promise that, once you sit down to read, you will not go unrewarded.

David Quammen's *Blood Line*
Stories of Fathers and Sons

Originally published in in *North Country Review* (Billings, MT), May/June 1989.

Blood Line: Stories of Fathers and Sons
David Quammen
Graywolf Press, St. Paul, Minnesota, 1988
Short fiction, 192 pages

In recent years, David Quammen has proven himself to be one of Montana's most gifted, versatile, and prolific young writers. The author of three well-received novels, *The Zolta Configuration, To Walk the Line,* and most recently, *The Soul of Viktor Tronko,* Quammen is best known for two collections of science essays drawn from his regular column in *Outside Magazine, Natural Acts* and *The Flight of the Iguana: A Sidelong View of Science and Nature,* just published by Delacorte Press. A frequent contributor to the *New York Times Book Review* and *Harper's,* Quammen was honored in 1987 with the National Magazine Award in Essays and Criticism. And now, with the publication of *Blood Line,* the Bozeman resident reveals his mastery of the short story form.

Set in Texas, Oregon, Mississippi, New England, and Montana, the three stories in *Blood Line* bring something rare to contemporary American fiction: An uncanny combination of superb storytelling, technical virtuosity, and extraordinary richness of emotion. Put simply, Quammen's stories are a joy to read, neither clever to the point of vacuity nor so understated as to communicate only oblique despair. These meditations on the profound connections between fathers and sons draw their energies, themes, and techniques from the grand tradition of the American short story, and yet they remain undeniably Quammen's own.

"Walking Out," the collection's first and perhaps best story, is the gripping tale of a father and his eleven-year-old son who climb into Montana's Crazy Mountains intent on shooting a bull moose and find instead death and a final, tragic understanding. As the story opens, the son, David, arrives in Livingston for a hunting trip with the father he both loves and fears. His parents are divorced, and except for his annual visit to Montana, he lives with his mother, that "fine beautiful lady" in Chicago. The father, never healed from the divorce, makes David the scapegoat for the grief and rage he still nurses. Overweight and insecure, afraid of his father's "solitary and characteristic bitterness," David, reluctantly – out of guilt and love – agrees to the hunt in the Crazies.

And as father and son bushwhack into the mountains, the story unfolds, quiet and disquieting. With shame, the boy recalls his ineffectual attempts to hunt blue grouse the year before; the father talks of his own first hunting experiences and how they left him shattered; the boy suffers sleepless through cruelly cold nights; they encounter a male grizzly with its aura of power and terror and authority; they stumble upon the carcass of a moose, bullet-riddled and "left to rot."

On the hunt's final day, they awaken to a fresh snowfall, and to the city boy, relieved to be almost free of the rigors of the hunt, the snow-clad woods seem "mysterious and benign and somehow comic." And then things go terribly wrong. In a scene of unbearable power, the boy's hand is savagely bitten by a grizzly cub and, minutes later, he accidentally shoots his father, shattering his knee. The long walk out begins, and a tragic and strangely healing new stage in the bond between father and son. No mere paraphrase can capture the compelling movement, the rich texture, the sheer readability of "Walking Out." Suffice it to say: This haunting, beautifully written, and uncompromisingly compassionate story should place David Quammen – once and for all time – in the august company of those American writers whose works truly matter.

The final two stories in *Blood Line* – "Nathan's Rime" and "Uriah's Letter" – reveal many of the virtues found in "Walking Out," but they don't share the same emotional poignancy. Both are ingeniously constructed, riveting spellbinders, but they seem more literary than "Walking Out," more distanced and dispassionate. And the relations between fathers and sons in these stories are darker, less resolved, less humane. "Nathan's Rime," with its Southern setting, its snakes and pigs and Baptist deacon and recurring images of decay, hints at the Gothic horror and humor of William Faulkner and faintly echoes the morbidly comic Hemingway story, "An Alpine Idyll." Nathan, abused and neglected by his snakeloving "daddy" throughout his childhood ("he was a man I did not like . . .") cannot escape the ties that bind sons to fathers. Even his father's death does not free him, and as "Nathan's Rime" begins, he is compelled to talk, "like a shrew eats," about a past that will not stay well buried.

William Faulkner's ghost arises again in "Uriah's Letter." Set in Hadrian, Mississippi, only a few miles from Oxford, Faulkner's hometown, and bearing all the telltale marks of the Faulkner style – long, riverine sentences, multiple narrators, memories of a heroic Civil War past, a spinster embittered by lost love, feuds between families, and rumors of incest – this novella-length story might almost have sprung from the pen of the Mississippi master himself. With uncanny exactitude (and undoubtedly as homage to a literary father for whom he has abiding respect), Quammen has written a story that could easily slip into the canon alongside such classic short novels as *Spotted Horses* and *The Bear*. In "Uriah's Letter," fathers – abandoned by their own parents – callously dispose of their sons (and daughters) in efforts to avenge ancient slights. Blinded by ambition and hate, they leave their children clinging "from habit not even to the defeat or the desolation, but to the very habit of clinging." Astonishing in its virtuosity, always suspenseful and rich in the darkest of humors, "Uriah's Letter" brings *Blood Line* to a satisfyingly Gothic close.

Anyone who cares about the fate of Montana literature will want to own David Quammen's remarkable first collection of short fiction.

Montana Spaces
Essays and Photographs in Celebration of Montana

Originally published in *North Country Review* (Billings, MT), May/June 1989.

Montana Spaces
Essays and Photographs in Celebration of Montana
Edited and with an introduction by William Kittredge
Photographs by John Smart; wood engravings by Emma Joy
    Dana
Montana Land Reliance, Helena/Nick Lyons Books, New York,
    1988
Essays, 198 pages

Montanans celebrate 100 years of statehood this coming year, and if the centennial results in nothing more than this superb collection of essays and photographs, it will have been profoundly worthwhile. Intended to celebrate Montana's first century and to "encourage a better understanding of the state and its heritage," *Montana Spaces* was conceived of and sponsored by the Montana Land Reliance, a nonprofit land trust founded by Montana ranchers and farmers to protect, through conservation easements, the state's "ecologically significant ranchlands."

Concerned always with quality, whether of the landscape or of literature and the photographic image, the Land Reliance placed its centennial project in able hands. Editor William Kittredge, one of the state's leading men of letters, has gathered together personal reflections, reminiscences, and essays about Montana and its spaces by nineteen writers who either live here or have strong ties to the state, among them such literary luminaries as Thomas McGuane, William Hjortsberg, Wallace Stegner, Gretel Ehrlich, Ralph Beer, David Quammen, Mary Clearman Blew, and David Long. And Helenan John Smart, whose photographs reside in the collections of the Art Institute of Chicago and New York's International Center of Photography, has contributed a portfolio of twenty-eight black-and-white images that capture the Montana landscape, and fabled Montana barrooms, with a sensitivity, exactitude, and sheer beauty that have rarely if ever been equaled.

In his introduction, editor Kittredge sketches, with quick,

incisive strokes, Montana's extraordinarily rich literary history. Montana storytellers, white and Indian, its novelists, poets, and essayists, notes Kittredge, help us to understand and celebrate ourselves and this place in which we live. Kittredge has written elsewhere that the "art of a region begins to come mature when it is no longer what we think it should be." Many of the nineteen essays in *Montana Spaces*, explicitly or by implication, subvert the received myths about Montana and the Wild West (as do much recent fiction, poetry, painting, and sculpture created here). No longer, these essays seem to say, is it valuable, or even healthy, to continue to glorify and idealize the Montana of dime novels and TV westerns.

As Ralph Beer writes in his essay "In Spite of Distance," we must resist, in our art and our lives, the "primitivism of mountain men, the romance of 'saving the ranch' and a chivalric code that rides exclusively on horseflesh at the expense of 'helpless' women." And after all David Long adds, in "Straight to the Actual," his fine study of Montana's contemporary visual artists, the "myths about the American West were largely manufactured, only ever true in severely limited ways, and so contradictory as to be no help at all."

After calling for an art that goes "straight to the actual," Long asks a pertinent question: "But what is the actual in our time? Wilderness or clearcut? Amber waves of grain or Minuteman silos?" The answer may well be: All of the above. The essays in *Montana Spaces* serve up slices of radically divergent actualities, the best of them probing beneath the surface of things to uncover subterranean, and often painful, truths about our Montana predicament.

In "Runoff," for example, Tom McGuane writes, in limpid prose, about fishing southwestern Montana's blue ribbon trout streams in early spring and exercising fish "whose memory has been dulled by the long winter." But though McGuane's essay is about pleasure, the pleasures of "three nice browns in a row," quiet water, and warm memories of a fly-fishing grandfather, it is also about an anger peculiarly Montanan: "I was thinking how many angry people, angry faces, you saw in these romantic landscapes. It was as though the dream had backfired in isolation."

That Montana rage McGuane speaks of, and the despair that so frequently attends it – products of 100 years of living on the periphery of American life, far from the centers of power, of being colonized, victimized, strip mined, and clearcut for the greater good of somewhere else – rear their heads in several other essays. Rancher Bill Stockton of Grass Range, one of the state's finest painters, expresses outrage most vehemently in "The Ghost Towns of My Time," a clear-eyed recitative of the violence done to Montana agriculturalists by railroads, politicians, and bankers. Don't bother to ranch, Stockton advises: "you can make a better living on welfare." Another rancher, poet Scott Hibbard, suggests that soon ranches will survive only as theme parks, relics of a vanished past. Hibbard later retracts this worst-case scenario, declaring that ranching can never die because it is "inseparable from the American character and imagination," but his despair is almost palpable.

To be victimized means, all too often, to victimize someone else, or to indulge in self-destruction. And as Mary Clearman Blew starkly points out in her account of a visit to Wahkpa Chu'gn, the *pishkun* or buffalo jump near Havre, the unrelenting vandalism of this prehistoric site suggests our refusal to acknowledge the role white Montanans have played in genocide, the suppression of the state's Native American cultures. Something lives here "that cannot examine itself," she writes, and "rather than admit it has a past – and therefore guilt – and mortality – it shuts itself away in indifference, or drunkenness, or chauvinism . . . ready to lash out on any provocation or hint of a threat." We must accept our past, Blew implies, before we can truly call this place home.

Rage, despair, and guilt are not the only themes sounded in *Montana Spaces*. William Hjortsberg writes, with great wit and insight of "The View from My Window"; Tim Cahill's "On the River of Cold Fires" turns a disastrous fishing trip into high comedy; and in "More than Skin Deep," Glenn Law examines his own love affair with Montana. Gretel Ehrlich's "River History" takes us on a spiritual, almost Zen-like journey through the Absaroka Mountains; Robert Sims Reid speaks of geology and paleontology and his own Midwestern roots; and in "The Gatekeepers," Beth Ferris writes movingly of a summer spent among the mountain goats of Glacier National Park. Ellen Meloy's ironic voice masks a deep fear that Montana's wild spaces will suffer the same fate as those in her native California; Charles F. Waterman recounts "Thirty Pretty Good Years" of hunting and fishing in Montana's mountains and streams;

and Alston Chase makes sense of sibling rivalry in "The Great White Trout."

But of all the pieces in *Montana Spaces*, four essays testify most tellingly to the growing maturity of Montana letters. In "Homestead," filmmaker Annick Smith writes, in beautifully detailed prose, of the loss of a husband, of the cherished homestead they had built together in the Blackfoot Valley, and of the healing that comes in dreams. David Quammen's "Strawberries Under Ice," ostensibly an essay on the properties of frozen water, is a complex meditation on the fragility of life and love, friendship and those "spectacular bits of Montana" Quammen claims as his own. Loving Montana "with pain and fear and pity" and yet desiring to live nowhere else, Quammen concludes, with the Russian mystic Leontiev, that only by placing it under ice can this troubled state be saved.

In Patrick Dawson's "Glory Holes," a family history unfolds, the story of five generations of Montanans: prospectors, homesteaders, uranium miners, ranchers, writers who "can't quite shake the illusion that the land still holds promise," seduced by the state's natural beauty and "most of all by our own brief history." A slice of that brief history comes alive in Wallace Stegner's delightful "That Great Falls Year." In a book in which almost everyone else writes of ranch life, wilderness, the rural, Stegner gives us an image of urban Montana circa 1920 as seen by an eleven-year-old boy fresh from the prairies of Saskatchewan. In Stegner's masterful hands, this tale of his own first encounter with lawns, sidewalks, electricity, and the disorienting rituals of city schooling resonates with wonder, compassion, and human connection, illuminating a realm of the Montana actual too often overlooked.

The essays in *Montana Spaces* create a richly textured image, and John Smart's twenty-eight photographs – superbly reproduced on the finest paper – only add to the verisimilitude and unruly beauty of that image. Ranging over the state from Grass Range to Porcupine Butte, from the Big Hole to the Missouri Breaks, Smart eschewed all the clichés of western landscape photography, saw with his own eyes, and went straight to the actual. Standing in the tradition of Stieglitz, Ansel Adams, Edward Weston, and most recently Robert Adams, Smart's subtly nuanced images present us with a new vision of our state, deeply felt and inescapable.

For producing *Montana Spaces*, the Montana Land Reliance deserves our gratitude. This important book is cause for celebration, centennial or not.

All Lessons are Fatal
Contemporary Montana Poetry, 1964–1989

A Talk

> Originally presented, in somewhat different form, during the
> panel on Montana poetry at *The Last Best Place* Conference,
> Carroll College, Helena, Montana, March 1989. This talk was in-
> tended as an introduction to, and critique of, the contemporary
> poetry section of the bestselling *The Last Best Place: A Montana
> Anthology* (Helena: Montana Historical Society Press, 1988). Also
> appearing on the panel were Montana poets Ripley Schemm
> Hugo, Paul Zarzyski, Dennice Scanlon, and Dave Thomas. A ver-
> sion of this essay was subsequently published in *North Country
> Review* (Billings, MT), Winter 1990.

Almost precisely twenty-five years ago, in the fall of 1964, Richard
Hugo arrived in Missoula to teach the writing of poetry at the
University of Montana, replacing the legendary and controversial
Leslie Fiedler. That same year, the University of Washington Press,
with its publication of the slim anthology, *Five Poets of the Pacific
Northwest* (featuring the work of Hugo, Kenneth O. Hanson, Carolyn
Kizer, David Wagoner, and William Stafford), served notice that this
region of the country was a hospitable environment for the writing
of expertly crafted and deeply human poetry. For many years, noted
the anthology's editor Robin Skelton, "the dominant feature of the
[Northwest's] poetic environment . . . was the presence of Theodore
Roethke . . . teacher and visionary. . . ." Roethke, the renowned poet
and professor of creative writing at the University of Washington in
Seattle, Skelton went on to argue, had had a much greater impact on
the region's poets than had its geography, geology, botany, and local
linguistic quirks combined. Through his exacting attention to detail,
his insistence on precise craftsmanship, wrote Skelton, Roethke had
led each youthful poet under his charge "toward the discovery and
exploitation of his unique voice."

Although the Dick Hugo who arrived in Missoula that autumn
twenty-five years back – an extraordinarily insecure man, untested
as a teacher, on the verge of divorce – would never have believed it

possible, his impact on Montana's poets and the state's poetic climate would be at least as powerful as Roethke's had been in Washington and Oregon. With Hugo's arrival in Missoula, Montana poetry could begin to come of age. Certainly, the state had already produced poets of talent (primary among them, the proto-feminist Butte writer, Mary MacLane, whose Whitmanesque celebrations of herself sometimes had the off-kilter charm of surrealist prose poems, and Grace Stone Coates, hidden away in Martinsdale, writing, like a latter-day Emily Dickinson, wry, witty poems about a life seemingly limited, but rich in imagination). And certainly, Leslie Fiedler had introduced Montanans, with a vengeance, to the difficulties and pleasures of modernist literature.

But Dick Hugo was the real thing: a living, breathing poet who quickly discovered that he loved to teach. As quickly, once they had heard of his humor, his warmth, his sly and merciless insights, students flocked to his classes. And they came to love this heavy-set man with the booming laugh, who looked, as he liked to brag, more like a truckdriver than a poet. For those who want a closer glimpse of Hugo the man, I recommend his posthumously published autobiography, *The Real West Marginal Way*, edited by Ripley Schemm Hugo and Jim and Lois Welch. In these autobiographical essays, Hugo was at his most naked, stripped of the masks he sometimes wore in his poems, and the book is enormously moving, at times hugely funny, "an extended meditation," writes William Matthews in his introduction, "on the relationship between the life and the work."

If you are interested in what Dick Hugo taught in his legendary writing workshops, you can turn to his collection of lectures and essays on poetry and pedagogy, *The Triggering Town*, published in 1979. And then, of course, there are the poems, in the eight individual volumes – from *A Run of Jacks* to *The Right Madness on Skye* – and in *Making Certain It Goes On: The Collected Poems of Richard Hugo*.

As Hugo's reputation grew, and more and more young writers came to Missoula for the privilege of studying with him, the University began to build a creative writing program. By the end of the 1960s, fueled by Hugo's popularity, the program had four full-time faculty members: two fiction writers, William Kittredge and Earl Ganz, Hugo, and another poet of quieter disposition but equal skill, Madeline DeFrees. A member of the Congregation of the Sisters of the Holy Names of Jesus and Mary until 1973, Madeline brought to her work a passion for scholarship, a meticulous sense of craft, and a love of the dense music of Gerard Manley Hopkins' poetry. Described as "cerebral, witty, and learned" by Pulitzer Prize winner Carolyn Kizer, Madeline leavened Dick Hugo's passionate embrace of the unfettered verbal imagination with an almost philosophical search for meaning and a playful, but exact sense of form. Both poets shared a love of the patterns sounds make, and while many of Hugo's poems emerged out of encounters with "triggering towns" – as he said, "the place triggers the mind to create the place" – Madeline writes of "imaginary ancestors," figures – historical or familial – to whom she feels a strong connection. In "Emily Dickinson and Gerard Manley Hopkins," for example, the two virginal and lonely souls take a formal cruise together; after all, DeFrees writes, "these brief affairs we label mid-Victorian,/ seduce the timid soul of wit's historian." A demanding and compassionate teacher, Madeline has published five books, including *When Sky Lets Go* (1978) and *Magpie on the Gallows* (1982). In the early 1980s, she left Montana to become Director of the Creative Writing Program at the University of Massachusetts at Amherst; she has since retired to Seattle, Washington.

A quick glance through the contemporary poetry section of *The Last Best Place* reveals the profound influence of Richard Hugo and Madeline DeFrees on Montana's poets. Of the thirty-two poets anthologized, twelve studied with the two poets, two – Ripley Schemm Hugo and the late Matthew Hansen – are members of Hugo's family, and then there are Hugo and DeFrees themselves. On the other hand, the remaining sixteen poets underscore the diversity, complexity, and richness of this state's poetic universe, and there are even those among the duo's students who stand outside what might be loosely called the University of Montana poetic tradition. Roger Dunsmore, for example, despite completing his Master of Fine Arts (MFA) under Hugo and DeFrees, early repudiated the strain of modernism they represented in favor of his own variant influenced by the American Zen poems of Gary Snyder (whose *Turtle Island* won the Pulitzer Prize for Poetry in 1975), classical Greek lyrics, and Native American song. As a professor in the University of Montana's Humanities program since the late Sixties and as a participant there in experimental Native American and environmental studies programs, Dunsmore has influenced many young writers. I, for one, claim Roger as my first poetry teacher, and his concerns, particularly his curiosity about and compassion for other cultures and his use of archival documents in his poems, have influenced my work deeply. Dunsmore's books include *On the Road to Sleeping Child Hotsprings* (1977), *The Sharp-Shinned Hawk* (1987), and *Blood House* (1987).

Other poets found their way to Missoula to teach for a quarter or a year while Hugo or DeFrees was on leave. These poets, among them Joan Stone, Tess Gallagher, John Haines, William Pitt Root, and Naomi Lazard, left their mark on students, wrote poems that added something to Montana literature, and moved on. Other poets – like Patrick Todd and Robert Sims Reid – received their MFAs in poetry from the University and made their homes in Missoula. Another Missoula poet, Dave Thomas, "traveled the old hippie, beatnik axis," working as a gandy dancer and construction worker, operating almost entirely outside the orbit of the university and its writing program.

And of course, Montana poetry hasn't meant only the Missoula writing scene. Ken McCullogh, author of *Migrations* and *Creosote,* taught at Bozeman's Montana State University during the early 1970s, and since 1975, Greg Keeler, witty poet and songwriter, has held the poet-in-residence chair at MSU. Bill Hoagland teaches at Northern Montana College, Minerva Allen works as a school administrator on the Fort Belknap Indian Reservation, Ed Lahey is a powerful voice from Butte, another Butte native Dennice Scanlon teaches school in Anaconda, folk poet Don Manker calls Broadus home, Paul Zarzyski cowboys near Augusta, and Wally McRae, the best-known of the contemporary cowboy poets, runs the Rocker 6 Ranch on Rosebud Creek.

Many of the other poets in *The Last Best Place* might be called Montanans in exile, living as far afield as San Diego and Anchorage, or as close by as Rock Springs, Wyoming, and Lewiston, Idaho. And then there are the Montana poets whose works didn't make it into the anthology, poets like the members of the Flatwillow Philosophical Society, who gather irregularly at the N-Bar Ranch near Grass Range to share their work (among them Wilbur and Elizabeth Wood of Roundup and N-Bar rancher Tom Elliott), and the former Helena-area poets Melissa Kwasny (now in San Francisco) and Susan Watson.

Watson, currently living in Greenwich, Connecticut, received the 1982 Montana Arts Council's First Book Award for her poetry collection *Birds That Stay*.

Even the briefest history of contemporary Montana poetry must include some mention of Montana publishing. Certainly, many of the poems included in *The Last Best Place* first appeared outside the state's boundaries, in periodicals like *The New Yorker* and Seattle's *Poetry Northwest* and in books published by houses in New York, Georgia, Idaho, and Washington state. But a number of the poems had their first publication in Montana magazines and in books created here; often those poems published in-state were written by the poets who stand on the margins of mainstream Montana poetry, the outsiders, the eccentrics, the anti-modernists, and the post-modernists, writers like Roger Dunsmore, Dave Thomas, Linda Weasel Head, Wally McRae, and a host of others lesser known.

Between the early 1970s and the early 1980s, Montana literary publishing was extraordinarily vital, a reflection no doubt of the energy flowing from the state's writing scene at the time. The University's writing program was at its peak, rated as one of the best in the nation; Dick Hugo had achieved national recognition, including a nomination for a National Book Award and appointment as editor of the Yale Younger Poets series; and the word had gotten out: Montana – Missoula, in particular – was a mecca for poets. The publishing explosion began with the founding of *CutBank,* the University's literary magazine, in 1972; initiated by David Long, today one of the state's finest fiction writers (and incidentally a fine poet), *CutBank* quickly developed a solid reputation, publishing poetry, fiction, translations, and reviews of consistent quality. Other magazines soon appeared on the scene: the first issue of *Montana Gothic,* another Missoula magazine, brought international surrealism to Montana in 1974, and in quick succession thereafter came the *Montana Review, GiltEdge,* and the *Portable Wall* (all of Missoula), Bozeman's *Corona,* and Helena's *Scratchgravel Hills.* The alternative statewide newspapers *Borrowed Times, Western Star,* and *Montana Eagle* published occasional poems and reviews of poetry collections by Montana writers. In book publishing, Missoula's Black Stone, SmokeRoot, Calliopea, and Owl Creek presses cranked out volumes of Montana poetry, many of them beautifully printed and bound by hand; in 1978, *CutBank* published

Where We Are: The Montana Poets Anthology, a collection of the works of over 70 poets; and the next year, Shaun Higgins of Helena released the first edition of Wally McRae's classic *It's Just Grass & Water* in his Regional Poets Series.

The little-known history of one of these Montana publishers – Peter Koch, the man behind *Montana Gothic* and Black Stone Press – suggests that Montana poetry has been even more diverse and unclassifiable than the already varied selection of poems in *The Last Best Place* might indicate. The term "regional" seems to get bandied about whenever we talk about Montana literature. Is there some characteristic peculiar to Montana writing that makes it readily identifiable as Montanan, or is it the case, as Missoula novelist Richard Ford has written in *Harper's* magazine, that the notion of regionalism is well-nigh meaningless, that the only distinction to be made is between good writing and bad writing? Bill Bevis, in his introduction to *The Last Best Place*'s contemporary poetry section, suggests that the only thing that separates Montana literature from the literature of other regions is not technique, but a greater emphasis on "landscape, weather, and naming of natural objects" and "a kind of humility, of submission to land and weather, that defines inland West, northern plains literature as a sort of subculture." Bevis, I think, is right as far as he goes: much of the poetry anthologized in *The Last Best Place* exhibits the characteristics he describes. The problem I have with this definition is that it limits what can be called Montana poetry, and I believe that the anthology reflects that limitation.

There exists a whole school of Montana poetry, a kind of "shadow" tradition, not one example of which is represented in the anthology – let's call it Montana surrealism. The poems in this tradition, many of them first published in Peter Koch's *Montana Gothic,* do not at all emphasize landscape, weather, or natural objects and reveal little humility toward the forces of the natural world. Instead, they focus on inner, psychic landscapes not grounded in the real, but in what Koch called the "marvelous."

The Montana surrealists – foremost among them Koch, Milo Miles, Craig Czury, Michael Poage, and Lee Bassett – were very active throughout most of the 1970s, publishing, theorizing, causing trouble. Scion of a Montana pioneer family, Peter Koch had studied and lived in San Francisco and Paris during the 1960s, establishing connections with the international surrealist movement and internalizing the French poststructuralist theory of the day, particularly that of Guy DeBord, leader of the Situationists. Upon his arrival in Missoula in 1974, Koch, with his wife Shelley Hoyt-Koch, established Black Stone Press and published the first issue of *Montana Gothic*. In that first issue, he launched an attack on the "specialization of poets, a cultural elite that dispense the captured words to the hungry mass. The inauguration of the Spectacle." Koch, it seemed, was horrified by the ways in which the mass media had rendered the world homogenous. "The ubiquitous image," he wrote, "is the 'beauty' that is conditioned into the mind of the beholder. . . . It is insulting to watch television, insulting to read the newspaper . . . insulting to open the mail. . . . 'Reality' has been reduced to one uninterrupted eightlane highway leading straight to the disneyland of harmless imitations and approved occupations." Perhaps Koch – a kind of regionalist himself – had returned to Montana in hopes that the spectacle of mass culture he had encountered in the cities, with its "oatmeal-like consistency," might be less overbearing here, that, in Montana, he and others of like mind might uncover "unprecedented extrusions of the marvelous." Koch saw himself as an archaeologist who would reveal "dangerous emanations" and saw much energy in an outlaw Montana tradition that included Lee Steen, "hermetic sculptor of Roundup"; the megalomania of the copper kings; the vitriolic tongue of Mary MacLean; "the perverse relic of Club Foot George's foot"; Jim Welch and the high-line mythos; anarchy in the Rocky Mountains.

Among the Montana surrealists, Koch was the only card-carrying member of the international surrealist movement. The others were young poets fascinated by the original surrealists and influenced by the leaping poetry of Minnesotan Robert Bly and Nobel Prize winner Pablo Neruda of Chile. Many of the Montanans' poems simply recapitulated what had been fresh forty years earlier in the poetry of French surrealists Andre Breton, Louis Aragon, and Philippe Soupault, but Montana poets like Michael Poage (whose books include *Born* and *Wings of Hair,* both from Koch's Black Stone Press), Craig Czury (author of *Janus Peeking,* winner of the Montana Arts Council's First Book Award in 1980), and Lee Bassett (whose many books include *Gauguin and Food, Hatsutaiken,* and *The Mapmaker's Lost Daughter* and who had little connection with the clique around

Koch) produced what were, to my mind, highly successful poems, poems in which startling images, macabre humor, and sometimes downright silliness combined to create what the surrealists called "convulsive" beauty, beautiful – in Lautreamont's memorable phrase – as "the unexpected meeting, on a dissecting table, of a sewing machine and an umbrella." Koch himself, usually so argumentative, wrote poems of a surpassing tenderness.

In addition to the surrealists, Koch published the work of Jane Bailey, one of Montana's rare erotic poets (including her book, *Pomegranate*), and he championed the "redneck work laments full of concrete noise and jackhammer dust" of Dave Thomas, regularly featuring his poems in *Montana Gothic* and designing and distributing Dave's first book, *Fossil Fuel,* published by the Montana Poets Cooperative in 1977.

Nineteen seventy-seven brought an end to Koch's dreams of a surrealist renaissance in Montana. In the sixth and final issue of the *Gothic,* he launched a vicious attack on the mainstream Montana writing community, pointing out that "we have here in Montana a sterling example of the repression of the imagination by what can fairly be judged an unconscious agent, the Writing Program at the University of Montana. . . . a state supported nursery under the direction of Richard Hugo." After that blast of vitriol, Koch packed his bags and returned to San Francisco, where he continues to work as a master printer.

The demise of *Montana Gothic* was not an isolated incident. By 1983, following Richard Hugo's death and Madeline DeFrees's departure for Massachusetts, most of Montana's little magazines and small presses had folded, and in general, Montana's poetry scene slipped into decline, with many poets leaving the state and few new ones arriving to take their places. *CutBank* survived, the most stable Montana literary journal of them all, and *Corona* and *The Portable Wall* (now in Billings) limped along, publishing extremely irregularly. Emily Strayer founded her Kutenai Press in Missoula, but with one notable exception, Montana literary publishing was deathly quiet.

The one notable exception was a magazine conceived, edited, and published by the poets Paul Piper of Missoula and Bill Borneman of Helena. Piper and Borneman's magazine perversely changed its name with each issue – in turn, it was called *Zetesis 1, Popular Poetix 2, African Golfer 3, Wrld Wr 4, 1733 South Fifth West,* until, with the sixth issue, its impish editors settled on the title, *Multiples.* And like Koch's *Gothic,* it published a coterie of avant gardists who cared little for regionalism and even less for the usual gratifications of poetry. Instead of surrealists, Borneman and Piper had ties with the Language Poets, perhaps the most controversial group of writers at work in the U.S. today. Heavily concentrated in San Francisco and the East Coast, the Language Poets, influenced by Russian Formalism and the cutting edge of French poetics, sought to lead the reader, in Borneman's words, beyond the "level of experience where things are crystallized out into definite shapes, and . . . into the 'vaporized world' of 'cryptic flux' where sundry thoughts are allowed to modify each other via 'chance' as well as by routine inferential patterns." Through tactics of non sequitur and fragmentation of syntax, these poets struggled to overcome what they saw as the tyranny of narrative and of sense. In addition to the Language Poets, Borneman and Piper published a handful of Montana writers, primarily outsiders like Craig Czury, Roger Dunsmore, and again, Dave Thomas, but perhaps most importantly, they continued what I see as a healthy tradition of bringing in from elsewhere modernist and postmodernist poetic strategies that stand in direct opposition to poetics as usual in Montana. Whether the Language Poets have much of an impact on Montana poets remains to be seen. Interestingly enough, neither Piper nor Borneman have succumbed to the formulas of the movement, and both of these talented poets are today producing very interesting work (none of which, incidentally, appears in *The Last Best Place*; to my mind, another important oversight). Borneman, the least regional writer I know, is a virtually uncategorizable artist. In addition to writing poems and other texts (including his remarkable 30-page "Guide Through World Chaos"), he is an accomplished songwriter, jazz guitarist, and visual artist. Piper, currently a graduate student in the University of Montana's creative writing program and a former editor of *CutBank,* writes and publishes prolifically, and his "Montana Notes" is, for my money, one of the finest (and wittiest) long poems written about this state.

An anthology can only hint at the richness of a literary tradition. I would have liked to see poems by Piper, Borneman, and the Montana surrealists in *The Last Best Place,* and others no doubt have their own favorites whom they feel were unjustly excluded. But the fact of the matter is: this is a magnificent anthology. If you are interested in further exploring the world of Montana poetry, I urge you to seek out *Where We Are: The Montana Poets Anthology*, to ransack your local library for books by individual poets, and to take advantage of that marvelous resource, the Regional Writers Project at the Yellowstone Art Center in Billings, which distributes the books of many Montana poets.

The relationship between place and literature is, and always will be, a complex and mediated one. It is essential that we as poets remain open to the places we inhabit, to experience, to emotion, and to idea, that we give up our expectations, however cherished, and embrace – with absolute honesty and unparalleled courage – whatever of the real remains to us. The late Robert Kelly, who called New York state home, admonished his fellow poets: "[try] to be humble/ to the place, not to think/ about it too much,/ to know it/ as it might let/ itself be known. . . ."

Michigan writer Jim Harrison, whose "Legends of the Fall," Bill Kittredge notes, is "regarded by a large public as one of the most vivid and compelling stories ever written about Montana" and whom I would like to claim as an honorary Montana poet (and one of the most vital), eloquently speaks of the juncture of perception, perspective, and place in his "After Reading Takahashi": "And all lessons are fatal: the great snowy owl / that flew in front of me so that / I ducked in the car; it will never happen again. / I've been warned by a snowy night, an owl, / the infinite black above and below me to look / at all creatures and things with a billion eyes, / not struggling with the single heartbeat / that is my life."

Today, the Montana poetry scene has a quiet strength. It may not seem as glamorous as it did during the glory years of the 1970s, but the poets who've survived that classic Montana cycle of boom and bust have matured, and their work glows with wisdom, humor, and compassion. The poets I know, whether natives or recent immigrants, seem entrenched for the long haul, writing often in isolation, determined to create poems that cater to no one but that speak to, and for, many of us. The success of *The Last Best Place* has brought Montana poetry a growing audience, and with any luck at all, this state will long continue to be a hospitable environment for the creation of expertly crafted and deeply human poetry.

The Montana–Paris Axis,
or Unpacking My Grandfather's Library
On the Track of a Bookish Tradition

Originally published in *Writing Montana: Literature under the Big Sky,* eds. Rick Newby and Suzanne Hunger (Helena, MT: Montana Center for the Book, 1996).

For John Hay Crowe, and for Agnes D. Regan

> *Poetic testimony reveals to us another world*
> *inside this world, the other world that is this*
> *world.*
>
> – Octavio Paz

In San Francisco in the mid-1980s, a book discussion group gathered to talk about Norman Maclean's *A River Runs through It.* Like many thousands of other readers since the book's release in 1976, the group's members found themselves entertained, instructed, and deeply moved by Maclean's tragic meditation on flyfishing and rivers and brotherly love set in the Montana of 1937. But the majority of them, having grown up in the Bay Area or other urban centers, noted that they had struggled – and failed – to believe that Montana's backwoods could support both a sheepherder whose chest hair grew through his union suit (because he had not taken it off all winter) *and* a Presbyterian minister who, when he'd finished fishing for the day, whiled away at streamside reading the New Testament in Greek, that a rodeo cowgirl turned whore with the name "Old Rawhide" could co-exist in the same world as a pair of young boys (and expert flyfishermen) who disdained Izaak Walton because his *Compleat Angler* revealed him to be "an Episcopalian and a bait fisherman."[1]

Only two of the reading group's members found this mixture of the crude and the refined, the unwashed and the literate unsurprising. The first, a young woman raised on a farm in Manitoba, spoke of her father's leatherbound Shakespeare, of his love for literature *and* the

---

1 Norman Maclean, *A River Runs Through It and Other Stories* (Chicago: University of Chicago Press, 1976), 5, 31, 94–96.

hard work of a farmer's life. The second, a fifth-generation Montanan born in Helena, found the others' incomprehension incomprehensible. Her grandmother – daughter of a mining engineer father and a Vassar-educated mother – had been raised in the rough-and-tumble mining camp of Montana's Alder Gulch and had then gone away to obtain a liberal education at the University of Wisconsin. In her prodigious memory, this beloved grandmother held thousands of lines of English and American poetry that she recited with passion and clarity. The young Montanan's entire family read voraciously; they valued literacy above almost every other virtue (except, perhaps, for kindness, generosity, and fairness) and sent their young to progressive schools – Dartmouth, Oberlin, Harvard, the University of Montana. The Montanan had spent her earliest years on Helena's Westside among elegant Victorian mansions built by early-day entrepreneurs whose fortunes came from gold, silver, cattle, and mercantile trade, and only a few blocks from the seedy south end of Last Chance where, as Ralph Beer has written, "the sheepherders and hard-luckers, the bums and healing rodeo riders" passed their days in "cheap hotels and derelict bars."[2] These disjunctions and juxtapositions seemed natural to her, and enlivening, made the remembered world of her childhood a fascinating place, she told the urbanites in her reading group. They shook their heads and said, "Not believable." The rough side, yes. But not the refined. That's not the West they'd come to imagine – purely primitive, untouched by civilization's curses and blessings.

Ethnographers call this urge to "rescue 'authenticity' out of destructive historical change" the "salvage paradigm." As James Clifford suggests, the salvage paradigm's underlying assumptions have everything to do with our desire to be redeemed (from an increasingly chaotic modern existence) and with our nostalgia for a purer (and non-existent) past, and almost nothing to do with the richness ("the multiple *histories* and *inventions*") of an actual culture.[3]

Damaging enough when the dominant culture tries to impinge its nostalgic definition of "authenticity" on a marginal culture (like Montana's), the salvage paradigm turns most destructive when the locals begin to ignore their own reality and buy in, instead, to the received

---

2   Ralph Beer, *The Blind Corral* (New York: Viking, 1986), 13-14.

3   James Clifford, "Of Other Peoples: Beyond the Salvage Paradigm" in *Discussions in Contemporary Culture: Number One,* ed. Hal Foster (Seattle: Bay Press, 1987), 121-122.

mythology. In 1949, in a much-maligned and often acute essay first published in *Partisan Review,* Leslie Fiedler noted that Montana ranch hands watched the "Hollywood version" of their lives – sanitized and sanctified, the cowboy's saga "transformed . . . into the national myth" – and they "*believed it all,*" though "going out from contemplating their idealized selves to get drunk or laid, they must somehow have felt the discrepancy, as failure or irony or God knows what."[4]

Over the past twenty years, Montana writers have done much to undermine, subvert, even lampoon the myths about Montana. Writers like William Kittredge, Ralph Beer, Mary Clearman Blew, Ivan Doig, Bill Stockton, Judy Blunt, Wallace McRae, and Thomas McGuane have pretty successfully deflated that idealized image of the cowboy and ranch life, giving us in exchange new images that enrich our imaginations and our lives. James Welch, Debra Earling, William Yellow Robe, and Vic Charlo tell us artfully crafted truths from Indian Country. And scores of other fine writers create wholly unexpected Montanas, playing with and against the myths (and sometimes simply ignoring them), opening fresh vistas and offering us pleasures undreamed of.

But still, there's one myth that hasn't wholly died. For worse and sometimes, arguably, for better, certain Montanans share the vision of those San Franciscan readers, that the Montana writer shouldn't know too much or at least shouldn't let on if he or she is well read, well traveled, too aware of trends and techniques that originate beyond the state's borders. And certainly, the Montana writer shouldn't depict a reality that strays too far from a generally accepted vision of what Montana might be: rough and ready, barely literate, beautiful but still, even in the 1990s, the ultimate frontier.

This self-imposed know-nothingism, a kind of censorship from within, has masked the very real sophistication of Montana's artists, allowing them to "pass" as authentic westerners, but all too often preventing them from being wholly themselves. In his myth-breaking study of Charlie Russell, Brian Dippie notes:

> [b]eneath the unchanging cowboy exterior . . . was a serious
> artist. It was a side Russell rarely revealed. He set up smoke
> screens, shied away from artsy conversation as pretentious

---

4   Leslie Fiedler, "Montana, or the End of Jean-Jacques Rousseau" in *An End to Innocence: Essays on Culture and Politics* (Boston: The Beacon Press, 1955), 136-137.

and maybe a bit effete, mocked those who were disposed to ponder "tech neque." A California writer who interviewed Russell in 1926 wrote that "it is the hardest thing in the world to get him to talk about art, especially his art, except in a joking way, when he can cover reality with a film of ridicule."

Among painter friends with whom he was comfortable, Russell did reveal a few long hairs. He was curious about technique, composition, ways to prepare a palette and mix colors. . . .[5]

This effacement of oneself as a professional artist, whether through silence or jocularity, can be seen as a complicated form of self-hatred, or merely the mask the artist wears to get the job done – and maintain friends – in a sometimes hostile (read: macho) environment. On some level, it's always a lonely compromise, hiding a central passion from those nearest you. Thank God, Charlie had friends like his beloved neighbor Josephine Tripp, with whom he could truly let his hair down and share his love of art and literature and exotic locales.

In his memoir, *Hole in the Sky*, William Kittredge describes how he drifted Into a telephonic affair with a "literary" woman who must have met some of the needs his eastern Oregon ranching community could not. They talked literature, they talked sex: "This was the life, I thought, because it was based on perfect candor." Kittredge was leaving what he had always known, in pursuit of a new, literary self he had created to match his actual desires: "I thought I would never be anyone if I didn't take care of myself." His marriage disintegrated in the face of "whatever it was that had gone haywire in my systems," and one day, Kittredge found himself alone in an empty house, empty save for many hundreds of books "and a few ashtrays":

An old friend came to help me box the books. "Jesus Christ," he said. "You'd be a smart son of a bitch if you read all of these."

Who had I led him to believe I was? Even my friends did not know me in my concealments.[6]

---

5   Brian W. Dippie, *Looking at Russell* (Fort Worth, Texas: Amon Carter Museum, 1987), 2.

6   William Kittredge, *Hole in the Sky: A Memoir* (New York: Alfred A. Knopf, 1992), 181-182, 206-208.

In the West, this tendency to conceal our true selves, especially if selfhood involves something beyond the most crude involvement in the arts, becomes second nature, and if it doesn't, there are those waiting to remind us that concealment is still the best strategy. Recently, a friend submitted a few poems in hopes of receiving a fellowship offered only to Montana writers. He did not receive the fellowship, which he could certainly understand, since Montana is aswarm with fine poets, fiction writers, playwrights, writers of essay and memoir. But being an inquisitive sort, and eager to learn from his experiences, he asked for the judges' comments on his work. He was astonished to learn that, though the judges thought his work "refreshing, sophisticated writing with an intriguing cerebral quality," they wanted to know, "Is it too scholarly – does artist really know this depth of poetry?" He inquired further and learned from staff members of the granting agency that one of the judges in particular (who had no doubt recently moved to Montana in search of simpler things) felt that my friend's work was not "Montanan" enough, that no one truly from Montana could "know this depth of poetry." A native Montanan educated in Montana schools, my friend was enraged and offended, not by his failure to receive a fellowship, but with the attitude embodied by the judges, that a Montana artist shouldn't, and perhaps couldn't, produce a sophisticated, allusive art. But there the message was, clear as the Montana sky: Conceal thyself.

This demand that we conceal ourselves derives, in no small part, from our desire for a world that coheres and comforts us in the face of the fractured existence that American (and Montana) life has become. But to give up that comforting coherence need not be a tragedy; to truly understand our lives, fragmented as they are, can be a blessing. As Norman Maclean has written, "Life is very persistent in splitting us into pieces," but through the writing – and reading – of literature, he adds, we can achieve "some kind of unity of the soul." In Maclean's view, that unity cannot be won at the expense of the complexity of what he calls "life itself": "I think a weakness of Montana stories has been that they have been too local, too true of Montana only. Montana stories should be true of Montana and of the world beyond."[7]

In an essay he calls "Roping from A to B," Tom McGuane critiques

---

7   Norman Maclean, "Montana Memory: Talk at the Institute of the Rockies" in *Norman Maclean*, eds. Ron McFarland and Hugh Nichols (Lewiston, ID: Confluence Press, 1988), 68, 73.

a literature that is too local from a slightly different point of view:

> The vulgarity we call the "sense of place" is a fairly nelly subinstance of schizophrenia, saving up facts, preferably inherited, about locale. It always made me very suspicious that no one from Yoknapatawpha ever went to Miami. Faulkner certainly left no stone unturned for himself; but the denizens of his books he locks up in this morbid, Cloud-Cuckoo-Land where everyone has mule trouble while the author rides up and down Sunset Strip in a convertible.[8]

McGuane goes on to explain that one of the reasons he took up roping was that "some cur said I had writer's hands, which really got me, as I am someone who wants to be a rugged guy in the West and not some horrid nancy with pink palms. . . just a message to other arty types out there in the Rocky Mountains: roping is a good fast way to acquire local-color hands."[9]

With his irony, loopy wit, and off-kilter characters who wander from Montana ranches to Key West to the Yale Club of New York City, McGuane practices what he preaches, merrily deconstructing and de-centering the image of Montana ranch life as strictly serious business. When he has Montana rancher Patrick Fitzpatrick in his fifth novel, *Nobody's Angel,* stop "at the calving shed a mile below the house" just to put a disk by jazz avant-garde saxophonist Ornette Coleman on the turntable – all the while ruminating on questions of race and technical virtuosity and cleverness – he undoubtedly establishes, for some readers and critics, a new standard for inappropriateness in Montana literature.[10] For others, his work represents liberation from the need to hide one's contradictions under a beaverslide haystacker.

". . . all honor to the books."
– Max Frisch

---

8   Thomas McGuane, "Roping, from A to B" in *An Outside Chance: Essays on Sport* (New York: Farrar, Straus and Giroux, 1980), 221.

9   Ibid., 222.

10   Thomas McGuane, *Nobody's Angel* (New York: Random House, 1981), 17.

Truth is, Montana has had – from the very beginning – what I want to call a "bookish" tradition, made up of individuals who are passionate about books and knowledge and the wider world. And this tradition of openness to experience and learning begins long before white folks first set foot on the American continent. In his introduction to the catalog of an exhibition of "elegant, subtle and sometimes hilarious" books made by Montana (and Berkeley, California) publisher and master letterpress printer Peter Koch, poet Robert Bringhurst writes:

> Along with coastal British Columbia and California, and the Colorado Plateau, Montana remains one of the culturally richest parts of aboriginal America. Speakers of Salishan and Siouan, Kutenaian, Algonkian and Uto-Aztecan languages converge there, and the boreal forest cultures meet the cultures of the Rocky Mountains and those of the high plains. Long before the first Europeans arrived, aboriginal trade routes led from the Bitterroot, the Big Hole and the Yellowstone to the west coast, the Ohio River Valley, the Pueblos and beyond. Even now, after centuries of destruction, it is one of the places where aboriginal oral literature remains alive. Few white Montanans have shared in this indigenous cultural matrix, except in the most superficial way. But the power of the place persists, drawing to it people, stories, languages and songs from around the world.[11]

One of the first offspring of the European and aboriginal cultures in this region might serve as the exemplar for the bookish westerner. Baptiste, the son of Sacajawea and Touissant Charbonneau, guides and interpreters for the Lewis and Clark expedition, was educated by both Protestant and Catholic clergy at William Clark's behest. In 1823, Prince Paul of Wurttemberg met Baptiste Charbonneau at a trading village on the Kansas River and took the young man to Europe, where he toured extensively. In 1829, Charbonneau returned to the West, working as a mountain man, guide, justice of the peace,

---

11   Robert Bringhurst, "Stepping Again into the Same Stream and Catching Different Fish: The Printing of Peter Koch" in *Peter Koch, Printer: Cowboy Surrealists, Maverick Poets & Pre-Socratic Philosophers* (New York & San Francisco: New York Public Library & San Francisco Public Library, 1995), 12.

and gold miner. "But in the early 1850's," writes John Ewers,

> [Baptiste Charbonneau] returned to his mother's people, the Shoshonis, in Wyoming, where he lived until his death in 1885. This French-Indian man of the world spoke English, French, Italian, Spanish, several Indian languages, and could use the sign language. He could discuss – with almost equal ease – French philosophy, Spanish dances, the trapping of beaver, or the uses of Indian medicine bundles.[12]

This frontier erudition – rich in contrasts and improbabilities – was not so unique as we might think. In the introduction to his extraordinary long poem, *Circling Back,* about the "West of the Rockies," Gary Holthaus notes that

> "Rocky Mountain College" is the name Jim Bridger, Osborne Russell, Joe Meek, and their friends gave their encampment near the Yellowstone in the winter of 1835. There they passed the time reading aloud to one another and in argument and debate, and there, Russell reported, "Some of my comrades who considered themselves Classical scholars have had some little added to their wisdom."[13]

Granville Stuart, another early role model for the bookish Montanan, came to the territory with his brother James in the late 1850s, seeking gold. "James and I were both great readers," Granville wrote in the first volume of his *Forty Years on the Frontier,* and after spending the bitter winter of 1860 at Gold Creek "without so much as an almanac to look at," the brothers "were famished for something to read." A party of Native Americans passing through told the Stuarts that a white man owning a trunk "full of books . . . was camped with all that wealth, in Bitter Root valley." The Stuarts "started for those books, a hundred and fifty miles away, without a house or anybody on the route, and with three big dangerous rivers to cross. . ." The brothers – after protracted and delicate negotiations – were able to obtain

---

12   John C. Ewers, *Indian Life on the Upper Missouri* (Norman: University of Oklahoma Press, 1968), 66-67.

13   Gary H. Holthaus, *Circling Back* (Salt Lake City: Peregrine Smith Books, 1984), xi.

"five books, for five dollars each," half of all the money they possessed – but then, after all, they "had the blessed books." The books included volumes of Shakespeare and Byron, "both fine illustrated editions"; a French Bible; a biography of Napoleon; and *Wealth of Nations* by Adam Smith. At the time he wrote his memoir, Stuart still owned all the books he'd purchased that spring except *Wealth of Nations*, which "being loose in the binding, has gradually disappeared, until only a few fragments remain."[14]

As it happens, the Bitterroot Valley was the site of one of the first permanent white settlements in what has become Montana, and the trader there, Major John Owen (who humbly named Fort Owen after himself), proved to be another book fancier. "The literary taste of some frontiersmen was of a surprisingly high order," noted George Weisel in his *Men and Trade on the Northwest Frontier,* basing his opinion on the inventory of Neil McArthur's trunk (McArthur owned the books the Stuarts happily purchased) and on the contents of John Owen's library at the fort, which included the works of Lord Byron, Dickens, Milton, Petrarch, Plutarch, Washington Irving, Sir Walter Scott, Charles Darwin, and Thomas Jefferson ("many volumes"), together with histories, almanacs, and *A Complete Dictionary of Poetical Quotations.*[15] Despite Owen's labors as trader, Indian agent for the Flathead tribe, keeper of a daily journal, and tireless traveler ("twenty-three thousand miles throughout the country"), "there still remains the mental picture," wrote Paul Phillips in his introduction to the Major's journals,

> of Owen sitting in his library at night, while the rest of the Fort people were deep in slumber. With his pipe in hand; his dog at his feet; his glass of grog at his elbow; and Lingard's *History of England* propped on the table before him; he studied the story of a history that was past, oblivious of the mighty history that he himself was shaping.[16]

---

14   Granville Stuart, *The Montana Frontier, 1852-1864,* ed. Paul C. Phillips (Lincoln: University of Nebraska Press, 1977 (1925]), 159-161.

15   George E. Weisel, *Men and Trade on the Northwest Frontier* (Missoula: Montana State University Press, 1955), 145, 247-249.

16   John Owen, *The Journals and Letters of Major John Owen, Pioneer of the Northwest, 1850-1871,* eds. Seymour Dunbar and Paul C. Phillips (New York: Edward Eberstadt, 1927), Vol. I, 13.

That Granville Stuart and John Owen, lovers of books, should write their own books – compiled by others though they may have been, out of journals and reminiscences after their authors' deaths – marks them as progenitors of a Montana literature both unrepentantly bookish and steeped in experience of an uncommon place. As Norman Maclean has written, "I have had the great fortune, then, of spending . . . my life in the beauty of the woods and books."[17]

Granville Stuart pitied those who did not live in Montana because they were "ignorant of the joys of going out poor in the morning and coming back rich in the evening (in imagination)."[18]

"Home-keeping youth have ever homely wits."
– William Shakespeare

Since the beginning of human history, the center has looked down upon the periphery, the major leagues have sneered at the minor, the capital has made fun of the provinces. This assumption of urban superiority and its contempt for those who live "elsewhere" is evident even in the ways we define certain terms relating to the margins. *The Random House Dictionary of the English Language* defines "provincialism" as "narrowness of mind, ignorance, or the like, considered as resulting from lack of exposure to cultural or intellectual activity," and the *Oxford English Dictionary* specifies further, "exhibiting the character, especially the narrowness of view or interest, associated with or attributed to inhabitants of 'the provinces'; wanting the culture or polish of the capital." And yet I've always liked to think of Montana as a province, and our literature as a provincial literature – for, to me, provincialism is the necessary condition out of which Montana's writers create a distinctive, richly universal art. My definition of provincialism, then: "Living far from the centers of established culture, but alive to all cultures; drawing

---

17   Maclean, "Montana Memory," 69.

18   Granville Stuart, "Montana As It Is" (1865) in *Frontier Omnibus*, ed. John W. Hakola (Missoula/Helena: Montana State University Press/Historical Society of Montana, 1962), 278.

upon both inner resources (cultivated in relative isolation) and received ideas (conceiving them afresh, even distorting them with little concern for convention); having the opportunity and the innocence to produce works that are out of the mainstream, eccentric, and vital."[19]

Joseph Kinsey Howard understood that, if Montana was provincial, its provincialism often led to creativity, and in his introduction to *Montana Margins,* he asserted that, while Montana's physical isolation has limited the state's economic development, its "cultural isolation has never been so complete as some Montanans and far too many in other regions thought it was." Provincialism, in its negative, know-nothing sense, he added,

> would have been fatal on the frontier. To survive, the newcomers had not only to adopt some of the aboriginal customs . . . but also to seize eagerly upon anything else, from anywhere, that would work, or even that might work – they were not afraid to try new things.[20]

Trying new things: Many artists from marginal cultures around the world have created works of substance and beauty out of their difference from the mainstream. Think of Kurt Schwitters, the great German master of collage, who formed his own, one-man movement, *Merz,* when his application to join the Dadaists of Berlin was rejected because his face was entirely too bourgeois. Schwitters, after all, did not live in Berlin, that "chaotic asphalt metropolis," but in Hannover which, wrote one of the Dadaists, "surpassed other German cities in only one respect: . . its petty bourgeois mentality."[21]

"It would be specious," writes Schwitters scholar John Elderfield, "to put too much down to [Schwitters's] provincial, and particularly Hannoverian, situation." Nevertheless, Elderfield adds,

---

19   For my discussion of provincialism here, I am indebted to the Yellowstone Art Center's Regional Writers Project, Billings, Montana, and to Donna Forbes, Gordon McConnell, Adrea Sukin, and Jet Holubek, who generously commissioned my talk, "In Praise of Provincialism" (presented September 25, 1986), for the museum's lecture series, "Written Locations: Views on Western Place."

20   Joseph Kinsey Howard, *Montana Margins: A State Anthology* (New Haven: Yale University Press, 1946), x.

21   Hans Richter, *Dada: Art and Anti-Art* (New York: Oxford University Press, 1965), 138; John Elderfield, *Kurt Schwitters* (London: Thames and Hudson, 1985), 170.

the contradictoriness of the way he lived, on the margins of bourgeois society (a society that was claustrophobic rather than chaotic), helps to account for the peculiarity of his literary themes, for his separateness from any aggressively modern or metropolitan avant-garde stance, in fact for the brand of provincial innocence that continually shows itself in what he did. His very eclecticism is that of an outsider, of someone independent of a mainstream taste. He nurtured his eclecticism as much as his provincialism. Indeed, both were an important part of his originality, for they gave him a happy freedom of mobility, and permitted him to achieve a level of artistic quality well beyond that of his more polemical contemporaries. . . . his very isolation seems to have strengthened his commitment to create an art that would match that of the metropolitan mainstream, but at the same time be all-inclusively personal and individual.[22]

Even further removed from the cultural capitals of Europe and North America, the Cuban writer Jose Lezama Lima is another artist whose strange and remarkable work helps define the qualities that characterize a lasting provincial art. Best known for his monumental novel, *Paradiso*, poet, essayist, and novelist Lezama Lima – in the words of Julio Cortazar – is "innocent of any direct tradition." Instead, Cortazar writes,

He assumes them all, from the Etruscan interpreting entrails to Leopold Bloom blowing his nose in a dirty handkerchief, without historic compromise, without being a French or an Austrian writer; he is a Cuban with only a handful of his own culture behind him and the rest is knowledge, pure and free, not a career responsibility. He can write whatever he pleases. He is not a chained slave, he is not required to write more, or better, or differently, he doesn't have to justify himself. His incredible gifts spring out of this innocent freedom, this free innocence. One has the feeling that [Lezama Lima] has come from another planet. . . . When the Innocent American makes

---

22   Elderfield, *Kurt Schwitters*, 170-171.

his appearance, the good savage who accumulates trinkets without suspecting that they are worthless or out of fashion, then . . . [there erupts] the primordial force of the stealer of fire.[23]

And, adds Mario Vargas Llosa, "It's hard to believe that this great expert on world literature and history, who speaks with the same picaresque familiarity about the desserts of Brittany, feminine Victorian fashions, and Viennese architecture, has left Cuba only twice . . . once to Mexico and once to Jamaica."[24] Viktor Shklovsky acknowledges this stay-at-home brand of provincialism (which is only geographical and never imaginative) in a discussion of the great Russian Andrei Bely, author of *Petersburg* and many other novels, "[I]t turns out that [he] had never crossed 'the frontiers of Switzerland.' No, he had only crossed the 'frontiers of his own self.'"[25]

"Peculiarity"/ "separateness"/ "independent of a mainstream taste"/ "happy freedom of mobility"/ "artistic quality well beyond that of. . . more polemical contemporaries"/ "all-inclusively personal and individual"/ "innocent freedom / free innocence"/ "the primordial force of the stealer of fire": the attributes of a complex, always engaging, and sometimes profound provincial art.

In their study of Franz Kafka and what constitutes a "minor" literature, French theorists Gilles Deleuze and the late Felix Guattari quote Kafka's diary entry for December 25, 1911, to bolster their claim that the emergence of a minor, provincial literature within a major language makes the "arid" parent language "vibrate with a new intensity": "A small nation's memory is not smaller than the memory of a large one and so can digest the existing material more thoroughly."[26]

---

23   Julio Cortazar, "To Reach Lezama Lima" in *Around the Day in Eighty Worlds,* tr. Thomas Christensen (San Francisco: North Point Press, 1986), 90-91.

24   Quoted in Severo Sarduy, *Written on a Body,* tr. Carol Maier (New York: Lumen Books, 1989), 69

25   Viktor Shklovsky, *Theory of Prose,* tr. Benjamin Sher (Elmwood Park, IL: Dalkey Archive Press, 1990), 175.

26   Gilles Deleuze and Felix Guattari, *Kafka: Toward a Minor Literature,* tr. Dana Polan (Minneapolis: University of Minnesota Press, 1986), 19; Franz Kafka, *The Diaries of Franz Kafka, 1910-1913,* tr. Joseph Kresh (New York: Schocken Books, 1948), 193.

Norman Maclean expresses it slightly differently: "You can't live in Montana without an extra amount of memory."[27] This excess of memory can lead, as in the case of Maclean himself, to a provincial literature rich in intensities, of pleasures savored and of losses grieved, of lives remembered and of an old language given new life.

"No people should have to depend on another and possibly hostile party to give its account to the world."
– D'Arcy McNickle

Straddling many worlds, D'Arcy McNickle – the Montana-born and -raised anthropologist, historian, and founder of a modern Native American literature – stands as perhaps the quintessential bookish Montanan, the exemplary provincial cosmopolitan. William Bevis writes of McNickle's vast culture in *Ten Tough Trips: Montana Writers and the West*:

> He knew the old world of Plenty-coups through the stories of the elders, and he knew also the modern world of European power and law. . . . In one chapter of *Wind [from an Enemy Sky]*, the rich white liberal, Adam Pell lunches with a U.S. Supreme Court justice at the Harvard Club in Boston. In the following chapter, old Two Sleeps, a Salish Indian, climbs up into the Mission Mountains for a vision quest, as worried for the future of his tribe as Adam Pell was for the future of the Constitution. . . . No other author in the history of American letters could have written those two chapters back to back, getting the dialogue right; no other American has had that kind of experience in both worlds and, therefore, that authority.[28]

Carlos Fuentes found the same breadth of knowledge and spirit, the same astonishing authority, in his old friend, the Argentine

<hr>

27   Maclean, "Montana Memory," 69.

28   William W. Bevis, *Ten Tough Trips: Montana Writers and the West* (Seattle: University of Washington Press, 1990), 92-93.

novelist Julio Cortazar: "He knew everything; he was the Latin American in Europe who showed the Europeans that he knew something more than they – and this was the fact that the Old World discovered the New World but had then been unable to imagine it."[29]

D'Arcy McNickle, ever hungry for knowledge, took his education where he could find it, painfully in mission schools (at St. Ignatius, Montana, and Chemawa, Oregon) and at the State University of Montana (Missoula), Oxford (for a brief period in the mid-1920s), and Columbia. Born to a Métis mother and a white father, he was an enrolled member of the Confederated Salish and Kootenai Tribes, and he spent his life working to give voice to Indian people, as writer, educator, and advocate in the political and cultural realms (he helped found the National Congress of American Indians, and he was the first program director for the Newberry Library's American Indian history center, now called the D'Arcy McNickle Center for the History of the American Indian in his honor). His Montana novels, *The Surrounded* (1936) and *Wind from an Enemy Sky* (1978), are among the most beautiful, and moving, in our literature.[30]

Once he left the Flathead reservation in the 1920s, D'Arcy McNickle never returned to live in his home country. "In his own eyes," writes his biographer Dorothy R. Parker, "he was a 'breed' from the frontier, untutored in the ways of the world," and "he wanted desperately to remake himself into a cultured man of the world." This ambition led him to Oxford and then to Paris, where he spent the winter of 1926.[31] We know almost nothing of his stay in Paris, but according to Parker, in an early draft of *The Surrounded* (entitled "The Hungry Generations"), his protagonist Archilde Leon spends some months in the "center of the civilized world," wandering "the streets and alleys near his rented room," trying to decide whether to return to Montana. While in Paris, Archilde discovers that racial prejudice is universal (he encounters anti-Semitism), and he discovers that, in studying history, "he was learning about actual happenings in the

---

29   Carlos Fuentes, back cover, *Around the Day in Eighty Worlds* by Julio Cortazar, tr. Thomas Christensen (San Francisco: North Point Press, 1986).

30   For all biographical details, I am indebted to McNickle biographer, Dorothy R. Parker. See *Singing an Indian Song: A Biography of D'Arcy McNickle* (Lincoln: University of Nebraska Press, 1992), and "D'Arcy McNickle: Native American Author, Montana Native Son," *Montana the Magazine of Western History* 45:2 (Spring 1995), 2-17.

31   Parker, *Singing an Indian Song*, 29, 36

past." This realization awakened Archilde (and McNickle, too) to written history (which filled him with "breathless excitement") and to the stories he had heard from his elders on the reservation.

As an artist, conjectures Parker, McNickle may well have discovered the works of American expatriate writers like Ernest Hemingway and Gertrude Stein while in Paris; certainly his prose echoes Hemingway's in its "simple plain phrases that brought his story before his listeners with the greatest clearness" [from "The Hungry Generations"].[32] As for thousands of expatriates, Paris – that "motley, bastard, heterogenous metropolis that belongs to no country"[33] – broadened the view for McNickle and helped to make him the extraordinary being he was to become, perhaps even deepened his understanding of the world he had left behind and about which he would soon write with so much feeling and power.

Another Montana artist, Bill Stockton of Grass Range – writer, painter, sheep rancher – spent time in Paris, studying art at the Ecole de la Grande Chaumiere, and in his essay, "Paris, 1948 – The End of an Era," Stockton recounts his experiences, describing the people, art, and ideas he encountered. And yet, throughout his essay, Stockton keeps coming back to central Montana, where the lessons he learned in Paris came to fruition and his art reached its maturity:

> I couldn't possibly imagine then that a few years later I would be sitting at the kitchen table in a cold, desolate shack in the middle of Montana making endless little variations on a line, and that I would finally turn to the naive, sensitive drawing of my children for inspiration. . . . I never dreamed that several years later I would look out my kitchen window on a bleak, winter landscape in Montana and there find inspiration for countless Avant Garde paintings and that I would dedicate several years trying to give these new forms style, purpose, and organization.[34]

---

32   Ibid., 40-42, 53.

33   Juan Goytisolo, "Why I Have Chosen to Live in Paris" in *Space in Motion* (New York: Lumen Books, 1987), 38

34   Bill Stockton, "Paris, 1948 – The End of an Era" (1961) in *The Arts in Montana,* ed. H. G. Merriam (Missoula: Mountain Press, 1977), 4-5, 7

In my study, in a niche in one of the bookshelves (placed just above a portrait of poet Richard Hugo at his typewriter), stands a *Plan de Paris par Arrondissement* that once belonged to Helena writer and thinker Frieda Fligelman. This guide to the streets of Paris – nearly identical in size and design to the one my wife and I purchased while on our honeymoon to the City of Light in 1993 – dates from the 1920s, the decade Fligelman spent in Paris, learning about life, writing poetry, and coming to some remarkable insights about the languages of non-western peoples.[35] The *Plan*'s pages have been annotated, with notes translating French francs to Belgian, lists of possible lodgings (Frieda pasted in an advertisement for "Furnished Rooms and kitchens, hot and cold water, lift, bathroom, telephone, 500fr. per month, 2 rue Labrouste" [her Paris address?]), and even her efforts to write Chinese characters. This little book, dog-eared and softened by the years, leaking pages, links me to a hidden tradition: that of the Montana artist in Paris, discovering the wider world ("the physical beauty and ultimately unanalyzable charm of a city which for centuries has been the refuge and the home for exiles. . ."[36]), preparing to bring home to Big Sky Country techniques and notions that can enrich our provincial art.

Here's a dirty little secret I've heard on the streets of Helena: that early in this century, a Montana couple visiting Paris stumbled upon Charlie Russell in the galleries of the Louvre. Russell greeted them warmly, but begged them not to mention to anyone back home that they'd caught him shamelessly studying the works of the masters in the capital of the decadent and the effete.

In the final pages of his *Ten Tough Trips*, William Bevis recalls how, as he sat in a Paris library reading the letters of James Fenimore Cooper, he could look up and see "a painting of an old man and two companions, with pack horses, on a bare rise of the plains.. . ." Signed by that provincial cosmopolitan, Charles M. Russell, the painting bore the title, *The World was all before Them*.[37]

In his *An Autobiographical Novel*, the poet Kenneth Rexroth

---

35   I am indebted to Alexandra Swaney and Arnie Malina for information about Frieda Fligelman. See Alexandra's essay on Frieda, "The Queen of Social Logic: the Life and Writing of Frieda Fligelman," in *Writing Montana: Literature Under the Big Sky*, and Arnie Malina's essay, "Frieda Fligelman: Commemorative Notes to a Life Completed," in *Scratchgravel Hills* 1 (1978), 10-18. See also *Notes for a Novel: The Selected Poems of Frieda Fligelman*, eds. Rick Newby & Alexandra Swaney (Helena: Drumlummon Institute, 2008).

36   Samuel Putnam, *Paris Was Our Mistress* (London: Plantin Publishers, 1947), 50.

37   Bevis, *Ten Tough Trips*, 206-27.

recounts that, while visiting Paris during 1925 (where he might have met D'Arcy McNickle and Frieda Fligelman), he encountered the American anarchist Alexander Berkman, who told him, "Go back. There is more for you in the Far West than there is here." Within a month, Rexroth was working as a fry cook in Billings, Montana, and a little later, as a wrangler for firefighting crews near Glacier National Park. It was there, among Montanans who were "amazingly literate and well informed" and yet had "all the characteristics which fiction and the movies made standard equipment" for western old-timers, that Rexroth began to hone the skills and sensitivities that would make him one of our greatest poets of the natural world.[38]

"These barren hills saw my mind's awakening."
– Mary MacLane

Sometimes Montana writers create works that take their place at the very cutting edge of world literature, influencing instead of influenced, pioneering new forms and new attitudes. In 1902, Mary MacLane – "of womankind and of nineteen years" – published her autobiographical novel, *The Story of Mary MacLane*, to much acclaim (and considerable shock). Selling nearly 100,000 copies in its first month and made up of equal parts Symbolist prose poem, Surrealist text, and young girl's intimate diary, *The Story of Mary MacLane* is said to have influenced D. H. Lawrence, Hart Crane, and Gertrude Stein and inspired a generation of American women to greater freedom of expression.

Alive to the possibilities of liberation from the strictures of Victorian America at the verge of a new century (possibly because she stood on the margins), MacLane gave eloquent and quirky, even transgressive, voice to the aspirations and anxieties of her contemporaries. She called herself the "Kid Primitive," and in keeping with her self-definition as a provincial artist, she pretended to be wholly original, to have sprung fully formed from the "dusty dreary wind-havocked waste" of Butte, even though she had graduated from Butte

---

38   Kenneth Rexroth, *An Autobiographical Novel* (New York: New Directions, 1969), 341-343, 356; Linda Hamalian, *A Life of Kenneth Rexroth* (New York: W. W. Norton & Company, 1991), 39, 45.

High School with "very good Latin, good French and Greek," and "a broad conception of History and Literature."

In a 1902 interview with Zona Gale of the *New York World*, she denied having read a single line of Walt Whitman, her most obvious literary ancestor. After much prompting, she admitted to admiring Virgil, Edgar Allan Poe, and Chaucer, along with the Russian "genius" Marie Bashkirtseff, though she asserted that "I am greater than she." When Gale encouraged her to read "Keats and Pater and Dante and Shakespeare" in order to find beautiful phrases, MacLane replied, like a true provincial who savors her own originality, her very primitiveness, "I don't have to do that. I have all those beautiful things in myself."

Upon MacLane's death in 1929, the *Chicagoan* wondered,

> How did it happen that a revolution in manners, a transvaluation of values in the female code of behavior, started, or seemed to start, with an unruly young woman who couldn't bear the sight of the tooth-brushes hanging up in the family bathroom in Butte, Montana? What seed fell upon that austere provincial soil to produce this amorous diarist with a narcissus complex? The New Woman has had many famous prophets, from Susan B. Anthony to Henrik Ibsen, but the origin of her wild young sister, the New Female, has not yet been carefully traced. The career of Mary MacLane is Chapter I in The History of Flapperism, ready-made for any ambitious sociologist.

In her interview with Gale, MacLane said, "I do not see any beauty in self restraint. Give something. If not yourself, then a pose. I gave myself."[39]

> *"Those crazy-eyed cowboys*
> *Lady, who romp you fantastically*
> *have sharp little knee caps*

---

39   *Tender Darkness: A Mary MacLane Anthology*, ed. Elisabeth Pruitt (Belmont, CA: Abernathy & Brown, 1993), vii, viii, 16, 19, 150, 132-133, 178-187. For a more complete discussion of MacLane, see Julia Watson's essay, "Engendering Montana Lives: Women's Autobiographical Writings," in *Writing Montana: Literature Under the Big Sky*.

> *beneath their horse sweat stinky*
> *faded jeans."*
>   – George Economou

When the talk turns to Montana literature, we seldom, if ever, mention the name George Economou. And yet this bookish Greek Montanan – poet, literary scholar, and translator – gives us, if not himself, then a fresh vision of Montana existence and offers to Montana writers technical means rarely encountered in our literature.[40]

In part, Economou's invisibility is his own doing, A member of what Ivan Doig calls the "Montana diaspora," Economou – born in Great Falls in 1934 – left Montana for an education at Colgate and Columbia universities and, to my knowledge, has never participated in Montana's literary community or seen himself as a Montana writer. At the same time, it seems that we expect Montana writers to be conservative in their aesthetic approach, and Economou is certainly never that. As with other consciously avant-garde Montana artists (I count here the Montana "cowboy surrealists" associated with Peter Koch's *Montana Gothic* during the 1970s, as well as the writers clustered around the Helena/Missoula literary journal, *Multiples*, in the 1980s[41]), we find it difficult to acknowledge the contributions of those whose works are ribald, experimental, rigorously modernist (discontinuous, constructed of fragments, rich in visual as well as verbal play), and bookish – even if they speak of Montana subjects and themes.

Economou's poetic work stands in the American modernist tradition of Ezra Pound, William Carlos Williams, and the poets of the Black Mountain school, particularly Charles Olson and Robert Creeley. More directly, he was the friend and eventual editor of Paul

---

40   I am grateful to another Greek Montanan, Penelope Helen Loucas of Roundup (and Tacoma), for introducing me to the poetry of George Economou in the late 1970s.

41   For a discussion of Koch and the surrealists, see my essay, "All Lessons Are Fatal: Contemporary Montana Poetry, 1964-1989," in this volume. For an overview of Koch's career, see Janice Braun and Robert Bringhurst, *Peter Koch, Printer: Cowboy Surrealists, Maverick Poets & Pre-Socratic Philosophers* (New York & San Francisco: New York Public Library & San Francisco Public Library, 1995), and Janice Braun, *Peter Koch, Printer: Recent Work* (Cambridge: The Houghton Library, Harvard University, 1995). See also Noelle Sullivan's essay, "Exquisite Magazine Corpses," in *Writing Montana: Literature Under the Big Sky* for a discussion of Koch's *Montana Gothic* and the *Multiples* series of magazines edited by W. R. Borneman and Paul S. Piper.

Blackburn,[42] the New York poet and translator who, following the principles outlined in Olson's essay, "Projective Verse," was in his own words, "working at speech rhythms, composition by field." Blackburn scholar Edith Jarolim notes further that Blackburn used the typewriter "as a means of notating the oral performance of a poem, on the analogy of a musical score. . . . More than anyone else associated with the Black Mountain aesthetic, he refined the use of punctuation, line breaks and text alignments that characterize the practice."[43]

George Economou, too, was composing by field, most markedly in his long poem, "Ameriki: Book One" (dedicated to the memory of Blackburn, who died in 1971), working to capture speech rhythms, bringing in fragments from historical documents, family diaries and conversations, Greek folksongs sung while fishing the streams of central Montana. This poem, on the simplest level the story of one immigrant family's America, is not constrained by any notion of what a regional literature must be. Woven of many strands, it reflects the complexities and discontinuities of Economou's experience. In the poem's prologue, he announces his method(s) of composition:

tape it (tap it)
transcribe it
type it
        but compose it
        feed it yourself, sweet compost
no bead drawn can bring that down
though you go down yourself in a heap –
                HA-AHHH![44]

An "economic comedy" Economou calls his poem, and in its pages, he traces the life of his father, an immigrant from Greece who arrives at Ellis Island in 1907 at the age of sixteen and for whom "work/ becomes the new/religion":

---

42   See Paul Blackburn, translator, *Proensa: An Anthology of Troubadour Poetry,* edited and introduced by George Economou (New York: Paragon House, 1986).

43   Edith Jarolim, introduction to *The Collected Poems of Paul Blackburn,* ed. Edith Jarolim (New York: Persea Books, 1985), xxiii.

44   George Economou, *Ameriki: Book One and Selected Earlier Poems* (New York: Sun, 1977), 3

OK, moving with the
railroads, yesteryear's
national seam, comes to
Missouri's headwaters
to spike ties, sweat
in the roundhouse, shine
 shoes, block hats,
weigh fruit, tend bar,
farm wheat, raise sheep
and shear them, drive
cattle to sell them.
      (KEEP IT MOVING)[45]

In the midst of all this motion, Economou finds time for a little recreation, to give complex and elegant shape to raw experience:

the act
      recalled/the act
of its recollection
            the act
of recording that recollection
become all one mosaic
                        one song worth singing:
to remember the walk down
into Pine Coulee
            is to remember
walking on air not rocks –
what joy in the mountains
man, what joy there is there
                        an Achaian daimon
sings out
            (in Cascade County now)
what joy there is in the mountains
hear the birdies tell it every day

and how they bear witness
these meadowlarks

---

45   Ibid., 7.

> their gut song in the trees
> and gut sings out of your hand
>
> you fish for trout
> crouch, sneak in the cool of the morning
> word & shadowless
> all gesture
> beside the brilliant stream
>
> That is the moment cast in the light
> of what?
> the day
> the memory
> rolled off the tongue for today & tomorrow
> sung in the mind's ear
> & heard anywhere
> that moment yields the flower in the seed
> light as air
> & hard as rock
> – *ingenium* –
> the wonderful
> engine by which we ever shape ourselves & world
> anew/
> rocks. birds. sorrows. fish.
> light. flowers. joys/
> to a self-surpassing music[46]

Economou, it seems, is obsessed with the ways we represent and personify nature. In his study, *The Goddess Natura in Medieval Literature,* he traces how the concept of a nature goddess as the "intermediary, subordinate, or vicar of God in the universe" is embodied in the poems of such medieval masters as Bernard Silvestris, Alan of Lille, Jean de Meun, and Chaucer.[47] In his own "Georgics," sometimes raunchy, sometimes tender, he talks of coyotes and rattlesnakes, sheep and Angus bulls, and the humans who live in nature

---

46   Ibid., 12-13.

47   George Economou, *The Goddess Natura in Medieval Literature* (Cambridge: Harvard University Press, 1972), 2

and sometimes "cultivate" it:

> Poor old earth we live off
> nobody here loves you
> but nobody
> not even the boy
> who looks over his
> shoulder to see if
> you curl and fold over
> properly against the
> steel concavity of the
> blades behind the tractor.
> Cussing out the gears
> he half remembers
> some old praise of you
> as he works at holding
> the wheel
>   in such a way
> it is no joy to see him sweat.[48]

With his complex mosaic, his self-surpassing music, these songs worth singing, George Economou adds something vital to the body of Montana literature, revealing the Achaian daimons that thrive in Cascade County, reminding us of "some old praise" that might serve to heal the earth. But he is never interested in the simple or the predictable. As he writes in a recent poem, "Even if you had a map, there would be surprises."[49]

> *"We may not make what we see, but what*
> *we see makes us."*
> – Lynda Sexson

The fictions of Lynda Sexson, Bozeman storyteller and scholar of

---

48   George Economou, *Landed Natures* (Los Angeles: Black Sparrow Press, 1969), 17.

49   George Economou, "Century Dead Center" in *Sulfur: A Literary Bi-Annual of the Whole Art* 34 (Spring 1994), 56.

religions, are rich in surprises. William Kittredge once wrote, "The art of a region begins to come mature when it is no longer what we think it should be,"[50] and with the publication of Sexson's *Margaret of the Imperfections* in 1988, Montana literature crossed over into its maturity, though too many Montanans missed the event.

None of Sexson's stories appeared in *The Last Best Place: A Montana Anthology*, and to my knowledge, the only Montana review her book received was in the *Bozeman Chronicle*, her hometown paper (*Margaret of the Imperfections* was reviewed widely outside the state, in *The New York Times Book Review*, *Chicago Tribune*, and *USA Today*, and it did receive the Pacific Northwest Booksellers Association Award for 1989).

Perhaps the reason for this lack of local attention lies with the fact that Sexson is not, in any limited sense, a "Montana" writer. Her magical stories are set in small towns that might be anywhere. As critic Guy Davenport notes, "If I didn't know she was American, I'd place these stories as coming from Scandinavia: by a compatriot of Andersen or Isak Dinesen."[51]

"I remember myself, long ago, as a tight little bud of a child," announces the narrator of Sexson's story, "Foxglove,"[52] and it seems that perhaps this is Sexson's greatest gift as a storyteller, the ability to enter, without condescension, the world of the child or the childlike. In "Starlings, Mute Swans, a Goose, an Impossible Angel, Evening Grosbeaks, an Ostrich, Some Ducks, and a Sparrow," the impossible angel – "She eats the lilacs and birds fly through her" – comes between a brother and his doting, jealous sister.[53] In "The Apocalypse of Mary the Unbeliever," eleven-year-old Mary, who was "developing breasts and suspicions, both of which she sought to conceal," observes with clear-eyed dispassion the growing religious fanaticism of her parents.[54] Whether she is writing, as in the lyrical title story, of a young woman who miraculously grows pearls all over her body, or as in "Hope Chest," of a slow-witted Dolores who waits in perpetual

---

50   William Kittredge, *Owning It All* (Saint Paul, MN: Graywolf Press, 1987), 176.

51   Guy Davenport, back cover of Sexson's *Margaret of the Imperfections* (New York: Persea Books, 1988).

52   Lynda Sexson, *Margaret of the Imperfections* (New York: Persea Books, 1988), 133.

53   Ibid., 19.

54   Ibid., 97.

hope for a marriage that will never come, Sexson treats her characters with absolute compassion and allows them their silliness, their joy, and their wisdom.

In the profoundly moving "Ice Cream Birth," a story set in Korea, Sexson's narrator, Claudia, writes of a street vendor, "She forgives me, I feel, all that is grotesque in my life and hers. . . . And she returns, to herself and to me, all our dignity."[55] In these miraculous stories – as close to magical realism as Montana literature gets – Sexson returns to all of us our dignity, and a refreshed sense of wonder.

"In searching out the sacred," Sexson notes in *Ordinarily Sacred*, her study of religious ritual and thought in the contemporary world, "one must examine what is overlooked." And then she says, among many profound and provocative things, "Art transcends its environment."[56] The stories in *Margaret of the Imperfections* may not tell us much about the external Montana of weather, mountains, and prairies, but the internal worlds they illuminate we overlook at the risk of our own spirits; they tell us, in Norman Maclean's phrase, of "life itself." And when we deny Lynda Sexson her proper place in the pantheon of Montana's finest writers, we deny our literature the maturity it has so recently achieved. For, as Guy Davenport says, "Lynda Sexson already has first-class citizenship in the republic of letters."[57]

"One book overlays another book, one life another."
–Maurice Blanchot

My maternal grandfather, Jack Crowe – a bookish Montanan, if ever there was one – died in January 1952, one year before I was born. Though I had not known him in life, throughout my childhood he was a beneficent presence, watching over me as I became a bookworm very much in his mold. "You're just like your grandfather," my mother would say, a touch of concern in her voice as I wandered off to read, abandoning my family in my quest for freshly imagined worlds.

---

55   Ibid., 37.

56   Lynda Sexson, *Ordinarily Sacred* (New York: Crossroad, 1982), 1 1, 76.

57   Ibid., 5

I have only one physical image of my grandfather; in a photograph that still sits on my parents' bedroom dresser, taken when he was about forty, Jack Crowe – his lean head finely boned and already bald – looks straight at the camera, his eyes kindly and intelligent behind wire-rimmed glasses (the very pair I keep in my study as a talisman). They are the eyes of a gentle man, a bookish man, someone who would pick up a book or magazine if ever the conversation stalled at suppertime, even if there were guests in the house.

Born in Ontario, Jack Crowe was brought at the age of three months to Montana, first to a homestead near Geyser, and later to a ranch on Little Belt Creek. Like so many of Montana's bookish folk (MacLane, Maclean, Doig), he claimed a Scottish heritage. Educated at schools in Ypsilanti, Michigan, and Missoula, he made a career as a teacher of history and Latin and as a school administrator in the towns of northwestern Montana: Troy (where my mother was born), Columbia Falls (where he served as superintendent of schools for many years), and Kalispell (where he ended his days). He was an ardent hunter, and during my youth, one emblem remained of his prowess: on my grandmother's living room floor in Kalispell lay a rug made from a black bear he had shot, its fur glossy and stiff and still smelling rankly of bear, its head lifelike, its teeth frozen in what I always took for a friendly grin.

But more than anything else in life (at least in my version of the man), Jack Crowe was passionate about books. He kept his favorites in a Mission-style oak cabinet, safe from dust and mice behind glass doors. This beautiful bookcase was my dream box, a repository, as Lynda Sexson might say, of the "stuff of the sacred." Not just a collector of books, Jack Crowe was a member of the anthropological category invented by French writer Jacques Roubaud, "*Homo lisens:* man who reads."[58] He would have understood, without reservation, the Austrian poet Ingeborg Bachmann when she declared, "Reading is a vice which can replace all other vices or temporarily take their place in more intensely helping people live."[59] And he would have nodded vigorously upon hearing Pierre Missac's dictum: "Those who roam

---

58   Jacques Roubaud, *The Great Fire of London: a story with interpolations and bifurcations* (Elmwood Park, IL: Dalkey Archive Press, 1991), 234

59   Ingeborg Bachmann, *Malina* (New York: Holmes & Meier, 1990), 57.

about in books do not worry about returning with empty hands."[60]

When, a few years back, I inherited two boxes of Jack Crowe's books *and* his beautiful bookcase, I felt myself coming home in some deep sense. As I opened the boxes and wandered among the dusty volumes, I sensed my bookish grandfather at every turn, his bald head bent over a book, his slender hands, his quiet presence, just as in those comforting childhood moments when I felt him beside me, the two of us – a kindly ghost and a young boy avid to live – reading from the same page. In his wonderful essay, "Unpacking My Library," Walter Benjamin tells us, "Actually inheritance is the soundest way of acquiring a collection,"[61] and I felt myself honored to be entrusted with the care of my grandfather's books.

The portion of Jack Crowe's library that passed into my hands was small but select: handsome sets of Teddy Roosevelt (including *A Book-Lover's Holidays in the Open*) and H. G. Wells; a leather-bound Shakespeare; *Gulliver's Travels*; two bound volumes of *Harper's Magazine* (1903–1904); an edition of Chaucer's *Troilus and Cressida* with wood engravings by Eric Gill; Virgil's *Aeneid*; Twain's *Personal Recollections of Joan of Arc*; and one of my boyhood favorites, a tattered tome entitled *Earth, Sea & Sky, or Marvels of the Universe*, a compendium of "Thrilling Adventures on Land and Sea," plus "Amazing Phenomena of the Solar and Starry Systems."

Sometimes, through his jottings in the margins and his underlinings, Jack Crowe talked to me. In his edition of *The Poetical Works of John Milton,* he prodded me to seek "life itself" in what I read; above a passage from "Paradise Regained," he wrote boldly, "This poem is only brain work & has no real color." On page 431 of Volume I of *The Library Magazine of Select Foreign Literature* (1879), near the end of Frederic Harrison's essay, "On the Choice of Books," my grandfather quietly encouraged my own bibliomania; with a check mark in soft pencil, he joined Harrison in declaring: "As the book exists, it must have the compliment paid it of being invited to the shelves." In my notebook, I placed Harrison's next to Walter Benjamin's, "To a book collector, you see, the true freedom

---

60   Pierre Missac, *Walter Benjamin's Passages,* tr. Shierry Weber Nicholsen (Cambridge: The MIT Press, 1995), 61.

61   Walter Benjamin, *Illuminations* (New York: Schocken Books, 1969), 66

of all books is somewhere on his shelves."[62]

By rights, I should be safeguarding my grandfather's books in his oak cabinet. Instead, I have chosen to keep another class of books behind those glass doors. Bookish Montanan though he was, my literate ancestor apparently had no interest in Montana's young literature. I did not find one Montana title among his books, a circumstance I cannot account for. Did the writings of his compatriots simply not interest him? Did he find meaning only in the literature deemed "great" by the academy? Did he somehow not hear the good news about the works of the new Montana writers of his day, writers like Dorothy Johnson and A. B. Guthrie, Jr., Grace Stone Coates and Joseph Kinsey Howard?

I will never know the answers to these questions, and so I have tried to carry on the bookish tradition my grandfather left to me, but with one difference: My bookishness – our Montana bookishness today – is global and local; it includes the classics, it includes the literatures of many cultures, and – cause for joy – it includes a mature and vibrant Montana literature. To celebrate this turn of events, I have turned Jack Crowe's beautiful cabinet into my Montana bookcase, a dream box filled to more than overflowing with the books of Montana's writers, young ones and dead ones, fiction writers and chroniclers of the "real," poets and philosophers, urban writers and rural writers, the famous and the obscure, all working together to offer us the multiple histories and inventions of an actual culture – our own.

---

62   Ibid., 64.

Writing Montana
Twenty-six Ways of Looking at a Literature

A Talk

Originally presented at the O'Connor Center for the Rocky Mountain West, University of Montana, Missoula, MT, March 1997.

Some months ago, Dr. Bill Farr [of the O'Connor Center for the Rocky Mountain West, University of Montana] asked me to talk to you tonight about the editorial process that culminated in the publication of the collection of essays, *Writing Montana: Literature under the Big Sky* [Montana Center for the Book, 1996], and about what that process taught me and my fellow editor, Suzanne Hunger, about the state of Montana's literature today.

On behalf of the Board of Directors of the Montana Center for the Book, I gladly accepted Dr. Farr's invitation – and then I realized, or rather remembered, that the process of editing *Writing Montana* had been as much an intuitive journey – with plenty of improvisation along the way – as it had been planned and logically carried out. With the process so recently completed, I asked myself, could I step back far enough to offer you a coherent image of what, in reality, sometimes seemed to verge on chaos? Given that I am always more comfortable with the fragmentary than with a false coherence, I offer the following fragments in hopes that they may prove helpful. They reflect my thinking alone. I cannot speak for Suzanne, or for the many others who helped make *Writing Montana* a reality.

In his introduction to *Montana Margins*, that wonderful precursor to *The Last Best Place: A Montana Anthology*, editor Joseph Kinsey Howard wrote: "Nothing is more personal than an anthology, and this one's pretensions to state and regional authenticity rest wholly upon the editor's judgments, with which few Montanans might agree." Bill Bevis, in his essay on the editing of *The Last Best Place* published in *Writing Montana*, goes on to say: "To assess any anthology . . . we should not ask if everyone, and all styles, were included. We should ask if it represented well a certain time, place, and preference. A great collection is not tasteless. The model is organic, not timeless."

Although *Writing Montana* is not an anthology, but rather a gathering of essays about one state's literature, I feel the need to join Howard and Bevis in offering my own apologetics: *Writing Montana* clearly reflects a time and place and its editors' preferences, preferences shaped – it must be said – by the climate generated and nurtured by previous efforts to define, analyze, and celebrate Montana's literary traditions. These efforts include H. G. Merriam's seminal literary journal *Frontier and Midland* (and scores of other little magazines over the years); Joe Howard's *Montana Margins*; the "Western Stories" issue of *TriOuarterly*, published in 1980 and edited by Bill Kittredge and Steven Krauzer; *Montana Spaces*, also edited by Bill Kittredge; *The Last Best Place*; *Circle of Women* edited by Mary Blew and Kim Barnes; and that groundbreaking work of Montana literary criticism, Bill Bevis's *Ten Tough Trips: Montana Writers and the West*. And then, of course, there are all those individual works of literature by Montana's many writers.

Some background, then. The time: the early-to-mid 1990s; the place: Helena, Montana; and the preferences: they will become more-or-less clear as I proceed. In our preface to *Writing Montana*, Suzanne and I note that in February 1992, the Montana Center for the Book hosted "Against the Grain: Organizing Montana's Writers," a gathering of representatives from more than a dozen Montana literary groups. In our preface, we noted:

> "Against the Grain" offered a disparate bunch of Montana writers – cowboy poets, rural humorists, romance novelists, writers of detective and science fiction, historians, and literary types from the state's universities – a rare opportunity to share information and common concerns, face to face.
>
> During the two days of "Against the Grain," we discovered that Montana's literary community is even more diverse, heterogenous, contentious, and lively than we dreamed possible – friendly tensions, bitter resentments, and traditional differences abound between urban and rural writers, among anti-modernists, modernists, and postmodernists, along geographic lines. Montana's

writers belong – we found – to what Spanish novelist Juan Goytisolo defines as a "plural literary space that [has] no boundaries" or what ethnomusicologist John Miller Chernoff calls a "diversified assembly," a community that seldom, perhaps never, speaks in a single voice – and yet remains a coherent, healthy community.

In our discussions with writers from every corner of the state, we discovered that *The Last Best Place: A Montana Anthology* frequently frames the ongoing conversation about Montana's literary culture. For some, it represents a (narrowly constructed) canon against which to define another, more inclusive canon; for others, it honors a meaningful (and remarkably diverse) tradition that feeds native pride and establishes a clear standard of quality for Montana's writers.

The board of the Montana Center for the Book had come to "Against the Grain" with a half-formed notion that we should publish a collection of essays on Montana's literature (especially since *The Last Best Place* had so dramatically increased Montanans' awareness of their state's literary traditions and since there was a very real shortage of venues for publishing commentary about those traditions.) But it was the unruly energy of the gathering itself that led us to move ahead with *Writing Montana.*

Given that beginning, how then did we come to assemble *Writing Montana*'s table of contents? We formed an editorial committee: Bob Clark, chief librarian at the Montana Historical Society; Richard Miller, Montana's State Librarian; Lewis and Clark Library's Debbie Schlesinger; Suzanne Hunger of the Carroll College English department; Richard Roeder, eminent historian and a member of the *Last Best Place* editorial board; Bill Borneman, bookseller and poet; and me.

We began with subjects – Native American literature, women's writing, urban voices – and we began with the names of potential essayists, writers who were already writing passionately and with insight about varied aspects of the state's literary traditions. We edited *Writing Montana* in the spirit of inclusion, but of course, in a book of 360 pages, we could only hint at the actual breadth and depth, the true richness, of Montana's literature. We shared a predilection, I think, for the overlooked, the under-appreciated, the repressed, and we wanted – at all costs – to avoid compiling a strictly academic collection. We sought experienced writers, not scholars necessarily, although a number of fine scholars contributed to the book, but sound thinkers and skilled stylists.

Some of those who had attended "Against the Grain" became prime candidates: Sue Hart, professor of English at Montana State University–Billings, a founder of the Montana Authors Coalition, and the prime mover behind the *Montana Literary Map*, published in 1991, proved to be the perfect choice to write an overview of the lively writing scene in eastern Montana. Romance novelist Sally Garrett Dingley of Dillon agreed to write an essay on Montana's genre writers but was sadly unable to complete it because of illness in her family. Two other attendees contributed to *Writing Montana's* group of ten essays on *The Last Best Place*: Mystery novelist and another founder of the Authors Coalition, Lise McClendon, also of Billings, and humorist and ranchwoman poet Gwen Petersen of Big Timber, a founder of Sagebrush Writers and the Montana Cowboy Poetry Gathering.

We asked part-time Helenan, regular *Northern Lights* contributor, and author of the Spur Award-winning *Raven's Exile*, Ellen Meloy, to survey Montana's nature writers, and with her usual wry elegance, she complied. Patrick Dawson of Billings took on a few sacred cows in his "Not Another Fish Story from Occupied Montana."

Ever since I encountered his "Glory Holes," in *Montana Spaces*, and his piece, "Our Literary Carpetbaggers," in *North Country Review*, Patrick Dawson has been one of my favorite Montana essayists, cranky and funny and fearless in the telling of his own truths. I almost never agree with Pat, on a logical level, but there is something in his work that commands your attention, that leaves you uncomfortable and sweaty and somehow exhilarated. It's the outrageousness of his opinions, those fierce nativist posturings, the barbed satire, the sheer excess of his style, as when he asserts, "It is a sad state of affairs when otherwise noble endeavors like fly fishing and writing are blamed for the ruination of a country. . . . In the arrogant tradition of Coronado, Custer, and Sir St. George Gore, so-called nature writers and pseudo-mystical white explorers wheel their new Volvos and Japanese 'sport-utility vehicles' over the mountain passes, through the canyons and prairies, and down our dusty streets, passing judgment and finding inspiration, acting like they are the first ones ever to see a sunset, glimpse a grizzly, snag a trout, or drink whisky from a tin cup."

Mentor of Montana fiction writers, former Missoulian Earl Ganz has long admired the works of Myron Brinig, the Butte writer described by H. G. Merriam as the "best native-born Montana novelist." As it happens, Ganz tells us in his beautifully crafted essay, "Brinig: The Truth Game," Myron Brinig was actually born in Minneapolis and came to Butte at the age of three, but he'd still written – in his *Wide Open Town* – "a wonderful book, a true picture of a great and terrible moment in history, the heyday of Butte, Montana, and the strike that marked the beginning of its decline." In "The Truth Game," Ganz looks at the man himself, his homosexuality, his ties with Mabel Dodge Luhan and her Taos circle, the pathos of a writer forgotten. In his eighties when Ganz became his friend and champion, Myron Brinig emerges – in Earl's masterful telling – as an enormously appealing, even tragic figure.

Roger Dunsmore has long been a student of American Indian traditions, and for *Writing Montana*, we selected from his collection of essays, *Earth's Mind: Essays on Native Literature* (forthcoming from the University of New Mexico Press this year), a meditation on the great Métis novelist DArcy McNickle and his phrase, "killing the water," from the 1978 novel, *Wind from an Enemy Sky*.

Helena historian and poet Noelle Sullivan had first caught our attention with an article on Montana's literary journals, written – I believe – for the *Bozeman Chronicle* in the early nineties, and we turned to her for an essay on the tradition of the little magazine in Montana. Her "Exquisite Magazine Corpses" covers the ground, from Merriam's *Frontier and Midland*, to eastern Montana efforts like *Alkali Flats* and *The Portable Wall* to purveyors of the arcane and the postmodern like Peter Koch's *Montana Gothic* and Borneman and Piper's *Multiples* series.

During my twenty years in Helena, I have been moved and fascinated by the life and work of Frieda Fligelman, scion of a Helena pioneer Jewish family, poet, and a founder of the discipline of sociolinguistics, and we turned to Alexandra Swaney – one of Frieda's protegees – for an essay on the self-described "Queen of Social Logic." Jazz composer and pianist, teacher, anthropologist – and now Montana's State Folklorist – Alexandra Swaney grew up in Helena and was befriended as a teenager by Frieda, "a small woman of birdlike energy and intensity, blue eyes sparkling with enthusiasm for the shape, direction, and portent of her latest idea, most likely related to her dearest obsession – the value of the great things spring-ing from the human mind: art, music, poetry, and especially, using human knowledge to better the human condition."

Educated under Alfred Kroeber, Franz Boaz, and Charles Beard at Columbia, Frieda was a member of the "Lost Generation," spending the 1920s in Paris, where – in collaboration with ethnolo-gist Henri Labouret – she applied techniques of linguistic analysis to the Fulani language of West Africa and demonstrated that non-west-ern languages were as complex as modern European languages and "sufficiently well developed and constructed to adapt to the demands of twentieth century life."

Frieda was also a poet, and during her lifetime – she died in Helena in 1978, at the age of 88 – she wrote 1,200 poems in English and "a few in French." She compiled these poems into a manuscript she variously entitled "Notes of a Lonesome Woman," "Notes for a Novel," and "Warning to Youth." She said that she had labelled her poems notes, even though they looked like poetry, because "the lin-ear form is a dress that can be worn by any idea. What is important about these pages is precisely that they are notes. Random notes are an aspect of life. They are just as legitimate a form as Alexandrines or sonnets."

In a self-portrait, she wrote:

She had a substitute
For beauty that is Freshness
And spring life –
She had the beauty
Of long weathered tints
On ancient monuments
Or shawls
Beauty that is chiseled in

By thought.

Ever the world citizen, she remained a Montanan. In Paris, she wrote in her poem, "Narrow Streets":

Our only view
In looking out on nature
Is seeing neighbors
Going through the necessary
Stupid things of life –
Eating and dressing
Shaving and playing cards.
Oh gosh! I'd give my bath-tub for ten miles of straight-lined prairie!

Frieda Fligelman and Myron Brinig, Sue Hart recently told me, were first cousins, and in fact, Frieda's father, the Helena entrepreneur Hermann Fligelman, paid for the passage of the Brinig family from Rumania to Montana.

As Missoulians may know, Henry Bugbee – now retired from the faculty of the Department of Philosophy at the university – has long been engaged in what he calls a "meditation of the place," and argues poet and bookseller Bill Borneman in his essay "A Philosophy of the Open Air," Bugbee's book, *The Inward Morning* – neither written in Montana nor about Montana – "marks the dawn of Montana philosophy." A famous walker and legendary fly fisherman, Bugbee describes his process of thinking: "weighed everything by the measure of the silent presence of rocks, spelled syllable by syllable by waters of manifold voice, and consolidated in the act of taking steps, each step a meditation steeped in reality." Bill Borneman concludes his essay: "Bugbee's form of instruction is like that of the waters of the river – now flowing, now frozen. By turns quiet and raging. Ultimately, his message seems to be: When there is nothing left to say and no one left to say it, what choice do we have but to listen harder. Listening itself becomes a language."

Julia Watson has very recently left the University of Montana to head up a women's studies program at a California university, and in a phone conversation, she told me that she saw her essay as a gift back to Montanans, and particularly to Montana women, for all they had given her in her years here. We asked Julia Watson to write an essay for our collection for at least two reasons: first, because we knew that she had done a tremendous amount of research on the autobiographical writings created by Montana women and had shared that research – and her insights – with many Montana communities through programs sponsored by the Montana Committee for the Humanities; and second, because we wanted to include a Montana scholar who was intimately familiar with the latest in literary theory and practice: poststructuralist, postmodernist, postfeminist, and we knew that Julia was, from her work as editor of such volumes as *De/ Colonizing the Subject: The Politics of Gender in Women's Autobiography* and *Theorizing Women's Autobiography; A Reader.*

Julia Watson's "Engendering Montana Lives: Women's Autobiographical Writing" is the longest essay in *Writing Montana* and, to my mind, a brilliant effort: exhaustively researched, passionately thought and felt, it leads us from the homesteading voices of Nannie Alderson and Evelyn Cameron, to native voices like Mourning Dove and Janet Campbell Hale, to the transgressive urban voices of Butte's Mary MacLane and the prostitute Madeleine, to those of our contemporaries Mary Blew and Cyra McFadden.

In her conclusion, Watson notes: "A startling fact: Every writer I have discussed is either an immigrant to or an emigrant from Montana; some are both. Many left because they found Montanans intolerant of women who didn't toe the line, whether it was a line for dutiful daughters or compliant prostitutes or dispossessed native women. Others came and stayed because their souls expanded in Montana's Big Sky as possibilities of self-discovery multiplied without the barriers of tradition in the East. Ideas of who and what is the Montana subject are now irretrievably multiple and heterogenous. And, as the generations of Montana women autobiographers I examined would suggest, always have been."

Where did we get the notion to ask a diverse group of Montana writers to assess, reexamine really, that Montana icon, *The Last Best Place: A Montana Anthology*? After all, for many Montanans, this extraordinary volume is literally a sacred text, our canon, beyond question. For those Montanans, *The Last Best Place* simply *is*, like a force of nature, bringing honor to Montana, and honoring our traditions and those who created them.

"One of the skewed advantages of a canon," writes Noelle Sullivan in her essay on Montana's literary journals, "is that it foments rebellion." This kind of rebellion, against literary standards and styles, I happen to think, is healthy, a sign of life in a literary culture. And by all accounts, Montana's literary culture is a vibrant and diverse and argumentative one.

Call it a perverse imp in my character, call me a troublemaker, but I was one of the first to take note of certain exclusions from *The Last Best Place*. In 1989, Clancy novelist Ralph Beer organized a *Last Best Place* conference at Helena's Carroll College, and he asked me to moderate the panel discussing the contemporary Montana poetry section in the anthology. In my introductory remarks, I offered a history of Montana poetry since 1964 (the year Richard Hugo came to Missoula), and while discussing the profound influence Hugo and the creative writing program at the university had had on the shape of Montana poetry, I noted that "Montana poetry has been even more diverse and unclassifiable than the already varied selection of poems in *The Last Best Place* might indicate." I went on to talk about "a kind of 'shadow' tradition" in Montana poetry, not one example of which was represented in the anthology.

The tradition I referred to was Montana surrealism, a school centered around Peter Koch's journal *Montana Gothic* published in Missoula during the 1970s. While not addressing Montana realities directly, this tradition drew its energies from, in Koch's words, "an outlaw Montana tradition that included Lee Steen, 'hermetic sculptor of Roundup'; the megalomania of the copper kings; the vitriolic tongue of Mary MacLane; 'the perverse relic of Club Foot George's foot'; Jim Welch and the high-line mythos; anarchy in the Rocky Mountains." My intention was not to denigrate *The Last Best Place* nor to demean its editors. I am very proud to have a poem in the anthology, and I consider that volume of 1,000-odd pages an extraordinary achievement for any culture, let alone one so young as our own. I simply wanted to expand the discussion of what constituted Montana poetry and to reclaim a tradition that was very important to my own work.

I was not the only Montana writer to call attention to the elements of Montana's literary diversity missing from *The Last Best*

Place. Some expressed their opinions in print, others in conversation, and in 1991, I published an essay on the rumblings over exclusions from *The Last Best Place* and another anthology, *Montana Spaces,* also published in 1988. This essay, "The Montana Canon and Its Discontents," appeared in the fourth *Writer's Northwest Handbook,* and in it, I noted, "progress in literary history is, as Viktor Shklovsky said, 'a succession of canonizations and displacements'; the canon being shaped, not only by considerations of form and of quality, but by the rise of new schools, new visions, new and contrary voices. And over the past two years, those Montana writers and constituencies even partially excluded from the newly constructed canon . . . have refused to be silenced, making their voices heard, sometimes politely, sometimes crudely, and often with great vehemence, wit, and anger. The displacements have already begun; what was definitive two years ago seems less than inclusive today." The excluded voices I mentioned in my essay were those of women, avant-gardists, and residents of the state's eastern counties.

By 1992, when the Center for the Book convened the "Against the Grain" gathering, it became clear that the most vocal critics of *The Last Best Place* were either from eastern Montana or wrote in popular genres (romance, science, and detective fiction, for example), and they were indeed vocal. We decided at that time to include in *Writing Montana* a kind of colloquium on *The Last Best Place.* We sought a balance between those who loved the book unreservedly and those who had criticized it (though often they loved it, too). We invited the anthology's entire editorial board to contribute (of the seven editors, Mary Blew, Bill Lang, and Bill Bevis chose to participate); we invited Margaret Kingsland, who had been so instrumental, as Executive Director of the Montana Committee of the Humanities, in making the anthology a reality; and we invited six other writers, ranging from fiction writer David Long of Kalispell to poet Wilbur Wood of Roundup; from novelist Melissa Kwasny of Jefferson City to poet and songwriter Greg Keeler of Bozeman; detective novelist Lise McClendon of Billings to ranchwoman poet Gwen Petersen of Big Timber. We sent each writer the following questions: "What has been *The Last Best Place*'s influence on Montana's literary culture? How has the book altered the ways the rest of the world views Montana? In hindsight, would you like to see certain writers or groups of writers added to or subtracted from *The Last Best Place*? As a result of the anthology's publication and the ensuing discussions about its contents, its forms, its exclusions and inclusions, how has your thinking about Montana's literary heritage changed over the past five years?"

In "*The Last Best Place*: Ten Views," the ten writers responded with eloquence and humor, brilliant defenses, sharp criticisms, a dialogue, and a short story. Together, they enlarge our view of Montana's centennial anthology, providing background on how the book was put together and effectively extending the range of Montana literature.

Paul Zarzyski straddles two poetic worlds, and in his essay, "The Lariati Versus/ Verses the Literati," he speaks to the differences and the common ground between contemporary, university-trained poets and the cowboy poets who have made their presence known throughout the West in recent years. Zarzyski came to Missoula twenty-some years ago to study with Dick Hugo, and he's stayed, writing his poems, competing as a bareback bronc rider, and in recent years, discovering affinities with the cowboy poets with whom he frequently performs.

Like most of us poets, Zarzyski has been eager to find an audience for his work, and in the passionate crowd at the third annual Elko Cowboy Poetry Gathering, the "self-described One-&-Only Polish-Hobo-Rodeo Poet of Flat Crick" found that audience. "[W]ith their robust laughter, I relaxed," writes Zarzyski. "I realized I'd come full circle back to the blue-collar world of my youth; somehow that world had discovered poetry while I was away and now was proud of me for bringing more of it back to them." In his concluding paragraph, he notes, "Thus far, I've discovered perhaps only a couple of square feet of common ground between the Literati and the Lariati. . . . My wish . . . is to nurture this small plot, and to witness it growing until it becomes a large enough 'stage' from which most any poet can speak the common language of, and to, the individuals who comprise the masses. And what we should be saying to them, again and again, is 'listen while we acknowledge and pay tribute to (Y)our lives.'" And Zarzyski's populist vision seems to be coming true. Friends who attended this year's Cowboy Poetry Gathering tell me that all sorts of writers, from the rural West at least – working cowboys and ranchers, the university trained and the self-taught, the free verse practitioners and the rhymers – are sharing the stage these days in Elko.

Richard Roeder, a member of the editorial board of *The Last Best Place*, one of Montana's preeminent historians, and a founder of the Montana Center for the Book, passed away on December 23, 1995. Only days before his death, he worked with my co-editor Suzanne Hunger to make the final corrections to his essay for *Writing Montana*, "The Genesis of *Montana Margins*." It was an essay he'd long wanted to write, given his profound admiration for Joseph Kinsey Howard, author of the classic popular histories, *Montana: High, Wide, and Handsome* and *Strange Empire*, and the editor of *Montana Margins*, the remarkable first anthology of Montana's literature published by Yale University Press in 1946.

Like Howard, Rich Roeder contributed greatly to our understanding of Montana's history and culture, as a co-author – with Bill Lang and Mike Malone – of *Montana: A History of Two Centuries*, a classic in its own right, and through his efforts in compiling the state's literary heritage in *The Last Best Place*. His essay tracing the creation of *Montana Margins* by an editor of genius can be seen as his final, tender contribution to the state he had adopted and grown to love.

Nicholas Vrooman, formerly Montana's state folklorist, shares with Rich Roeder a passion for the work of Joseph Kinsey Howard; most recently, he supplied a new introduction to the softcover edition of *Strange Empire* published by the Minnesota Historical Society in 1994. In *Writing Montana*, Vrooman tells us of Donald Hollowbreast, the Northern Cheyenne newspaper columnist who, since the 1950s, has served as a culture bearer for his tribe. Rendered deaf by the global flu epidemic of the teens, Hollowbreast gathered the information for his columns by sign language, that "beautiful dance of hands, a literary art unto itself," and in hundreds of columns, he "found a way to pass on, keep alive, and discuss on a community-wide basis, elements of life that comprise the very nature of being Cheyenne." In writing of the Sacred Buffalo Hat Bundle, Hollowbreast notes, "There are versions of the history":

> One of them is that the bundle came from the Black Mountain, north, in the ice flows north of Hudson's Bay country, somewhere back up towards the ice flows. When a man came with that bundle the Northern Lights were

flashing. And he came with the bundle to look for people who were good people. The instructions were that you go south, and when you see a camp of people, you sit on a hill and you watch them. You can tell whether this bundle will go to them. You can tell by the manner of the people. He came and sat on a hill, watched the people. And he didn't like the way they were, they were not compassionate. So, he left, continued south. He came to another camp, and he watched them, also. He didn't like what he saw, so, he continued south. The fourth camp he saw, he saw compassion, he saw people that were good people. So, he says, Here's where I'll go. And he came to the people with this bundle.

In "Landscape with Figures: The Georgic in Montana Literature," Helena native Maile Meloy traces another kind of history, that of "the farming or ranching family memoir, and the novel that reads like such a memoir," and how that literary tradition was influenced, shaped, inspired by the seminal works of Wallace Stegner. Part of Meloy's undergraduate thesis at Harvard, her essay makes the point that while "Montana's literary inheritance, the romantic West, has been reimagined thoroughly and intelligently by a generation of writers who have taken western work as their subject," "the Montana narrative still exists largely within the bounds of a decorum that disallows literary playfulness, sex, extensive allusion, 'mouthiness,' the excessively articulate."

Scott Mainwaring, a Helena bookseller, is articulate, even mouthy, about what he does and doesn't like in the detective fiction he discusses in his essay, "Montana Mysteries: A Partial Bibliography," and he seldom shows compassion in his judgments. Mainwaring read something over fifty Montana mysteries before sitting down to write, and maybe all that reading made him cranky. His bibliography covers the usual suspects – Crumley, Jackson, Bob Reid, Krauzer, Burke, McClendon, Prowell, Guthrie, and Hugo – as well as lesser-known locals like Grace and Olive Barnett, Margaret Scherf, and Muriel Bradley – and even such improbable national and international figures as Elliot Paul and Rex Stout.

In his note on A. B. Guthrie's four mysteries, Mainwaring writes: "Guthrie disowned his first book, the cowboy mystery

Murders at Moon Dance. The University of Nebraska brought it back into print in 1993 after his death. Why they reprinted this thing is not so puzzling if one reads his other mysteries; it is no less mediocre than the later ones."

During the 1980s, Laurie Mercier was Montana's state oral historian, interviewing hundreds of Montanans from all walks of life. More recently, she completed her doctoral dissertation on working-class society and culture in the "City of Whispers," Anaconda, Montana. Mercier seemed like the logical choice when we were looking for someone to write about Montana's oral traditions, and especially working-class oral traditions. Her essay, "In Search of Working-Class Voices: Montana's Oral Literature," presents oral narratives by two Anacondans, Tom Dickson and Katie Dewing, and these storytellers offer, in Mercier's words, "a critical perspective as well as unique patois and rhetorical skills." Because "working-class Montanans seldom wrote about their lives," we must turn to the oral record, captured by historians and folklorists, for their stories. Luckily, Mercier notes, "Working-class cultures valued visiting and camaraderie and provided opportunities and listeners to shape and polish stories, jokes, and reflections."

In 1988, Mary Clearman Blew presented a paper at the Montana Historical Society's annual conference. She called her paper, "There Ain't No Such Thing as a Woman in Montana," and she had written it in response to an essay on contemporary Montana fiction writers published in *Montana Spaces*. That essay did not mention, among the new writers cited, one woman. Reading more closely, Blew found – applying, tongue somewhat in cheek, the techniques of feminist hermeneutics – "traces of the excluded other," three brief references in which women or girls were either rescued or kidnapped, "acted upon and passed around like token[s] in a game, but essentially unretained." Blew concluded her remarks with the assertion, "There is such a thing as a woman who writes fiction in Montana. She is largely invisible. She's Pat Henley, Lynda Sexson, Linda Peavey, Ruth McLaughlin. She's enrolled in a fiction writing class somewhere, and she's probably keeping quiet."

In *Writing Montana*'s final essay, "Writing and Fire," Mary Blew reassesses the situation for Montana's women writers, and the news is good. Blew writes: "Ultimately, out of the twenty-three essayists and fiction writers that we included in *The Last Best Place* the only women were Cyra McFadden, Patricia Henley, Debra Earling, and myself. It is amazing to think that only ten years ago our list was so short. I look back and wonder if we saw the sparks."

In the course of her essay, Blew discusses the works of fourteen women writers of fiction or personal essay who make Montana their home full or part-time. She pays special attention to the writings of Annick Smith, Deirdre McNamer, Leslie Ryan, Judy Blunt, and her co-editor of *Circle of Women*, Kim Barnes, and of course, there are many others. Blew speaks for all of us when she concludes, "Maybe fires never seem to be coming closer until the moment they consume us. For now, we write; we cherish what we have; we celebrate our increasingly rich and diverse voices. Our future flickers outside the rim of vision."

What is a book like *Writing Montana* for? Why do we expend all this energy to compile, examine, and celebrate our home-grown literature? Does it matter in the long run, in the big picture? Montanan-in-exile Jim Grady, author of *Six Days of the Condor* and other novels and screenplays, offers one answer, perhaps the most important of all. In a recent letter that found its way to me after he'd acquired and read *Writing Montana*, Grady writes from his home in Silver Spring, Maryland:

> Growing up in Shelby in the 1950's meant denying many things, most of all that I would *without blinking* kill to write books and movies as the work of my life. Such denial was logical, for even among the families who read in that place and that time (of whom there were surprisingly many), knowledge of writers as actual people was the stuff of novels written by New Yorkers and Hollywood fantasies. "Everyone" knew that writers (a) starved; (b) were drunks or drug addicts or worse (whatever worse was, who dared contemplate?) (c) were nobody any of us would ever or could ever know. I knew about being poor and I knew about alcoholism, and clearly, there were no writers that I knew, so to dream of becoming one/ admit to being one. Well, that was something I kept secret.
>
> Of course, there were rumors of someone named

Guthrie and a woman who wrote *The Hanging Tree,* but clearly, they were gypsies of fate, and not really Montanans like us.

If nothing else, the mere existence of *Writing Montana* and before it, *The Last Best Place,* create the chance of realistic hope being delivered at a tender age to some other dreamer living in someplace like Harlem or Belt or Sunburst – or maybe even Shelby. . . .

What Is This "New" Montana Story?

Originally published as the introduction to *The New Montana Story: An Anthology,* ed. Rick Newby (Helena, MT: Riverbend Publishing, 2003).

"Make It New!" trumpeted Ezra Pound, that native-born westerner who fled Idaho at age two and never looked back. Pound tells us – in his Canto 53 – that Tching Tang, an innovative leader of ancient China, wrote "Make It New!" (a Confucian precept) on his bathtub, where he was sure to see it every day. Morrison's *Chinese Dictionary* defines the phrase Tching inscribed on his tub thusly: "Fresh . . . to restore or increase what is good." In Canto 53, Pound further refines – in the context of his efforts to invigorate the literature of his time – his understanding of the Chinese ideogram:

> Day by day make it new
> cut underbrush
> pile the logs
> keep it growing.

Pound's slogan, drawn from the deep past, became the rallying cry for literary modernism, but often it was interpreted to mean that the past has no value and that only the new – which represents an absolute rupture with earlier artistic styles and notions – can possess life, energy, substance. However, new scholarship indicates, as art historians John E. Bowlt and Olga Matich put it, that the new in twentieth-century art and literature "did not suddenly 'arrive' . . . but [instead it] maintained organic connections with the more remote and recent past and then nourished what came thereafter." Pound, who venerated many traditions, felt similarly; he sought to renovate his own literary tradition by reattaching it to its roots and enriching it with elements from other cultures. He wanted to increase what was good and, above all, to "keep it growing."

In compiling *The New Montana Story,* I have tried to bear in mind this vision of "newness." Some of these stories represent more radical breaks with the immediate past than others, but most of them skillfully extend a tradition that has yet to show signs of flagging – it is, after all, scarcely one hundred years young.

The New Montana Story showcases the works of what I am calling the third wave of modern Montana storytellers. The first wave, of course, included such legendary western writers as Frank Bird Linderman, Mildred Walker, Walter Van Tilburg Clark, Grace Stone Coates, A. B. Guthrie, Jr., and Dorothy Johnson. Through the 1950s, these masters, together with prescient educators and editors like H. G. Merriam, Joseph Kinsey Howard, and Leslie Fiedler, nurtured a small but vibrant literary community and laid the groundwork for the Montana storytelling traditions that flourish today.

With the advent of the 1960s, a new wave of extraordinary Montana writers emerged, some of them native born, others settling under Guthrie's Big Sky in search of quietude, natural beauty, cheap rents, and the comradeship of the ever-growing community of fellow writers. This second wave boasts such talents as the late Norman Maclean, Ivan Doig, William Kittredge, Mary Clearman Blew, James Welch, Annick Smith, James Crumley, Jon Jackson, Thomas McGuane, William Hjortsberg, Richard Ford, and Cyra McFadden. By crafting world-class stories, stories that resonate with readers everywhere, this band of writers set a high standard for all future Montana storytellers.

The third wave of writers – most at mid-career, though some are considerably younger – range from such well-known names as Pete Fromm, Melanie Rae Thon, David Long, Deirdre McNamer, and Ralph Beer to writers just emerging like Maile Meloy, Noelle Sullivan, and Aaron Parrett. Some are the students or protégés of the preceding generation, but others come from quite different backgrounds, bringing new strains into Montana literature. Their stories – and here I define "story" as narrative prose, whether fictional or not – include short stories (some very short, indeed), excerpts from novels, memoirs, and personal essays.

My selection process for *The New Montana Story* has been highly personal, colored by my own tastes, this historical moment, and my background as a poet and editor (who happens to relish a good story, wherever it may appear). Another editor might have chosen quite a different group of stories. That said, I have – in making my selections – operated on the principle of inclusiveness, although no anthology, of course, can be truly inclusive. This means that I have tried to assemble a genuinely diverse group of stories, diverse both formally and in terms of subject matter and tone. The one restriction I have allowed is that every story must, in some way, relate to Montana reality – however each author prefers to define that reality. My goal has been to achieve a balance between humor and drama, tight plotting and acute psychological portraiture, fabulist excursions and pure realism. Due to length limitations and financial realities, I have had to exclude scores of fine Montana writers, and to them I offer my heartfelt regrets.

Not only are the writers of the third wave "new" in the sense that many have not been previously anthologized – nor have their works become widely known outside a small circle – but they also craft stories that renovate the rich Montana tradition – *keeping it growing, increasing what is good.* They take on new subjects, for example, keeping us abreast of shifts, both slight and profound, in Montana reality. Some of the stories, like Dee McNamer's "Virgin Everything," take into account – to hilarious *and* heartbreaking effect – the displacements and distortions brought on by technology and globalization, Montana's status as a vacation wonderland for the world's elites, and the dire condition of our economy. Others, like Ellen Meloy's "A Map for Hummingbirds," underscore the migratory nature of our 21st century lives, while still others, like Pete Fromm's "Cranes," explore the emotional impact, even in isolated Montana, of AIDS, that postmodern plague.

Another aspect of the new has to do with tone, with a lessening of anxiety and an infusion of humor. Ken Egan, writing about A. B. Guthrie and what he calls the "Siren Song of Apocalypse" in Montana literature, notes, "It's difficult to imagine a less humorous tradition of writing than that practiced in Montana." In "Landscape with Figures: The Georgic in Montana Literature," an essay published in 1996, Maile Meloy notes that Montana's modern writers have been "anxious about language, its excesses, its uncertainties, its playfulness" and prey to an "underlying fear of appearing 'mouthy.'" The result, as Bill Bevis argues, in a reassessment of *The Last Best Place: A Montana Anthology,* has not been altogether negative, far from it. It has brought us, in Bevis's words, the "endurance, the realism, the various forms of terse eloquence" that have distinguished Montana writing.

But that tendency, admirable as it has been, appears to be diminishing. Many of the stories here – balanced by a number that are powerfully dark and terse and grave – sport plenty of humor and verbal play. Tom Harpole's rambunctious and affectionate "My Cat Chuck," for example, recalls Montana's hilarious folktale tradition, collected in anthologies like H. G. Merriam's *Way Out West: Reminiscences and Tales* (1969) and *An Ornery Bunch: Tales and Anecdotes Collected by the W.P.A. Montana Writers' Project* (1999). David Horgan's "A Lot of Living to Do" is a joyous take on questions of aging and memory and the creative spirit. Other stories, like Robert Lee's "Big Ears," use humor to ward off, and cope with, a failure of courage. Lynda Sexson's "This Is How We Got to Be Three Pods and a Pea" is an exercise in sheer play – a magisterial parable as mysterious and dense as anything in Kafka, but infinitely lighter in spirit.

The new Montana story is increasingly told by women. As Melissa Kwasny has pointed out, scarcely fifteen years ago, the Contemporary Fiction section in *The Last Best Place* included only four women out of its twenty-three writers. Since then, Mary Clearman Blew, almost single-handedly, has worked to correct the balance, both by spreading the good word about Montana's women writers in essays and talks like "There Ain't No Such Thing as a Woman in Montana" and "Writing and Fire" and through editing, with Kim Barnes, the anthology, *Circle of Women: An Anthology of Contemporary Western Women Writers* (1994), which included more than a dozen Montanans.

Fourteen of the thirty-one writers in *The New Montana Story*, I'm happy to say, are women, and their perspectives render the new Montana story that much more diverse, adventuresome, and truly open to the farthest reaches of Montana experience. To mention only a few: Caroline Patterson chronicles, in "Fruit in Good Season," the downward spiral of a woman implacably out of step with the constraints of her community. Debra Magpie Earling offers her own haunting brand of magic realism on the Flathead Reservation. With "A Black Convertible," Elizabeth Wood has crafted the pure expression of a yearning for broader horizons, for the open road. Melanie Rae Thon speaks, in astonishing prose, of unbreakable familial ties and tensions. And Noelle Sullivan appropriates the voice of Margaret Bourke White as she photographed Fort Peck Dam, and the people who built it, for the first issue of *Life Magazine* in 1936.

Rural existence has always provided rich material for Montana stories, and here Ralph Beer, Tom Elliott, and Kim Zupan spin widely divergent tales about life on the ranch. These writers know whereof they speak: Beer and Elliott are long-time ranchers, and Zupan spent a decade as a professional rodeo cowboy. It is a pleasure to re-encounter Beer's muscular prose, studded with particulars and rich with that terse eloquence Bill Bevis has celebrated. Among the first of the third-wave Montana storytellers to reach a national audience (William Kittredge and Steve Krauzer included his story "Riders" in a special "Western Stories" issue of *TriQuarterly* in 1980), Beer tells the story of a Métis ranch hand who honors the bonds of friendship, even unto death. Mortality, in its myriad forms, is the theme of Tom Elliott's "Journey of Small Deaths," as it takes us from the home ranch in central Montana to a Texas café to the realm of dreams.

For me, the fiction of Kim Zupan was among the most bracing of my discoveries as I edited *The New Montana Story*. I'm only sorry that I hadn't discovered his work earlier. His story here, "Shelterbelt," excerpted from the unpublished novel, "Why Do the Heathen Rage," appears at first glance to resemble the Gothic work of southern writers like William Faulkner and Cormac McCarthy – his prose is an overpowering onrush of language, filled with neologisms and archaic phrasings, "writerly" in ways that Montana literature has generally not been – and yet as I entered Zupan's world, I found myself astonished and deeply moved by his evocation of the austere beauty of the Missouri Breaks and of "an old man grieving with such perfection."

Themes of grief and loss shape many of the stories in *The New Montana Story*. In "Four Lean Hounds, ca. 1976," Maile Meloy traces, with great subtlety and emotional insight, the impacts of an accidental death upon those left behind. Paul Piper, in his story, "Snow Country," recounts – within a brief span – the process of a dying that is hauntingly beautiful and full of hope. Aaron Parrett, in unadorned, unrelenting prose, tells of another kind of loss, another kind of hope: the leaving behind of an abusive father. Neil McMahon, in an excerpt from his unpublished novel, "Journeyman," portrays a champion boxer who learns what it is to lose, while in Allen Jones's "A Fine Spring Day, with Regrets," a young fisherman discovers the true meaning of ownership. And in "Dogs and Dogs," the story of a homeless man and his canine companion, Phil Condon explores the redemptive power of letting go.

Non-fictional voices have grown increasingly important in recent Montana literature, and I've included personal essays and memoirs in *The New Montana Story* to represent this vital trend. With considerable humor, Ruth McLaughlin tells of growing up poor and resourceful on the northeastern Montana homestead settled by her Scandinavian grandparents. Native New Yorker Florence Williams discovers her Jewish roots in her adopted home of Helena, and Fred Haefele ruefully examines Montana's often bizarre image in the national media. Painter and bird hunter Sandra Dal Poggetto attempts to reconcile "my attraction to gun powder with my love of powdered pigment."

Montana's past has long served to stimulate the imaginations of Montana's storytellers, and I've included stories that make skillful use of that rich and conflicted history. In "The Last Photograph of Lyle Pettibone," David Long tells the complex story of labor struggles in a northwestern Montana lumbering town early in the twentieth century. In an excerpt from Matt Pavelich's novel-in-progress, "Our Savage," we witness the migration of Serbian immigrants upriver from New Orleans to the mines and brothels of brawling Butte. And in "Manus Dugan," a profile of genuine heroism, Ron Fischer takes us inside the horror and exaltation of the Speculator Mine disaster.

I have included, too, a few stories that stray far afield from the realistic tradition. Maile Meloy traces the origin of this postmodern impulse to William Kittredge's memoir *Hole in the Sky* (1992) – "what Montana literature sounds like when it makes its first attempts at playfulness and self-consciousness." The formal experiments I've chosen – "mouthy" and anti-narrative – include Bill Borneman's infinitely looping and loopy "Bill Bongo's Party," a meditation on rhythm and language and place, and Melissa Kwasny's lyrically fractured "A Woman among Them, Painting," which tells of the love between two women – who meet again and again through history and around the world, in an empty room in a small plague-ridden city, "in a stone village in the most civilized country in Europe," "over a hundred years ago on the plains of Montana." In "Warrior," Krys Holmes reveals how a child's grief and fear of loss can stimulate her imaginative powers, even her sense of play.

Playful and grieving, men and women, open to the new but steeped in tradition, the writers of the third wave of modern Montana storytelling – shaped, challenged, and instructed by the rigor, ambition, and sheer accomplishment of their forbears – have been writing a new Montana story that is richly diverse, often altogether surprising, and as a clear mark of their Montana citizenship, superbly crafted. The new Montana story is, as it always has been, many stories: some rural, others urban, some about deep roots, others about the loss of any sense of home, some boisterously funny, others sad beyond bearing. This is as it should be. With skill and heart and power, Montana's storytellers continue to tell us about individual lives in ways that touch us all, no matter where we live or what our experience. In Norman Maclean's phrase, their stories, perhaps now more than ever, are "true of Montana and of the world beyond."

A Regionalism that Travels
Further Thoughts on Montana Literature

Presented, in somewhat different form, to Dr. William Farr and the Hon. Pat Williams' Regionalism class, O'Connor Center for the Rocky Mountain West, University of Montana, Autumn 2002, and in the Dean's Lecture Series, University of Montana–Helena, December 2003. Some of the material in this talk is drawn from my essay, "Bookmen on the Montana Frontier," presented to the Colophon Club of San Francisco, May 2001. Versions of "Bookmen on the Montana Frontier" then appeared in *Rendezvous* (Montana Committee for the Humanities, Missoula, MT), Spring 2001; *Montana the Magazine of Western History* (Helena, MT), Spring 2002; and *Book Club of California Quarterly* (San Francisco, CA), Winter 2001–2002.

In a review of *The New Montana Story,* the anthology I recently compiled and edited, the freelance writer Janet Henderson made this critical point, "The delightful diversity of the . . . writing [in *The New Montana Story*] calls into question the efficacy of regional labels for literature. While most of the writing here escapes the dangers of regional writing, isn't it possible that continuing to categorize it could limit it? There is a chauvinism that underlies our pride in being Montanans, and it bodes well that most of these writers are not perpetuating that quality." She said further, underscoring her point, "Debra Earling's poetic American Indian story contrasts beautifully with David Horgan's wacky ultra-contemporary voice that tells a story with no effort whatsoever to be distinctly Montanan. [Horgan] offers hope that perhaps we are outgrowing regionalism, bit by bit."

Despite Henderson's excellent point, I still think that celebrating, and continually pushing the boundaries of, our regional literature remains important, even crucial to our sense of ourselves and our place in the world. Perhaps the following remarks will help explain why I feel that the notion of regionalism remains useful.

So, to begin:

In 1925, the *Nation* published its prize poem for that year. The poet was Eli Siegel, and he had entitled his poem, "Hot Afternoons Have Been in Montana." The poet, a resident of the East Coast, had no firsthand experience of Montana; rather, as he wrote, "Very early the wideness of Montana on the map had taken me. A hot afternoon in that wideness; that uncrowdedness; that United States!" "Hot Afternoons Have Been" was not really a poem about Montana, but rather a celebration of American places far from cultural centers, of the importance and validity of individual experiences wherever they may take place ("a person," wrote Siegel, "is a history, a being, and a possibility of aesthetic opposites.")

His poem, which today seems oddly expressed and certainly naïve, made an impact. It asserted Americanness, the equality and vitality of provincial existence, at a time when many American writers still looked to Europe for their models. As William Carlos Williams – the great American modernist poet of place and champion of a uniquely American idiom – wrote of "Hot Afternoons," "I say definitely that that single poem, out of a thousand others written in the past quarter century, secures our place in the cultural world."

The poem was a great leveler. In it, Siegel wrote, "In Montana, men eat and have bodies paining them . . . /Was not Montana here in the Middles Ages, when old Rome/was at its oldest, when/Aristotle wrote/ . . . in Paris/men and women wrote of philosophy who were elegant,/witty and thought spirit was of matter . . ./Samuel Johnson was/in London then; Pitt was in England; men lived in Montana,/Honolulu, Argentina, and near the Cape of Good Hope;/O life of man, O, Earth. . . ./Afternoons have to do with the whole world;/And the beauty of mind, feeling knowingly the whole world!"

At about the same time that Siegel was penning his ode to an imaginary Montana, a young professor at the University of Montana, H. G. Merriam – raised a Westerner in Colorado and one of the first crop of Rhodes Scholars – began to "encourage his students," as his granddaughter Ginny has written, "to tell real stories of Montana. Eastern writers have voices, he knew. What about ours, uniquely Western?" Like Eli Siegel, Merriam believed that even Montanans could have beautiful minds, capable of expressing with distinction their particular experience in this particular place. He sought to nurture this regional expression, both by founding the second creative writing program in the nation (after Harvard's) and publishing a literary journal, *Frontier* (later *Frontier and Midland*) devoted to the new western writing.

In 1930, he wrote to Grace Stone Coates, the wonderful poet and fiction writer from Martinsdale, Montana, who assisted him in editing the magazine: "I know very definitely what I hope to have started, and that is a vigorous burst of development in regional writing. That's what I'm working for. And I genuinely believe that's what we stand a good chance of getting. To my mind regionalism is to be the next vitalizing influence in American letters. Northwest life has richness, variety, freshness – why should we out here [not] be in the front line of the skirmish?"

Merriam, of course, did not invent literary regionalism. Instead, he was the leader, in the Northern Rockies, of an intellectual movement encompassing regional consciousness – emphasizing regional characteristics over national ones – that had considerable currency during the Depression years. And his intentionality, his drive to create a truly regional literature, bore fruit, among talented students like Dorothy Johnson, A. B. Guthrie, Jr., and D'Arcy McNickle and among the writers he published in *Frontier and Midland,* writers like Grace Stone Coates, Frank Bird Linderman, and Wallace Stegner.

As Mary Clearman Blew points out, from her vantage point today at the University of Idaho, one person can profoundly influence the quality of writing in a state or region. And because Merriam was in Missoula, and because other great teachers and advocates of a robust and sophisticated regional literature followed him – Leslie Fiedler, Richard Hugo, Madeline DeFrees, Bill Kittredge, and Dee McNamer to name a few – Montana literature, perhaps more than those of its immediate neighbors, has prospered. Idaho, for example, as Mary Blew asserts, "is not Montana. . . . [It has] less tradition and a lower profile," fewer well-established literary institutions, and she notes, "a disproportionate number of the current Idaho writers hold MFA degrees from the University of Montana." Why is this? Blew hazards that it may be because "Idaho is marked by isolation: isolation between the races, isolation between north and south, and the psychic isolation of our deep differences in politics and religion and economics."

Now you might argue that Montana, too, is marked by isolation, that what makes us exceptional, both good and bad, is our distance from everything that matters: "that wideness, that uncrowdedness" that Siegel celebrated. But one of the tensions – and strengths, I will argue – in Montana cultural life is the clash between our nostalgia for a romanticized, isolated past and the reality of our connectedness with information, goods, and people from elsewhere. Many feel that, in losing our isolation, we become too much like everywhere else, deterritorialized, denatured. In 1887, E. V. Smalley mourned this loss. He wrote:

> The railroad was the great epoch-making factor in the history of Montana. It took much of the romance and adventure from Montana life, it took away the sense of remoteness and daring, made life more commonplace, . . . set people to traveling, . . . and introduced a new population which knows not the ways of the "old-timer."

Smalley was, ironically enough, a publicist for the Northern Pacific Railway. Other examples of this powerful nostalgia include the painter and storyteller Charlie Russell's eloquent rage over "trails plowed under," and in A. B. Guthrie's *Big Sky*, mountain man Boone Caudill's dream, in the words of Bill Farr and Bill Bevis, to live "happy and free in a wild West"; Boone did not "hanker to live in no anthill."

My argument today will be that the power of the arts in Montana stems from the tension between our isolation and our travels, together with the permission cultural leaders like H. G. Merriam have given us to cultivate our own stories and visions: freely, unashamedly. This is a subject that is near and dear to me – this question of what I provisionally call a dynamic provincialism: a regionalism that travels.

Let me briefly lay out a few ideas from the ethnographer, James Clifford, on the subject of travel and regional identity, and then read you a little folkloric parable about how we Montanans have been known to (playfully) construct our identities. James Clifford, who teaches in the History of Consciousness Program at UC-Santa Cruz, is the author of *The Predicament of Culture: Twentieth-Century Ethnography, Literature, and Art,* a book that has greatly influenced my thinking about these matters. In his more recent *Routes: Travel and Translation in the Late Twentieth Century,* Clifford sets out, in the essay "Traveling Cultures," to more accurately define what the term "local" means, in all its complexity. Here's what he has to say:

> Twentieth-century ethnography . . . has become increasingly wary of certain localizing strategies in the construction and representation of "cultures." . . . [Of course s]ome strategy of localization is inevitable if significantly different ways of life are to be represented. But "local" in whose terms? How is significant difference politically articulated, and challenged? Who determines where (and when) a community draws its lines, names its insiders and outsiders? . . . once the representational challenge is seen to be the portrayal and understanding of local/global historical encounters, co-productions, dominations, and resistances, one needs to focus on hybrid, cosmopolitan experiences as much as on rooted, native ones.
>
> To press the point: Why not focus on any culture's farthest range of travel while *also* looking at its centers . . . ? How do groups negotiate themselves in external relationships, and how is a culture also a site of travel for others? . . . To what extent is one group's core another's periphery? If we looked at the matter in this way, there would be no question of relegating to the margins a long list of actors: missionaries, . . . literate or educated informants, people of mixed blood, . . . merchants, explorers, prospectors, tourists, travelers, . . . entertainers, migrant laborers, recent immigrants. . . . Ex-centric natives.

And speaking of ex-centric natives, here is that parable I promised, which plays with what "local" means in Montana. This story
comes from the collection of folklore collected by the WPA Montana
Writers Project during the 1930s, now housed in the Montana State
University Libraries in Bozeman. I stumbled upon it while helping
to select the pieces for the collection of folktales, *An Ornery Bunch.*
This story didn't make it into the anthology, but I've always loved it.
It belongs to the subcategory of Montana tales that poke fun at the
gullibility of dudes. It comes from Anne Hawkins's text, "Dances of
Pioneer Days":

> One met many notable characters at the old-time western
> dances. There was "Four-Eyes," so called because of his
> glasses. He had several degrees from Harvard, but he had
> tired of the effete east and come west to be a cowpuncher.
> "Four-eyes" attended every dance within riding distance,
> and I remember at one dance there was a young lady who
> said she was from the "East" (in reality from Posey County,
> Nebraska) whom "Four-Eyes" was quite attentive to. He
> was "stringing" Miss Posey County along at a great rate,
> making her believe that he was a poor dog of a cowpuncher
> born over on Bacon creek, and seldom off his range. Miss
> Posey County was *so* sorry for him. Wouldn't he come east
> some time? She'd be delighted to show him around; the east
> had so much of culture and art that the westerner missed.
> "Four-Eyes" expressed himself as being greatly in her debt
> and admitted that he had a hankering for the higher things
> in life and then asked Miss Posey County if they had hous-
> es on both sides of the street in the cities, and she said, "Oh,
> yes indeed, Mr. 'Four-Eyes,' they build that way you know."

Bookishness is a kind of travel, and long before H. G. Merriam found
his way to Montana, the very earliest EuroAmerican Montanans were
laying the groundwork for a truly literate culture, a culture where the
bold notion that local writers might have something important, even
vital, to say did not seem entirely foreign or laughable. What follows

is a little meditation on bookishness as a western way of being: In the opening moments of the 1976 Arthur Penn film, *Missouri Breaks,* starring Marlon Brando as a bounty hunter and Jack Nicholson as a horse thief, screenwriter Tom McGuane has David Braxton, the rancher who has hired Brando, proudly tell a visitor: "The first time we saw this country, it was buffalo grass and blue-joint up to the stirrups. By the second year we had eight-thousand Texas half-bred cattle and thirty-five hundred volumes of English literature in my library."

A few scenes later, after supervising the hanging of his visitor, who has turned out to be a horse rustler, Braxton – in need of relaxation after his grim work – asks his daughter, "Honey, pull down *Tristram Shandy* for me again, would you?"

Is Braxton a wholly fabricated character, a product solely of McGuane's book-infatuated imagination, or does this filmic bookman on the Montana frontier have some basis in the historical record? And if he did exist, what does his existence tell us about the character of the mining and ranching frontier on the endless prairies and in the mineral-rich mountains of early Montana? Can we find him believable, or merely a magic realist touch in a postmodern Western, given the images we've come to cherish of rugged Montana, a place purely primitive, untouched by civilization's curses and blessings? After all, as painter Sandra Dal Poggetto reminds us in a recent essay, urban collegians at the University of Chicago called students from the rural West, like Dal Poggetto's great aunt Pearl fresh from the high plains of Colorado, "barbs," "their barbarian ways a source of amusement and ridicule for the civilized young ladies."

David Braxton is, in fact, modeled closely on a real-life barbarian by the name of Granville Stuart, a Scottish-American bibliophile, miner, rancher, vigilante, and dreamer sometimes called "Mr. Montana," who claimed direct descendance from Mary Stuart, Queen of Scots. Stuart came to Montana early, with his brother James, after a less-than-successful foray into the California goldfields, and the two brothers, though they never achieved much material success in Montana, left an indelible mark on the place.

Granville Stuart had no shame about his passion for books, and the following story, told by cattleman Nick Bielenberg to A. J. Noyes, reveals the ambivalence Stuart's fellow Montanans felt in the face of his unbridled bookishness (an undeniable hunger for books mixed with deep mistrust of the distraction from the work at hand that reading inevitably entailed):

> Quite a number of years ago I bought some cattle of Granville Stuart. We had to move them across the country to the railroad. Granville was along . . . but as far as making a hand was concerned he was no good. He was always a great fellow to read. He thought it would be a good thing to take a whole lot of books for the cowpunchers' enjoyment. Darned if I know how many he had, but anyway a sack full. The way those cowboys would tackle those books was a caution. They would come into camp and pick up a book and the cook would holler "Grub Pile" till he was red in the face and he could never get all those fellows to come at the same time. Just as soon as a fellow would drop a book some other galoot would grab it. The cook called me aside one day and told me he was going to quit as the boys thought more of Granville's books than they did of his grub. It would never do to lose a good cook . . . and I told him not to say anything and I would see that [the books] would cause him no more trouble. It was the next day that we arrived at the Yellowstone so I gathered up the books and threw them into the river, thus starting the first circulating library ever known in Montana.

Granville Stuart's missionary zeal for reading – and he did have a library of some 3,000 volumes on the DHS Ranch in the Judith Basin – was shared by his rancher neighbor, fifteen miles distant, James Fergus, another Scot who possessed his own "splendid library and the leading periodicals." The reading materials in both ranchers' libraries, wrote Granville, were "at the disposal of everybody." Perhaps it is no fluke that Granville finished out his working life as head of the Butte, Montana, Public Library.

In actual fact, neither Granville Stuart nor the anti-bibliophile Nick Bielenberg was oblivious to the history each was shaping, and they sought to record it. Some, like Stuart, wrote his own books; others, like Bielenberg, told their folktales and anecdotes to scribes like A. J. Noyes.

Folklorist Lynn Rudloff writes, "People are story-telling animals. Cultures create identities through narratives." Granville Stuart himself launched his first effort to shape his new culture's identity in 1865, when he wrote and published *Montana As It Is,* the "first printed account of Montana after the territory was organized." Sadly, most of the edition was lost in transit to the West, and apparently only a few copies remain in existence.

Though he wrote several more manuscripts (most published posthumously, under the editorship of the ubiquitous Paul Phillips; the largest, a 314,000-word illustrated history of Montana, proved unpublishable), Granville Stuart failed to find worldly success in any of his endeavors, except perhaps in the improbable career of diplomacy. Even his promising time on the DHS Ranch, as cattle baron and leader of the band of vigilantes, Stuart's Stranglers, ended in disaster with the dread winter of 1886–87 and the death of somewhere between two- thirds and three-quarters of his herd. He recovered from this bankruptcy (and the death of his first wife, Awbonnie Tookanka, a Shoshoni woman and mother of his eleven children), in 1894, when he found himself appointed by President Grover Cleveland as U.S. Envoy Extraordinary and Minister Plenipotentiary to Paraguay and Uruguay. Granville returned to Montana four years later when Republican William McKinley replaced Cleveland, a Democrat, but before heading home, always fascinated by South America, Granville toured the continent, acquiring trunkloads of books along the way. He spent his last years in Butte, working as city librarian and writing the memoirs that would establish his immortality. As William Kittredge and Steven Krauser have noted, he was not simply, at the end, "a kindly old gent, surrounded by the books he loved all his life and fondly . . . recalling pioneer days"; instead, he was a "more complex man, an often impractical visionary . . . entrapped in contrary dreams, . . . and deeply angered by the paucity of his rewards." He died in 1918, the year before H. G. Merriam arrived to teach at the state university in Missoula.

I'd like to conclude with a few reflections on the questions, "Why do we care about our regional arts anyway? How do they matter? Isn't art just art, and don't we live in an era of homogeneity, of undifferentiation and displacement, where any regional differences are simply marketing gimmicks or the last spasms of a dying authenticity?"

For the last year and a half, as I compiled and edited *The New Montana Story,* I tried to keep these questions in mind. In *The New Montana Story,* I've sought to showcase what I call the third wave of modern Montana storytellers. First, of course, came such legendary western masters as Frank Bird Linderman, A. B. Guthrie, Jr., Walter Van Tilburg Clark, and Dorothy Johnson. Then the 1960s brought a new generation of extraordinary writers of fiction and memoir. Prominent among this second wave of modern Montana writers are such talents as Norman Maclean, Ivan Doig, William Kittredge, Mary Clearman Blew, James Welch, Annick Smith, James Crumley, Jon Jackson, Thomas McGuane, William Hjortsberg, Richard Ford, and Cyra McFadden.

What I've found in compiling my anthology is that the third wave of writers – shaped, challenged, and instructed by the rigor, ambition, and sheer accomplishment of the previous generation – has been writing a new Montana story that is richly diverse, sometimes altogether surprising, and as a clear mark of their Montana citizenship, superbly crafted.

The art critic Lucy Lippard writes in her book, *The Lure of the Local,* that "place is . . . the locus of desire." To put it another way, the local is a place we love, with the richly conflicted and enduring love we usually reserve for family. As I read through dozens of stories in the process of selecting those I wanted for *The New Montana Story,* I felt as though I was caught in a web of contending voices, each eager for my attention, each worthy of my love. Yes, things sometimes got a little discordant – but it was a great pleasure, this swimming among stories, this love fest, and I felt each evening, as fragments of narratives darted through my brain, that this web was becoming part of me, that in some way my experience of Montana as a place now included them all – the lyrical and the harsh, the outright funny and the sorrowing – and that this web would forever sustain me, in my place, no matter where I might travel.

To paraphrase Lynn Rudloff, we forge our identities through

the stories we tell about our place(s) in the world. And because we are free to choose those stories, we may as well give up on the nostalgic, on false stories that lead us astray, and instead choose those that, when inscribed upon our bodies, help us to more fully live. These stories are rarely predictable; they have little to do with local color or with the more banal aspects of what Tom McGuane castigated as a "sense of place"; they may frighten, offend, or challenge us. But they tell us truly who we are. James Clifford has written: "To know who you are means knowing where you are. Your world has a center you carry with you."

If you are lucky, as I think we are in Montana, the art of your place embraces what is essential in the local, takes into passionate account all of your travels and encounters, and allows you, in Eli Siegel's words, to "feel knowingly the whole world." H. G. Merriam might not recognize the multiple histories and inventions embodied in our new Montana stories, but surely, he could not help drawing satisfaction from the clear evidence that the regional literature he dreamed of – rich, various, and fresh – has so vigorously flourished.

Fine Print: Greg Keeler and Some Publishers

Originally published in *Kinesis* 3 (Whitefish, MT), Winter 1991.

Greg Keeler is one of Montana's most versatile literary talents – poet, song writer and singer, author of truly excessive musicals, a kindly and hilarious latter-day troubadour – and his work attracts publishers like a hatch of salmon flies draws rainbow trout.

Most recently, landscape painter Russell Chatham's Clark City Press of Livingston, Montana, has brought forth Keeler's *Epiphany at Goofy's Gas* (1991), a collection of 120 pages and some 60 poems, its cover (featuring an uncharacteristic, non-landscape Chatham oil, *Pigeons*) perhaps the most striking yet from Clark City's talented designer Anne Garner. Like Keeler's earlier full-length books from Idaho's Confluence Press, *Epiphany* covers a lot of territory, from "Chickadee Dejection" to "Wooly Worm Invective," from "Llamas in the Landscape" to "Erzurum, Turkey," and it offers its readers, as Gary Snyder says, much "wit, spit, and intelligence."

Epiphany at Goofy's Gas is available at fine bookstores everywhere, but another of Keeler's recent publications, *New, Improved Coyote* (1990), is a stunning art object limited to 150 copies and available only from the publisher and a few rare book dealers. Printed letterpress and hand bound by Stephanie Newman at Pumpernickel Press in Keeler's hometown of Bozeman, *New, Improved Coyote* qualifies as one of the finest examples of book art ever crafted in Montana, and its $300 price tag puts it in the same category as an original print, small painting, or ceramic sculpture.

Anyone enamored of fine book-making will find *New, Improved Coyote* a worthy object of desire; at the same time, it matches, with its antic colors and slightly crazed, slightly classical design, Keeler's revisionist takes on the Native American trickster: "Coyote sat in front of/ the typewriter disguised/ as a white middle-class/ slob cashing in on an/ Indian tradition."

Stephanie Newman, Assistant Professor of Graphic Design at Montana State University founded her Pumpernickel Press in Madison, Wisconsin, where she received her Master of Fine Arts under the tutelage of Walter Hamady, the letterpress printer, designer, and book artist whose classes and exuberant example have had a vivifying impact on many young American publishers of fine, limited-edition books.

Newman designed, illustrated, made the paper for, printed, and bound the first two books she produced under her Pumpernickel imprint. *New, Improved Coyote* is similarly handcrafted. Newman is again listed as designer, printer, and binder, but this time, she has farmed out the illustrations to Bozeman artist Fran Noel. They are three brightly colored litho-serigraphs – original prints bound into the book – with titles like "Coyote Wails on Silver Creek During a Lunar Eclipse" and "Coyote Hooks a Racist Rainbow at the Aquarium Pool." The papers used in the book are exotic, with names like Momi, Moriki, Ogura, and Ingres Antique, vividly textured, and ranging in color from eggplant purple to a mustard yellow. The typefaces are Lydian and Swing Bold printed in various inks, including a truly lurid, slightly darker-than-lime green, and the concertina binding revolves around a Montana dogwood stick secured by neon-hued fish line. All in all, the package is perfectly suited to its contents: "Coyote looked at/ the sun and asked, / 'What am I?' / After a few minutes/ the sun answered, / 'You're blind.'"

At least one Greg Keeler poem has caught the eye of yet another letterpress printer with strong Montana ties. In 1991, Peter Koch of Berkeley, California – wildly nostalgic for the trout streams and open spaces of his native state – launched his Hormone Derange Editions, a series of letterpress broadsides featuring texts by Montana writers, with Keeler's "Lament o' the Laundromat."

Perhaps not entirely politically correct, "Lament" tells, in the voice of a love-struck male, the story of his encounter in a laundromat with a "lady fair" who, sadly, ignored his advances, even when he expressed "my wild astonishment/ At our matching bowling shirts" and even when he "mad to desperation . . . seized her fresh dried underpants/ And drew them o'er my head." Measuring approximately 25 inches by 8 inches, the broadside features illustrations (by Zahid Sardar) of a washing machine and of a man's head, bespectacled, bearded, and crowned by a pair of pink panties.

Koch has since produced two more broadsides in the Hormone Derange series, both featuring poems by Missoula's Dave Thomas, the moving "A Memory from Last Summer," with a wood engraving by Missoula artist Dirk Lee ("a brother," Thomas has written, "in the struggle to give obscurity a decent name"), and "The Ten Thousand Things," the powerful Thomas poem included in *The Last Best Place: A Montana Anthology.*

Peter Koch, scion of a Montana frontier family, made his first mark in Montana publishing when he and his wife, Shelley Hoyt-Koch, returned – after studies and wanderings – to his hometown of Missoula in 1974. There, they founded Black Stone Press and the literary journal, *Montana Gothic,* and between 1974 and 1977, Koch published, in handsome letterpress editions, books by a handful of Montana poets, most prominently Michael Poage (*Born, Wings of Hair,* and *Handbook of Ornament*) and Jane Bailey (*Pomegranate*). He also designed and distributed Dave Thomas' first book, *Fossil Fuel* (1977).

Since departing Montana in 1977 and making his home in the San Francisco Bay area, Koch has kept busy, designing and printing exquisitely crafted books for private clients (his *Cheri* by Colette, in the classic Janet Flanner translation, created for George F. Ritchie of San Francisco, is one of my favorites; limited to an edition of 120 copies, it features Tovil handmade paper and deeply satisfying typography). He also designs and prints letterpress business cards, announcements, broadsides, pamphlets, brochures, and other elegant ephemera for the University of California Press, Fine Print Magazine, North Point Press, Stanford University Library, and many others.

In recent years, Koch has also occasionally indulged in his own publishing projects, including *Point Lobos* (1987), a portfolio of fifteen poems by Robinson Jeffers and fifteen photographs by Wolf Von dem Bussche. With an introduction by legendary California poet (and printer) William Everson, *Point Lobos,* printed letterpress on 18" x 22" sheets of a French mouldmade paper, is housed in a box of three-quarter-inch native black walnut and protected by a "removable Solander box constructed by Klaus-Ullrich Roetscher of archival materials covered with German linen." Truly for collectors only, *Point Lobos* costs well over $1,000.

Other recent Koch projects are his stunningly austere *The fragments of Herakleitos* (1990), with translations by the great Kentucky polymath Guy Davenport, printed in an edition of 113 copies; a book of previously unpublished works by San Francisco's late poet laureate

Robert Duncan, *Notebook Poems: 1953* (1992), created with the help of students at San Francisco State's The Press at Tuscany Alley, where Koch served as master printer; and a sculpture of lead and fired clay, with accompanying book, *Diogenes of Sinope*, translations by classicist and art critic, Tom McEvilley.

Koch now maintains a studio in Berkeley, a large and friendly space crowded with five letterpresses, including a huge automatic Heidelberg cylinder press, and prints and paintings by his favorite Montana artists, mavericks like Dirk Lee and Troy Dalton. There, like many expatriated Montanans, he nourishes his nostalgia for his home state to "a fine and excruciating pitch."

"Now I know, " he wrote to the Billings literary journal, *The Portable Wall,* in 1990, "that cutthroat trout and deer steak and Jack Daniels are mighty fine . . . I miss the rivers so much I dream about fishing." The results of Koch's "fine" nostalgia are these elegant and improbable Hormone Derange Editions, each bringing us a fresh Montana voice.

That Greg Keeler's poems – "lunatic masterpieces," David Quammen calls them – excite some of Montana's, and the West's, best publishers, "just as a farmer might be/ excited upon finding a spud/ shaped like the Virgin Mary," means that our world gets graced with some extraordinary books and broadsides, sonic, tactile, and visual wonders. May Mr. Keeler continue to pursue his lunacy.

Ken Egan's *Hope and Dread in Montana Literature*

Originally published in *Oregon Historical Quarterly,* Portland, OR, Summer 2004.

Hope and Dread in Montana Literature
Ken Egan, Jr.
University of Nevada Press, 2003
Literary criticism, 232 pages

This important study participates in the rethinking, even revisioning, of western culture called for by Wallace Stegner when he urged his fellow westerners to "Dream other dreams, and better" ("A Geography of Hope" in *A Society to Match the Scenery,* Holthaus, Limerick, Wilkinson, and Munson, eds., 229). Ken Egan, for many years professor of English at Rocky Mountain College in Billings, Montana, takes as his starting point that string of bizarre events not so long ago, when the Freemen, Ted Kaczynski, and the Militia of Montana captured the national imagination – and Big Sky Country seemed a place inhabited solely by violent paranoids.

Montana, of course, is populated by a diversity of peoples, many of whom abhor the extreme attitudes and behaviors of their most militant neighbors, but nevertheless, Egan argues, most Montanans share with these fringe elements the "sense of lacerating manipulation by outside forces, quest for a world apart, and attraction to violence as a solution" (xv). Egan then proceeds to examine, in the state's brief but rich literary tradition, the roots of such apocalyptic thinking and to seek out, within that same tradition, "alternative ways of responding to our crises" (xvii).

Egan sees Montana literature as profoundly dialectical. "Side by side with tales of woe," he writes, "move tales of endurance and even recovery" (xviii). Ranging across the entire history of Montana literature – and skillfully placing specific works within regional, national, and even global contexts – Egan first leads the reader through a prehistory of the state's literature, where both Native Americans and early settlers (Two Leggings, Pretty-shield, Plenty Coups, Garcia, Alderson) acknowledge terrible losses while maintaining at least a mordant sense of humor, and thence to the mid-century modern tragic tradition (Guthrie, McNickle, Hugo, Howard, Toole), in which the losses and failures appear irrevocable – and strangely seductive. These catastrophists, Egan argues, however beguiling, may not have served us well. "Visions of cataclysm," he writes, "can contribute to a culture of despair and thereby disempower as much as empower the reader" (109).

Egan concludes his study with examples of what he calls "pragmatic comedies," works by such recent masters as James Welch, Mary Clearman Blew, William Kittredge, Deirdre McNamer, and Ivan Doig, whose voices espouse "engaged, careful, concrete, caring responses to the pressures that continue to exert themselves on the rural West" (109–110). These novels and memoirs, in the tradition of Wallace Stegner, offer (mostly) unsentimental hopes – often through the discovery of deep connections to family and place – in the face of entirely real and often profound displacements, losses, and seismic economic shifts.

I can't say that I came away from *Hope and Dread* entirely agreeing with Ken Egan's thesis. I found myself wondering whether a region's literature, however pragmatic, can eradicate persistent myths. As Wallace Stegner said of the mythic cowboy, whom he wanted to bury, "He is a faster gun than I am. He is too attractive to the daydreaming imagination." (*The American West as Living Space*, 79). And I feel more than reluctant to dismiss the work, apocalyptic or otherwise, of such extraordinary (and beloved) writers as Richard Hugo or Joseph Kinsey Howard.

But that said, *Hope and Dread in Montana Literature* is a wonderful book, fluidly written, splendidly researched, witty, and riddled with insights large and small. As Egan clearly knows, Montana literature has always cut close to the real, however much it has partaken of foolish dreams, and one of the lovely things about the book is Egan's insistence on bringing to bear his own experience as a deeply rooted Montanan. His inclusion of Montana philosophers and historians is appropriate and refreshing, his focus on women writers is exemplary, and his tribute to James Welch, both for his brilliance as a writer and for his service to the broader Montana community, is worth the price of the book.

Hope and Dread in Montana Literature seems destined to stand on the shelf next to William W. Bevis's *Ten Tough Trips, The Last Best*

Place, and all those other Montana classics about which Ken Egan writes with such clear-eyed passion.

Truer to History

Bookishness as a Western Way of Being

Originally published as the preface to *Splendid on a Large Scale: The Writings of Hans Peter Gyllembourg Koch, Montana Territory, 1869–1874,* ed. Kim Allen Scott (Helena, MT: Bedrock Editions/ Drumlummon Institute, 2010).

When Hans Peter Gyllembourg Koch first arrived at Fort Musselshell, Montana Territory, in the spring of 1869, he knew at once that he had come to a strange, even barbarous place. As he landed, he beheld a sight

> . . . which was certainly calculated to shock the nerves of any eastern tenderfoot. Along the brink of the river bank on both sides of the landing a row of stakes was planted, and each stake carried a white, grinning Indian skull. They were evidently the pride of the inhabitants, and a little to one side, as if guarding them, stood a trapper, well known throughout eastern Montana, by the sobriquet of "Liver-eating Johnson." He was leaning on a crutch, with one leg bandaged, and the day being hot his entire dress consisted in a scant, much shrunken, red undershirt, reaching just below his hips. His matted hair and bushy beard fluttered in the breeze, and his giant frame and limbs, so freely exposed to view, formed an exceedingly impressive and characteristic picture.

Although Koch, in many ways, shared the prejudices and anxieties of his fellow EuroAmerican settlers, he was to become an exceptional Montanan, a pioneer whose story "deserved publication," in the words of historian Carleton B. Cone, "as an antidote to Hollywood's version of the settlement of the West and truer to history." Cone, a specialist in European history (with a passion for the West), was the first scholar to edit Koch's writings, and, late in life, he encouraged Koch's great-grandson, Peter Rutledge Koch, to move forward with the publication of this book. After all, he wrote the younger Koch,

> Peter was a middle class man of substance, better educated
> than most of the western settlers . . . [and] interested in the
> refinements of life. . . . Peter never herded cattle or wore a
> six shooter or sat in a saloon drinking & playing cards. The
> kind of people who did that didn't build the West.

While his claim (that cowboy culture played no role in the building of the West) can certainly be disputed, Carl Cone was right about Hans Peter Koch possessing a unique perspective on the character of the emerging frontier. Now, nearly seventy years after Cone began his work on these diaries and letters, the present volume, *Splendid on a Large Scale: The Writings of Hans Peter Gyellembourg Koch, Montana Territory, 1869–1874,* superbly edited by historian Kim Allen Scott, brings us a voice, alternately terse and eloquent, that offers testimony to a life lived in diligent pursuit, not only of material success, but also of a deep understanding – scientific, historical, and literary – of the place this Danish immigrant had chosen as his home.

Peter was not a bourgeois defined solely by his respectability and gentility. He embodied, in fact, the combination of rough and refined that gave the emergent EuroAmerican culture of the Northern Rockies its tension and savor. He had, after all, started out his time in Montana as a woodhawk on the Missouri, cutting fuel for the steamboats that plied the great river, and he was a trader at an isolated post on the Musselshell before he became a "substantial" banker. Like his fellow Montanans Granville Stuart and James Fergus, he was a classic western bookman, in love with this wild new country and, at the same time, passionate about the knowledge (and pleasure) to be found in books. And like Stuart and Fergus, he was an avid collector.

In September 1872, Peter wrote his fiancée, Laurentze, then living in Mississippi, that he was "enthusiastic on the subject of Montana, her beauties and resources. . . . I want to collect everything in regard to our territory. I expect it will be our home for our life, and the closer we study it and the better we know it, the more likely we will be to succeed." Not unlike his peer, the great California bookman Hubert Howe Bancroft (both men died in 1918), but on a smaller scale, Peter Koch assiduously collected the literature of exploration, and in this volume, Peter Rutledge Koch, in his essay,

"Unpacking My Great-Grandfather's Library," traces the history of that remarkable collection.

As his son Elers Koch would note, Peter believed "in a broad and liberal education. He emphasized the humanities as well as science." His passion for education and book culture led him to help establish the Agricultural College of the State of Montana, today Montana State University and the public library in his adoptive hometown of Bozeman. In February 1873, he wrote Laurentze,

> Here I am sitting in our new library-room which we have just opened. . . . It is really a beautiful hall. . . . We have two chandeliers with a shade-lamp over the reading tables in the centre of the room. On the middle of one wall is a large book-shelf, containing as yet only about 150 volumes, but with what we buy East and donations we hope to reach one thousand volumes before next winter. . . . I don't know anything in which I have taken so much interest for many years.

He called upon his future father-in-law, Christian Koch, to help him build the Bozeman library. He wrote to Christian, asking for both books and periodicals:

> I know you have got a great many books which you will never read again, and which nobody else (except perhaps Laurentze) cares about or will ever open. Now I should appreciate them very much, whether poetry, novels or scientific works (particularly the latter). . . . I shouldn't ask you if it wasn't that Laurie will, before long I hope, derive as much benefit from it as anybody. I wish also that you would send me some Southern papers sometimes. We have some fifty or sixty papers on our files but none from Louisiana or Mississippi.

By the spring of 1873, he could report that "we have got 4,500 volumes of books on the way, which will be a great help."

In his public spiritedness and as the "compelling, moving, driving force behind the movement for a newer education," Peter Koch possessed, in the words of the 1919 Bozeman *Weekly Exponent,* "the intelligence of an aristocrat and the heart of a democrat." Peter's drive to collect "everything in regard to our territory" extended beyond the assembling of private and public libraries. He aggressively collected all manner of material related to his new home, and he befriended the men charged with documenting and preserving the wonders of the West, figures like Nathaniel Langford, the first superintendent of Yellowstone National Park; Langford's fellow explorer Ferdinand Hayden; and the great documentary photographer William Henry Jackson. In October 1872, he wrote to Laurentze:

> I like Dr Hayden very much and I take so much interest in his explorations. . . . He has promised me copies of all his former reports as soon as he gets to Washington, he gave me to-day also some stereoscopic views, which I will send you soon, and he gave me a copy of his last report (the same you have got). . . . He had me sent some more meteorological instruments the other day, and I hope to get a barometer from the U.S. Coast Survey.
>
> . . . I will write to Jackson, the photographer of the expedition, to send you some stereoscopic views, as soon as he has been home long enough to take copies. You will notice that I am anxious you shall have an idea of our territory, and I am indeed in love with it. . . . I will admit it has a . . . rigorous climate; but then again we have weather, and are having it now, which cannot be equalled anywhere in the world. An autumn day here is perfect. . . .

He asked his fiancée to help broaden his search: "I wish when you run across any articles on Montana or surrounding countries in newspaper or magazines that you would save them for me." Again, he asserted his intention to "collect everything in regard to our territory." And he contributed his own accounts of life in Montana, penning articles for both Danish and American publications (for an example of this occasional journalism, see his article, "Life at Muscleshell in 1869 and 1870"; originally published in the second volume of *The Contributions to the Historical Society of Montana* in 1896, this narrative does a great deal to fill in gaps in the more immediate, but necessarily more fragmentary account of this period found in Peter's letters).

Peter saw the physical world as another text to be read, if only he could learn enough, and he noted that, during his time as a surveyor, he'd acquired a copy of George Lyell's *Student's Elements of Geology*, since "surveying through these mountains gives one a good opportunity to studying it, and I see so many things puzzling to me. . . . It is impossible to travel through Montana without wanting to know something of geology." His curiosity extended broadly. He became an accomplished botanist, and he was always seeking the fossil record. In 1874, he reported that he had not "succeeded in finding any fossils . . . although I never go out without breaking up rocks to look for them."

Peter's studious efforts to understand his new home did not foreclose a more purely experiential appreciation of the place. One fine fall day in 1873, he wrote to Laurentze:

> You have no idea how much there is in this wild life that I enjoy. If I were 10 years younger it would be terribly easy for me to turn into a half savage and spend my life on the prairie. The sense of freedom one has out here when he gets up, where he can look around for a hundred miles and not see his neighbor's smoke, is perfectly splendid. Some mornings when I am riding all alone, I cannot help putting my mare at a gallop and singing loud.

Heretofore, Hans Peter Koch has been known, if he is remembered at all, for his yeoman's work on behalf of an emerging literate culture in this new land. But with the publication of *Splendid on a Large Scale*, we now have him as author, a man of many parts who has left us this wonderfully articulate account of his first years in a new country – as unlikely frontiersman, often reluctant businessman, aspiring naturalist, avid bookman, and yearning lover (he and Laurentze did not marry until October 1874).

It is with great pleasure that Drumlummon Institute, in collaboration with Peter Rutledge Koch and our good friends at Bedrock Editions, brings these important texts – until now buried in archives and miscellaneous publications – to those who love the history and lore of the American West. It seems fair to say that Hans Peter Koch's letters and diaries (as "antidote to Hollywood's version of the settlement of the West") stand among the most richly nuanced, fluent, and intimate accounts we have of the early days of white settlement in Montana Territory.

The Flavor of Words
The Selected Poems of Grace Stone Coates

Originally published as the preface to *Food of Gods and Starvelings: The Selected Poems of Grace Stone Coates,* eds. Lee Rostad & Rick Newby (Helena, MT: Drumlummon Institute, 2007).

When Lee Rostad first approached me about publishing a volume of selected poems by Grace Stone Coates, I knew this had to be the perfect choice as the first book published by Drumlummon Institute. Grace Stone Coates of Martinsdale was not only a Montana writer whose poems and stories resonated far beyond the state's borders, but she had been instrumental in the nurturing of a homegrown literary tradition – through her work as an editor with Harold G. Merriam and his seminal regional journal, *Frontier* (later *Frontier and Midland)* at the University of Montana. And Drumlummon Institute aims, in our own modest way, both to continue the grand tradition of Merriam's *Frontier and Midland* (through our online journal of Montana arts and culture, *Drumlummon Views)* and to extend the reach of Montana's arts and letters far beyond this place, through the journal and our books.

As Lee Rostad notes in her fine introduction below, Grace Stone Coates was soon forgotten after her death in 1976, but since 1985 and the publication of Lee's *Honey Wine and Hunger Root: Grace Stone Coates* (a slender selection of Grace's poems, together with a biographical essay), Grace has reemerged as a powerful voice of Montana and American literature. Her inclusion in *The Last Best Place: A Montana Anthology* (1988) cemented that reemergence, and in subsequent years, with the republication by the University of Nebraska Press of her classic novel, *Black Cherries,* and the release in 2004 of Lee Rostad's award-winning *Grace Stone Coates: A Biography in Letters,* we have been able to witness firsthand Grace's prowess as a storyteller and as an astonishing correspondent who touched the lives of many of our finest writers, from William Saroyan to Frank Bird Linderman to Taylor Gordon. We only lacked a substantial selection of her poetry to fully appreciate all dimensions of this wonderfully passionate, profoundly witty, and often moving writer.

This book stands somewhere between a volume of collected

poems and the usual "selected" poems, which offers only a taste from the various stages of a poet's lifetime of work. After much thought, Lee Rostad and I decided that we wanted to give readers as large a sampling of Grace's best poetic work as cost and good sense would allow. For this reason, we have included all of the poems in Grace's two published volumes of verse, *Mead and Mangel-Wurzel* and *Portulacas in the Wheat*. These two excellent collections have been out of print since the early 1930s, and copies of the first editions, when they can be found, sell for as much as $160. Even Lee Rostad's *Honey Wine and Hunger Root* is hard to find and can cost $95 on the rare book market. In addition to the complete texts of those two published collections, we include a final section of more than seventy "uncollected" poems culled from literary magazines and Grace's manuscripts (out of many more than twice that many). This book is quite simply intended for lovers of poetry, who will – we trust – find much to love here.

Through her role as Grace's literary executor, Lee Rostad has long known the full range of the poetry of Grace Stone Coates. My acquaintanceship with the work is relatively new, and my reading of Grace's poems has been a startling and deeply rewarding journey of discovery. Grace Stone Coates was not a nice lady poet. Her honesty is unremitting and sly; she once wrote, "I put a little lunar caustic in the honey sometimes." Her take on the dance between men and women, especially within the circle of married life, is unsettling, lucid, and ruthless. And yet her deep tenderness for those close to her, especially her husband Henderson, comes through in poems like "To H – " and "For a Hunter's Safety." She was not interested in grand gestures, but rather in the drama of daily life. As she wrote, "[A] carved cherry pit means as much to me as those faces that insult the Black Hills."

Trying to capture the essence of her poetic work, H. G. Merriam wrote to Grace:

> You like brittle emotion, hard crystal thot, subtle and experimental wording. You also delight in phrases, in the flavor of words. You prefer tempered emotions – tempered not necessarily by living but by thinking.

Irony – that gap between what is said and what is understood, generating humor or a wince – was her frequent weapon and, as one critic put it, her "armour." Lee Rostad points out in her introduction that Grace often found her own work "hilarious." She was as hard on herself as on her neighbors (who never understood her poet's need to be "alertly intent keeping quiet"; they would barge in, cautioning her, "Don't sit doing nothing, it makes one so blue").

Grace had tremendous range, and her poetic output includes short lyrics, long narratives, satires, laments over losses, history poems infused by her intimate knowledge of Montana history, odes to the natural world, sly parables, and "voice" poems (where she entered into the consciousness of another). She ceased writing poetry in mid-life, but two decades later, she could assure H. G. Merriam that she had found "a degree of tranquility, an inner happiness that persists even when I'm tired or irritated or momentarily crying outside. Sometimes I feel luminous inside. . . . I'm still convinced that the creative principle of the universe is laughter." I for one am grateful that Grace Stone Coates has left us her luminous poems – and that she retained throughout a belief in the healing power of laughter, finally finding an "inner happiness" that tears could not wash away.

I want to thank Lee and Phil Rostad for their unstinting support of this project. Lee Rostad has been the exemplary literary executor. It is through her efforts, her abiding passion for the life and work of Grace Stone Coates, that we now have in print so much of the mature work of this remarkable writer. The legacy of Grace Stone Coates has benefited, too, from the championing of her work by other scholars and editors, especially Richard Roeder, Mary Clearman Blew, and Caroline Patterson.

A Few Words on the Poetics of Frieda Fligelman

Originally published as the preface to *Notes for a Novel: The Selected Poems of Frieda Fligelman,* eds. Alexandra Swaney & Rick Newby (Helena: Drumlummon Institute, 2008).

> *To great writers, finished works weigh lighter than those fragments on which they labor their entire lives.*
>
> – Walter Benjamin

> *What is important about these pages is precisely that they are notes. Random notes are an aspect of life. They are just as legitimate a form as Alexandrines or sonnets.*
>
> – Frieda Fligelman

> *A song, a spirit, a white star that moves across the heaven to mark the end of a world epoch or to presage some coming glory.*
>
> – H. D. (Hilda Doolittle)

As Alexandra Swaney and I made our selection from Frieda Fligelman's more than 1,200 poems (her lifetime's assemblage of "random notes"), it became increasingly clear that, like her age-peers H.D. (Hilda Doolittle) and Marianne Moore (H.D. was born in 1886, Moore in 1887, and Frieda in 1890), Frieda stands in a grand tradition of women poets who, from antiquity, have expressed their personal visions with concision and clarity, distilling, refining, singing.

Like H.D. and Moore, Frieda possesses a truly modern voice. And like the work of Moore and H.D., Frieda's "notes" arise out of – in the words of critic Jeanne Kammer – "habits of privacy, camouflage, and indirection," resulting in "linguistic compression" and daring juxtapositions. Like her fellow Montanan, that "amorous diarist with a Narcissus complex," Mary MacLane of Butte (born in 1881) – whose works are said to have influenced D. H. Lawrence, Ernest Hemingway, and Gertrude Stein – Frieda Fligelman wrote from a westerner's sense of independence and ebullient possibility.

When speaking of Frieda's modernity, too much cannot be made of her upbringing in late nineteenth- and early twentieth-century Montana where, as historian Paula Petrik has written, the "frontier had shaped a new vision of what was necessary and possible for women." In the Helena of Frieda's youth, the Victorian "cult of true womanhood" lost some of its power, and young women absorbed, in Petrik's words, "values more commonly associated with masculine society – independence, work, and participation in public life." Clearly, Frieda was among those female Montanans who most thoroughly internalized the new values. As her younger sister Belle Fligelman Winestine recalls, "Frieda was the one who said that instead of going to finishing school, we were going to college. . . . When our parents saw how terribly she wanted to go, they were willing to send her. And, of course, when she went, I would be the one to go too."

Both Frieda and Belle plunged into the women's suffrage movement in Montana. Belle gave speeches on street corners, and Frieda was among those who set up and ran suffrage booths at the Montana State Fairs of 1911 and 1912. Montana's women won the vote in 1914, and in 1916, Montana suffragist Jeannette Rankin was the first woman elected to the United States Congress (Belle Fligelman traveled to Washington with Rankin, serving as her chief assistant).

As a western woman, Frieda felt her responsibility to participate in public life deeply, and from early adulthood she was passionate about social reform. In 1911, she wrote to Randolph Bourne, the great American social critic and theorist of an anti-war ethic ("War is the health of the state" was his slogan), that she intended "doing good *with* people" rather than a more paternalistic "*for*" or "*to*". In her work as a pioneering sociolinguist, she sought to reform Euro-American perceptions of so-called "primitive" languages, and as one reviewer wrote in 1933, her pioneering work on Fulani vocabulary "will give pause to those who maintain the insufficiency of African vernaculars for the development of a higher culture."

Not only a truthteller who helped lay the groundwork, through activism and example, for enormous changes in the lives of women and in the western world's understanding of other cultures, Frieda Fligelman may well be one of the most remarkable unknown poets of the American West. Frieda had only published a handful of poems in her lifetime (primarily in an exceedingly slim volume she entitled *Beyond the Mores,* printed letterpress and hand bound in 1965 by Athé Press in Berkeley). Just as she sought to demonstrate the sophistication and complexity of Fulani and other African languages, she hoped – through her poems – to give voice to "thousands [who] have had these experiences, however inarticulately." With her unstinting honesty and her anguish modulated by wit, she modeled a new (and often difficult) way of being. It is our hope that this volume will bring Frieda's notes to an audience ready to hear this story of a woman ahead of her time, a woman certainly lonesome but also always "fascinated by the possibilities of life."

Having written those 1,200 poems, Frieda Fligelman presented us with a daunting challenge. How were we to select a representative group of poems that showcased her best work, illumined her central concerns as a poet, and honored the carefully thought-out architecture of her manuscript?

At first, as editors, we sought to select only Frieda's most concentrated and skillfully crafted poems, but upon reflection, we felt that this approach was too conventional for the work of such a free (and iconoclastic) spirit and would lose the full range of Frieda's emotion (especially the darker humors). After all, *Notes for a Novel* is not simply the gathering of a life's work in poetry, but rather a consciously constructed text, with each poem placed just so, after much deliberation.

While we could not include even half of her poems, we felt that to abandon her set of categories was to do irreversible violence to her intention. And so, we have preserved her book's eccentric architecture, with its imaginatively titled subsets, its several (and often recurring) themes, and its balance between density and a lightness that signals triumph over all obstacles (and there were many).

Over her lifetime, Frieda kept a record of the order in which she wrote her poems, but in the manuscript she left at her death, she shattered any chronological order, carefully rearranging her notes according to theme. Nevertheless, she must have felt that it was important that the reader know her original order. Therefore, she provided the numbers you will find in brackets to the right of the title of each poem; these indicate each note's place in her original, chronological order. Thus, a poem written in the 1920s (say, #200) might find itself immediately following a poem written in the 1960s (#1021) followed by another from the 1940s (#626). The only poems that do not have these numbers are the final two, which did not appear in her final typescript but are printed in her little book, *Beyond the Mores.* We include these two poems because Frieda sometimes read them aloud in her final years and because they capture the absolute freshness of her spirit, even at the end.

Many thanks to those who have believed in the importance of Frieda Fligelman's testimony to a life lived fully (despite many disappointments). Above all others, Alexandra Swaney has shepherded Frieda's literary legacy with great care, love, and grace. As Frieda's literary executor, Alex has ensured the preservation of Frieda's papers at the University of Montana and the Montana Historical Society, and she has written with candor, heart, and insight about both Frieda's pioneering work in sociolinguistics and her prowess as a poet (see Alex's introductory essay to this book). *Notes for a Novel* stands as a monument not only to Frieda's wit, her indefatigable spirit, her heartbreak, and her darting intellect, but also to Alexandra Swaney's passionate championing of a nearly forgotten figure whose voice remains vividly modern today.

Many thanks are also due to Caroline Patterson for including a sampling of Frieda's poems in her anthology, *Montana Women Writers: A Geography of the Heart,* and to Tami Haaland of Montana State University–Billings for recognizing Frieda's work through her Montana Poetry Project. We are grateful to Harriet Rochlin, a leading scholar of the Jewish experience in the American West, for contributing her insightful foreword. And our gratitude goes to Arnie Malina, for permission to reprint his fine essay on Frieda. Arnie was among the very earliest champions of Frieda's life and poetry.

Sources

Jeanne E. Abrams, *Jewish Women Pioneering the Frontier Trail: A History in the American West* (New York: New York University Press, 2006).

Walter Benjamin, "One-Way Street," *Reflections: Essays, Aphorisms, Autobiographical Writings,* ed. Peter Demetz (New York: Harcourt Brace Jovanovich, 1978).

H.D. (Hilda Doolittle), *Notes on Thought & Vision & The Wise Sappho* (San Francisco: City Lights Books, 1982).

Rachel Blau Duplessis, *H.D.: The Career of That Struggle* (Bloomington: Indiana University Press, 1986).

Mary MacLane, *Tender Darkness: A Mary MacLane Anthology,* ed. Elizabeth Pruitt (Belmont, CA: Abernathy & Brown, 1993).

Paula Petrik, *No Step Backward: Women and Family on the Rocky Mountain Mining Frontier* (Helena: Montana Historical Society, 1987, 1990).

Christine Stansell, *American Moderns: Bohemian New York and the Creation of a New Century* (New York: Macmillan, 2001).

Elizabeth Cady Stanton, Susan Brownell Anthony, Matilda Joslyn Gage, and Ida Husted Harper, *The History of Woman Suffrage* (Rochester, NY: Susan B. Anthony, 1922).

A. W., review of Frieda Fligelman, "Moral Vocabulary of an Unwritten Language (Fulani)," in *Journal of the Royal African Society,* 32:127 (April 1933), 216–217.

Against the Terrible Dismembering
The Poetry of Roger Dunsmore

Originally published as the introduction to Roger Dunsmore, *On the Chinese Wall: New & Selected Poems, 1966–2018*, ed. Rick Newby (Helena, MT: Drumlummon Institute, 2018).

When Roger Dunsmore was seeking his Master of Fine Arts in poetry in the late 1960s, he was a mature student who knew his own mind. One day, in the hallway of the English department at the University of Montana, he told a fellow student that his search for spiritual meaning was always more important to him than poetry, and that if the poems ever got in the way of his life of the spirit, he would gladly set the poems aside. The brilliant poet Madeline DeFrees, one of his principal teachers, overheard the conversation and chastised Roger for his lack of commitment to a poetic vocation. Having both a spiritual vocation and a poetic one herself – DeFrees had spent nearly 40 years as a Sister of the Holy Names of Jesus and Mary – Madeline knew the choice Roger described could be very real. (In 1973, she would formally turn away from her vows and wholeheartedly embrace teaching and writing.)

Fortunately, Roger Dunsmore has never had to make that choice. Poetry, for him, became a spiritual practice, "a form of sanity." As he told a reporter, "It probably saved my life. Before I started writing I had no way, no vehicle to express or explore what I was feeling. Poetry has given me that."[1] Perhaps he would agree with Matsuo Bashō, who once wrote: "In this poor body, composed of one hundred bones and nine openings, is something called spirit, a flimsy curtain blown this way and that by the slightest breeze. It is spirit, such as it is, which led me to poetry, at first little more than a pastime, then the whole business of my life."[2]

In the essay that follows, I attempt to set out the path that led Roger Dunsmore to the way of poetry. His poems speak for themselves, but the story of his coming to poetry is a singular one.

---

1   "Montana Western's Roger Dunsmore earns Humanities Montana award," University of Montana Western website; https://www.umwestern.edu/scholarship-grant-research-news/1202-montana-westerns-roger-dunsmore-earns-humanities-montana-award.html

2   Quoted in Lucien Stryk, introduction, *On Love and Barley: Haiku of Bashō*, tr. Lucien Stryk (London: Penguin, 1985), 10.

❈ ❈ ❈

*The innocence of the notion that we should or can
separate the best from the worst is disastrous.*

Roger Dunsmore, "All My Stories Are Here:
Four Montana Poets"[3]

For more than fifty years, poet, scholar, and teacher Roger Dunsmore
has brought to American letters a unique and subversive vision.
He has articulated that vision in his courses in humanities, Native
American literature, and wilderness studies at the University of
Montana (both Missoula and Dillon campuses) and through his
books and essays. To hundreds, if not thousands, of students, Roger
is regarded as a warmly human, boundary-shattering, and ever-challenging teacher. He does not hesitate to befriend his students, and
his classes are known for their sense of intellectual and experiential intimacy and for a shared search for new meanings in old stories. Together students and professor interrogate the four gospels of
the New Testament; Aristotle's *Nicomachean Ethics*; the fragments
of Greek poet/soldier Archilochos; the teachings of Black Elk, the
Oglala Lakota medicine man and devout Catholic; the antics of ritual clowns in many cultures; the voices of the San Bushmen of the
Kalahari, the Mbuti (pygmies) of the Congo, and the Senoi of the
Malay Peninsula; Taoist texts; and Zen parables.

As a poet who is always also a scholar, a teacher, and a seeker,
Roger Dunsmore has brought to his place in the world a nuanced, unvarnished, and nakedly forthright sensibility, filled with humor, anguish, and abiding love. This book, his *New & Selected Poems,* caps a
life generously and consciously lived. By attending – with respect and
passion – to the voices of the Other, Roger's poems give us our own
world in its full complexity. This wild richness is marked equally by

---

3   Roger Dunsmore, "All My Stories Are Here: Four Montana Poets," *Drumlummon Views:
The Online Journal of Montana Arts & Culture,* Spring/Summer 2006, Vol. 1, Nos. 1–2, 128;
https://www.mtmemory.org/nodes/view/91841?keywords=Drumlummon%20Views&
type=all&highlights=WyJkcnVtbHVtbW9uIiwidmlld3MiXQ==&lsk=83893f8a889b51974e
915fe328e377ac A considerably briefer version of this essay appeared in *All Our Stories Are
Here: Critical Perspectives on Montana Literature,* ed. Brady Harrison (Lincoln: University of
Nebraska Press, 2009).

horror and beauty, by wisdom and the most profound human failings.

Although he is a much-loved and admired figure in Montana's literary world, Roger's maverick oeuvre has never received the critical acclaim it deserves. Despite this relative lack of recognition, Roger has continued to forge his singular texts, texts that celebrate "the small things, the ordinary things that are always extraordinary if only we can see."[4] His powerful and moving poems are acts of *remembering,* and remembering, as he notes, "is a way to honor what holds back the terrible dismembering."[5] Perhaps now, as Roger achieves the grand age of eighty, *On the Chinese Wall: New & Selected Poems, 1966–2017* will bring his poetic work the wider readership it deserves and secure his place as an important, even essential, voice from the Northern Rockies/High Plains of western North America.

> *I weighed everything by the measure of the silent presence of things, clarified in the racing clouds, clarified by the cry of hawks, solidified in the presence of rocks, spelled syllable by syllable by waters of manifold voice, and consolidated in the act of taking steps, each step a meditation steeped in reality.*
>
> Henry G. Bugbee, Jr.,
> *The Inward Morning:
> A Philosophical Exploration
> in Journal Form*[6]

Roger Dunsmore did not begin as a poet. Rather, he became, in his late teens, a spiritual seeker. He recalls:

> I had been converted to fundamentalist Christianity at the end of my senior year of high school in Pittsburgh and

---

4   Roger Dunsmore, *Blood House* (Vancouver, BC: Pulp Press, 1987), back cover.

5   Ibid., 85.

6   Henry G. Bugbee, Jr., *The Inward Morning: A Philosophical Exploration in Journal Form* (State College, PA: Bald Eagle Press, 1958; New York, NY: Collier Books, 1961; Athens: University of Georgia Press, 1999), 139.

spent the first two years at the university engaged, through an inter-varsity Christian organization, in trying to bring other students to Christ. I nearly flunked out my freshman year because my attention and energy were so focused on this effort.[7]

By his junior year at Penn State, Roger had "worked my way intellectually free of that religious form." Instead of finding security in the "conventional answers of fundamentalism," he fell instead "in love with the questions potential converts raised for me." Also, he recalls, his undergraduate studies in philosophy, psychology, and the sociology of religion offered perspectives "on the limits of the Christian enterprise as I was experiencing it." Nevertheless, he continued, as did many young Americans at the start of the 1960s, "to search for some sense of wholeness and meaning beyond the normal avenues of career, money, marriage, etc."[8] Despite his rejection of the Christian path, as he wrote later, "the energy of that initial experience continued to fuel [my] ongoing search toward fuller consciousness."[9]

In graduate school at Penn State, where he studied literature and philosophy, Roger found a mentor who would become essential to the development of his character, his thought, and his understanding of the spiritual. Philosopher of religions Henry Bugbee (1915–1999) spent a year at Penn State as a guest lecturer (he had been at Harvard and was now at the University of Montana), and Roger quickly saw that the charismatic Bugbee "spoke about matters of religious experience with a depth and insight I had never heard or imagined before."[10]

Henry Bugbee, who had published the remarkable *The Inward Morning: A Philosophical Exploration in Journal Form* in 1958,[11] was denied tenure by Harvard the previous year because he did not publish enough. Truthfully, Bugbee had no interest in publishing the sort

---

7   Roger Dunsmore, email to Rick Newby, February 15, 2018.

8   Ibid.

9   Roger Dunsmore, "The Autobiography (Apology) of a Convicted/Conflicted Eco-Poet" (unpublished talk).

10   Dunsmore, email to Newby, February 15, 2018.

11   For the rest of Bugbee's published writings, see Henry G. Bugbee, Jr., *Wilderness in America: Philosophical Essays,* ed. David W. Rodick (New York, NY: Fordham University Press, 2017).

of closely argued analytic papers that were the standard philosophical fare of the time. As Roger Dunsmore recalls, Bugbee "had left places like . . . Harvard, because he wanted a larger life than academia offered, and he wanted to be outdoors in real country too."[12] The philosopher Bruce Wilshire writes:

> Despite his great knowledge of the history of western philosophy that *The Inward Morning* evidences on nearly every page, Bugbee derives also from an ancient preliterate tradition of rumination, counseling of elders, storytelling. Or as if a Paleolithic hunter were about to die, and is making a final reckoning of his life.
>
> Bugbee's critique of academic-analytic philosophy flows seamlessly from his ruminating, his turning things over in his mind to find what deeply moves him, renders him whole, grounded, his thought like a prayer or a vow, momentous. Abstraction and argument too easily become abstractedness. . . .[13]

Bugbee's work represented the melding of a form of existentialism his mentor Gabriel Marcel called neo-Socratic with Asian modes of thinking and being, especially Taoism and the discipline of Zen Buddhism. When D. T. Suzuki, the great interpreter of Zen for the West, lectured in the early 1950s at Harvard and elsewhere in the Northeast, Bugbee was able to spend considerable time with him in conversation. Bugbee was especially taken by the Zen notion of "pure experience," identifying "enlightened consciousness with a kind of immediacy prior to all reflection," the Buddhist concept of "No-mind."[14] Scholar of comparative religions Huston Smith has called *The Inward Morning* "the most Daoist western book I know."[15]

Roger Dunsmore spent as much time as he could with the

---

12   Dunsmore, email to Newby, February 15, 2018.

13   Bruce Wilshire, *The Primal Roots of American Philosophy: Pragmatism, Phenomenology, and Native American Thought* (State College: Penn State University Press, 2000), 159–160.

14   Andrew Feenberg, "Zen Existentialism: Bugbee's Japanese Influence," in *Wilderness and the Heart: Henry Bugbee's Philosophy of Place, Presence, and Memory*, ed. Edward F. Mooney (Athens: University of Georgia Press, 1999), 82.

15   Quoted in Edward F. Mooney, "Bugbee, Henry Greenwood, Jr.," John R. Shook, *The Dictionary of Modern American Philosophers*, vol. 4 (London: Thoemmes, 2005), 383.

philosopher while Bugbee was at Penn State, taking two classes from him, Contemporary Religious Thought and Oriental Thought. For the latter he recalls, "I took no other class so that I could concentrate on his work."[16] For Roger, Henry Bugbee's engagement with wilderness, both the idea and the reality, would prove to be crucial – especially when both men found themselves in the wilds of Montana soon thereafter.

Philosopher Daniel Conway notes that *The Inward Morning* "appeals to a sense of wilderness that resonates familiarly with popular appreciations of the North American Western frontier" and readers are "likely to find themselves very much at home in the wilderness settings Bugbee so eloquently describes and in the yearnings for spiritual communion they evoke." At the same time, Bugbee spoke of wilderness in a very different sense, inspired by his encounters with Asian ways of thinking. Conway argues, "This sense of wilderness discloses reality as a depthless mystery, which calls to us and conveys the unresolved fluency of our existence."[17] If we acknowledge this mystery, Bugbee asserted, "Our true home is wilderness, even the world of every day."[18]

David Hinton, translator of Chinese poets and sages, notes that this experience of wilderness is not entirely alien to Americans, and in fact, the tradition of American poets embracing/enacting wilderness that Hinton describes in his recent study, *The Wilds of Poetry: Adventures in Mind and Landscape,* is dazzling proof of this. Hinton traces this tradition back to Henry David Thoreau's failed attempt to climb Maine's Mount Ktaadn, where the great Transcendentalist had an "experience of existential *contact*" with absolute wilderness: "all the explanations and assumptions fell away and he was confronted with the inexplicable thusness of things, this immediate reality, unknowable and unsayable, reality that is pure question, pure mystery."[19]

Both senses of wilderness would deeply engage Roger Dunsmore, especially as he developed his own poetic voice – he certainly stands in the tradition Hinton describes, especially the

---

16   Dunsmore, email to Newby, February 15, 2018.

17   Daniel W. Conway, "The Wilderness of Henry Bugbee," *The Journal of Speculative Philosophy* 17.4 (2003), 259.

18   Bugbee, *The Inward Morning,* 83 (University of Georgia Press edition).

19   David Hinton, *The Wilds of Poetry: Adventures in Mind and Landscape* (Boulder, CO: Shambhala Publications, 2017), 1.

lineage that includes Robinson Jeffers, Kenneth Rexroth, and Gary Snyder – and as he helped to create the Round River Program for Environmental Education and the Wilderness and Civilization Program at the University of Montana.

In a personal essay written in 2006, Roger would quote, as evidence of what he had "gleaned from [Bugbee's] thought," the following passage from *The Inward Morning*:

> What thing is eternal and infinite other than perishable things themselves? . . . Our failure to appreciate our union with the whole of nature is our failure to love the finite truly.[20]

> *It is a Montana landscape I see when I close my eyes, its people I imagine understanding or, more often, misunderstanding me. And in this sense I have to think of myself as a Western writer.*
>
> Leslie A. Fiedler[21]

For Roger Dunsmore, all roads would now lead to the American West. Henry Bugbee, after leaving Harvard in 1954, was hired three years later by the Philosophy Department at the University of Montana, Missoula. And through Bugbee's good graces, in 1963, Roger was taken on at UM to teach freshman composition. While at Penn State, Roger had met a second mentor with powerful ties to the University of Montana, the controversial and influential literary critic Leslie Fiedler. Fiedler (1917–2003) presented a series of lectures at State College that, in Roger's words, "blew me away." Roger's first year at Montana was Fiedler's last, after twenty-odd years in Missoula; Fiedler would go on to serve as Samuel Langhorne Clemens Professor of English at the State University of New York at

20   Quoted in Roger Dunsmore, "From the Great Lakes to the Backbone of the World: Roger Dunsmore on His Life and His Work," *Roger Dunsmore: Greatest Hits, 1969–2006* (Columbus, OH: Pudding House, 2007), 7. For original, see *The Inward Morning*, 136 (University of Georgia Press edition).

21   Quoted in Prem Kumari Srivastava, *Leslie Fiedler: Critic, Provocateur, Pop Culture Guru* (Jefferson, NC: McFarland & Co., 2014), 114.

Buffalo, where he gained additional fame (and notoriety). Impressed by Fiedler's fierce brilliance, Roger "sat in on every lecture he gave that year, especially the majority of the Humanities sequence weekly lectures, Homer to Sartre." And as Fiedler was packing up his office, Roger asked him if he "would put in a good word for me with the Dean so that I could teach half time in Humanities from 1964 on, which he did."[22]

When, in 2012, he received the Humanities Montana Hero Award, Roger acknowledged to the *Missoulian* newspaper:

> [Fiedler] was a WWII vet who'd do Indian leg wrestling at the bars on Woody Street. He was the kind of guy the Legislature was howling about. He's the guy that made room for me to come into the humanities program at UM, and I owe him a real debt.[23]

As role model, what did Leslie Fiedler have to offer the young Roger Dunsmore? Yang to Henry Bugbee's yin, Fiedler – called the "greatest wild man in American letters"[24] – loved to provoke, to outrage, to tease out the complexities and contradictions in a given text. More to the point, as he famously wrote, "I have . . . a low tolerance for detached chronicling and cool analysis. It is, I suppose, partly my own unregenerate nature. I long for the raised voice, the howl of rage or love."[25]

In his credo, "Toward an Amateur Criticism," published in 1950 in the *Kenyon Review,* Fiedler outlined his preferred critical approach:

> I am opposed to the dogged anti-Romanticism of much

---

22   Dunsmore, email to Newby, February 15, 2018.

23   Martin Kidston, "UM professor Roger Dunsmore honored for teaching, writing," *The Missoulian* (Missoula, MT), Aug 17, 2012; http://missoulian.com/news/local/um-profes-sor-roger-dunsmore-honored-for-teaching-writing/article_34f8c568-e80b-11e1-ae37-001a4b-cf887a.html

24   Brady Harrison, "Love, death, and the deep, abiding happiness of Edgar Allan Poe, or, Leslie Fiedler at Montana State University (and SUNY-Buffalo)," *The Montana Professor* 19.1, Fall 2008; http://mtprof.msun.edu

25   Christopher Lehmann-Haupt, "Leslie Fiedler Dies at 85; Provocative Literary Critic," *New York Times,* January 31, 2003; https://www.nytimes.com/2003/01/31/books/leslie-fiedler-dies-at-85-provocative-literary-critic.html

> contemporary criticism which leads to a contempt for
> the imagination, and is often grounded in a kind of *lump-*
> *en*-nominalism that would grant only a second-class "re-
> ality" to works of art. . . . I propose a mode of criticism
> more congruous with the sort of literature we admire, a
> criticism as wary of bureaucratization, as respectful of the
> mythic and mysterious, as dedicated to a language at once
> idiosyncratic and humane as, say, *Moby Dick* or the novels
> of Kafka.[26]

Mark Winchell, his biographer, has noted, "[b]efore Fiedler, hardly any literary critics discussed race and sexuality in American literature. Since him, they hardly talk about anything else."[27] University of Montana professor of English Brady Harrison adds: "A pioneer in what would become such fields as gender studies, queer theory, Western studies, postmodern literary studies, and more, Fiedler was ahead of his time and must be numbered among the greatest American scholars of the twentieth century."[28] Christopher Lehmann-Haupt, writing in the *New York Times,* called Fiedler "the maverick man of letters" who "attempted to tear away traditional masks of literary discourse and engage . . . deeper autobiographical and psychological considerations."[29]

Besides offering Roger Dunsmore a new way of thinking and writing about literature and culture generally, Fiedler – a self-described "literary anthropologist"[30] – possessed a passionate interest in the Native American communities he encountered in the West, a

---

26   Leslie Fielder, "Toward an Amateur Criticism," *The Kenyon Review,* 12:4 (Autumn 1950), 561–562. Fiedler's urge to write criticism as "idiosyncratic and humane" as any work of literature rhymes perfectly with Henry Bugbee's assertion: "Certainly anyone who throws his entire personality into his work must to some extent adopt an aesthetic attitude and medium" (from Henry G. Bugbee, Jr., *In Demonstration of the Spirit* [Princeton University, 1936], unpublished undergraduate thesis).

27   Quoted in Andrew Rosenheim, "Leslie Fiedler: Celebrity Critic Who Liked to Provoke," *The Independent* (UK), February 3, 2003; https://www.independent.co.uk/news/obituaries/leslie-fiedler-36224.html

28   Harrison, "Love, death, and the deep, abiding happiness of Edgar Allan Poe,"; http://mtprof.msun.edu

29   Lehmann-Haupt, "Leslie Fiedler Dies"; https://www.nytimes.com/2003/01/31/books/leslie-fiedler-dies-at-85-provocative-literary-critic.html

30   See Leslie A. Fielder, preface, *The Return of the Vanishing American* (New York: Stein & Day, 1968), 7.

passion that Roger would come to share in profound and important ways. Fiedler, in his 1948 essay, "Montana; or the End of Jean-Jacques Rousseau," railed against the treatment of Montana's Indians and concluded, "so long as the [white] Montanan fails to come to terms with the Indian, despised and outcast in his open-air ghettos, just so long will he be incapable of coming to terms with his own real past, of making the adjustment between myth and reality upon which a successful culture depends." In 1956, in appreciation of his advocacy for Native American rights, the Blackfeet tribe adopted Fiedler and gave him the honorific, Heavy Runner, after the peacemaker Chief Heavy Runner, who was killed in the brutal Marias (Baker) Massacre of 1870.[31]

Both Henry Bugbee and Leslie Fiedler, in Roger's words, "believed that the university as an institution needed 'mavericks' in order to keep it alive and to get beyond mere academics. . . . ,"[32] a belief the younger man would hold dear throughout his working life. But before he truly settled into university life, the maverick Roger Dunsmore had to journey far from the mountains and rivers of western Montana. In 1966, his "disastrous" first marriage fell apart, and at the same time, he lost his position at UM. Determined "to take in the light that had filled Homer, Sappho, Archilochos, Sophocles, Euripides, Socrates, and other Greeks,"[33] he caught a Yugoslavian freighter heading across the North Atlantic, accompanied by a trunk full of books.

He recalls, "I wanted to drink in that [Grecian] light, breathe it, bathe in it, let it devour me like it had the faces of the ancient marble lions still roaring at the sky in Delos." Despite mentors like Bugbee and Fiedler (or more likely because of their influence), he "felt lost in much of the language and ideas of conceptual academic talk." He needed new ways of being, of perceiving, and of expressing.[34]

---

31   Leslie Fiedler, "Montana, or the End of Jean-Jacques Rousseau," *An End to Innocence: Essays on Culture and Politics* (Boston: The Beacon Press, 1955), 141. Fiedler dedicated *The Return of the Vanishing American,* his 1968 study of the role of Indians in American literature, myth, and reality, to "the Blackfoot Tribe Who Adopted Me."

32   Dunsmore, email to Newby, February 15, 2018.

33   Dunsmore, "From the Great Lakes to the Backbone of the World," *Greatest Hits,* 8.

34   Ibid., 8, 9.

He writes:

> So I drank through the winter of 1966–67 in the little tav-
> ernas on the island of Mykonos. . . . Out of this new experi-
> ence on my own far from home, family, and work, and out
> of my memory, I hoped to find the necessary fragments on
> which to build: a self and world. Poetry was the vehicle. . . .
> The act of poetry became for me the practice of trying to
> enter into the life of perishable things more fully. Poetry
> required an attention to the concrete and a lyricism that I
> rarely found elsewhere.[35]

> *Can your learned head take leaven*
> *From the wisdom of your heart?*
>   Lao Tzu, *Tao Te Ching*, tr. Witter Bynner[36]

As he entered into a life of poetry, Roger solidified what he calls a
"matrix or nuclear source . . . out of which I am still receiving energy
and guidance." He elaborates:

> That matrix is composed of the thought of Henry Bugbee
> with his insights into religion founded on deep connection
> to nature (deep ecology?) . . . ; united with reading the ear-
> ly poems of Gary Snyder in the old Donald Allen anthol-
> ogy, *New American Poetry* . . . with reading the little/big
> Zen book, *Zen Flesh, Zen Bones* by Paul Reps; with reading
> *Black Elk Speaks* while on [that] Yugoslavian freighter . . .
> and hoping to find Martin Buber, having read *I and Thou*,
> to be my teacher (he died while I was on that freighter
> bound for Europe); and determined to take a wrecking ball
> to the whole intellectual framework I had taken in from
> my public education for the last twenty-four years; and to
> rebuild from that rubble, using only the fragments that

---

35   Ibid., 9, 8.

36   *The Way of Life According to Lao Tzu*, tr. Witter Bynner (New York: Capricorn Books, 1962), 30.

seemed infused with intense reality and light and authenticity. That matrix.[37]

The poets from other cultures and times that Roger found most congenial as he began to write – Archilochos of Paros (7th century BC), the ancient Greek mercenary and poet with the "nettle tongue"[38]; the Roman Catullus (ca. 84–ca. 54 BC), the first "modern" poet in the Western tradition, "speaking as close to his actual self and emotions as many twentieth-century poets"[39]; and the Japanese master Ikkyū (1394–1481), who was "always bent on crushing any ideal of self or conduct, any theory or belief"[40] – each stood well outside the dominant cultures of their times. A modern poet was the first to show Roger the potential of poetry to contradict, from an ethical stance, the norms of society and to speak truth to power.

When he first encountered e. e. cummings' antiwar poem, "i sing of Olaf glad and big,"[41] Roger hadn't written any poetry. But he instantly recognized a kindred spirit and saw the possibilities for writing poems that were not simply aesthetic objects. Cummings' poem was, as Roger has written, "about the beating to death of a conscientious objector by the Army. . . . It includes lines like 'I will not kiss your fucking flag' and 'there is some shit I will not eat.' This is not mammering around. It cares about message and has a narrative structure and is radical. I saw that poetry could matter. It mattered to cummings & it mattered to me & it could be about witness to what is wrong and what is right in this cockeyed world."[42]

Like cummings, the Greek Archilochos looked at "warfare… in terms of raw survival, not in terms of the religion of the nation-state." In an essay on poets at war, from ancient Greece to World War One to the Vietnam conflict, Roger goes on to assert: "[Archilochos] is

37   Roger Dunsmore, email to Rick Newby, February 16, 2018.

38   Guy Davenport, introduction, *7 Greeks: Translations by Guy Davenport: Archilochos • Sappho • Alkman • Anakreon • Herakleitos • Diogenes • Herondas* (New York: New Directions, 1995), 2.

39   Roger Dunsmore, "Minotaur: Caius Valerius Catullus & the Labyrinth of Desire," unpublished essay.

40   Stephen Berg, foreword, *Crow with No Mouth: Ikkyū, 15th Century Zen Master,* tr. Stephen Berg (Port Townsend, WA: Copper Canyon Press, 1989.

41   e. e. cummings, "i sing of Olaf glad and big,"*100 Selected Poems* (New York: Grove Press, 1959), poem XXX, 37-38.

42   Roger Dunsmore, email to Leo Francovich, Gonzaga University, July 12, 2017.

the first poet in our tradition to speak as himself, directly out of his own experience."[43] Archilochos' most famous poem gives us a soldier's unvarnished experience on the battlefield:

> *Some Saian mountaineer*
> *Struts today with my shield.*
> *I threw it down by a bush and ran*
> *When the fighting got hot.*
> *Life seemed somehow more precious.*
> *It was a beautiful shield.*
> *I know where I can buy another*
> *Exactly like it, just as round.*[44]

When in 1964 Guy Davenport's translations of the poems of Archilochos were first published,[45] Roger notes, "critics thought [that Davenport] had invented them, along with some bogus Greek poet with a made-up name, Archilochos, whose writings were far from what they had come to expect from the expression of the Greek warrior ideal."[46]

It was a similar irreverence that drew Roger to the poems of Catullus – "the brilliance of their obscenities and the emotional directness of his voice." Catullus was a great admirer of Archilochos, but the Roman offered greater range of subject and tone, especially in his longer poems. Roger notes: "It is Catullus' ability to reach two thousand years forward, to us, with his intensely emotional, highly crafted poems of love and hate, coupled with his ability to reach two thousand years backward into the primordial, dreamlike origin myth of Europe, that makes him so significant." Roger felt a great sympathy with Catullus' "spirit of grief, anger, humor, and direct expression around the failures of erotic love, or despair at our history, our separation from the oldest powers." This melding of history, myth, and the personal, the ancient and the modern, would mark Roger's poetic

---

43   Roger Dunsmore, "Three Soldier Poets," *Gathering on Full Exhale: The Catastrophic Miracle Called Consciousness* (unpublished essay collection).

44   Guy Davenport, *7 Greeks: Translations by Guy Davenport,* fragment 79, 39.

45   See Guy Davenport, translator, *Carmina Archilochi* (Berkeley: University of California Press, 1964).

46   Dunsmore, "Three Soldier Poets," *Gathering on Full Exhale.*

work from the start.[47]

The eccentric, sometimes scandalous Japanese poet Ikkyū remains one of Roger's favorite voices. Ikkyū's combination of earthiness, humor, and hard-earned wisdom set him apart from many Zen masters. Poet and translator Lucien Stryk writes: "He never pretended to be saintly, took his passions as a natural part of life. . . . After a disappointing day he would rush from the temple to a bar, wind up at a brothel. After which there was often a crisis of self-doubt." Despite his all-too-human failings, this reputation for "always spitting in the face of orthodoxy," Ikkyū remains revered as an illustrious master and profound Zen poet.[48] For Roger, Ikkyū's fierce honesty and contradictory humanity rendered him an important model, a kindred spirit. The Lakota holy man, John (Fire) Lame Deer, another of Roger's admirations, once said: "A medicine man shouldn't be a saint. He should experience all the ups and downs, the despair and joy, the magic and the reality, the courage and the fear, of his people. . . ."[49]

The poet Gary Snyder, since Roger first encountered his work in *The New American Poetry, 1945–1960,* has been a mentor, a friend, and an inspiration. For many in the counterculture, Gary Snyder has been a kind of holy man, but one who is always down to earth, full of good humor and kindly wisdom, one who lives the life he preaches with tremendous commitment and generosity. As Roger notes, "people would tell me that my early poems sounded like Snyder, which bothered me and which I denied. . . . embarrassed at how much I owed him and struggling to find my own voice, but standing on his more than adequate shoulders." Anyone reading this volume will see, not Snyder imitations, even in the early poems, but rather shared concerns between the two men: a passionate interest in First Peoples, a dedication to wilderness *and* the notion of wildness, a love of Asian spiritual and poetic traditions, and rapt attention to the voices of

---

47   Dunsmore, "Minotaur: Caius Valerius Catullus."

48   Lucien Stryk, preface, *Crow with No Mouth: Ikkyū,* tr. Stephen Berg, 9–10, 11.

49   Richard Erdoes, *Lame Deer, Seeker of Visions.* (New York: Simon and Schuster, 1972), 68. Quoted in Roger Dunsmore, "The Gift of John (Fire) Lame Deer," *Gathering on Full Exhale: The Catastrophic Miracle Called Consciousness* (unpublished essay collection).

working men and women.

During his time at the University of Montana, Roger invited Snyder several times to Missoula, once with his old Beat comrade Allen Ginsberg, and another with his Dharma sidekick Nanao Sakaki, the "Japanese wandering poet."[50] On his part, in a letter to one of Roger's colleagues, Snyder wrote that he saw "Roger Dunsmore as one of the very small number of genuinely original and craftsmanly poetic talents of this decade. . . . from the very beginning I was brought up short by the skillfulness and strength of Roger's book *On the Road to Sleeping Child Hot Springs.*" Snyder further acknowledged the importance of Roger's essay on the "impact of *Black Elk Speaks* on aspects of contemporary writing and thinking."[51] In his most recent collection of poems, *The Present Moment* (2015), Snyder thanks Roger as one among those who have been "challengers, teachers, and friends to my various works."[52]

Roger signals the importance of Snyder's work and thought to his own project when he dedicates *On the Chinese Wall: New & Selected Poems, 1966–2017,* to the "Great Subculture, which reaches far back beyond the stone age cave paintings of Europe, back beyond the roots of the Tao and the time before Jonah in the belly of the whale." In a famous essay, "Why Tribe," Snyder named this tradition and sought to define it. In Snyder's words, the Great Subculture "has taught that man's natural being is to be trusted and followed; that we need not look to a model or rule imposed from outside in searching for the center; that in following the grain one is being truly 'moral.'"[53] Roger has followed the grain with integrity and grit, always seeking to broaden the conversation about what it means to be human.

50   Roger Dunsmore, introduction, *The Poetics of Wilderness: Proceedings of the 22ⁿᵈ Annual Wilderness Lecture Series,* ed. Roger Dunsmore (University of Montana Wilderness Institute, 2002), 5.

51   Gary Snyder, letter to Maxine Van de Wetering, Humanities Department, University of Montana, November 15, 1977.

52   Gary Snyder, *This Present Moment: New Poems* (Berkeley: Counterpoint, 2015), 73.

53   Gary Snyder, "Why Tribe," *Earth House Hold* (New York: New Directions, 1969), 115.

> *The capacity to share one consciousness, to feel what the others are feeling in the chest and the belly goes far beyond the family and the clan. It extends to every aspect of the environment within which the people live, to the rocks and the winds.*
> Roger Dunsmore, *Earth's Mind*[54]

Central to the matrix that has fueled Roger Dunsmore's thinking and imagination since the early 1960s is that strand represented by his encounter with *Black Elk Speaks* (which had just been rediscovered and a new edition printed in 1961). While Leslie Fiedler's advocacy for Montana's Indians may have been an influence, it was Henry Bugbee who led Roger to engage deeply with Native American ways of thinking and being. Roger writes:

> I made a conscious decision to not work in Western philosophy because of the problem of sounding like a watered-down Bugbee, but to instead take what I had learned from him and apply it in the area of American Indian literature and thought. *Black Elk Speaks* was the perfect text for doing just that (talk about a religious perspective grounded in the natural world!) and I built my work with American Indian materials off that marriage – fusing Bugbee with Black Elk.[55]

Perhaps more than anything, critic and Roger's former colleague Alan Weltzien writes, "Dunsmore's poetry embraces the marginalized and indigenous in teaching us to listen to their stories, which belong in our cultural center."[56] To be clear, this is not just some form of new postmodern colonialism. In his foreword to Roger's *Earth's Mind: Essays on Native Literature,* Vine Deloria, Jr. (1933–2005), argues:

---

54   Roger Dunsmore, introduction, *Earth's Mind: Essays in Native Literature* (Albuquerque: University of New Mexico Press, 1997), 13.

55   Dunsmore, email to Newby, February 15, 2018.

56   O. Alan Weltzien, "From the Unvoiced Margins to the Center: The Populist Poetics of Roger Dunsmore," *These Living Songs: Reading Montana Poetry,* eds. Lisa D. Simon and Brady Harrison (Missoula: University of Montana Press, 2014), 74.

> [Roger Dunsmore] is not a summertime "experiencer" of Indians rushing back to the coast to crank out a first-hand (albeit briefly experienced) story about Indians. Rather he reflects on his years in the West, ponders the meanings of his memories, and produces a set of essays that asks us to consider whether we have learned anything or thought anything after our encounter with Indians. This offering is therefore a new turn of events in literature on Indians – the proposal to go where few people have gone . . . – and to consider what various messages from Indians might actually mean.[57]

Deloria, author of the classic *Custer Died for Your Sins: An Indian Manifesto,* says of Roger's essays: "So we have thoughts – thought-provoking and engendering thoughts – reflections, meditations, and finally realizations"[58] – an approach very much like Henry Bugbee's "ruminating, his turning things over in his mind to find what deeply moves him, renders him whole, grounded, his thought like a prayer or a vow."[59] For Roger, this encounter with native literatures was the "track of a beginner's journey on the path of earth's mind."[60]

*Composing a poem is a way of leaving the self
behind and getting involved in something larger.*
Robert Bringhurst, "Poetry and Thinking"[61]

---

57   Vine Deloria, Jr., foreword, Dunsmore, *Earth's Mind,* vii.

58   Ibid., viii.

59   Wilshire, *The Primal Roots of American Philosophy,* 160.

60   Dunsmore, introduction, *Earth's Mind,* 1.

61   Robert Bringhurst, "Poetry and Thinking," *Drumlummon Views: The Online Journal of Montana Arts & Culture,* Fall 2006–Winter 2007, Vol. 1, No. 3, 171; https://www.mtmemory. org/nodes/view/91842?keywords=Drumlummon%20Views&type=all&highlights=WyJkcn-VtbHVtbW9uIiwidmlld3MiXQ==&lsk=83893f8a889b51974e915fe328e377ac See also Robert Bringhurst, *The Tree of Meaning: Thirteen Talks* (Kentville, Nova Scotia: Gaspereau Press, 2006), 139–158.

More even than his essays, Roger Dunsmore's poems can be seen as a form of prayer, an effort to stay whole, grounded within a universe that persistently challenges, instructs, terrifies, and enchants him. From his first collection, *On the Road to Sleeping Child Hot Springs,* onward, Roger has sought to heal himself through his poems.

On the Road to Sleeping Child Hot Springs appeared in 1972, and as Gary Snyder noted above, it was the work of a mature poet, beautifully crafted and striking in its (sometimes brutally) honest engagement with the most difficult of subjects. Take, for example, "February Beach," an alternately tender and terrifying poem about every parent's potential for child abuse. The speaker tells the daughter he once snatched high overhead and slammed "hard into your crib/three, four times,/wanting to bash you/against the wall or floor":

> Now I know we must return,
> you riding my shoulders,
> clutching my ears, my curly hair
> with your laughter,
> return to those cracked nights
> to rout that murderer
> or wander forever in icy rooms.

The poem ends in tenderness:

> There are lovers on the beach,
> one man and one woman
> clutched together near rocks
> at the far end.
> They want the night's first freshness
> after all that rain.

Despite the evident quality of *On the Road to Sleeping Child Hot Springs,* Roger was not satisfied with his first book, and so he spent the next four years revising, rewriting, and honing the poems of the first edition. In 1977, Pulp Press of British Columbia published a second, radically altered version of *On the Road.* This is characteristic of Roger. As Alan Weltzien notes, "Dunsmore doesn't consider his poems complete after publication; he habitually revises, sometimes publishing a newer version."[62] (In fact, Roger has revised a number of the poems in this volume, including some of those that he'd already revised for the second edition of *On the Road.*)

An example of this revision can be seen in one of the most powerful long poems in *On the Road,* "A Year on Grant Creek." In the first edition, "A Year on Grant Creek" was puzzling, nature images jammed against images of great violence, like a double exposure with neither photograph in focus:

> Rabbit tracks,
> hollowed out snow places
> where deer slept warm together.
> The mountain at night –
> a village exploding
> jagged tin flowers in your womb.
> Wind like a train thru the trees
> rubs creaking limbs.

In the second edition, "A Year on Grant Creek" came into focus. The violent dream images have been given a human context: we encounter a Greek woman who has suffered great physical and mental anguish. An artist, she fills painting after painting with "ripped open tin flowers/or a village growing inside a womb/the instant before it is bombed":

> And later you send two watercolors,
> flowers blooming the first dream
> that isn't blood.

And now the nature images, which seemed so out of place in the first version, have been skillfully subordinated to the real subject of the poem:

> Rats, and a bear in the plum tree,
> startle my sleep,
> the splintered trunk white in the moonlight
> like your large, unmilked breasts

---

62   Weltzien, "From the Unvoiced Margins," *These Living Songs,* 68.

and limp wrists and close-cropped hair.
You must be married by now.
You must be forty at least.
Maybe your black hair is long again,
and your dreams calm.
Here, orange larches fire the earth. . . .

The poems in *On the Road to Sleeping Child Hot Springs* take into account Roger's experiences in Europe during the 1960s and acknowledge the impact of his return to Montana after being hired to teach full-time in the Humanities program. Some simply offer snapshots of the Montana experience:

Greyhound

At the urinal in the Butte station
the man next to me pisses blood.
It foams up over the drain.
Two guys just put it back in their pants
and walk away.

Across the aisle
a Crow Indian with a beat-up face panhandles the passengers
and a runaway boy and girl,
barefoot, clothes in grocery sacks,
hold each other in their sleep.

Published in 1987, *Blood House* marks, in a very personal way, Roger Dunsmore's deepening engagement with the Native American world. During these years, he was married to Nancy Neal, and even though he had lived in Montana for 15 years, he writes, "I did not know where I was until we started going home to Glasgow . . . to visit [Nancy's] mother." He continues, "*Blood House* contains the poems of those years, expressing what I was learning about and from Indian people, from the land, and from my new family."[63]

---

63 Dunsmore, "From the Great Lakes to the Backbone of the World," *Greatest Hits*, 11.

The poems in *Blood House* speak in many and various voices, the voices of Spanish conquistadors, Native American elders living out their days in sterile nursing homes, prison inmates, a reservation schoolteacher, Che Guevara (and the Aymara Indians, with whom Che "did not connect"), family, and friends. These compelling voices – by turns quiet and boisterous, meditative and enraged, loving and estranged – tell us what it means to be human in a world endangered by humans. And by their particularity, they give us a Montana rarely evoked, a Montana where an old Indian woman stuffs her vagina with paper "so the whitemen couldn't hurt you anymore," where "we leave no pieces of flesh from our arms,/no beads or bright cloth,/ only a dime on the sleeping buffalo," where "I'm still working at Bill's one-stop/and waiting for Donna's water to break," where "there's lot-sa stories they wouldn't want told."

Roger's courage in telling the stories "they" don't want us to hear is perhaps his greatest gift, but in many ways, the "personal" poems in Blood House's final section are its most moving and imme-diate. In these poems, people die (a farmer in a car wreck near Malta, an unborn child through abortion); another child, the poet's son, is born and brings great joy; the child's placenta – the blood house of the title – is planted in the garden ("Your mother calls it death,/bury-ing the part that housed you/ . . Second birth/of every birth"); to an Indian friend, the eating of tripe signifies rebirth; and another kind of death – the poet's divorce – brings the circle around again.

Special mention must be made of the long poem, "Navajo High School," included in this volume. This poem first appeared in Roger's 1997 collection, *Earth's Mind: Essays in Native Literature,* as part of the essay, "Columbus Day Revisited: American Indian Literature and Historical/Linguistic Truth." It recounts, in poetic form, Roger's life-changing experience, in 1988, as scholar in residence for the Arizona Humanities Council at Tuba City High School, the largest Indian high school in the United States. This effort, in which Roger sought to (re)introduce Navajo and Hopi students to their own cul-ture, was met with resistance by teachers, administrators, and par-ents. But in the end, through persistence and the support of key members of the faculty, Roger was able to convince the principal of the district that the "only way to reach national achievement standards was to restore Indian identity – and thereby to restore cultural wholeness to Tuba City students." Most controversial were texts by Native American writers that Roger introduced in his classes, texts that expressed rage at the burying of Native American history and culture, texts like Jimmy Durham's "Columbus Day" –

"In school I was taught the names
Columbus, Cortez, and Pizzaro and
a dozen other filthy murderers."

As Roger reports in his poem, when a teacher complained:

"The students don't need that.
They have too many negatives in their lives already.
Our responsibility is to give positive images,
not to dig up old hurts."

A young woman student answers:

"Yes, there are parts of our history
that are painful, that hurt.
Of course it is difficult
to learn these things.
But we can endure that pain
because they are the truth.
That's all we need from our teachers,
the truth."

Roger's efforts drew the attention of reporter Richard E. Meyer, staff writer for the *Los Angeles Times,* and on July 28, 1989, the *Times* published Meyer's lengthy, provocatively titled article, "Lesson in Controversy: Teaching the Navajo to be Navajo." Meyer reported:

Dunsmore told Indian students that knowing who they were was as important as learning English and math and science in order to be part of the white man's world. "You do not have to make a choice between being Indian and being successful," he said. "You can be both. You can be of two minds. In fact, you must be both.

"And, as a result, you will have advantages over people who are just one or the other."[64]

The school district was finally won over, and the scholar in residence program continued for another year, with the Hopi poet Ramson Lomatewama succeeding Roger in the position.

Italo Calvino has written that immersion in another culture, "polymorphous and complex," can be like "falling in love."[65] In *Tiger Hill*, Roger tells us of just such an encounter: a pair of rapturous and melancholy sojourns he spent in China during the 1990s. The China Dunsmore traversed was just awakening to certain freedoms, but it still suffered the aftershocks of a troubled history. Despite these traumas and his own near-death experience, Dunsmore returned with poems and stories. He tells us not only of "gingko trees, old as gods" and coffins "like little boats/carved with lotus flowers," but also of newfound Chinese friends, with whom he shared confidences, laughter, and sorrows. And in this world where nothing was familiar, his thoughts – fluttering "like prayer flags" – sometimes drifted back to loved ones at home: his mother, his son, a revered mentor, the dying father of his wife Jenni. This extraordinary book, steeped in the realities and dreams of two equal but separate worlds, attends the living and the dead with grace, humility, and, above all, abiding love.

Here, with the poem "Mountain Ash," Roger pays homage to Henry Bugbee, the philosopher who opened so many doors for him. The poem concludes:

> You raise your first glass of ale
> for the day, old teacher and friend
> I have not come often enough to see.

---

64   Richard E. Meyer, "Lesson in Controversy: Teaching the Navajo to be Navajo," *Los Angeles Times*, July 28, 1989; http://articles.latimes.com/1989-07-28/news/mn-99_1_navajo-culture

65   Italo Calvino, "The Cloven Communist," *Hermit in Paris: Autobiographical Writings* (New York: Pantheon, 2003), 125.

We drink to this not dying,
your eyes like a cat's
there in the sheltered arbor
those last days of summer.

Now there are no words.
These crows, this wind-chime,
open a door.
A soft breeze blows
your wax-wing heart
into the bright silence
of mountain ash.

With *You're Just Dirt* (now renamed for this volume *We're Just Dirt*), Roger once again brings us powerful poems revealing Montana's rich and dark history, beautiful lyrics celebrating the natural world and love between humans, poems in the voices of underdogs and outlaws, and fierce articulations of his understanding of Native American culture. Whether he is writing about prisoners in the state prison at Deer Lodge, the flight of a hummingbird, moments of unbearable grief, a Sioux winter count, or the "patience of bears," he continues to offer us poems, rich in particulars and infinitely tender, that celebrate a shared humanity and sing the dailiness of a life that claims his most profound affection. This collection reflects his new partnership with the painter, poet, and Yoga teacher Jenni Fallein.

As the poet Craig Czury writes in his preface to *You're Just Dirt,* we can read Roger's poems "as guy lines to steady [our] way of seeing and receiving the unexpected gifts of this world, naming the known, naming the unknown."[66]

---

66   Craig Czury, preface, Roger Dunsmore, *You're Just Dirt: Poems,* Montana Poets Series, Vol. 1 (Kanona, NY: FootHills Publishing, 2010), 7.

> *Understanding the ordinary*
> *is called Enlightenment.*
> Lao Tzu, *Tao Te Ching #16,*
> composed by Roger Dunsmore

As the nearly 50 poems – all written since 2010 – in the *New Poems* section of this volume attest, Roger Dunsmore's commitment to poetry has only deepened in recent years. These new poems reflect a greater expansiveness and sense of play. There are poems about torture in Central America and elegies for friends and family, but more often, the poems reflect a true recognition of the pleasures, mysteries, and delights of the ordinary. There are tender, philosophical love poems for his wife Jenni. In "Taking in the Morning," he writes: "My wife sleeps beside me./The boat's sail lines move slightly./Just because all this, even the rocks,/changes, just because all nations,/species, galaxies, are impermanent,/doesn't mean it's all illusion." Other poems offer exuberant or rueful celebrations of domesticity, as in "Home Improvement" or "Pecan Pie Kills Lonesome."

A marvelous group of poems focuses on the non-human creatures in Roger's world: wild bulls ("Old Jock on the Loose"), bears ("Blind Harry and the 3 Bears"), crows ("Crow's Feet"), whales ("Easter Morning Hump Backs") and one friendly wolverine named Henry ("Oreo Cookies").

Once again, we hear the voices of working folk ("Crew Boss" and "Plastered"), of a World War II veteran who visits the daughter of a Japanese soldier he killed "hand-to-hand/in a fox hole/in a war/half a world away" ("Veteran's Day"), of Roger's old friend, Salish elder Frances Vanderburg, who tells him the true names of the landforms in her native place ("Changing the Names").

The wilderness remains essential to Roger. In several poems, he honors the natural world we still find relatively untouched in Glacier National Park ("*Nature's a Killer*" and "Remembered") and the Bob Marshall Wilderness ("On the Chinese Wall"). He tenders a last request: "when I lay dying/place me/on the flat warm stones/this beach/waves pounding in."

Roger Dunsmore is a master poet of our time and place.

❊   ❊   ❊

Only that day dawns to which we are awake.
There is more day to dawn. The sun is but a
morning star.
                    Henry David Thoreau, *Walden*[67]

I have known Roger Dunsmore since I was 18, for almost five decades. Roger was my first poet-mentor, and a stalwart friend from
the very beginning. He not only introduced me to the life of poetry,
but – as he did with so many of his students – to a life of the mind
that sought connections everywhere, among cultures, between the
high and the low, the sacred and profane, the beautiful and the un-
gainly. And now, with the publication of *On the Chinese Wall: New
and Selected Poems, 1966–2018,* we can see the fruits of Roger's long
search for meaning. His spiritual search is embodied in these poems,
and for this marvelous body of work, we can be ever grateful.

As I conclude this essay, I receive, a few days before his 80th
birthday, a note from Roger. He writes, "Absolutely beautiful spring
day here today – I worked outside putting together a new fence to
keep the chickens out of our gardens. I find that I love the work –
rough carpentry plus digging post holes by hand, and the satisfaction
of physical accomplishment – even mixing the concrete by hand in
a wheelbarrow, just doing it the old fashioned way, depending on
those skills inherited from the older generation, and using a few of
my grandfather's hand tools. So I'm tired but satisfied."[68]

And after his recent return from a journey to Australia and New
Zealand, Roger sends me his latest poem. He calls it "Approaching
Eighty," and it offers the hard-earned wisdom of a man who, like his
beloved Ikkyū, has never pretended to be saintly, a man who remains
in love with rough carpentry and the unruly realities of this world:

---

67   Henry David Thoreau, *Walden, or Life in the Woods* (Ticknor & Fields, 1862), 440.

68   Roger Dunsmore, email to Rick Newby, April 20, 2018.

Take your time, Dunsy,
curl of Indian Ocean waves
gently breaks in and out
in its inexorable rhythm,
wise and moonstruck
beyond any human knowing.

You have all the time in the world, Dunsy,
and none –
litter of seaweed at the tide-line,
green tea in a bottle,
turquoise waves.
Take your time.

(After visiting the massacre site of Noongar People at Pinjarra,
Western Australia)

Debra Magpie Earling's *The Lost Journals of Sacajawea*

Originally published, in somewhat different form, in *We Proceeded On,* the official publication of the Lewis and Clark Trail Foundation, Inc., ed. Caroline Patterson, Great Falls, MT, Summer 2012.

The Lost Journals of Sacajewea
Debra Magpie Earling
Photo-interventions by Peter Rutledge Koch
Editions Koch, Berkeley, 2010
65 numbered and 5 *hors commerce* copies, $3,500
An additional suite of prints suitable for exhibition is available.

In the spring of 2005, at the peak of the Lewis & Clark Bicentennial, the Missoula (Montana) Art Museum launched the exhibition, *Native Perspectives on the Trail: A Contemporary American Indian Portfolio.* Alongside the prints by such leading Native American visual artists as Jaune Quick-to-See Smith, Neil Parsons, Dwight Billedeaux, Molly Murphy, and Corwin "Corky" Clairmont, there appeared the text of a powerfully haunting poem entitled "The Lost Journals of Sacagawea," by Bitterroot Salish novelist Debra Magpie Earling.

At that time, master letterpress printer and book artist Peter Koch, a native Montanan who makes his home in Northern California, was also exhibiting a Lewis & Clark–themed body of work at MAM. Koch's suite of Iris prints, entitled *Nature Morte,* offered – like Earling's poem and most of the work in *Native Perspectives on the Trail* – a highly critical, even jaundiced, and certainly irreverent interpretation of the impact of the Corps of Discovery on the landscapes and cultures of the American West.

Earling and Koch recognized each other as kindred spirits and began immediately to plan the project that has become this extraordinary book. Earling extended her original text into a full-throated voicing of sorrow and rage over the legacy of abuse of Native women and of destruction of the Native world that revolved around the vast herds of bison, a place and time when even "the bones of the earth [could not] stand the weight of buffalo running."

In Earling's telling, Sacajewea's *"is the story Lewis and Clark won't be writing down."* It is a harrowing story; as Earling has noted elsewhere, "The stories I feel called to write often reveal the darkest side of the human heart." Her novel, the award-winning *Perma Red,* unflinchingly depicts life on Montana's Salish-Kootenai Reservation in the 1940s, both the beauties and often brutal realities of that life. Here, again, she is unflinching:

> The white men don't see the wives who are hidden
> in the lodges at the edges of lost
> the women who carried the small-pox dead
> to scaffolds
> losing their fingers
> in purging fires
> of children
> or women who gather bundles of sticks
> in the frost-bitten winters of fever.
> They are witches
> who crawl hump-backed
> their hands only palms/the webbed feet of ducks/work
> dogs to carry meat.
> > This is the life left to unfortunate women.

Earling's work, as James Welch has written, can be "startlingly spiritual," and within the voice of her imagined Sacajewea, we sense a spiritual strength in the face of extremity that, quite simply, moves beyond rage or bitterness to a quiet acknowledgment of the importance of telling our stories, but especially those that might otherwise be lost.

> With all these stories of loss
> rivers as wide
> as a smile remembered
> when rain changes the brief night with your face.

> When rain

> the pattern of a hundred faces, a thousand faces, all the lost,
> all the dead keep showing up
> on the highway
> beneath the lip of trembling leaves
> in the wind tossed rivers

In the flooding waters
In the myriad tales of rain
no one is lost from us.

To surround and embrace this astonishing text, Peter Koch has constructed an equally extraordinary container. His self-styled "photo-interventions" make great use of the early photographic record of EuroAmerican incursion into the Northern Plains/Rockies and of the Native peoples and great bison herds that those EuroAmericans encountered. Images by L. A. Huffman, F. Jay Haynes, S. J. Morrow, and anonymous photographers, printed on Twinrocker Da Vinci hand-made paper, perfectly attend Earling's text, forging tensions, offering evidence, tendering us a glance at an austere, troubling, and gorgeous world. The cover is printed on a smoked buffalo rawhide paper designed and hand-made especially for this edition, and the spine of *The Lost Journals of Sacajewea* is beaded with trade beads and small caliber cartridge cases.

Peter Koch, founder of the Codex Foundation which every other year sponsors the internationally renowned Codex Book Fair and Conference at the University of California Berkeley, has created a great many books as works of fine art in his forty-year career, but none of them can match the alchemy of this bringing together of text and type, paper and binding. At $3,500, *The Lost Journals of Sacajewea* is not for everyone, but copies can be found in libraries and museums across the land, from the Montana Historical Society to the University of Chicago to Yale. Perhaps one day soon, a smart publisher will bring out a trade edition.

Let Sacajewea have the last words:

They are stacking the bones of buffalo
Mountains of dead buffalo rotting
Bones, more bones ...... a great white fire rising
over the vast land
they once roamed.

Cathedral of bones.
In the murky dust
of buffalo
the cities rise.

Annie Connole's *The Spring: A Mythic Memoir*

Originally published in *High Desert Journal,* Spring 2021.

The Spring
A Mythic Memoir
Annie Connole
Chin Music Press, 2021
Memoir/prose poem, 112 pages
Hardcover

> *Every natural fact is a symbol of some spiritual fact.*
> – Ralph Waldo Emerson, "Nature"

With this remarkable first book, writer Annie Connole, Montana born and raised, brings us a work of surpassing grace, tenderness, and power. *The Spring* is truly a book of the West, but unlike so many texts within the western and specifically Montana narrative tradition, it relies not upon a gritty realism, but rather speaks out of an inclusive sense of the Real, one that embraces our dreams, the rich array of animals with whom we share this western landscape, and the spirits of both the living and the dead. Though it is subtitled "A Mythic Memoir," I prefer to think of *The Spring* as an extended prose poem, one that must be read in a single sitting – only in this way, can we experience the full force of the text's quietly gripping arc.

With echoes of Native American animal tales, Australian Aboriginal Dreamtime stories, and even European and American folk narratives that feature animals as co-equal residents of our world, *The Spring* makes little distinction between the human and animal realms. Here, the narrator and her partner, the painter, continually encounter and engage with a myriad of non-human creatures wild and domesticated. Bodies of water, too, play their roles: the spring of the title, high mountain lakes, the Missouri, Gardiner, and Lamar rivers. Beginning in the mountain town of Phillipsburg, Montana, the elliptical narrative takes us to Yellowstone National Park, briefly to New York City, and then to Joshua Tree, California, where the Mojave and Colorado deserts meet, and the narrator can escape the "minefield of memory up north."

The central action of *The Spring* is told quietly, simply: "[T]he painter jumps into the spring on a full moon night. I never see his face again, except in dreams. He becomes light." The text, a fable the narrator tells herself – and us – follows her struggle to find some sort of peace after her beloved partner chooses to end his own life. No explanation is given for the painter's choice, but perhaps, as with so many suicides, any such explanation is always partial. Instead, the narrator, attended by her animal allies and mentors, haunted by memories and profound disquiet, descends into the depths of grief and then, ever so slowly, begins to heal.

It is a common enough story, but here, it is told in fresh and startling ways, and in the telling, works its themes and images deep into the reader's mind and heart. Through indirection and disjunction, "animal communions," dream imagery, and sheer beauty, *The Spring* asks us to share the narrator's journey, connecting us to our own griefs and opening us to possibilities of redemption and solace. In working this magic, Annie Connole represents a new and compelling voice arising out of the American West.

The animals in *The Spring* are not just part of the scenery. Not simply emblems of some human yearning, they signal changes, they join the narrator's journey as allies or teachers, they comfort and frighten and transform. They are absolutely central to the story, more so than any humans other than the narrator and the painter. In fact, nearly every one of the brief prose poems (that, by accretion, make up the larger narrative) has as its title an animal's name: Snake, Deer, Mountain Lion, Frog, Cat, Horse, Owl, Swan, Old Black Dog, Tadpole, Bear, Horse, Dragonfly, Moose, Sparrow, Fox, Bluebird, Rabbit, Goat, Dove, White Alpaca, Wolf, and Buffalo.

In "Bluebird," the narrator tells us:

For many meals, for many years, I sat across the table
from the painter. Bluebird's royal blue coat is reminiscent
of the painter's Mediterranean blue eyes and oxford shirt.
Like the painter's majestic eyebrows, Bluebird's thick
black eyebrows look as though they have been painted
on in two broad strokes. Eyebrows, thick and sleek, were
the painter's most notable feature.

*As I finish my soup, I reach out to Bluebird. He flutters
again, startled, and moves to a branch by my side. Still
watching me as I watch him.*

The Spring, illustrated with Connole's own photographs, is truly a spiritual text, a haunting meditation that can help us to survive
our own unbearable losses. Annie Connole writes:

*I move through new and old tracks of Yellowstone.
Many happy returns. But on this trip, I am alone,
hunting ghosts, hunting things I cannot name, hunting
elusive silhouettes with a steady knock on the inside of
my heart drumming a low beat.*

Pioneering Montana
Visual Modernism

Theodore Waddell, Isabelle Johnson, and Early Montana Modernism

Originally published as part of my monographic essay, "Theodore Waddell: Life & Work," in Rick Newby, the Hon. Pat Williams, Robyn Peterson, Bob Durden, Donna Forbes, Mark Browning, Gordon McConnell, Paul Zarzyski, Scott McMillion, Patrick Zentz, William Hjortsberg, Greg Keeler, and Brian Petersen, *Theodore Waddell – My Montana: Paintings & Sculpture, 1959–2016* (Helena: Drumlummon Institute, 2017).

In June 1991, two longtime friends, both painters who happened to be ranchers, mounted an exhibition in Absarokee, Montana. Held in the little farming community's two banks, the exhibition showcased the work of two of Montana's foremost modernists, Isabelle Johnson, age 90, and her most renowned student, Theodore Waddell, 50. A review in the *Billings Gazette* noted that the show included ten works by each artist:

> watercolors, oil[s], wood cuts, pen and ink sketches plus inventive drawings of oil and graphite by Waddell. Both artists – reflecting their native Montana – depict nature, horses, cattle, sheep. Their style[s] are very different but reactions from viewer[s] are similar – Waddell's called "bold," Johnson's called "full of life."

As *Gazette* reviewer Lucile Moses pointed out, when Waddell entered Eastern Montana College in 1959, he soon enrolled in a painting class with Isabelle Johnson (1901–1992), and the two – despite their forty-year age difference – became lifelong friends.[1] Waddell had planned to be an architect, but he recalls, "Within a month or less [of studying with Johnson], I decided that I didn't want to do anything other than make art."[2]

Until recently, Isabelle Johnson's life and work have attracted very little scholarship, but with the publication of *"A Lonely Business": Isabelle Johnson's Montana* (Yellowstone Art Museum, 2015), we now

---

1   Lucile Moses, "Old Friends Stage a New Show," *Billings Gazette, Enjoy* section, June 28, 1991, 12.

2   Theodore Waddell, note to Rick Newby, October 1, 2013.

know a great deal more about Johnson's education and influences, the trajectory of her career, her aesthetic philosophy, and the full range of her body of work, which included not only her renowned landscapes, scenes from ranch life, and studies of trees and flowing water, but also accomplished academic works from her student years and arresting images of Indian powwows and city life.[3] In his contribution to *"A Lonely Business,"* Theodore Waddell writes, "I don't think there is any way to over-estimate the influence of Isabelle on all of us."

By all accounts, Johnson was an inspiring and rigorous teacher. Waddell remembers, "Izzie we called her, not to her face – it was a term of endearment. She would take several of us to her house downtown and give us hot chocolate and talk about art." As a freshman, Waddell was "working for the art department, checking out tools [and] . . . working for the railroad on the freight dock, loading freight from 4pm until 3am." Johnson worried about him not getting enough rest, so she "bought a cot for me to take naps in the tool room."[4] Waddell recalls, "She was a figurative painter, but she had this loose, graphic way of applying the paint that drew me to her."[5]

Waddell's friend and fellow painter, the late Jim Poor (1936– 2014), credits Johnson with "opening [my] eyes to modernism."[6] Poor, who studied with Johnson earlier than Waddell, has said that Johnson's teaching style represented an "exciting, vivid attitude toward art in touch with life and earth." She was "ahead of her time in teaching the creative process" and always "very, very respectful of each student."[7] Another Johnson student, painter Donna Loos, recalls: "[S]he felt it was a requirement of her job that she push us and lead us to look in other directions that were not traditional, and she did it without saying a mean word about [Charles M.] Russell or any other traditional painter. . . .[S]he opened up our minds until we did

---

3   See Robyn G. Peterson, Bob Durden, Patricia Vettel-Becker, Donna Forbes, Theodore Waddell, and Peter Halstead, *"A Lonely Business": Isabelle Johnson's Montana* (Billings: Yellowstone Art Museum, 2015).

4   Waddell, email to Newby, February 22, 2013.

5   Quoted in Jaci Webb, "Ted Waddell: Redefining the Label of 'Western Artist,'" *Billings Gazette,* November 17, 2014, 1.

6   Quoted in Bob Durden, *Jim Poor: Confluences* (Great Falls, MT: Paris Gibson Square Museum of Art, 2009), 1.

7   Quoted in Rick Newby, "Artists Who Also Teach, Part II," *State of the Arts,* Montana Arts Council, January/February 2000, 22–23.

it by ourselves."[8]

Isabelle Johnson partook of a distinctly Montana tradition, that of accomplished artists who are also working ranchers. Johnson's family ranch lay in the gorgeous Stillwater country of south-central Montana, and Isabelle's parents, Albert and Irene, both hardworking immigrants from Norway, made a success of the Albert Johnson Land Company, running sheep from 1911 until 1942 and then cattle until their deaths in the late 1950s. Always enterprising, Albert Johnson introduced the first McCormick binder into the Stillwater country, and in the early twentieth century, "because of the demand for draft horses in this newly developing land," Albert and his neighbors "sent to France for a thoroughbred Percheron stallion, named Thomas; the price, $4,000." Isabelle recalled that her father built a "special barn and corral for Thomas . . . and was his devoted guardian for more than 10 years. . . . the Stillwater became noted for its prized draft horses."[9] After her parents died, Isabelle continued to run the ranch with her two sisters, Grace and Pearl, and her brother Ingwald, who served as the principal manager.

At the same time, Johnson had her own career, as historian, teacher, and painter. She received a B.A. in History from the University of Montana and an M.A. from Columbia University, and she taught history and the social sciences in the Billings public schools for some years. But as she turned her passionate attention to the art of painting, she studied variously at the Otis Art Institute, Los Angeles; the Los Angeles County Museum School; the University of Southern California; the Art Students League, New York; Columbia University School of Painting and Sculpture; and the Colorado Springs Fine Arts Center.

By all accounts, the key moment in her journey toward painting came in 1946 when she was selected to participate in an experimental program at Skowhegan, Maine. Organized by Henry Varnum Poor, the influential painter, designer, architect, ceramist, and thinker, this program – limited to twenty-five participants – was a precursor to the important Skowhegan School of Painting and Sculpture, which Poor co-founded that same year.

---

8   Quoted in Robyn G. Peterson, "Introduction and Acknowledgments," Peterson, et al, "A Lonely Business," 3.

9   Isabelle Johnson, "Folks Called Johnson," in Jim Annin, *They Gazed on the Beartooths,* Volume 1 (Billings, MT: J. Annin, 1964), 272.

As Terry Melton, first director of the Yellowstone Art Center (now Museum), noted in 1971, "Poor's inquiring and inventive experimentations affected and continue[d] to affect the painting attitudes of Isabelle Johnson's work."[10] Perhaps even more important was Poor's advice about *where* Johnson should settle. Curator Gordon McConnell writes, "When she talked with Poor about pursuing opportunities in the East he told her, 'You go home. You belong to the West. The West needs you. Montana is a desert of art. You go home and make it bloom.'"[11]

Isabelle was able, during a 1954 sabbatical from her teaching duties at Eastern Montana College, to spend a year touring Europe, where she undoubtedly encountered the works of her principal influence, Paul Cezanne and where, during her time in Paris, she spent day after day studying the masterworks in the Louvre. From all of her travels and studies – as poet and photographer Peter Halstead writes – Isabelle "brought home the light from distant worlds. The Hudson River light of Thomas Moran; the chalk glaze of Cezanne; the yellowed clay of the Camargue; the arid, blocky hills and river-like fields of Winslow Homer."[12]

Isabelle Johnson is often called Montana's first modernist painter, but that is not strictly correct. It is perhaps more accurate to call her Montana's first native-born modernist who went on to become an influential teacher within the state – and thereby, in Henry Varnum Poor's words, helping to "make [Montana] bloom" with visual expressions congruent with the modern age.

Modernism was indeed slow to come to Montana. In 1920, the Great Northern Railway first brought German painter and designer Winold Reiss (1886–1953), with his Art Deco–inflected style, to Glacier National Park. Alongside his accomplishments as a portraitist of Montana's Blackfeet, Mexican revolutionaries, and notable figures of the Harlem Renaissance, Reiss is considered one of the

---

10   Terry Melton, *Paintings by Isabelle Johnson* (Fort Worth, TX: Amon Carter Museum of Western Art, 1971), unpaginated.

11   Gordon McConnell, *Yellowstone Art Museum: The Montana Collection* (Billings, MT: Yellowstone Art Museum, 1998), 28.

12   Peter Halstead, "Photographing Isabelle," in Peterson, et al, *"A Lonely Business,"* 42.

first modernist interior designers in the United States. His design for The Crillon, New York, has been called the "first modern restaurant decoration in the U.S.A."[13] Reiss would have a powerful impact on several Montana painters, especially portraitist Elizabeth Lochrie (1890–1981), through the art school he ran in Glacier Park during the 1930s.

Even earlier, in 1913, another German modernist Julius Seyler (1873–1958) came to Montana to paint. A shirttail relative of Louis W. Hill, the Great Northern Railway magnate, Seyler is often characterized as a Post-Impressionist, standing alongside masters like Cezanne, Van Gogh, and Gauguin; one of his works, *Nordischer Fischerhafen* (*Nordic Fishing Port*), appeared in the famous Armory show, the 1913 exhibition that first introduced modernism to a broad American audience.[14]

As historian William Farr writes, Julius Seyler differed markedly, because of his "experimental leanings," from most painters brought to northern Montana by the Great Northern. More commonly, the GN artists depicted "Glacier's scenic grandeur in decidedly realistic terms." Farr adds, "[T]here remained a decidedly loose, sketchy, or incomplete character to much of Seyler's painting that did not sit well in the popular appreciation."[15] Montana painting wouldn't see such experimental leanings and expressive brushwork again until Isabelle Johnson appeared on the scene in the early 1940s.

In the early twentieth century, American-born proto- and premodernists like Joseph Henry Sharp (1859–1953) and Maynard Dixon (1875–1946) also brought modernist elements to their work painted in Montana. Sharp, known as the spiritual founder of the Taos Society of Artists, did not travel very far down the modernist road (unlike many of his Taos colleagues), but his Montana work – especially his magisterial landscapes and scenes of Crow Indian life – hover somewhere between a more traditional European approach,

---

13   Robert Kashey, *Winold Reiss, 1886–1953: Works on Paper: Architectural Designs, Fantasies and Portraits* (New York: Shepherd Gallery, 1986), unpaginated.

14   See Milton W. Brown, *The Story of the Armory Show* (Washington, DC: The Joseph H. Hirshhorn Foundation, 1963), 289.

15   William E. Farr, "Julius Seyler: Painting the Blackfeet, Painting Glacier Park, 1913–1914," *Montana The Magazine of Western History* 51:2 (Summer 2001), 61. For a full treatment of Seyler's Montana sojourn, see William E. Farr, *Julius Seyler and the Blackfeet: An Impressionist at Glacier National Park*, Charles M. Russell Center Series on Art and Photography of the American West, Book 7 (Tulsa: University of Oklahoma Press, 2009).

learned during his academic studies in Antwerp and Munich, and the looser impressionism he encountered in Paris. Thomas Minckler, in his study of Sharp's late floral still lifes, notes that he knows of only one truly modernist still life in Sharp's entire oeuvre, the graphically bold, angular *Carnations* (no date).[16]

Maynard Dixon, who would become a pure modernist by the mid-1920s, came to Montana in 1917, again under the auspices of the Great Northern Railway, and the work that emerged during that summer partook, in the words of art historian Donald Hagerty, of "a postimpressionist style, with a vigorous, bold, and forceful presentation." In 1915, Dixon had encountered, at the Panama-Pacific International Exposition, San Francisco, some of the latest European avant garde works, several of which had been featured in the Armory Show two years earlier. Hagerty notes that "Dixon credited the exposition's modernist art with revising his ideas about color and the use of space."[17] His magnificent *Home of the Blackfeet,* painted in 1938, remains perhaps the most powerful evocation of his Montana stay.

In the summer of 1916, even the great American portraitist John Singer Sargent (1856–1925) – whom Theodore Waddell has claimed as an important influence – traveled to Glacier National Park. Though he seems quite conservative today, in the early twentieth century Sargent was considered daring, especially in his nearly "scientific attitude to his material."[18] He was, in the words of fellow painter Kenyon Cox, "a modern of the moderns and, in the broadest sense of the word, a thorough impressionist." [19]

Although Sargent reported from Glacier that "it is delicious to be here among crags and glaciers and pine woods," he apparently did not paint any Montana scenes, but instead waited until he had traveled into the Canadian Rockies, where the "scenery is grander

16   See Thomas Minckler, *In Poetic Silence: The Floral Paintings of Joseph Henry Sharp,* ed. Rick Newby (Tucson, AZ: Settlers West Galleries, 2010), 133.

17   Donald J. Hagerty, "Maynard Dixon and a Changing West, 1917–1935," *Montana The Magazine of Western History* 51:2 (Summer 2001), 43, 42.

18   Sarah Burns, *Inventing the Modern Artist: Art and Culture in Gilded Age America* (New Haven, CT: Yale University Press, 1996), 177.

19   Kenyon Cox, "Two Ways of Painting," *Bulletin of the Metropolitan Museum of Art* 7:11 (November 1912), 205.

still."[20] There, at Lake O'Hara, Alberta, he would paint one of his few pure landscapes that has, notes Canadian art historian Bruce Hugh Russell, "always been considered one of Sargent's finest paintings." Russell continues, "Apart from the brilliant virtuosity of his brush work, it is his idiosyncratic composition which results in its success . . . avoiding the clichés of mountain tops delineated against the sky, and . . . cropping visual comprehension of the extent of the lake's perimeter."[21]

Theodore Waddell's daughter, the curator Shanna Shelby, writes that her father was "greatly influenced" by Sargent, especially in terms of the "application of paint." She continues:

> Waddell learned how Sargent executed the depth of space by working with not only tonal range but also texture. The astute observer can compare how depth is achieved by both artists by using smooth brushstrokes in dark tones and heavy strokes with more paint in lighter colors. It may seem absurd to compare Sargent's elegant socialites to Waddell's Angus portraits; however the subject is second-ary to process. As technique it makes perfect sense.[22]

Isabelle Johnson's closest competitor for the role of Montana's first resident modernist painter was surely Fra Dana, another woman rancher whose life and art have been thoroughly documented in *Fra Dana: American Impressionist in the Rockies* (Montana Museum of Art & Culture, 2011) by Montana scholars Valerie Hedquist and the late Sue Hart.[23] Dana was born in 1874 in Terre Haute, Indiana, but by 1892, her family had moved to Dayton, Wyoming, in the foothills of the Big Horn Mountains, near Sheridan. There she was to meet rancher Edwin Lester Dana, and they would marry in 1896. At the

---

20   John Singer Sargent, letter to Evan Charteris, July 25, 1916, quoted in Bruce Hugh Russell, "John Singer Sargent in the Canadian Rockies: 1916," *The Beaver: Canada's History Magazine* 77: 6 (December 1997/January 1998), 4.

21   Bruce Hugh Russell, "John Singer Sargent in the Canadian Rockies: 1916," *The Beaver: Canada's History Magazine* 77: 6 (December 1997/January 1998), 4.

22   Shanna Shelby, "A Daughter's Perspective," in Terry Oldham, Theodore Waddell, Terry Melton, Shanna Shelby, and Kirk Robertson, *Angus Anthem: Theodore Waddell* (St. Joseph, MO: Albrecht-Kemper Museum of Art, 2009), 15.

23   See Sue Hart and Valerie Hedquist, *Fra Dana: American Impressionist in the Rockies* (Missoula: Montana Museum of Art & Culture, 2011).

same time that she was putting down roots in the West, Fra Dana had always aspired to be a painter, and between 1890 and 1893, she studied at the Cincinnati Art Academy.

A fascinating and complex figure, Dana would go on to spend considerable time in New York, where she studied with the preeminent late-19th-century American artist William Merritt Chase, and Paris, where she encountered the pioneering collectors of advanced art, Leo and Gertrude Stein. Dana was a classic Impressionist, and she appears to have had little interest in more avant-garde approaches, even though her best artist friend, Alfred Maurer (1868–1932), has been called the first American Fauvist.

For some years Dana divided her time between the vast Dana ranch, the 2A (home to the largest purebred Hereford herd in North America), at Pass Creek, Montana, on the Crow Reservation and the artistic life in New York and Europe. Unlike Isabelle Johnson, who found her ranch origins congenial, indeed a natural way of being, Fra Dana had deeply mixed feelings about finding herself isolated from the great centers of art. Dana appreciated, and sometimes loved, ranch life, but she also wrote, heartbreakingly:

> If my life is to be bounded by Pass Creek, how can I stand it? I am full enough of life to want friends, music, painting, the theater; all the stimulus of modern movements. . . . I will go back to the ranch and never ask to go away again and try to content myself with the flowers and books, both of which I love. But the loneliness![24]

In another diary entry, written after a "wet, tired, dirty" day of spaying heifers, she wrote, "I speak no more of my vanished dreams."[25] Like noted 20th century Montana poet and novelist, Grace Stone Coates of Martinsdale, who also lamented her loneliness in

---

24   Fra Dana, unpublished journal, September 28, 1911, transcribed by Mildred Walker and quoted in Valerie Hedquist, "Travels with Fra: From Pass Creek to Paris," Hart and Hedquist, *Fra Dana: American Impressionist in the Rockies*, 71–72.

25   Fra Dana, unpublished journal, undated, transcribed by Mildred Walker and quoted in Ripley Hugo, *Writing for Her Life: The Novelist Mildred Walker* (Lincoln: University of Nebraska Press, 2003), 106.

this "alien land," [26] Dana could be downright dismissive of her ad-opted state. In 1907, she confided to her diary, "Beauty of any kind is a thing held cheap out here in this land of hard realities and glaring sun and alkali. There are no nuances."[27] As a mark perhaps of her ambivalence, Dana painted very few Montana scenes, and her strongest works are richly evocative domestic interiors, often featuring a gentlewoman at her leisure, drinking tea or reading the newspaper.

Beyond her art, which was little known during her lifetime, Fra Dana's greatest contribution to the culture of Montana has undoubtedly been the gift – upon her death in 1948 – of her personal art collection to the Montana Museum of Art & Culture, University of Montana. Besides her own lovely work, including portraits, still lifes, florals, domestic scenes, and a handful of landscapes, her collection includes significant works by William Merritt Chase, Alfred Maurer, Douglas John Connah, Joseph Henry Sharp, Hans Kleiber, and E. W. Gollings, as well as French prints (Daumier and Forain) and more than thirty works of Asian art, including Ming Dynasty watercolors and *ukiyo-e* prints by the Japanese masters Hiroshige, Hokusai, and Utamaro.

While artists like Reiss, Kleiber, Sharp, Dixon, and Fra Dana are certainly important in Montana's art historical record, it was Isabelle Johnson who most directly forged the path to the vibrant and diverse Montana art world of the early 21st century. Unlike Fra Dana, Johnson when she looked at the Montana landscape saw nothing, but nuance. As art historian Patricia Vettel-Becker writes about Johnson's 1965 oil, *Little River, Winter,* in *"A Lonely Business,"* "it is a rather unremarkable site [judging by a contemporary photograph], but through her painting she has transfigured it, forcing the viewer to focus on what often goes unnoticed in winter scenes, primarily color. The blues, oranges, and greens that may be missed upon casual glance

---

26   See Lee Rostad, "From An Alien Land: An Introduction," in *Food of Gods and Starve-lings: The Selected Poems of Grace Stone Coates,* eds. Lee Rostad and Rick Newby (Helena: Drumlummon Institute, 2007), 17–29.

27   Quoted in Erika Doss, "'I *Must* Paint': Women Artists of the Rocky Mountain Region," in *Independent Spirits: Women Painters of American West, 1890–1945,* ed. Patricia Trenton (Berkeley: University of California Press, 1995), 222.

are here wrestled into view through bold strokes of pigment."[28]

Johnson conveyed this sensitivity to the subtleties of apparently "unremarkable" landscapes to all of her students (and to Theodore Waddell in particular). She admired French Symbolist painter Gustave Moreau (1826–1898) as "one of the greatest modern teachers"; Moreau's students at Paris' *École des Beaux-Arts* had included Henri Matisse and Georges Rouault. In an essay on color, Johnson quoted Moreau in expressing her own ideas of what a young painter should pursue to achieve depth, intimacy, even profundity through the mindful use of color. Moreau had written:

> [Y]ou must think color imaginatively. You must copy nature imaginatively; this is what makes the artist. Color should be considered, pondered, reflective, inventive . . . . Believe me, the only painting that will endure is that which has been dreamed about, thought about, reflected on, created in the mind and not simply with manual facility.[29]

In a 1952 essay addressed to amateur painters, Johnson insisted that the amateur need be "neither a dabbler nor dilettante," but instead should strive to become a serious painter who happens to not "paint for a living," but always learns new things, always perfects his or her craft, always strives for new freedoms:

> Soon the amateur learns that a work of art is a "thing created nearest to the heart's desire." He ceases to think of the postcard, the calendar, the theatrical illustration. He forgets there were ever such things as so-called rules and senses that his work is not a copying of nature but a putting together of elements to create a work of art which responds to its own laws of being rather than to an order imposed by the outer world of our senses.[30]

---

28 Patricia Vettel-Becker, "Isabelle Johnson and the Visual Poetics of Home," in Peterson, et al, *"A Lonely Business,"* 31.

29 Gustave Moreau, quoted in Isabelle Johnson, "That Wonderful World of Color," *The Arts in Montana*, ed. H. G. Merriam (Missoula, MT: Mountain Press, 1977), 40.

30 Isabelle Johnson, "For What is the Amateur Painter Working?", *The Arts in Montana*, ed. Merriam, 170, 172.

During the same time that he was studying with Isabelle Johnson, Ted Waddell had another series of encounters that helped cement his commitment to a specifically Montana modernism and community of Montana contemporary artists. In 1960, when he was only seventeen, his friend, Mac Lewis, a graduate student at Eastern, took him to Bozeman to meet the painters Robert (1920–1990) and Gennie DeWeese (1921–2007), painter and printmaker Jessie Wilber (1912–1989), and ceramist Frances Senska (1914–2009).

As he's written, "My association with them lasted for a lifetime," and of the DeWeeses in particular, he says, "I always say that the DeWeeses saw me through puberty, mid life crisis, and Medicare. It was great to visit them. They would sit at the kitchen table, smoking hand-rolled cigarettes and making art. It was everywhere, oozing from their pores. . . . they both had immense ability and great personalities." Of Bob DeWeese, he recalls, "He was cool, one of the first artists I knew who had a downtown studio, over the [VFW Club]. His early etchings were magic."[31] Gennie DeWeese was an equally accomplished artist, and she possessed an ability, in both her landscapes and her domestic scenes, to create – in the words of art historian Julie Codell – "a rich painted surface with bold graphic lines that describe and abstract at the same time,"[32] something she shared with the later Theodore Waddell.

Waddell says of Senska and Wilber, both professors of art at Montana State University, along with Bob DeWeese:

> I met Frances and Jessie at the same time as I met the DeWeeses. Frances and Jessie brought modernism to Montana in the late 40s. Frances was, as you know, called the Mother of Potters as she taught all the good ones, [Peter] Voulkos (1924–2002), [Rudy]Autio (1926–2007), [John] Takehara (1929–2009), and countless others. . . . I saw them as often as I could. I traded Frances pots for sculpture. . . . I bought her pots whenever I could. She was always kind and always showed up for all art events whenever she could.[33]

---

31   Theodore Waddell, email to Rick Newby, February 22, 2013.

32   Julie F. Codell, "Scene/Seen Out the Window: The Works of Gennie DeWeese," *Gennie DeWeese: Retrospective* (Missoula, MT: Art Museum of Missoula, 1996), 10.

33   Theodore Waddell, email to Rick Newby, February 22, 2013.

In the ceramics world of the mid-century American West, Frances Senska figured large in the dispersion of aesthetic and pedagogical approaches introduced by European émigré artists, especially those associated with the German Bauhaus. As the child of Presbyterian missionaries, perhaps she found it natural to serve as a missionary for modernism.

Senska went on transmit her modernist approach to Peter Voulkos and Rudy Autio, two of the most important ceramic artists to emerge in the postwar United States. Both Autio and Voulkos went on to distinguished teaching careers during which they, in turn, influenced hundreds of students. Of particular importance to Ted Waddell's story, at the University of Montana, Autio established a zone of radical freedom in the studio, encouraging his students to experiment and teaching by example.

These elder modern artists who welcomed the seventeen-year-old Ted Waddell so warmly (and whom he took to calling his art aunts and uncles) made up the core of a Montana modern art community that grew slowly during the 1940s, 50s, and 60s and has since expanded exponentially. Waddell recalls:

> It seemed like the art world was pretty finite during the 60s. . . . [T]he number of artists who were serious were few, and most of them knew each other. It was nothing to drive halfway across the state to attend someone's opening. During those years, we all shared what we knew.[34]

Rancher, painter, sculptor, and writer (author of the classic *Today I Baled Some Hay to Feed the Sheep the Coyotes Eat*), Bill Stockton (1921–2002) was one of Isabelle Johnson's true peers. Waddell remembers:

> I was very taken with Bill's notions about art and the fact that he had studied in Paris seemed mystical and magical. . . . I don't know how directly Bill influenced me visually as our work was radically different in most ways. Having said that, we shared a love of the landscape and animals. Bill's use of a nearly abstract approach to his work did have an

---

34 Ibid.

impact on me. I have always admired his draftsmanship.[35]

Having encountered this small band of committed modernists, Ted Waddell must have felt that life as a contemporary artist in Montana might, in fact, be possible.

---

35   Ibid.

"A Beautiful Spirit"

Origins of the Archie Bray Foundation for the Ceramic Arts

Researched & written with Chere Jiusto

Originally published in Garth Clark, Peter Held, Rick Newby & Chere Jiusto, Patricia Failing, & Janet Koplos, *A Ceramic Continuum: Fifty Years of the Archie Bray Influence,* ed. Peter Held (Helena, MT, and Seattle, WA: Holter Museum of Art/University of Washington Press, 2001). Excerpts from this essay appeared in *Montana the Magazine of Western History,* Helena, MT, Spring 2001, and *American Craft,* New York, NY, April/May 2001.

> "Origin is an eddy in the process of becoming."
> – Walter Benjamin[1]

"You get notorious," said Peter Meloy, "when you start a pottery in the middle of the wilderness."[2] Meloy – at age ninety – was remembering the beginnings of his own backyard pottery in the late 1940s in the small town of Helena, Montana.[3] But he might as well have been talking about Helena's Archie Bray Foundation for the Ceramic Arts, which Meloy helped to found in 1951.

Over the past half century, the Bray – as the foundation is familiarly known – has certainly achieved renown, and even a little notoriety, in the American ceramics world and beyond. That it has flourished for fifty years in the wilds of Montana, and that from its very beginnings it has played an important role in the development of contemporary ceramics, is cause for wonder, even astonishment. How was it that a band of strong-willed Montanans – in the midst of the conformist 1950s and with relatively little access to technical information about the making of pottery and ceramic sculpture – came to create this world-class haven for lovers and practitioners of the ceramic arts?

The search for origins, German cultural critic Walter Benjamin

---

1   Walter Benjamin, *The Origin of German Tragic Drama* (London: NLB, 1977), 45.

2   Peter Meloy, conversation with Chere Jiusto and Rick Newby, July 2, 1998. In August 1998, Peter Meloy, the last surviving co-founder of the Archie Bray Foundation, passed away. We dedicate this essay to his memory.

3   Peter Meloy, interview by Martin Holt, Helena, MT, June 19, 1977, Archie Bray Foundation for the Ceramic Arts Archives, Helena, MT (ABFA).

has written, "needs to be recognized as a process of restoration and reestablishment, but, on the other hand . . . as something imperfect and incomplete."[4] While much remains to be learned about the origins of the Archie Bray Foundation, our aim is to begin to restore and reestablish – to reinterpret and reinvigorate, with the aid of new research – the events of fifty years ago, when a brickmaker, a lawyer, and a salesman created a "place to work for all who are seriously interested in any of the Ceramic Arts."[5]

Ten Million Bricks

> "Western Clay Plays Role in Growth, Beauty of
> Capital City"
> – *Helena Independent Record,* July 22, 1945

The story begins in a rough-and-ready Montana gold camp that refused to dwindle and die. Instead of a ghost town, Helena grew into a center for mining, transportation, and commerce, and it became Montana's territorial and then state capital. Situated on the eastern edge of the Rockies, the prospering town – originally constructed of wood and canvas – sought greater solidity.

Brick and stone homes and business blocks became symbols of status, and frequent fires – as many as nine in the mining camp's first decade, 1864–1874 – prompted the town fathers to require that only masonry buildings be built downtown. By 1869, Helena's business district boasted seventy-five structures built of granite and brick, and during the 1880s, the town's entrepreneurs displayed their wealth by commissioning lavish mansions – many of them built of brick – on Helena's prestigious west side.[6]

All this construction created a market for locally made brick, and in 1880, Nicholas Kessler – a local brewer and part-time maker of bricks since 1866 – went into the business in a big way, buying a

---

4   Benjamin, *Origin of German Tragic Drama*, 45.

5   Archie Bray, Sr., letter to Branson Stevenson, 1951, ABFA.

6   Chere Jiusto, *The Heart of Helena* (Helena, MT: Montana State Historic Preservation Office, 1989), 5; Marguerite Greenfield, *The Old Fire Bell on Tower Hill* (Helena: Committee on Landmarks, n.d.); and Paula Petrik, *No Step Backward: Women and Family on the Rocky Mountain Frontier, Helena, Montana, 1865– 1900* (Helena: Montana Historical Society Press, 1987), 6–7, 14–15.

pair of brickmaking machines and launching Kessler Brick and Tile Works. At first, Kessler ran his brick works next to his brewery, on the western outskirts of Helena, but in 1885, he purchased the neighboring brick business operated by Charles C. Thurston and moved his operation to Thurston's yard, just off today's Country Club Road.

In 1884, Charles Thurston had hired a skilled brickmaker by the name of Charles H. Bray. Born in Tavistock, Devonshire, England, in 1864 (the year gold was discovered at Helena), Charles Bray had served an apprenticeship with a British brickmaker before coming to the United States in 1880. After Nicholas Kessler purchased the Thurston yard, he installed Bray as his plant manager. Bray enlarged and updated the plant, improving the kilns and adding a steam engine to power wet-mud brick presses and a dry-clay press. He also added sewer pipe and tile, decorative brick, and flowerpots to the Kessler product line. The Kessler Brick and Tile Works prospered under Charles Bray's direction, and as Nicholas Kessler's son, Charles, would later assert, "No less than 90 per cent of the brick of which Helena's buildings were constructed were made at these Brick Yards."[7]

By the 1890s, the only other brick and tile manufacturer in Helena was the Switzer Brick and Terra-Cotta Company, which operated fifteen miles west of Helena, at Blossburg. The Blossburg clay pits produced a blue clay body of commercial quality, and in 1905, the Switzer and Kessler brickmaking operations merged, forming the Western Clay Manufacturing Company. Operating under the ownership of another Kessler son, Frederick, and Jacob Switzer, Western Clay retained Charles Bray as general manager. Bray kept the brickmaking operation – now consolidated at the Kessler yard, with clay coming from Blossburg by rail – up to the minute. He constructed beehive kilns that still grace the brickyard, as well as extensive drying sheds. A 250-horsepower Corliss steam engine ran the plant. Employing upwards of 50 workers, Western Clay produced fire, sidewalk, ornamental, paving, and pressed brick; culvert and sewer pipe; lawn vases and flowerpots; clay tile; flue linings; and even hollow tile for grain silos. By 1918, production ran

---

7   Charles N. Kessler, "A few remarks at the occasion of the opening of the First Branch of the Archie Bray Foundation, at the Western Clay Manufacturing Company Plant, west of Helena, Montana," October 20, 1951, ABFA.

as high as 10 million bricks and tiles annually.

In 1920, Charles Bray purchased the Switzer interest in the company, and eight years later, he bought out the Kessler family, becoming sole owner. Upon Charles's death in 1931, his son Archie stepped in as general manager and president of Western Clay.

Groomed to lead the enterprise in a new century, Archie Bray learned brickmaking at his father's knee, intuitively absorbing the nineteenth-century practices of molding and "burning" brick. He combined this practical knowledge with the technical training he received in the Ohio State University ceramics engineering program, reputed to be the finest in the nation. Archie continued his father's innovations, converting the coal-fired boiler and kilns to natural gas in 1931. And under his direction, Western Clay continued as Montana's preeminent brick producer, even at the peak of the Great Depression.

Only after World War II did the demand for brick and other ceramic products – with the rise of new building technologies and materials – begin to shrink. At the same time, Archie Bray, a long-time patron of the arts, had become obsessed by a vision. Next door to the Western Clay plant, Archie would found a center for the ceramic arts with the support of friends who shared his vision and helped to carry it further.[8]

Three Friends

> "... they were just plain three close friends. And
> they were the three trustees of the original Archie
> Bray Foundation when it opened."
>
> – Betty Bray Galusha

A complex figure, Archie Bray was a hardheaded businessman who supported the arts and loved to garden, a member of Helena's cultural and business elites who delighted in meeting visiting

---

8   For our discussion of the history of Western Clay Manufacturing Company, we are indebted to Fred Quivik, whose study, *The Western Clay Manufacturing Company: An Historical Analysis of the Plant and Its Development* (Butte, MT: Renewable Technologies, Inc., 1985), proved invaluable. See also "Bray Was Born While Miners' Picks Tapped Golden Flood of Last Chance," *The Townsend* (MT) *Star*, undated clipping, scrapbooks, ABFA.; Duane W. Bowler, "Western Clay Plays Role in Growth, Beauty of Capital City," *Helena Independent Record*, July 22, 1945; Archie Bray, Jr., interview by Martin Holt, Los Angeles, CA, August 3, 1978, ABFA; and Chere Jiusto, "Brickyards to Potshards," *More From the Quarries of Last Chance Gulch* (Helena: *Helena Independent Record*, 1995), 106–109.

celebrities dressed in his dusty brickyard clothes, "a resourceful man and very determined."[9]

As a young man, Archie had wanted to become a physician, but his father instead insisted that he be trained as a ceramic engineer. One family legend has it that the "bitter battle" of wills between father and son ended the day Charles Bray "took a buggy whip and whipped [Archie] until it cut the shirt off his back. . . . from that time forth, it was understood that he would go and be a ceramic engineer, which he did."[10]

From an early age, Archie had also nursed a fond regard for the arts, especially the performing arts. This was another passion his family did not share or understand, and the one concession Archie's parents made to his artistic bent was to allow him to take piano lessons. Music would continue to be Archie's first love – "He was a nut on symphonic and operatic music. . . . he liked the French composers," recalled a friend – and as an adult, he traveled every winter to New York City to immerse himself in opera and the theater.[11]

Not content with finding culture elsewhere, Archie Bray sought to bring the "finer arts to his home town." For some six years – at the same time that he worked long hours as manager of the brickyard – he single-handedly sponsored concerts in Helena. Sometimes, he lost considerable sums, as when a savage Montana blizzard limited the audience for a vocal recital to thirty-two hardy souls. He was always, recalls his daughter, Betty Bray Galusha, "hocking the life insurance and mortgaging the house . . ." to cover such losses. Finally, he linked his efforts to the national Community Concert Association series. The Community Concerts were "run as a business" – a "saving grace" for the Bray family finances.[12] The series brought to Helena such luminaries as Nelson Eddy, Jascha Heifetz, and Paul Robeson,

---

9   Archie Bray, Jr., Holt interview, ABFA.

10   Archie Bray, Jr., Holt interview, ABFA.

11   Archie Bray, Jr., Holt interview, ABFA; "Archie Bray, Sr., Helena Industrialist and Patron of Fine Arts, Dies at Home Today After Illness," *Helena Independent Record,* February 17, 1953; Al Gaskill, "The Man in the Brown Derby," *Helena Independent Record,* April 17, 1960; and Meloy, Holt interview, ABFA.

12   Archie Bray, Jr., Holt interview, ABFA; and Betty Bray Galusha, interview by Martin Holt, Denver, CO, May 10, 1978, ABFA.

along with many lesser-known performers.[13] Always dressed in his dusty workingman's clothes, Archie chauffeured the artists about town, and he befriended many of them, inviting them into his home. These brief but intense contacts meant a great deal to him, and sometimes, when he talked about the artists he had known, "tears would almost come into his eyes. . . ."[14]

In 1936, Archie's passion for theater led him to Peter Meloy, future co-conspirator. That year, Meloy's brother Henry – known as "Hank" – had returned to the family ranch near Townsend, Montana (about thirty miles from Helena), to spend the summer painting and drawing. Educated at the Art Institute of Chicago and later a painting instructor at Columbia University, Hank had brought his girlfriend home with him, a New York actress named Ruth March. Hank and Ruth hadn't enough money to buy return train tickets to New York, and in those depression years, "there was no money in the family." But Ruth had just appeared in an off-Broadway play, *The Drunkard,* and the resourceful duo – with help from Peter and neighbors – put on the play in the loft of a horse barn. The play raised the necessary train fare, and among those traveling from Helena to swell the audience was Archie Bray. A few days later, Archie and Norman and Belle Winestine – prominent members of Helena's small, tightly knit intelligentsia – returned to the Meloy ranch to discuss bringing *The Drunkard* to Helena.[15]

Nothing came of the effort to take *The Drunkard* on the road, but these first encounters between Archie Bray and the Meloys bore fruit in the early 1940s, after Peter Meloy had settled in Helena.[16] Peter and Hank again crossed paths with the owner of the Western Clay brickyard; this time, a mutual interest in clay brought them

---

13   Archie Bray, Jr., Holt interview, ABFA; Betty Bray Galusha, Holt interview, ABFA; and "Members of Community Concert Association Have Been Given Opportunity to Enjoy Big Names of Entertainment World," *Helena Independent Record,* undated clipping, scrapbooks, ABFA.

14   Peter Meloy, "Archie Bray and The Archie Bray Foundation," unpublished reminiscence, July 1997, ABFA

15   Peter Meloy, "Archie Bray and The Archie Bray Foundation," ABFA; Peter Meloy, interview by Chere Jiusto and Rick Newby, July 2, 1998, ABFA; Meloy, Holt interview, ABFA; and Alexandra Swaney, "The Queen of Social Logic: The Life and Writing of Frieda Fligelman," *Writing Montana: Literature under the Big Sky,* eds. Rick Newby & Suzanne Hunger (Helena: Montana Center for the Book, 1996), 103.

16   Peter Meloy maintained a lively interest in the theater, and between 1939 and the early 40s, he directed the Helena Little Theatre. See Vivian Paladin and Jean Baucus, *Helena: An Illustrated History* (1983; Helena: Montana Historical Society Press, 1996), 185.

together. The Meloys had been fascinated by ceramics since their youth. In Peter's telling, drought and depression had left the Meloy family with "plenty of free time," and so he and Hank had turned to digging clay from a clay bank they'd discovered on the ranch. Firing the pots they made in the ranch blacksmith forge proved a dismal failure, and by the time the Meloys re-encountered Archie, they were determined to find a better way to fire their work. They visited the brickyard to buy clay from the Blossburg pits, and after Hank had sculpted a horse from this "very plastic" clay body, they asked Archie if they could fire it in one of the beehive kilns. Archie agreed. Though the firing wasn't entirely successful, the friendship between Archie and the Meloy brothers was launched.

Hank Meloy spent most of each year in New York, teaching at Columbia and meeting many leading artists of the day, from George Grosz to Willem de Kooning. He painted prodigiously: "sensitive landscapes and horses of rural Montana . . ." as well as "urbane and lively studies of nudes and abstract color compositions. . . ." He continued to spend summers back home where, in addition to his painting, he sculpted an occasional ceramic figure and decorated his brother's plates and bowls. He died suddenly in 1951, at the age of forty-nine.[17] As Rudy Autio – another major player in the Archie Bray Foundation story – has testified, Hank was an artist of "sublime ability" who influenced the younger sculptor "profoundly."[18]

Peter Meloy, on the other hand, stayed in Helena, working as a prominent attorney and district judge. He made pots in his off hours and built a "small ceramic workshop" in his backyard, where he installed his own electric kiln, one of the first in Montana. Archie Bray spent many evenings with the Meloys, talking "about building the pottery . . . talking about music. . . ." Together they hatched a plan to start a pottery at the brickyard. "When I think back on [Archie's] visits," Peter Meloy has written, "it seems that he had found a place

---

17   See Donna Forbes, Rudy and Lela Autio, and Gordon McConnell, *Henry Meloy: Five Themes: 1945–1951* (Billings, MT: Yellowstone Art Center, 1990); and *Henry Meloy: Notes, Henry Meloy: Non-Objectives, Henry Meloy: Landscapes,* and *Henry Meloy: Portrait Drawings,* all published by the Henry Meloy Educational Trust, Helena, MT, n.d. The bulk of Henry Meloy's artistic output not in private hands is held by the School of Fine Arts, the University of Montana, Missoula.

18   Rudy Autio, artist's statement, *Northwest Ceramics Today* (Boise, ID: Boise State University, 1987), 8.

where he could give expression to his dreams."[19]

A second Montana potter was also serving as confidant for Archie's thoughts "about building the pottery." Branson Stevenson of Great Falls was a man of many parts: world traveler, printmaker, painter, sculptor, potter, oilman, salesman, and inventor. He first met Archie in 1947. As Montana branch manager for Socony Vacuum Oil Company (later Mobil Oil), Branson visited the Western Clay plant regularly and sold Archie "steam cylinder oil and so forth." Always the art patron, Archie bought some of Branson's etchings, and the two men inevitably started talking about their growing interest in the ceramic arts.[20]

Stevenson had first studied pottery with Sister Mary Trinitas Morin, a Sister of Providence and the head of the Division of Arts at the Great Falls (Montana) College of Education, today the University of Great Falls. Educated at the Art Institute of Chicago and the Catholic University of America, where she received her Master of Fine Arts, Sister Trinitas was adept in many different media, mastering the arts and crafts of metal and ceramic sculpture, silversmithing, woodcarving, stained glass, pottery, weaving, and calligraphy.

An innovative and visionary artist with a fondness for found materials, Sister Trinitas was the first Montana educator to set up a kiln on a Montana college campus. During the late 1940s, she led students around the state to dig and test native clays, and by example, she "stimulated the teaching of pottery in the schools." Besides teaching Branson the fundamentals of pottery, Sister Trinitas convinced him to study with Marguerite Wildenhain, the Bauhaus-trained potter whose school at Pond Farm, California, influenced many American potters from mid-century onward.[21]

Not a college graduate, Branson Stevenson prided himself on his "curiosity, individuality, enthusiasm and skill," and as an artist, his greatest strength was as a technician and innovator. Always seeking "new and practical ways of creating art and the tools to perfect his art," he made several technical contributions to his chosen avocation.

---

19   Meloy, Holt interview, ABFA; and Meloy, "Archie Bray and The Archie Bray Foundation," ABFA.

20   Branson Stevenson, interview by Martin Holt, Great Falls, MT, August 2, 1978, ABFA; and Herbert C. Anderson, Jr., *The Life, the Times and the Art of Branson Graves Stevenson* (Raynesford, MT: Janher Publishing Inc., 1979), 213–214.

21   Sister Providencia, *Life Sketch of Sister Mary Trinitas Morin, F.C.S.P.* (Great Falls, MT: College of Great Falls, 1965); and Anderson, *Branson Graves Stevenson*, 223, 224.

Perhaps his most important was the wax resist process commonly used today, which utilized a water-soluble wax, Ceremul A, that Branson marketed for Socony Oil. Used industrially for such things as coating milk cartons, Ceremul A – in wax resist – was far superior to the traditional paraffin for several reasons: paraffin had to be heated and was a fire hazard, was difficult to apply, and hardened quickly, while Ceremul A could be used straight from the container, brushed on easily, kept glazes from sticking to the waxed surface, and completely evaporated during firing, leaving behind only the potter's intended design.[22]

Besides his inventiveness, curiosity, and enthusiasm, Stevenson possessed a great gift for friendship. He maintained friendships, usually through extensive correspondence, around the globe, from Central America – where he had spent a part of his youth and young adulthood – to Japan to Great Britain. One of his correspondents was Bernard Leach, the British writer and potter. Early in 1950, Stevenson had read in *Time* magazine that an exhibition of Leach's pots was traveling to Washington, D.C. Never shy, Branson wrote to Leach at his St. Ives pottery and asked if, during the following summer, the potter would be willing to loan the same group of pots to the Northern Montana State Fair at Great Falls. Leach agreed, and his work was an "outstanding feature" of the fair that summer.[23] Branson later attended a Leach workshop in Minnesota, and the friendship was cemented, especially when Branson introduced Leach to Ceremul A, markedly easing the challenges of wax resist decoration for the British master.[24] Leach would often trade his stoneware pots to Branson for supplies of the wax (not then available in England).[25]

In 1951, as Archie Bray set in motion his plans for a foundation for the ceramic arts, Branson began another extensive correspondence, this time with Archie, serving as sounding board for the brickmaker's plans, dreams, and frustrations.[26]

---

22 Anderson, *Branson Graves Stevenson*, 223–224, 229, 240.

23 "Famous Ceramic Artists Hold Seminar at Helena," *Great Falls Tribune*, undated clipping, scrapbooks, ABFA.

24 Stevenson, Holt interview, ABFA.

25 Anderson, *Branson Graves Stevenson*, 224.

26 Archie Bray, Sr.'s letters to Branson Stevenson, dating from early 1951 to February 1953, survive in the Archie Bray Foundation Archives and provide invaluable insight into Archie's thought processes from the time the foundation began until his death. Branson's letters to Archie do not appear to have survived.

Two Brash Young Men and Their Teacher

"We got this rumor that somebody up at this
brickyard was thinking of building a pottery."

– Frances Senska

By 1951, the Helena potteries – Peter Meloy's modest backyard pottery and Archie Bray's grand dream (on the cusp of realization) – were indeed getting notorious. That spring, two young ceramics-savvy Montanans – Rudy Autio and Pete Voulkos – drove up to Helena from Bozeman. They had heard through Peter Meloy that "there was a chance to work at a pottery. . . ." As Frances Senska – the pair's pottery teacher at Montana State College – recalled, Archie Bray immediately "latched onto [Autio and Voulkos], and they latched onto him, and they worked in a corner of the drying shed that summer." To pay their way, the young men worked in the brickyard during the day. At night, they turned their talents to making pots and ceramic sculpture from the Blossburg clay. And they jumped in to help Archie build the pottery he'd long dreamed of constructing next door to the brickyard.[27]

During the late 1940s, Autio and Voulkos – both veterans – studied art at Montana State College (MSC) in Bozeman, and they were lucky enough to arrive on campus the same year (1946) as did Frances Senska, their first ceramics instructor. "I started teaching ceramics," recalled Senska, "with the merest little scrap of knowledge. I had had just two quarters of ceramics when I started teaching. I just learned it right along with the class."[28]

In fact, despite her relative inexperience, Frances Senska would introduce to Montana many of the aesthetic and pedagogical ideas brought to the United States by European artists who had fled their homelands during the World War II era.[29] Senska had

27   Rudy Autio, interview by Chere Jiusto and Rick Newby, Missoula, MT, November 3, 1998, ABFA; Frances Senska and Jessie Wilber, interview by Martin Holt, Bozeman, MT, July 16, 1979, ABFA; and Peter Voulkos, interview by Martin Holt, Oakland, CA, August 7, 1978, ABFA.

28   Senska/Wilber, Holt interview, ABFA.

29   See Marcia Y. Manhart, "The Emergence of the American Craftsman – a la BA, BFA, MA, and MFA" in *A Neglected History: 20th Century American Craft* (New York: American Craft Museum, 1990), 21.

received her training in fine arts at the University of Iowa, earning her B.A. in 1935 and her M.A. in 1939. She had first encountered clay in Africa, where – as the child of Presbyterian missionaries – she had spent her first fifteen years. But it was not until World War II, during her Navy service, that she took her first pottery course, studying with Edith Heath at the California Labor School.

In the summer of 1946, just before coming to Bozeman, she took a second pottery course, this time from Finnish potter Maija Grotell at the Cranbrook Academy of Art in Michigan. Grotell believed that each potter should find his or her own approach – "I am against influence," she said – and she hesitated to critique her students' work, instead encouraging them to search and inquire. She taught, said Senska, "more by example, than by instruction."[30]

Another European emigre profoundly affected Frances's thinking about design and pedagogy. He was the Hungarian Laszlo Moholy-Nagy, the Bauhaus master who founded a New Bauhaus in Chicago in 1937. By the time Frances studied industrial design with Moholy-Nagy, the New Bauhaus had failed, and he was directing the Chicago Institute of Design, which bore the stamp of his program of "intellectual integration." Vehemently opposed to specialization (which he felt isolated people and deadened the emotions), Moholy-Nagy sought to produce "many-sided amateurs with their own ideas and practical skills." Frances embraced this attitude, calling him a great teacher because "he never told anyone anything couldn't be done." "He'd say, 'Well, try it,'" she recalled. "'You might find out something.'"[31]

Frances brought the hands-off teaching approaches of Maija Grotell and Moholy-Nagy to Montana State College, where she "instructed . . . told them things," but "didn't try to force any style." She could be directive, as when Pete Voulkos "was doing something he could just as well have done in high school industrial arts, and I

---

30   Susan D. Harris and Ted Vogel, *Heroes, Icons, History and Memory: 1998 NCECA Honors and Fellows Exhibition,* Modern Art Museum of Fort Worth (National Council on Education for the Ceramic Arts, 1998), 87–88; Garth Clark, *American Ceramics: 1876 to the Present* (London: Booth-Clibborn Editions, 1987), 270; and Frances Senska, interview by Chere Jiusto and Rick Newby, Bozeman, MT, June 9, 1998, ABFA.

31   Senska/Wilber, Holt interview, ABFA; Senska, Jiusto/Newby interview, ABFA; Marcia Y. Manhart, "Charting A New Educational Vision," *Craft in the Machine Age: The History of Twentieth-Century American Craft, 1920–1945* (New York: Harry N. Abrams/American Craft Museum, 1995), 69; and Krisztina Passuth, *Moholy-Nagy* (New York: Thames and Hudson, 1985), 205–206.

said, 'You know, it's been done. Come into the twentieth century.'" And noted Frances, "He did!"[32]

Frances's teaching style worked perfectly for her two star students. Like many older students coming out of the military at that time who were, in the words of Marcia Manhart, "more self-assured than the usual undergraduates,"[33] Rudy Autio and Pete Voulkos seemed remarkably focused.[34] Frances recalled that both men "moved very fast into their own thing." Pete Voulkos "always did everything just a little bit better than everybody else," while Rudy Autio was "inner directed" and often worked by himself – which was "perfectly alright" with Frances, since he was already "an excellent craftsman"[35] and "he's always been a mature artist, sort of quiet, polite, and curious."[36]

Both Pete Voulkos and Rudy Autio were Montana natives whose parents had immigrated to the United States. Pete's parents, Efrosine and Harry, were Greek and had come to Bozeman in the 1920s. Harry was soon regarded as Bozeman's finest chef, while Efrosine raised the five Voulkos children. Pete was the family rebel, sometimes skipping school to play pool or fish in the nearby blue-ribbon trout streams, but during the depression years, he labored extraordinarily hard – at as many as five jobs at once – to help support his family. In doing so, he developed an awesome capacity for work.

Physically powerful and mechanically adept, Pete sought a congenial career. Always a night person, he'd heard that "artists don't have to get up in the morning," and after serving in the Pacific theater as an Army Air Corps nose gunner, he returned to Bozeman and took advantage of the G.I. Bill, enrolling himself in the MSC art department. At first determined to become a commercial artist, he took painting courses from Jessie Wilber and Bob DeWeese, talented modernist painters who influenced and befriended the driven young artist. Wilber and DeWeese were soon disappointed,

---

32   Senska, Jiusto/Newby interview, ABFA.

33   Manhart, "The Emergence of the American Craftsman," 23.

34   Senska/Wilber, Holt interview, ABFA.

35   Senska/Wilber, Holt interview, ABFA.

36   Frances Senska, interview by Matthew Kangas, Bozeman, MT, August 5, 1982, quoted in Matthew Kangas, *Rudy Autio: A Retrospective* (Helena: Montana Historical Society Press, 1983), 7–8.

however, when – in his junior year – Voulkos took his first ceramics course from Frances Senska.[37] "That was it," recalled Frances. "That's what he wanted to do."[38]

By the time he graduated from MSC in 1951, Pete was starting to sell his pots and to win awards in national competitions, including a purchase prize in the Fifteenth National Ceramic Exhibition (1950), Syracuse Museum of Fine Arts. In January 1951, he went on to graduate school in ceramics at the California College of Arts and Crafts (CCAC), Oakland.[39]

Rudy Autio came from Butte, Montana, the brawling copper camp known as the "Richest Hill on Earth." His parents, Arne and Selma, were natives of Finland, and Rudy spoke Finnish before he mastered English. A Navy veteran, Rudy fell in love with and married a fellow MSC art student, Lela Moniger, a native of Great Falls, Montana.

Unlike Pete, Rudy was not initially enraptured with clay. As he noted, "I was interested in becoming a sculptor, and I didn't care for this crafty stuff and making pottery. . . ."[40] His early work, Frances Senska remembered, had "this very strong northern, Nordic kind of imagery, a Finnish, almost Oriental look to it . . . always different from what everyone else was doing."[41] After leaving MSC in 1950 (he received a B.S. in Applied Art), Rudy went directly to graduate school in sculpture at Washington State University, Pullman. It was the summer after Rudy's first year at WSU – and Pete's at CCAC – that the two young men took that fateful trip to Helena and found themselves hard at work in Archie Bray's brickyard.[42]

---

37 Rose Slivka, "The Artist and His Work: Risk and Revelation," in Rose Slivka and Karen Tsujimoto, *The Art of Peter Voulkos* (Tokyo/Oakland, CA: Kodansha International/The Oakland Museum, 1995),34–35.

38 Senska/Wilber, Holt interview, ABFA.

39 Slivka and Tsujimoto, *The Art of Peter Voulkos,* 161.

40 Autio, Jiusto/Newby interview, ABFA.

41 Senska/Wilber, Holt interview, ABFA.

42 Kangas, *Rudy Autio,* 5–8, 69.

Archie's Vision

> "According to leading authorities, Pottery, Inc.,
> is the only place of its kind, not only in
> the United States but in the world."
> – *Helena Independent Record,* October 7, 1951

While Pete Voulkos and Rudy Autio labored in his brickyard, Archie Bray – in conversation with Peter Meloy and Branson Stevenson – finalized his plans for "the first branch of the Archie Bray Foundation," which he called Pottery, Inc. In an undated letter to Branson, Archie described his vision for the foundation:

> Somehow lets keep it all on the plane we dreamed – lets be practical too, lets keep it all in good fun, to roll along the whole idea built around – "A place to work for all who are seriously interested in any of the Ceramic Arts." To be high standards – to keep it nice – that it may always be a delight to turn to – to walk inside the Pottery and leave outside somewhere – outside the big gate – up town – anywhere – the cares of every day. Each time we walk in the door to walk into a place of art – of simple things not problems, good people, lovely people all tuned to the right spirit. That somewhere thru it all will permeate a beautiful spirit . . . carrying on and forwarding the intentions, the aims and the life of the Foundation. Can we do it? What a joy it is to do it.[43]

According to the local paper, "Bray had dreamed and planned" the pottery "for so long" that he needed no building plans, and "long before the structure was begun, he would explain [the pottery floor plan] to friends by scratching it out on the ground with the heel of his shoe."[44]

The pottery building, as it emerged from Archie's imaginings, was to be well-equipped, featuring five rooms covering 2,400 square feet. A museum space would house exhibits and a library of ceramics

---

43   Archie Bray, Sr., letter to Branson Stevenson, n.d., ABFA.

44   Dorothy Helton, "Pottery, Inc., Is Realization of Years of Planning by Archie Bray, Patron of Arts," *Helena Independent Record,* October 7, 1951.

books. The main pottery room would "contain wheels, drying racks, areas for sculpturing and tables . . . for hand work," while the kiln room would feature three gas kilns, including a salt kiln and a "muffle" kiln intended for porcelain and high-fire glazes. An electric kiln – cutting-edge technology for the time – would be used to test porcelains and Montana clays, and the glaze room came complete with a "power-ventilated glaze booth."[45]

The pottery was merely the "first branch" of Archie's foundation, representing only a third of his expansive vision. He intended to build two more structures, one for painters and printmakers and the other for the performing arts. The theater would seat three hundred and host plays, theater workshops, and "concerts by small musical aggregations."[46]

Given Archie's interest in the resurgence of the crafts, his vision may well have emerged out of his reading of the works of William Morris and like-minded thinkers. The founder of the English Arts and Crafts movement, Morris had championed a return to beautiful works skillfully crafted by hand, as antidotes to the shoddy workmanship and inferior products of the Industrial Age. Almost certainly, Archie had read Bernard Leach's influential book, *A Potter's Book,* which carried forward Morris's ideas – coupled with a healthy infusion of techniques and philosophical approaches from Asia. From its publication in 1940, *A Potter's Book* was considered the "potter's bible," and Archie's friend Branson Stevenson corresponded regularly with Leach.[47] Leach's pottery at St. Ives, Cornwall, was considered a model for other studio potters, and it may well have served – at least in imagination – as Archie's ideal as he planned his own center.

As a practicing industrialist, Archie stood somewhere between Leach – who disdained industrial products and even modernist institutions like the Bauhaus that sought to bring art to the industrial process[48] – and figures like Bauhaus master Moholy-Nagy, whose

---

45   "Pottery Building, Composed of Five Rooms, Offers Serious Artists Facilities for Every Type of Ceramics," *Helena Independent Record,* October 7, 1951.

46   Helton, "Pottery, Inc., Is Realization."

47   The first letter still surviving – in the Archie Bray Foundation Archives – from Bernard Leach to Branson Stevenson dates from March 15, 1951, but internal evidence indicates that the two men had been corresponding for some time before that date.

48   Bernard Leach, *A Potter's Book* (1940; Levittown, NY: Transatlantic Arts, 1976), 14–15.

slogan was "Not Against Technical Progress, But With It."[49] Archie initially insisted that "there would be no commercializing of the art output" from his pottery, but that when demand developed for multiples of an object created at the foundation, "the molds are turned over to the Western Clay company . . . and there the production becomes a wholesale business."[50] As time passed, Archie refined his position regarding the development of commercial products at the pottery and, in fact, insisted that the artist-craftsmen and -women he hired devote a portion of their time to commercial work. This in turn led to tensions with the artists and frustration for Archie. At the foundation's beginnings, however, everything operated on the level of idealism and good will and everyone involved pitched in wholeheartedly to help Archie realize his dream.

From the Ground Up

> "So one night [Archie] came out and said,
> 'I've got the foundation laid for it.'"
> – Peter Meloy

With the arrival of Pete Voulkos, Rudy Autio, and Kelly Wong, another MSC graduate hired for the summer of 1951, Archie had no need – and no excuse – to put off building his long-envisioned pottery building. The three young artists pitched in, as did Branson Stevenson, who took "his three weeks of Socony vacation" to help out, "laying brick, building the main stack and flues in the pottery, and working on the construction of the gas fired, downdraft, open fire kiln."[51] Interested members of the Helena community came out to lay a line of brick or two. Frances Senska and Jessie Wilber drove over from Bozeman, and Jessie contributed "special tile" – still on the front of the pottery – that depicted kilns and "what would be happening in the building." Frances later wrote that "so many amateurs laid brick for those walls, it's a wonder they remain standing."[52]

---

49   Laszlo Moholy-Nagy, "Education and the Bauhaus," in Passuth, *Moholy-Nagy,* 346.

50   Dorothy Helton, "Pottery, Inc. Has Enjoyed Widespread Recognition During Its First Big Year," *Helena Independent Record,* undated clipping, scrapbooks, ABFA.

51   Anderson, *Branson Graves Stevenson,* 227

52   Senska/Wilber, Holt interview, ABFA; and Frances Senska, "Pottery in a Brickyard," *American Craft,* February/March 1982, 33.

And in his letters to Branson that summer, Archie would frequently close with "Lots of Brick to Lay, Branson, Lots of Brick" – a litany that Branson inscribed on a tile he installed in the pottery's wall.

Pete and Rudy made plenty of pots that summer, "using . . . the local clays." They fired their pots in the beehive kilns, stacking them on top of the bricks and salting them along with the brick. As resident sculptor, Rudy also sculpted a "heroic" ceramic bust of Archie Bray, which made him look like "some sort of Roman senator."[53] They spent much of the summer "laying brick mostly, 'til we got up to where the roof plates go on." Then it was September, time for them to return to graduate school. Brickyard carpenters "set up the roof," and by late October, Archie Bray's pottery was ready for its grand opening.[54]

Peter Meloy drew up the papers for the Archie Bray Foundation, naming Archie Bray, Sr., Peter Meloy, and Branson Stevenson as the first board of directors. With the paperwork begun and a roof on the pottery building, Archie set October 20, 1951, as the date for a gala opening dinner. Invitations went out to all those who had helped lay brick, to potters and artists in the region, and to local supporters. In photos of the opening banquet, some forty celebrants sit at formal, white-clothed tables set up in the pottery's main room. During the joyful evening, Charles Kessler offered a brief history of the brickyard,[55] and Branson Stevenson – serving as toastmaster – spoke about the foundation and its aims. Archie later described Branson's remarks as "beautifully done, so very sensitive, so much as I want everyone to see it."[56] Peter Meloy presented Archie with a pot by Bernard Leach, and Rudy Autio unveiled a plaque – created in secret by Autio, Voulkos, and Meloy at the Meloy pottery – that read:

> The helpers in the building of this pottery dedicate their
> work to the sincere wish that the work produced here will
> be the result of a serious effort to create those fine things as
> are so much a part of the life and interests of the man who
> is making this pottery possible.

53   Autio, Jiusto/Newby interview, ABFA. Rudy Autio's bust of Archie now rests in Robert Harrison's *A Potter's Shrine* on the grounds of the Archie Bray Foundation.

54   Voulkos, Holt interview, ABFA.

55   Charles N. Kessler, "A few remarks at the occasion of the opening of the First Branch of the Archie Bray Foundation," ABFA.

56   Archie Bray, Sr., letter to Branson Stevenson, ca. October 26, 1951, ABFA.

After dinner, Archie showed a film on making pots and conducted tours of the facilities. And Pete Voulkos "threw the first pot in the new building." One of those attending the dinner that night was a new arrival to the Archie Bray Foundation, a young California potter named Lillian Boschen.[57]

The First Resident Director

> "Miss Lillian Boschen . . . has arrived
> in Helena to take charge of
> the Archie Bray foundation. . . ."
>> – *Helena Independent Record,* n.d.

In early October 1951, the Archie Bray Foundation issued a press release, announcing that a Miss Lillian Boschen would be teaching classes in "sculpting, hand-modeling, and wheel-throwing" at Pottery, Inc. Boschen had met Frances Senska while the two women were in the Navy, and like Pete Voulkos, Boschen had studied at the California College of Arts and Crafts. She had also taken courses at the San Francisco Art Institute and at Mills College, working under Carlton Ball. Both Voulkos and Senska had recommended her to Archie Bray as a worthy first director for the freshly completed pottery – replacing Voulkos and Autio while they finished up graduate school.[58]

Apparently, when Pete Voulkos headed back to Oakland for his final year at CCAC, Archie had not yet decided whether to invite him back to the foundation. There never seemed to be a question as to whether Rudy Autio would come back the following summer as resident sculptor, but it appears that there was room (and funds) for only one resident potter, and Archie had to choose between Lillian and Pete. As early as late October 1951, Archie agonized over the decision in a letter to Branson.[59]

In early December of that year, Archie again pondered the decision candidly and at length in another letter to Branson, writing

---

57   "Pottery, Inc., Dedicated During Banquet in New Building Saturday Evening; Forty Attend," *Helena Independent Record,* October 28, 1951.

58   "Young Woman Has Arrived in City To Take Charge of Archie Bray Foundation," *Helena Independent Record,* undated clipping, scrapbooks, ABFA.

59   Archie Bray, Sr., letter to Branson Stevenson, October 26, 1951, ABFA.

that he preferred Lillian "in many ways":

> Her attention to detail which Pete did not display, her
> willingness to do little things which Pete would look on as a
> nuisance and her willingness to follow my directions which I
> *think* Pete would not.

On the other hand, Archie understood that Pete – with his charisma, extraordinary throwing abilities, and growing list of national awards – "could be played up as a feature . . . and to me this is a big factor, almost enough to determine my decision." "I want the place," he added, "to as rapidly as possible become known as a real centre."

As he struggled with his decision, Archie began to think of "keeping both of them."[60] On December 17, Archie told Branson that he had wired Voulkos that "we would look for him here just as soon as he could come,"[61] but in another December letter, he reiterated how pleased he was with Lillian's work, teaching, and attitude, adding that "I can hardly afford a staff of 2 specialists."[62]

By March 1952, Archie was no longer getting along with Lillian Boschen. In a letter dated March 6, he told Branson, "She cannot see . . . that everything she does should be for the interest of the Foundation. The least direction on my part and she pouts and pouts. . . . she wanted to go on filling the big kiln to her heart's content and to hell with what I wanted done" (which was to use the same kiln to fire an order of flowerpots for a local nursery). "Perhaps," Archie admitted to Branson, "I have handled labor too long, expect my decisions . . . to be followed – *willingly*." He concluded ominously, "I will have co-operation or I will start anew."[63]

Lillian stayed on at the Bray into the spring, but by summer, her name no longer appeared in Archie's letters. She went on to open a pottery in Virginia City, Montana, which she ran for several years.[64] Archie's frustrations with the artists in the pottery did not end with Lillian's departure.

---

60   Archie Bray, Sr., letter to Branson Stevenson, December 2, 1951, ABFA.

61   Archie Bray, Sr., letter to Branson Stevenson, December 17, 1951, ABFA.

62   Archie Bray, Sr., letter to Branson Stevenson, December 1951, ABFA.

63   Archie Bray, Sr., letter to Branson Stevenson, March 6, 1952, ABFA.

64   Senska/Wilber, Holt interview, ABFA.

"And so I say – Problems"

> "... I didn't want problems in my Pottery.
> I did so want it to always have
> a feeling for me of delight and pleasure. ...
> Not a place of rules and conditions and
> situations and worries."
>
> – Archie Bray, Sr., letter to
> Branson Stevenson, December 1951

Despite Archie's deep and very real passion for the arts and artists – and despite his eccentricities, such as always wearing his dirty work clothes – he was first and foremost a businessman, with a deeply rooted work ethic. His daughter recalled that he "never slept ... more than four hours, five hours in his life. ... He got up at 5:30 [a.m.], 6:00, and went to work and came home perhaps 1:00 [a.m.], 2:00, and that was it."[65] With the creation of the pottery, his workload only increased, and as he struggled to make the pottery self-sustaining, his frustrations grew.

"These Potters are a problem!" Archie wrote Branson in April 1952. He could not understand their disdain for making flowerpots and other production ware.[66] According to Rudy Autio, "they were quite handsome products, [but] we didn't ... particularly care for it. Turned out to be busywork and it ... didn't really pay the bills. ... we wasted a lot of effort doing it."[67]

Archie was incensed, too, by Pete Voulkos's night-owl approach to work – at 3 p.m., Archie told Branson in disbelief, "Pete and Mrs. Pete are up town for *breakfast!!*"[68] Pete saw things differently. He would "work day and night," making his own pots and keeping up "a production on the side. ... I would make a dozen of this, a dozen of that, a dozen of that every day. And then I'd work on my own things. Usually late at night." Between working on his own pots, teaching classes, and keeping up the production line ("I became very facile ... to the point that it got to be a little boring. ..."), Voulkos was working "about eight

---

65   Betty Bray Galusha, Holt interview, ABFA.

66   Archie Bray, Sr., letter to Branson Stevenson, April 10, 1952.

67   Autio, Jiusto/Newby interview, ABFA.

68   Archie Bray, Sr., letter to Branson Stevenson, April 10, 1952.

days every week."[69] Although he failed to recognize the strain that harsh working conditions and exhausting schedules placed on the artists, at one point, Archie did grant that, for Pete Voulkos, "being behind is his way of getting things done."[70] But until the end of his life, Archie would complain to Branson about the potters' work habits.

The potters, on the other hand, did not like the Archie Bray Foundation policy that the Foundation receive all income from sales of the pots made on the premises, except for those created for "shows and exhibitions." And apparently, as artists with pride of authorship, the potters bridled at the suggestion that their individual work be stamped with the official ABF stamp.[71]

There were aesthetic differences, too, and differences over how the foundation should present itself to the larger world. Influenced increasingly by modernism and the sobering realities of the Atomic Age, Pete and Rudy made what Archie dismissed as "ribs, guts and belly buttons Art." Their works of this period seem tame today – certainly when compared to the two artists' category-shattering work of the late 1950s and early 1960s – but to Archie they were making "a lot of crooked crazy shaped pots."[72] Relatively minor scraps over the Bray's image and direction reflected Rudy and Pete's need to define themselves and their work against what they perceived as Archie and Branson's more craft-oriented and commercial approach. These struggles only prefigured more profound battles to come, battles that would radically alter the character of American ceramic art.

The First Big Year

> "The artistic venture . . . now has the
> toehold it needs to expand and further develop."
> – *Helena Independent Record*, n.d.

Meanwhile the Bray was becoming known as "a real centre," as Archie had hoped. Locally, the classes taught by Lillian and Pete

---

69   Voulkos, Holt interview, ABFA.

70   Archie Bray, Sr., letter to Branson Stevenson, November 5, 1952, ABFA.

71   Archie Bray, Sr., letter to Branson Stevenson, December 1951, ABFA; and Archie Bray, Sr., letter to Branson Stevenson, Spring 1952, ABFA.

72   Archie Bray, Sr., letter to Branson Stevenson, December 23, 1952, ABFA.

brought in enthusiastic students from Helena and the surrounding region, and Pete's wife, Peggy, taught enameling classes and produced enameled ashtrays and other products to raise funds for the foundation. Archie began working to obtain college-level accreditation for Bray courses. And despite the potters' resistance, Archie succeeded in developing a market for ABF production ware, which included flowerpots, honey jars, and ashtrays. Orders poured in for ashtrays and a planter and iron tripod set (designed by Lillian Boschen) from shops in Texas and Oregon, as well as from Gump's, the famous San Francisco gift store.[73] And in downtown Helena, the bookshop of Susan Eaker, Archie's close friend, served as the local outlet for Bray products.

A skilled marketer, Archie hosted the Bray's first open house on January 1, 1952, and though the temperature was 12 degrees below zero, seventy-five people braved the elements for the event. "A lovely affair," Archie wrote Branson. "Everyone was pleased, stayed on and on. . . ." At least two visitors made donations to the foundation fund, and the first person in the door wanted to buy an electric kiln for his wife and daughter.[74]

In both 1951 and 1952, the Archie Bray Foundation took its show on the road, traveling to the North Montana State Fair in Great Falls. In 1951, Autio and Voulkos demonstrated their throwing and sculpture techniques and displayed the "first salt glazed pottery ever produced in Montana." The following August, Rudy and Pete were joined by Peggy Voulkos and Doris Strachan (who had been hired for the summer as Pete's assistant), and the quartet of Bray residents showed fairgoers "clay working, wheel throwing, modeling, sculpture, enameling on metals, and firing."[75]

Closer to home, Archie continued his involvement with the Community Concerts series, and as the local paper reported, "every Community Concert artist . . . visited the pottery and inscribed his or her name on small ceramic tablets, which comprise the 'guest

---

73   Archie Bray, Sr., letter to Branson Stevenson, 1952, ABFA

74   Archie Bray, Sr., letter to Branson Stevenson, January 1, 1952, ABFA.

75   *Great Falls Tribune,* August 6, 1951; and Helton, "Pottery, Inc. Has Enjoyed Widespread Recognition During Its First Big Year," *Helena Independent Record,* undated clipping, scrapbooks, ABFA.

book."[76] A news photographer was often on hand, and features on the performers' visits regularly appeared in the local paper, helping to keep the Bray in the public eye.

Like Archie, Branson Stevenson had marketing in his blood, and during his travels across the United States, he persistently spread the word about the Archie Bray Foundation. Perhaps his greatest coup came in 1952 when, during a business trip to New York, he visited America House, the "leading craft shop" in the country and a precursor to the American Craft Museum. There he met Mrs. Aileen Vanderbilt Webb, America House's founder and the force behind the American Craftsmen's Cooperative Council. Dedicated to "elevating the status of the crafts in America," Mrs. Webb invited the potters of the Archie Bray Foundation to display their wares at America House in a special exhibition.[77]

As events unfolded, the Bray exhibition, entitled "Potters and Glazes of Montana," spent a month during the fall of 1952 at America House and then went on to the Metropolitan Museum of Art. According to the *Helena Independent Record,* the potters included in the show were Pete and Peggy Voulkos, Manuel Neri (who, like Voulkos and Boschen, had studied at the California College of Arts and Crafts and was visiting the Bray that year), Branson Stevenson, Maxine Blackmer, and several local potters taking classes at the Bray. Some of these Montana pots – together with others by Frances Senska, Jessie Wilber, and Peter Meloy – would later tour Europe and Asia in an America House–curated exhibition, "Handcrafts in the United States," sponsored by the State Department.[78]

On October 18, 1952, the Archie Bray Foundation celebrated its dynamic first year with another banquet. Again, forty celebrants gathered in the pottery building. With the recent America House show under its belt and with Pete Voulkos continuing to win national prizes for his pots – his work appeared in seven exhibitions in 1952, from the 17th Ceramic National at the Syracuse Museum to

---

76   Helton, "Pottery, Inc. Has Enjoyed Widespread Recognition During Its First Big Year," *Helena Independent Record,* undated clipping, scrapbooks, ABFA. Apparently, the ceramic guest book has been lost.

77   *Craft in the Machine Age,* 249.

78   Anderson, *Branson Graves Stevenson,* 229; *Great Falls Tribune,* June 22, 1952; and "Exhibit of Montana Made Pottery From Archie Bray Foundation Being Shown in New York City," *Helena Independent Record,* August 31, 1952.

a one-man show at Gump's of San Francisco – the "thriving" foundation could legitimately claim that it had "become known from coast to coast."[79]

Leach, Hamada, Yanagi

> You know that we felt that a start had been
> made . . . that held out a greater promise than in any
> other place which we visited in America.
> – Bernard Leach, letter to Peter Meloy, n.d.

Archie Bray and his fellow board members had always planned to sponsor workshops by renowned ceramic artists at the foundation. Their first choice was Bernard Leach, the British potter, writer, and thinker who ardently championed the notion of the "artist-potter." In the artist-potter's work, Leach maintained, "there is a unity of design and execution, a co-operation of hand and undivided personality, for designer and craftsman are one."[80] This attitude was central to the thinking of the three founders, and they wanted to hear more.

In early 1952, Branson Stevenson learned that Bernard Leach would be touring the United States late in the year. Branson wrote Leach, asking if he might be interested in making a stop at the Archie Bray Foundation – to present lectures and demonstrate his approach to pottery-making. On March 20, Leach replied cautiously, wondering if a Montana stop would conflict with another workshop – arranged by Alix and Warren Mackenzie – already scheduled for St. Paul, Minnesota.[81] Branson assured Leach that St. Paul and Helena were 1,047 miles apart and that, moreover, he could travel by train to Montana and on to his next stop in California, at no extra cost.[82]

Leach discussed the matter with the Mackenzies, and on April 24, he wrote Branson that since he was already visiting three "centres" on his tour – the scheduled stops were Black Mountain College in

79   Helton, "Pottery, Inc. Has Enjoyed Widespread Recognition During Its First Big Year," *Helena Independent Record,* undated clipping, scrapbooks, ABFA.; Slivka and Tsujimoto, *Peter Voulkos,* 174; and "Pete Voulkos Plans To Show Wares At Two Exhibits," *Helena Independent Record,* June 4, 1952.

80   Leach, *A Potter's Book,* 1–2.

81   Bernard Leach, letter to Branson Stevenson and Archie Bray, March 20, 1952, ABFA.

82   Branson Stevenson, letter to Bernard Leach, April 17, 1952, ABFA.

North Carolina, the St. Paul Gallery and School of Art in Minnesota, and Chouinard Art Institute in Los Angeles – he shouldn't add a fourth without the consent of the original sites. And besides, he noted, he didn't think he wanted to face a fourth, "so I tentatively suggest that we might . . . come for a week just friendly-wise . . . to sit around and talk shop, from the warm side of the window pane. . . ." In this letter, Leach told Branson that he was traveling with two Japanese friends, Shoji Hamada, reputed to be Japan's leading potter, and Soetsu Yanagi, director of the Museum of Folk-craft in Tokyo.[83]

Branson wrote back immediately, conveying both his and Archie's delight and promising an "interestingly restful" time.[84] As things developed, the difficulties over a conflict with the other sites seemed to evaporate. Leach decided to go ahead and make the Archie Bray Foundation a fourth "centre" at which he, Yanagi, and Hamada would make a full presentation. In September 1952, Archie issued a press release announcing Leach's impending visit, scheduled for early December.[85] In a letter to Branson, Archie noted his intention to send personal invitations to "75–100 people we know – folks – potters who are truly interested."[86]

By the first week of December, when Leach, Hamada, and Yanagi arrived in Helena, sixty interested folks had signed up for the workshop.[87] They came to Helena from as far away as Grand Junction, Colorado, though most hailed from Montana, with significant contingents traveling from Butte, Missoula, Great Falls, and Bozeman. Several were arts educators, including Frances Senska, Jessie Wilber, and Bob DeWeese of Montana State College and Sister Trinitas from the Great Falls College of Education.

The two-day workshop, held over a weekend, featured throwing demonstrations (sometimes simultaneous) by Leach and Hamada, two lectures by Yanagi ("The Responsibility of the Craftsman" and "Mystery of Beauty," which were subsequently published as

---

83   Bernard Leach, letter to Branson Stevenson, April 24, 1952, ABFA.

84   Branson Stevenson, letter to Bernard Leach, May 1, 1952, ABFA.

85   "Famous English Potter Will Visit Pottery," *Helena Independent Record,* undated clipping, scrapbooks, ABFA.

86   Archie Bray, Sr., letter to Branson Stevenson, September 14, 1952, ABFA.

87   Sign-up list, "Visit and demonstration and lectures by Bernard Leach, Shoji Hamada, Dr. Yanagi, Week of Dec 1-1952," ABFA.

pamphlets by Peter Meloy),[88] and films and slides portraying the ceramic traditions of Japan and England.

Much has been made of the 1952 tour by Leach, Hamada, and Yanagi. Ceramic historian Garth Clark notes that the "seminars at the Archie Bray Foundation . . . and at Black Mountain College . . . proved to be particularly far-reaching." Frances Senska has called the Bray visit "very influential," while Rudy Autio terms it "very significant . . . at least for me."[89] What was it that so impressed and stimulated the American ceramists who attended these workshops?

After all, two years earlier, Bernard Leach had – as Frances Senska put it – "made everybody in the country mad" when he declared that he saw little potential in American ceramics, noting that its practitioners lacked a cultural taproot.[90] Young Americans like Senska saw their own predicament differently: "We came from so many different places, and could give our own spin to whatever we were doing. . . . [In America] you can select any tradition you want and follow it, or make up your own as you go along."[91] Rudy Autio said of Leach, "I don't think he had a great deal of respect for the American potter at the time, and . . . that's the reason we didn't like him." Pete Voulkos, while admitting that Leach had written a "brilliant book," said of the British potter, "He had this quasi Oriental thing, but he was basically a jug maker from Europe."[92] Earlier in the year, at Black Mountain College, Leach had annoyed his hosts by being "rather stuffy and grand" and refusing – at first – to throw any pots because the local clays and kilns weren't what he was accustomed to.[93] At Helena, Leach bemused the rough-and-ready Montanans by wearing his tweeds and a tie even while throwing pots, and he "never

<hr>

88   These little pamphlets – now extremely rare – were edited by Helena merchant Norman Winestine. Winestine had served as European correspondent for *The Nation* while living in Paris during the 1920s. In 1983, Ken Ferguson reissued the two essays as one pamphlet entitled *Two Essays: Soetsu Yanagi,* with the "Proceeds to Benefit the Archie Bray Foundation."

89   Clark, *American Ceramics,* 101; Senska/Wilber, Holt interview, ABFA; and Autio, Jiusto/ Newby interview, ABFA.

90   Bernard Leach, "American Impressions," *Craft Horizons,* Winter 1950.

91   Senska, Jiusto/Newby interview, ABFA; and Senska/Wilber, Holt interview, ABFA.

92   Rudy Autio and Peter Voulkos, interviewed in the video, *Revolutions of the Wheel: The Great Move West,* Vol. 2 (Los Angeles, CA: Queens Row, 1998).

93   Martin Duberman, *Black Mountain: An Exploration in Community* (1972; New York: W. W. Norton, 1993), 364.

once . . . got a spot of clay on him."[94]

Certainly, the philosophical approach of Soetsu Yanagi struck a chord. For Rudy Autio, who at that time "didn't care for this crafty stuff," the encounter with Yanagi was revelatory, introducing him to a cultural tradition in which "pottery making has been for centuries regarded as a true art, of equal dignity with the fine arts."[95] Autio recalled that Yanagi talked about "Zen and the art of gutsiness and of letting things happen . . . There was total involvement, of making it right. . . . And simplicity, economy, no fussing. . . . I began to look at ceramic art in a more professional way. . . ." Autio also remembered that in "walking around the [brick]yard with Dr. Yanagi . . . I began to see how he appreciated things like salt glaze on sewer tile."[96]

As a founder of the *Mingei* movement in Japan, which championed a "true craft . . . rooted in common, everyday utensils made by unknown craftsmen,"[97] Yanagi argued that individual artists should "brighten their goods rather than themselves. . . ." Yanagi was well aware of the forces that militated against such a return to selflessness – "We may call these modern times the Age of Signatures" – but still he called for setting the "individual artist free from his individuality." Only if craftsmen were to let go of their need to be recognized, Yanagi claimed, would society enter into a "golden age of craft . . . when beautiful unsigned goods [are] sold cheaply and widely used."[98] For many of the American potters in the 1952 workshops – and especially those like Voulkos and Autio, who were working hard to establish their reputations – Yanagi's vision must have seemed hopelessly Utopian.

For both Autio and Voulkos, it was the living example of Shoji Hamada that most affected and influenced them. As he had at Black Mountain – where he used the "clay and glazes available" with sureness and delight[99] – Hamada proved wonderfully adaptable to local conditions in Helena. Frances Senska remembered that "they went

---

94   Voulkos, *The Great Move West.*

95   Soetsu Yanagi, introduction to Bernard Leach's *A Potter's Book,* xv.

96   Autio, Jiusto/Newby interview, ABFA.

97   Gerry Williams, "The Japanese Pottery Tradition and Its Influence on American Ceramics," *American Craft* (April/May 1998): 54.

98   Soetsu Yanagi, "The Responsibility of the Craftsman," *Two Essays,* 7–12.

99   Duberman, *Black Mountain,* 364.

out to do watercolors, and it was cold, and the water froze on the paper. And Hamada was so tickled [by the] effect of the watercolor freezing on the paper."[100] As Rudy Autio watched Hamada at the wheel, he "saw that there was more to pottery making than just making pots and selling 'em in some kind of dime store. I saw . . . the true connection with the work. . . ." After the workshop, Autio "tried to make Hamada pots for a while, and it didn't work all that well, but it did in a way. And certainly left some impact."[101] Autio has said elsewhere, "Shoji Hamada, more than any other person, gave me an insight into what clay was about."[102]

But for Pete Voulkos, the example of Hamada was even more profound – and more intimate. Because Hamada did not use a kick wheel – "he always used a Japanese wheel you'd turn by hand" – he asked Voulkos to kick the wheel for him. "I was right there," Voulkos remembers, "and had my head down with his, and he'd tell me to kick faster or slower, so I was just watching his hands. . . . How often do you get close to a living legend like he was?"

As the son of a chef, Voulkos had always paid attention to the deftness of cooks. "I'd watch short-order cooks. . . . They just had all this dexterity, as they walked by, they'd flip something over, they'd wipe something off, I always marveled at that." And like the short-order heroes of Voulkos's youth, Shoji Hamada "never missed a stroke."

Technically, Voulkos took a great deal from his encounter with Hamada. "I especially liked when he would decorate with his brushes using the slips right onto the greenware. I'd never seen that before. So I started using Japanese brushes all the time." He responded immediately, too, to the spontaneity that Hamada embodied, to the freedom of the master potter's forms. After the workshop, Voulkos remembered, "[my pots] started to loosen up a little bit . . . the forms started to change. I got to be able to handle more clay."[103] Gerry Williams, long-time editor of *Studio Potter*, has written that Voulkos's peers noted the "subtle softening changes" that appeared in the Montana potter's work after he witnessed Hamada's "casual but

---

100   Senksa, Jiusto/Newby interview, ABFA.

101   Autio, Jiusto/Newby interview, ABFA.

102   Autio, The *Great Move West*.

103   Voulkos, Holt interview, ABFA; and Voulkos, *The Great Move West*.

artful throwing" that December.[104]

Though the Montana ceramists found much to criticize in the person and attitudes of Bernard Leach, upon hearing of Archie Bray's death in February 1953, Leach wrote to Peter Meloy, sending his condolences – "We gained a real feeling of friendship & respect for Archie during those days in Helena" – and lauding the Bray Foundation. "You know," Leach wrote, "that we felt that a start had been made under Pete Voulkos that held out a greater promise than in any other place which we visited in America."[105]

Architectural Ceramics

> "That was my picture of being a sculptor, to do
> heroic statuary for public buildings."
>
> – Rudy Autio

Clearly, from the beginning, pottery making had been a focus at the Archie Bray Foundation, but a second ceramic art form – murals made of fired clay – also played an important role in the foundation's first years. Rudy Autio single-handedly brought this emphasis to the Bray. Inspired while in graduate school by Mexican muralists Diego Rivera and Jose Clement Orozco, Rudy began to develop the skills needed to produce large-scale ceramic murals. "I was a handy sculptor. . . but firing with clay was a different matter." Luckily for Rudy, "Archie was interested in my sculptural potential, so he used to go out talking to . . . people who wanted to buy his brick, and [he] says, 'I got a kid here that can make a plaque for you if you buy my brick. . . .'" Archie's strategy worked, and often an architect or builder would receive, along with an order of brick, one of Rudy's sculptural wall pieces as a "kind of dividend."

Though his "first efforts were pretty dismal," Rudy soon learned how to "model and cast in terra cotta" and to create plaques and murals using carved brick:

> . . . carved brick, we got the idea of doing that over in the
> yard. . . . We altered the [brickmaking] machinery a little

---

104   Williams, "The Japanese Pottery Tradition and Its Influence," 57.

105   Bernard Leach, letter to Peter Meloy, n.d., Peter G. Meloy Papers, Montana Historical Society Archives, Helena, MT.

bit, and I . . . started to make some blocks that I set up on easels, and started to carve those. . . . That turned out to be a pretty good way of doing things . . . for buildings because they were structural at the same time [that] they were decorative. . . . Then they'd be fired in the brick kiln and I would number them and put 'em on a truck, deliver them to the site and they went up with the brick work. . . . Carved brick was a good thing for me, you know. It started to pay my way there for awhile.[106]

During the 1950s, Rudy created wall plaques for Montana State University's new humanities building, Missoula; the veterinary research building at Montana State College, Bozeman; First United Methodist Church, Great Falls; St. Gabriel's Catholic Church, Chinook; Gold Hill Lutheran Church, Butte; and other Montana churches, schools, libraries, and banks.[107]

Sadly, it was the opportunity to create a mural for the brand-new Charles Russell Gallery in Great Falls that brought the aesthetic and personal differences at the early Bray most clearly (and painfully) to the surface. Branson Stevenson – an acquaintance of cowboy artist Charles M. Russell and a close friend of Russell's sole protege, Joe DeYong – served as the first chairman of the museum's board, and with Archie's help, he convinced his fellow board members that a tile-and-brick mural – "the whole to be an abstract design" – would be just the thing for the museum's entrance. Almost immediately, conflict erupted over the mural's character. The museum envisioned the mural including a replica of Russell's signature, but Peter Meloy, Pete Voulkos, and Rudy all opined, "in one voice," that that was a "lousy" idea" and would ruin the building.

Though Rudy had done "a dozen or more sketches" for the mural and was conscious of the need to moderate his work for such a commission – "If I did something for architecture, I usually pulled my claws in a little. . . ." – Branson got involved, perhaps because the museum board disliked the younger artist's designs. In any case, Branson put forth his own design, and Voulkos and Autio – in Archie's testimony – declared that Branson's "design for the Russell building

---

106   Autio, Jiusto/Newby interview, ABFA.

107   For a more thorough discussion of Autio's public works, see Kangas, *Rudy Autio,* 11–15, 68.

was lousy, that it would hurt them to do it, that they would not put their name on anything of the sort" and that they would "go to Great Falls and tell the architect and the committee the whole thing was lousy." After further negotiations, Archie told Branson that the two young ceramists had come around, saying that they "would do the job – modified. Little angels, wings and all." But Archie told them to forget any modifications: "The thing has been booted around enough now, it stays as it is set now."

However, in Archie's final letter to Branson, dated February 2, 1953, only eight days before the former's death, it is clear that the issue was still not settled. Archie hastened to assure Branson that Pete and Rudy had nothing but "respect and love for you . . . tho at times they do go off the deep end. . . . they are young and . . . sometimes without a grain of sense." Archie noted that he was glad that a design involving a horse had been vetoed. Ultimately, Rudy's "idea of the repeat pattern and done in Indian style" was the design finally approved by the museum.[108] The finished mural, as critic Matthew Kangas notes, features a "repeated eight-tile module, alternating black and red, using stylized prehistoric petroglyphs incised into wet bricks." Public art almost always involves compromise, but creating the C. M. Russell Gallery mural – though the result, in Kangas's words, was a "significant work" – must have left all parties feeling dissatisfied.[109]

Art for Art's Sake

"No ribs guts and belly buttons – No ART!"
– Archie Bray, Sr., letter to
Branson Stevenson, January 23, 1953

Increasingly, the aesthetic and philosophical gulf between Archie Bray – who was rooted in nineteenth-century brickmaking traditions and steeped in Bernard Leach's theories of the "artist-craftsman" – and Pete and Rudy – with their forward-looking, even revolutionary modernist sensibilities – widened. Archie Bray began to dislike the attention that Pete Voulkos was receiving, both locally and

---

108   Autio, Jiusto/Newby interview, ABFA; and Archie Bray, Sr., letters to Branson Stevenson, September 18, 1952; September 19, 1952; November 5, 1952; December 23, 1952; and February 9, 1953, ABFA.

109   Kangas, *Rudy Autio*, 11.

nationally. He felt that the focus of attention should be on the foundation that bore his name – or on his old friend, Branson Stevenson. In a January 1953 letter to Branson, he wrote:

> All of them can talk of Voulkos and Pete Meloy too, but the work you do . . . is so far ahead of any anyone is doing in all Montana! . . . But for fun let's be exact. Voulkos has 2 glazes. . . . No matter what shape, what size, what anything – maybe some red iron slip, then the 2 glazes. . . . But you have done more experimental work than they will ever accomplish. 45 glazes! Lovely colors. Lovely effects and shadings. Lovely shapes. A keen alert interest, always something new![110]

In early 1953, Branson published an article on his experimental approach, "Clays and Glazes of Montana," in *Craft Horizons*; and another Stevenson article, "Art from the Ground Up," appeared that spring in the *Quarterly of the Montana Institute of the Arts*. In both, Branson celebrated the many glazes he'd concocted from the "seemingly inexhaustible minerals of Montana's field and roadside" and he sought to share "some of our enthusiasm for this down-to-earthy art-craft."[111]

The young artist-craftsmen in residence at the Archie Bray Foundation did not share Branson's enthusiasm. Like many artists of their generation, including the Abstract Expressionists they would soon emulate, they were radically individualistic and sought a sophisticated expression, not something "down-to-earthy." In a 1954 article, also published in the M.I.A. quarterly, Lela and Rudy Autio profiled Peter Voulkos. They wrote:

> Pete has never made a fetish of glazing techniques. In fact, he does not do exhaustive glaze testing, relying instead on a half dozen glazes which he uses excellently. While he values a thorough knowledge of the technical end of pottery, the main objectives in his work are strictly esthetic.

---

110   Archie Bray, Sr., letter to Branson Stevenson, January 19, 1953.

111   Branson Stevenson, "Clays and Glazes of Montana," *Craft Horizons* (January/February 1953), 42–43; and Branson Stevenson, "Art from the Ground Up," *Quarterly of the Montana Institute of the Arts* (Spring 1953), 4–6, 37.

. . . There are few potters who have used native clays and earth glazes to the extent that Pete has used them. . . . Pete now thinks that digging clay is nonsense if it is cheaper and more practical to buy it. . . . In contrast . . . are the purists who dig and refine their clay . . . and perhaps spend so much time "grubbing the earth" they have little to show for their effort.[112]

The differences between the old and new guard – over artistic freedom, over Archie's push for production ware, over distinctions between art and craft – surfaced dramatically in Susan Eaker's bookstore in late January 1953. In a letter to Branson, Archie wrote that Eaker – whose store was the Helena outlet for Bray production ware and who was Archie's confidant (and thus aware of his frustrations) – had called the foundation, asking for more enameled ashtrays made by a Bray volunteer.

Eaker wanted the ashtrays immediately, before the legislature adjourned and the legislative wives – her best customers – went home. And she made it clear – using Archie's colorful phrase – that she wanted "no ribs guts and belly buttons – No ART!" Pete and Rudy went into town to talk things over with Eaker. As Eaker told it, the Bray resident artists arrived empty-handed and "started to argue" with her, asserting that the "enamels should all be scrapped – no one should ever see them!" Pete and Rudy said that they "were not going to bastardize their art to suit people's taste." Eaker, who was locally famous for her excitability, "tore into them." "Who are you to set yourselves as the last word as to what is good or bad art?" she demanded. And "what is to become of the institution you are working for?" When Pete and Rudy told Eaker, "we don't intend to sell our art here . . . no store [in Helena] is worthy of it," Eaker became "overheated and practically showed them the door."

Archie asked Branson, "Why do they do it? . . . They have forgotten everything Leach and Hamada told them – forgotten why??" And to think, bemoaned Archie, that "Leach said Pete had promise." To make matters worse, he went on, "none of them now say Leach was so good" and in fact, one of them had gone so far as to call

---

112   Lela and Rudy Autio, "Peter H. Voulkos, Potter," *Quarterly of the Montana Institute of the Arts* (Fall 1954), 3–6.

"Leach's stuff . . . crap!!!"[113]

In 1957, with ruthless candor, Pete Voulkos clarified his revolutionary position regarding the relationship between art and craft, when he served as juror for an exhibition of works by the "Designer-Craftsmen of the Mississippi Basin." Only three years after leaving Helena, Voulkos had become – according to the show's catalog – "Leader and envy of every pedestrian potter, . . . Vigorous breaker of meaningless boundaries, Scourge of the dull and too-often-repeated." In his juror's statement, he said:

> Lack of stimulation leading to lack of conviction, idea and intensification seem to be the general rule of the . . . show. . . . not only this show but most craft shows. . . . A few techniques at hand, seemingly passed off for art. . . . people associated with craft work tend to confine themselves in a very tight little sphere refusing for some reason the contamination of any of the fields of creativity. . . .[114]

The Death of Archie Bray, Sr.

> "A kindly and conscientious man,
> devoted to his friends and his city,
> was Archie C. Bray, who died far too long
> before the three score and ten milestone of life."
> – *Helena Independent Record*, n.d.

In January 1953, Archie Bray somehow damaged his leg and found himself in the local hospital with phlebitis. "I can't remember bruising [my leg]," he wrote Branson, "can't remember squeezing it, can't remember anything which would indicate an injury. I asked about long hours, over work and all that. It is hard to say. . . ."[115]

After a month of enforced rest, during which he fought complications that included bouts of the flu and pneumonia, he "seemed to be getting along fine." During that month, he did his best to keep

---

113   Archie Bray, Sr., letter to Branson Stevenson, January 23, 1953, ABFA.

114   *Catalog to an Exhibition of Works by Designer-Craftsmen of the Mississippi Basin* (Chicago: Art Institute of Chicago/Midwest Designer-Craftsmen, 1957).

115   Archie Bray, Sr., letter to Branson Stevenson, January 19, 1953.

the brickyard and foundation running from his hospital sickbed. Finally, he was allowed to go home.

On the drive across town, Archie, Sr., asked his son a favor. "Drive me out to the brickyard, and let me take a look." Archie, Jr., had just been "carefully admonished by the doctors . . . [to] take him directly home," and so he refused. His father lived "another three or four days," and "then all of a sudden" the morning of February 17, 1953, Archie Bray, Sr., died instantaneously of an embolism. He was sixty-six years old.[116]

As a prominent Montana "industrialist and ardent patron of the fine arts," Archie was eulogized at length in the local paper. He was remembered for his industriousness, his love of gardens and the performing arts, and his civicmindedness. But perhaps most importantly, wrote his eulogist, "Mr. Bray died with his life's ambition partly attained in the establishment of Pottery, Inc., as part of the Archie Bray Foundation. . . ."[117]

Branson Stevenson and Peter Meloy served as pallbearers in Archie's funeral. Nearly fifty years later, Peter Meloy would say, "I want you to know that you've got to give Archie Bray a lot of credit. . . . The main thing is, two things, one is that Archie had the idea of art; secondly he had the clay."[118] Branson Stevenson remembered that "Archie wanted people to pass through the doorway into a place of art and appreciate the simple philosophies of art as people will do if they are of the same spirit." "Archie Bray's vision," added Branson, "became reality."[119]

In remembering Archie Bray, both Rudy Autio and Pete Voulkos understood clearly his importance to their own lives and to the history of American ceramics. Rudy recalled that, though Archie sometimes found the young artists unmanageable and their art incomprehensible, he showed remarkable restraint, "considering his background and the way he saw art. . . . he knew art had to move. . . . he called the stuff that we did ribs, guts, and bellybuttons. . . . He was

---

116   Archie Bray, Jr., Holt interview, ABFA.

117   "Archie Bray, Sr., Helena Industrialist and Patron of Fine Arts, Dies at Home Today After Illness," *Helena Independent Record,* February 17, 1953.

118   Meloy, Jiusto/Newby interview, ABFA.

119   Anderson, *Branson Graves Stevenson,* 227.

pretty good. He didn't say much."[120]

And Pete has said, Archie "started a great thing. And was very instrumental for me, for Rudy, because he gave us a place to work. . . . he was a very generous man in all ways. . . . He'd always stop in at the pottery, and he would bring us food. He was always getting imported foods. . . . And every time he'd get a big shipment in, he'd always throw a little bit our way. . . . to us he was a hell of a great guy."[121]

The Foundation Without Archie

> "Then, just by plain default, I found myself
> in charge of the brickyard and all
> the various other operations."
>
> – Archie Bray, Jr.

Like his father before him, Archie Bray, Jr., had grown up in the brickyard. As a young man, he had witnessed the building of the pottery, but he had never been an enthusiastic supporter of his father's foundation. In fact, in September 1952, Archie, Sr., wrote to Branson Stevenson, "My son is terribly disturbed! He cannot see the possibilities [of the pottery]. . . . my son's opposition . . . in no way makes the task easy – I am tired of going up stream all the while." After Archie, Sr.'s death, however, Archie, Jr., honored his father's wishes and continued to support the pottery. "My father wanted it to continue," he said, "and I was going to do everything I could to see that he was not disappointed." Rudy Autio has said of Archie, Jr., "He was the one who saw to it that [the] Bray Foundation survived, more than anyone else. . . . he was so loyal to the place, even though he didn't like it. . . . [After Archie, Sr.'s death] he came to me and told me that, 'we'll see that you're okay, don't worry about it.'"[122]

Rudy and Archie, Jr., had a "good relationship," but Pete Voulkos found that, "after Archie died . . . I started getting these politically sort of off-beat pressures from the rest of the family, and they were very unsympathetic to this whole idea, and it became very

---

120   Autio, Jiusto/Newby interview, ABFA.

121   Voulkos, Holt interview, ABFA.

122   Archie Bray, Sr., letter to Branson Stevenson, September 19, 1952; Archie Bray, Jr., Holt interview, ABFA; and Autio, Jiusto/Newby interview, ABFA.

tough and boring and monotonous. . . ."[123]

On the surface at least, life at the Bray continued much as before. While Rudy worked on a variety of architectural projects, Pete maintained the line of Bray production ware and persevered in sending out his own work to competitions. In April 1953, Pete's pots were featured in a solo exhibition at the University of Florida, Gainesville, and later in the year, examples of his work appeared in a pair of national exhibitions, *Good Design,* at the Museum of Modern Art in New York, and *Designer Craftsmen U.S.A. 1953,* in which Pete won first place in ceramics.[124]

Black Mountain College

> "Art does not seek to describe but to enact."
>
> – Charles Olson[125]

Pete Voulkos's growing reputation led him – in the summer of 1953 – to take part in a transformative experience, one that was "so beautiful and so new to me that . . . I just really got turned on."[126] Karen Karnes and David Weinrib, the ceramics faculty at North Carolina's Black Mountain College, invited Pete to spend three weeks teaching a workshop at the renowned (and impoverished) experimental college. Dominated between 1933 and 1949 by former Bauhaus master Josef Albers, Black Mountain College was, despite its small size and limited resources, a "unique creative community where the most vital work being done was in the arts."[127] When Voulkos arrived in early summer, the poet Charles Olson was directing the college and a remarkable cast of American artists – including such figures as potters Karnes, Weinrib, and M. C. Richards, dancer/choreographer Merce Cunningham, composers John Cage and David Tudor, and painters

---

123   Autio, Jiusto/Newby interview, ABFA; and Voulkos, Holt interview, ABFA.

124   Slivka and Tsujimoto, *Peter Voulkos,* 162.

125   Charles Olson, "Human Universe," *Selected Writings* (New York: New Directions, 1966), 61.

126   Peter Voulkos, interview by Mary Emma Harris, Berkeley, CA, December 24, 1971, Black Mountain College Research Project Papers, North Carolina State Archives (NCSA), Raleigh.

127   Mary Emma Harris, *The Arts at Black Mountain College* (Cambridge, MA: The MIT Press, 1987), 170.

Jack Tworkov and Esteban Vicente – made the place "just fantastic" for Voulkos. "Every night there was something happening . . . dance or readings . . . painting critiques and, you know, little sorts of seminars. . . . It was very exciting." When he arrived, Voulkos was making "pretty straight pottery," not "very inspired." Voulkos said of his weeks at Black Mountain:

> . . . watching these pros in action . . . you begin to feel it. . . . They're loose, and . . . they begin to invent within their form. . . . Well, my total commitment kind of formed. . . . [T]hat whole Black Mountain trip . . . put it all in context . . . really turning on about what form is about. . . . So that helped me . . . later when I . . . just forgot about that whole . . . idea of pottery being just . . . craftsmanship. . . ."[128]

At Black Mountain, Pete made his own mark as an artist of remarkable skill and drive. "[T]hey'd come over and watch me," he recalls, "they couldn't believe me, either."[129] Rector Charles Olson, a mythomaniac whose enthusiasms, according to Karen Karnes, were often out of proportion, found in Pete the "personification of the American West," building up an "elaborate iconography" around the young Montanan. Olson had assumed that Pete's "dark looks and taciturn manner" signified a Native American heritage, and when Pete told Olson that he was Greek, the larger-than-life poet (he stood six feet seven) "promptly restructured his theory, drawing Greco-Indian comparisons of mythic proportions."[130]

After his three weeks at Black Mountain, Pete drove up to New York City with fellow westerner M. C. Richards (she hailed from Weiser, Idaho). Pete stayed with Richards and David Tudor while he toured the city, a place in which he felt totally at home, as though "I'd been there before." He visited the museums – "I'd never been in a museum" – and he "met . . . just about all the artists that were . . . important at that time," among them Willem de Kooning (who was "sort of aloof") and Franz Kline. Kline had been a hero to Pete, and he met and talked with the painter at the Cedar Bar, the famous

---

128   Voulkos, Harris interview , NCSA.

129   Voulkos, *The Great Move West.*

130   Harris, *The Arts at Black Mountain College,* 174; and Duberman, *Black Mountain,* 365.

Abstract Expressionist hangout where Kline was "holding forth every day."[131]

According to Rudy Autio, when Pete returned to Helena, "it was just like he was transformed. You could almost see it on his face, there was a kind of glow. . . ." Abstract Expressionism, Rudy added, was "the glove [Pete] had to put his hand into." In Autio's telling, Pete's work "changed very dramatically, and he started, instead of these nice pretty bottles," to make wilder pots with a "whole bunch of different thrown elements [attached to] the main body . . . and cut walls." Pete continued to throw the Bray's production ware and he was still making "pretty" pots for competitions. But like the artists he'd met at Black Mountain, he had begun to invent within his own form.

Rudy, too, was stimulated by the ideas Pete brought back from North Carolina, though he'd "been doing things with slab construction all the time. . . . since I was doing sculpture. I wasn't a potter." Abstract Expressionism was most definitely "in the wind," with its emphasis on gesture and the "emotional spirit of the moment."[132]

Marguerite Wildenhain

> "[Marguerite Wildenhain] was pretty arrogant, and she didn't like the fact that she was being outclassed by our growing and famous Peter Voulkos."
>
> – Rudy Autio

After the death of Archie, Sr., the Bray continued to host workshops by well-known ceramic artists. Between 1953 and 1956, Antonio Prieto, Carlton Ball, Kathleen Horsman, and Rex Mason all presented successful workshops at the Helena pottery, and up-and-coming ceramic artists like Robert Sperry and Muriel Guest spent time there making pots. But perhaps the most important workshop, after the Leach/Yanagi/Hamada visit, would be the 1954 visitation by the legendary Bauhaus potter and proprietor of Pond Farm, Marguerite Wildenhain. Though Wildenhain's visit produced a negative reaction,

---

131   Voulkos, Harris interview, NCSA.

132   Autio, *The Great Move West*; and Autio, Jiusto/Newby interview, ABFA.

it had a positive impact. It helped to push forward the ceramic revolution just begun by Pete Voulkos and Rudy Autio. For the young
ceramists, Wildenhain proved an articulate and powerful enemy
against whom to define their emerging positions as avant gardists of
clay and propagandists for total aesthetic freedom.

Marguerite Wildenhain had been among the very first pottery
students at Germany's Weimar Bauhaus in 1919. Though the main
Bauhaus campus was at Weimar, the pottery had been set up, for
practical reasons, at nearby Dornburg under the direction of veteran
potter Max Krehan and Master of Form Gerhard Marcks, a sculptor.
Krehan – "unaware of the current debates about art and society" –
ran the workshop on a traditional apprenticeship basis, and Marcks,
more conservative than his Bauhaus peers, had little faith in the latest progressive thinking about education.[133] According to Frances
Senska, who had studied with the Bauhaus potter at Pond Farm in
1950, Wildenhain disliked another Bauhaus master, the pedagogical-
ly progressive Laszlo Moholy-Nagy, because, in her view, he was "too
naive" in his willingness to let students "try anything."[134]

The Marguerite Wildenhain who arrived in Helena in May
1954 for a week-long workshop was, according to Rudy Autio, arrogant, authoritarian, and intolerant. Rather than let students "try
anything," she insisted that there were "certain ways you hold your
hand. . . . And there was nothing in between that she would allow,
you know, 'my way is the only way.'" She believed firmly in a long
apprenticeship, "six or seven years under a tough master before we
knew what the hell we were doing," and she was offended by these
young Montana upstarts who "just went ahead and did it."

To add insult to injury, Wildenhain – in Rudy's opinion –
"couldn't throw as well" as Pete, and someone in the workshop audience called out, "'Ah, Pete can do better than that,' . . . and she was
just livid. . . ." Soon, Rudy continued, "people were gathering around
Pete and kind of ignoring Marguerite. . . . He was the new guy, the
new kid on the block who was doing real well." As Pete remembers it,
Marguerite "had this feeling that I was a sort of trouble maker, that

<hr>

133   Elaine Levin, "The Legacy of Marguerite Wildenhain," *Ceramics Monthly*, 45:6 (June/
July/August 1997): 71; Frank Whitford, *Bauhaus* (New York: Thames and Hudson, 1984).
74–75; and Magdalena Droste, *Bauhaus, 1919–1933* (Berlin: Bauhaus-Archiv Museum fur
Gestaltung/Benedikt Taschen Verlag, 1990), 68.

134   Senska/Wilber, Holt interview, ABFA.

I'd thrown something into the stew that shouldn't be there."

In Rudy's assessment, "it was a funny workshop. I did admire a few things. . . . She could throw her work very thin . . . and she could pull handles in a very nice way." But her "strict philosophy of having to apprentice" and her dogmatism made no sense to Autio and Voulkos, who were "into dogma-free living and being able to express yourself any way possible."[135]

The End of an Era

> "But the whole thing changed at that
> point, you know, after Archie had died."
>
> – Peter Voulkos

Relations between Pete Voulkos and Archie Bray, Jr., continued to be strained, and in mid-1954, when Pete received an offer from Millard Sheets to head up the new ceramics program at the Los Angeles County Art Institute, he jumped at the chance. At the Otis (as the institute is popularly known), Peter Voulkos proceeded on the path he'd begun in Montana. He ran his program, in the words of Rose Slivka, "in his usual style, as a free-wheeling place where energies and enthusiasms were high and contagious and everyone there caught the spirit."[136] Pete continued to spend summers at the Bray, at least through 1955, and in 1975, he returned to Helena in triumph – as perhaps the most famous ceramic artist in the world – to teach his own workshop.

Mutual respect existed between Archie, Jr., and Rudy, and Rudy stayed on as resident director of the pottery through 1956. Soon after the Wildenhain workshop, two of the potters who attended – Jim and Nan McKinnell of Seattle – moved to Helena to work at the Bray. Both "proficient potters," they had just returned from a two-year European tour, during which they had "studied under master potters in France, England, and Scotland." The McKinnells taught the community classes and helped Rudy make the production ware. A ceramics engineer, Jim tested clays for the brickyard, and as Archie, Jr., remembers, he "contributed a good . . . bit." The McKinnells did

---

135   Autio and Voulkos, *The Great Move West;* and Autio, Jiusto/Newby interview, ABFA.

136   Slivka, "The Artist and His Work" in Slivka and Tsujimoto, *Peter Voulkos,* 39.

not consider themselves avant garde artists, and their work, noted Archie, Jr., "appealed more to what people did want."[137]

On occasion, tension would develop between Jim McKinnell and Rudy, because – though Rudy was in charge – Jim was "well trained, and . . . he was a little contemptuous of us because we were totally ignorant about technical shit. . . ." Jim, Rudy remembers, "didn't feel that he had to nourish the glaze problems of everyone . . . 'cause he was sort of paying his way here . . . and helping a lot." But, adds Rudy, "during those hard days at Bray's, you know, cold, it was winter, and we were crammed together, and it was a dusty little pottery shop, and every day we'd be there close to each other, and after a while, little things would start to get in the way, your morale kind of went down." Some of the stress was caused, in Rudy's recollection, because the resident potters "didn't know where the money was coming from . . . it got too tight."[138]

Finally weary of "making $200 a month and trying to live on that," Rudy decided to leave the Bray. Pete Voulkos had been encouraging him to move to Los Angeles, and Rudy took his young family to California. Though a number of L.A. architects were interested in his carved-brick murals and he soon found a job in a kiln factory as a lab technician, Rudy stayed only a few months. Homesick for Montana and determined to work as an artist, he sent a telegram to K. Ross Toole, director of the Montana Historical Society, and Toole hired him on the spot to create exhibits and work as a curator. In 1957, Carl McFarlane, president of the state university at Missoula, offered Rudy a position teaching ceramics in the art department. Rudy accepted, and as he put it, a "whole new world began over here."[139] From 1957 to his retirement in 1984, Rudy Autio influenced generations of ceramic artists – as a dedicated teacher and as "clay artist, painter, and visual innovator."[140] Rudy, too, would return to the Bray. In fact, he remained a staunch supporter through the years, teaching workshops, serving on the foundation's board of directors, and

---

137   John H. Nickerson, Jr., "An Incomplete History of the Archie Bray Foundation," master's thesis, State University of New York College of Ceramics, Alfred University, 1969; and Archie Bray, Jr., Holt interview, ABFA.

138   Autio, Jiusto/Newby interview, ABFA.

139   Autio, Jiusto/Newby interview, ABFA

140   Michael G. Rubin, foreword, *Rudy Autio: Work, 1983–1996* (Missoula, MT: White Swan Press, 1989), 3.

regularly donating his art to foundation fundraising events.

In May 1957, the McKinnells left the Archie Bray Foundation, to set up a studio in Deerfield, Massachusetts. With Archie and the first resident artists gone, the stage was vacated, ready for the next era – and the next set of players – in the history of the Archie Bray Foundation.

"thru it all will permeate a beautiful spirit"

> "To make the origin gain ground: vocation of all origin."
> – Edmond Jabes[141]

Despite the battles over aesthetics and work habits, despite the cold and the financial challenges, the first years of the Archie Bray Foundation established – in an astonishingly short time – all the elements that today make the mature foundation, in Rudy Autio's words, a "very important center." First and foremost, the vision that Archie Bray articulated in his letters to Branson Stevenson – and during those evenings at the Meloy home – remains as vital at the start of the twenty-first century as it was fifty years ago.

Still a "place to work for all who are seriously interested in any of the Ceramic Arts," the Bray welcomes – just as it did in the early 1950s – ceramic artists from across the United States. And just as Archie, Branson, and Peter Meloy invited masters from England, Germany, Scotland, and Japan to present workshops and work in the pottery, so does the current Bray maintain an international character, with ceramists visiting from Siberia and Thailand, Korea and Finland, Roumania and Taiwan.

Archie Bray, by treating ceramic sculptors and makers of pots as equals, established an inclusiveness that transcends genres. And the early battles over distinctions between art and craft, between "lovely" glazes and "crooked crazy shaped pots," have sensitized the place to the need for tolerance, rendering it truly welcoming to all aesthetic approaches.

Idealistic and practical, good fun and a place where much

---

141   Edmond Jabes, *From the Book to the Book: An Edmond Jabes Reader,* trans. Rosmarie Waldrop, Pierre Joris, Anthony Rudolf, & Keith Waldrop (Hanover, NH: Weslayan University Press, 1991), 201.

good work is done, the Archie Bray Foundation for the Ceramic Arts today stands as a worthy memorial to the "life and interests of the man who [made] this pottery possible." It is, indeed, a "place of art – of simple things [and] good people. . . ." And though there will forever be problems, "thru it all" still permeates that beautiful spirit of which Archie Bray dreamed fifty years ago.

Missionaries for Modernism

George and Elinor Poindexter and Montana's Poindexter Collections of Postwar American Painting

Originally published in Ben Mitchell, Rick Newby, and Andrea Pappas, *The Most Difficult Journey: The Poindexter Collections of American Modernist Painting* (Billings, MT: Yellowstone Art Museum, 2002).

> *Seeing [Willem de Kooning's] pictures more or less every day, they slowly became beautiful, and then they stayed beautiful.*
>
> – Edwin Denby[1]

In 1957, the fledgling Poindexter Gallery, situated at 21 West 56th Street in New York City, launched an ambitious exhibition, *The Thirties: Painting in New York.* Founded two years earlier by arts patron Elinor Poindexter, the Poindexter Gallery specialized in the New York School (mostly second-generation Abstract Expressionists), together with outlanders like Washington, D.C., Color Field painter Gene Davis and Californians Richard Diebenkorn, James Weeks, and Paul Harris. With *The Thirties*, curated by painter Pat Passlof, the Poindexter sought – as "one of the galleries which must explain, defend and promote the more advanced manifestations of contemporary art" – to "present works from an archaic period, in an effort to recapture a climate which quickened the development of a significant trend in American art."[2]

The works in the show were not the expected Thirties images. Instead of representing the "neo-plastic, the social realist, and the regionalist" schools predominant at the time, they were "unfamiliar" works that had helped lead to a "new conception," the first truly American art: Abstract Expressionism.[3]

The artists included ranged from such early American modernists as Joseph Stella, Milton Avery, and Stuart Davis to first generation

---

1 Edwin Denby, untitled essay, in *The Thirties: Painting in New York,* ed. Pat Passlof (New York: Poindexter Gallery, 1957).

2 Introduction, *The Thirties.*

3 Ibid.

Abstract Expressionists like Jackson Pollock, Willem de Kooning, Jack Tworkov, Arshile Gorky, Lee Krasner, Milton Resnick, and Franz Kline to others less classifiable, including the radically individual Earl Kerkam and the hugely influential teacher of painters, Hans Hofmann.

Not academic in approach, nor "recreating the total picture of an era" (that was for museums), *The Thirties* aimed at the "sharpening of a memory, the evocation of a time. . . ." To that end, the show's catalog brought together, alongside reproductions of the works exhibited and photographs from the period, quotations from artists, poets, critics, and hangers-on who had immersed themselves in New York's impoverished but dynamic art scene during the Great Depression.[4]

Included was a rich essay by poet and dance critic Edwin Denby, who meditated upon the impact of having lived next door to the young Willem de Kooning. He spent much time in de Kooning's loft, where he remembered "people talking intently and listening intently and then everybody burst out laughing and started off intent on another tack." Despite the poverty and the almost complete lack of critical attention – "everybody drank coffee and nobody had shows" – Denby recalled that "we were all happy to be in a city the beauty of which was unknown, uncosy, and not small scale."[5]

Lawrence Campbell, writing in *Art in America* many years later, cited *The Thirties* as a "remarkable exhibition . . . of great historical interest." While Elinor Poindexter has noted that the show, patently educational in character and with few of the paintings for sale, was intended as marketing, to "help make [our] name known," it established a theme in the lives of the Poindexter Gallery and of Elinor and her husband, Everton Gentry "George" Poindexter. Collectively, they were to be missionaries for the "more advanced manifestations of contemporary art," and they would carry their passion not only into the canyons of Manhattan, but to the farthest reaches of the American continent – George's home state of Montana.[6]

---

4   Ibid.

5   Denby essay, *The Thirties*.

6   Lawrence Campbell, "Pat Passlof at Elizabeth Harris," *Art in America* 82 (January 1994): 104; Elinor Poindexter, interview by Paul Cummings, September 9, 1970, Oral History Collection, Archives of American Art, Smithsonian Institution, Washington, D.C (hereafter OHC, AAA); introduction, *The Thirties*.

> *Good collections often have strange pockets. . . . A significant collection is not a question of representation but of a specific point of view.*
>
> – Pontus Hulten[7]

In 1960, Michael S. Kennedy, director of the Montana Historical Society in Helena, found himself faced with a startling proposition. Montana native and New York commodity broker Everton Gentry "George" Poindexter wanted to give the state historical society a painting in memory of his father, Joseph Boyd Poindexter, a former Montana attorney general and governor of Hawaii Territory. The offer to donate the memorial was not startling, but the choice of painting certainly was.

Poindexter was offering a painting by Abstract Expressionist Willem de Kooning, from the Dutch-born artist's famed and controversial "Woman" series: a "voluptuous seated figure," in one curator's words, that "radiates the excitement, anxiety, and ferociousness with which de Kooning endowed a classic theme, the female nude."[8] Whatever his misgivings might have been, Kennedy did not blink; he accepted the gift by return mail.

Montana at mid-century was not on the cutting edge of contemporary painting. While a few painters, some in the state's universities, others on farflung ranches, were carrying the torch for modernism, many of the state's citizens still thought that the visual arts began and ended with the oils, watercolors, bronzes, and drawings wrought by Montana's own "Cowboy Artist," Charles M. Russell. In the 1950s and early 1960s, as pioneering Montana modernist painter Gennie DeWeese has said, "Charlie Russell was god."[9] And the Montana Historical Society had a serious investment in the primacy of Russell's aesthetic; it was home to the Malcolm S. Mackay Collection of Charles M. Russell Art, purchased by the Society six years earlier, in 1955, from a family of New York stockbrokers who

---

7   Pontus Hulten, quoted by Ingrid Sischy, *Artforum* (December 1981): 68.

8   Nancy Tieken, *Montana's Best-kept Secret: The Poindexter Collection of Modern American Masters* (Denver, CO: Denver Art Museum, 1998), 5.

9   Gennie DeWeese, interview by author, October 17, 1999. See also Rick Newby, "Grizzly Bears and Art Openings: Montana's DeWeese Family," *Montana Magazine* 158 (November/ December 1999): 18–23.

were also Montana ranchers.[10]

Pleased by Kennedy's ready acceptance of his gift, George Poindexter began, in the autumn of 1960, to outline a plan to send Montana's sole art museum a contemporary art show to complement the unveiling of de Kooning's *Woman*; by January 1962, that plan had evolved into a much more ambitious scheme, to loan the Montana Historical Society, with an eye to future donation, a significant portion of Poindexter's personal collection, "about a hundred pictures in all. . . ." Poindexter was realistic about his collection; some of the works, he wrote, "aren't good enough to have in a permanent collection," and the collection, in his view, was "over balanced" by the works of two painters "not typical of the [Abstract Expressionist] movement": Robert DeNiro, Sr., and Earl Kerkam. Poindexter noted that he was continuing to collect, with a focus on the "new generation . . . just emerging out of Abstract Expressionism." He also wrote that he hoped to persuade his friends to "add to the collection from time to time"; he further suggested that, by working the "tax angle," he could convince other collectors and successful artists like Robert Motherwell to donate works, thereby creating "one of the good collections in the country."[11]

By return mail, Michael Kennedy expressed delight at the thought of receiving what he was already referring to as the Poindexter Collection of the Montana Historical Society. He and his staff, he confessed, were "simply amazed at the extent" of the collection. Some imbalance was natural in any personal collection, he wrote, adding that both DeNiro and Kerkam were "brilliant, in my judgment." A month later, Kennedy wrote Poindexter that, though he was being circumspect about the gift until they had worked out the final details, he was announcing, in speeches around Montana, that "we stand on the threshold of the acquisition of what . . . may well be the largest collection of the American school, the abstract expressionist, . . . west of the Mississippi River."[12]

---

10   See Kirby Lambert, "Montana's Last Best Chance: The Malcolm S. Mackay Collection of Charles M. Russell Art," in *Russell's West: The C. M. Russell Museum Magazine* 5 (2000): 3–9.

11   George Poindexter, letter to Michael Kennedy, Jan. 12, 1962, Poindexter Collection Files, Montana Historical Society Museum (hereafter MHSM); George Poindexter, letter to Michael Kennedy, September 10, 1962, MHSM.

12   Michael Kennedy, letter to George Poindexter, January 17, 1962, MHSM; Michael Kennedy, letter to George Poindexter, February 15, 1962, MHSM.

In August 1962, George Poindexter shipped the first works from his collection to Helena. This first installment included thirty-five works: oils, pastels, gouaches, watercolors, drawings, and a solitary photograph by Abstract Expressionist photographer Aaron Siskind. Represented were such important artists as Jackson Pollock, Adolph Gottlieb, Richard Diebenkorn, Phillip Guston, Franz Kline, Jack Tworkov, Arshile Gorky, and Robert Natkin. The group included three more works by Willem de Kooning, as well as several paintings each by DeNiro and Kerkam. By October 1 of that year, Poindexter had shipped the Society another twenty-six pieces, bringing the Poindexter Collection tally up to sixty-one. This second group included works by artists Al Held, Milton Resnick, Joe Steffanelli, Herman Cherry, and a solitary woman, Sonia Gechtoff.

"They are all American Contemporary painters," wrote Poindexter in a letter to the executive secretary of the Montana Alumni Association (he had attended Montana State University, Missoula, 1918–1920, before transferring to New York's Columbia University), "and some of the pictures are masterpieces." In the same letter, he expressed the reasons for his generosity:

> I have been collecting these pictures for ten years and I love them all. My reason for giving them away is because my whole family were always Montanians at heart and I'd like to do something for the state. I believe the collection is good enough and varied enough to have an effect on Montana's cultural climate.[13]

Poindexter made it clear that the Montana Historical Society should make his collection "also available to the educational institutions of the State of Montana" and to other institutions designated by the Society's director. He was loaning the collection in memory of his father, Joseph Boyd Poindexter who, besides serving as a judge in Montana's Fifth Judicial District and as Montana attorney general, had been governor of the Territory of Hawaii at the time of the Pearl Harbor attack, and of his maternal grandfather, Everton Judson Conger, an early Montana circuit judge and the officer in charge of the detail that captured John Wilkes Booth following the

---

13   George Poindexter, letter to Robert Hingham, August 10, 1962, MHSM.

assassination of Abraham Lincoln.[14]

> [The Poindexter-Orr Ranch was] *among the first*
> *to bring stock . . . into Montana, and their opera-*
> *tions have been conducted upon a most extensive*
> *scale, cattle, horses and sheep of the highest grade*
> *being raised in large numbers. . . . no firm in the*
> *state was better known or had a higher reputation.*
> *– Progressive Men of the State of Montana*[15]

George Poindexter did have deep Montana roots. In addition to his politically prominent father and maternal grandfather, his paternal grandfather, Thomas Watson Poindexter, was a successful merchant, proprietor of the T. W. Poindexter and Sons Mercantile Company in the southwestern Montana town of Dillon. But perhaps more importantly for George's sense of himself as a Montanan, his great-uncle, Philip H. Poindexter, had founded one of Montana's earliest and most extensive cattle and sheep ranches with business partner William C. Orr in 1864, not far from the river Captain Meriwether Lewis had christened Philanthropy sixty years earlier (today the Ruby River).

The Poindexter-Orr Ranch, set in the broad and beautiful Big Hole Valley, was an empire unto itself; it even had its own fort, built in 1868 to defend against the never-materialized threat of marauding Indians. The Poindexter-Orr brand, the Square and Compass, was the first to be registered in Montana Territory, and the ranch was successful enough that both Poindexter and Orr built sizeable mansions for their families; the twenty-room Poindexter home, dubbed "The Cottonwoods," featured eight fireplaces, wide staircases, and paneled walls, and the three-story Orr house, built of stone, was modeled on the Florida governor's mansion. Besides vast herds of sheep and cattle, the thriving ranchers raised fine horses with names like Voltaire, Fortune, and Nabob, and their horse herd included Percherons, Normans, and Clydesdales imported from England and French

---

14   George Poindexter, "Statement of Purpose, Poindexter Collection of Contemporary American Paintings," October 1, 1962, MHSM.

15   "Philip H. Poindexter," *Progressive Men of the State of Montana* (Chicago: A. W. Bowen and Company, 1903), 496, 497.

coach horses. In 1944, the Poindexters and Orrs sold the ranch to C. B. Mace. Today the spread, known as the Beaverhead Ranch and part of Koch Industries' vast Matador Cattle Company properties, covers 250,000 acres, and its fences extend for more than 2,000 miles.

The Poindexters, having come to Montana from the California and Oregon gold rushes, were indisputably important citizens in their new home. They left their mark everywhere. In and around Dillon, the Poindexters placed the family name on a street, a relay stage station, a country school, even a slough; and for many years, a Poindexter published the *Dillon Examiner*. And the Poindexter and Orr families donated the land upon which the State Normal School in Dillon (today Western Montana College of The University of Montana) was built.[16]

"Today I am the possessor of over forty paint-
ings ... and I prize them more than anything else
I own. I have broken through the barrier of space
and color and the experience has changed my life."
                               – George Poindexter[17]

How was it, then, that George Poindexter, a hardheaded commodities broker, "raised," as he put it, "in the cultural desert of Western Montana" and in Hawaii, "two thousand miles from the nearest ballet," became such a passionate exponent of an art, postwar American

---

16   For my discussion of the Poindexter-Orr Ranch and the Poindexter family in Montana, I am indebted to the following sources: Patrick Dawson, et al, *The Montana Cowboy: Legends of the Big Sky Country* (Helena, MT: Stoecklein Publishing, 1998); Robert Fletcher, *Free Grass to Fences* (New York: University Publishers, 1960); *The History of Beaverhead County, Montana*, vols. 1 & 2 (Dillon, MT: Beaverhead County History Book Association, 1990 & 1997); John Lincoln, *Rich Grass and Sweet Water: Ranch Life with the Koch Matador Cattle Company* (College Station: Texas A&M University Press, 1989); Michael P. Malone, Richard B. Roeder, and William L. Lang, *Montana: A History of Two Centuries*, rev. ed. (Seattle: University of Washington Press, 1991); Al Noyes, *History of Southern Montana*, hypertext edition, Chapter XVII (www.montana-vigilantes.org/noyeshtml/chapters/chapter17.html); "Orr, Poindexter early cattle kings," *Dillon* (Montana) *Tribune-Examiner*, September 3, 1980; "Philip H. Poindexter," *Progressive Men of . . . Montana*, 496–98; Poindexter Family Papers, Beaverhead County Museum and Historical Society; and "The Square and Compass Brand," unattributed reminiscence, Joseph Boyd Poindexter Papers, 1935–1942, SC 1980, Montana Historical Society Archives (hereafter MHSA).

17   George Poindexter, *One Man's Journey through Space – and Color* (Helena, MT: Montana Historical Society, 1988), 1

painting, and specifically the New York School, that many found difficult, if not incomprehensible? In an essay, "One Man's Journey through Space – and Color," written before his first contact with the Montana Historical Society, he attempted to explain his conversion from antagonistic skeptic to proselytizer for abstraction. "One Man's Journey" was intended for an audience of food chemists gathered at an Institute of Food Technology convention. Poindexter had brought a group of abstract paintings to show the chemists, telling them that

> for 362 days of the year I have to listen to you talk food chemistry about which I know nothing. So for 3 days you have to listen to me talk about art about which you know nothing.[18]

The story Poindexter told was one of tenacity, courage, and ultimately great satisfaction. His "most difficult journey" had begun when a friend showed him a Paul Klee painting she had recently purchased. George thought Klee must surely be a child (and not a very talented one), and when his friend told him the Swiss artist was famous and that she had been lucky to buy the painting for $500, he thought she was "ready for a sanitarium." A trip to Paris only deepened his consternation. First, he discovered that the paintings he had brought back, by some "genius" he had discovered in Montparnasse, were absolutely worthless and that the "big daubs of color any child could do better" he'd summarily rejected proved to be by Nicolas de Stael, the "best French painter since Picasso." He learned something else, that Paris

> was no longer the place to buy the works of unknown painters. New York, the very place where I lived, had superceded Paris. . . . A small group of painters called Abstract Expressionists had upset the painting apple cart by a new approach sometimes called action painting. Artists were flocking to New York from all over the world to study with the new masters. . . .[19]

Poindexter looked at the paintings by these new masters and

---

18   George Poindexter, *One Man's Journey*, 1; George Poindexter, letter to Mrs. Michael Kennedy, October 6, 1960, MHSM.

19   George Poindexter, *One Man's Journey*, 1–2.

found that their "weird shapes and messy colors were beyond me." But instead of giving up, the stubborn businessman decided to figure out the new art or expose it as a sham. He signed up for a painting class with Polish-born Jack Tworkov, one of the "least understandable" of the new painters. To his surprise,

> Jack turned out to be serious, intelligent and articulate. . . . Now I'll find out, I thought, Jack will tell me. But that wasn't the way it happened. The first thing I learned was that neither Jack nor anyone else could tell me. It was something I had to dig out for myself. But how?[20]

Tworkov told him, "Just keep on painting and looking and it will come to you." But despite his best efforts – he went to exhibition openings, met many of the artists, and read the art magazines – Poindexter "still didn't understand any of it." Finally, Tworkov suggested that he buy a painting or two, not one of his difficult ones, but something easier. Tworkov suggested a large abstract by Robert Goodnough. Poindexter, afraid he would back out if he hesitated, bought the painting and took it home where, after a quick glance, he turned it to the wall. "I was flabbergasted," he recalled. "It looked like . . . nine square feet of black and white chicken feathers with a little blood dripped on them. . . . I didn't have the nerve to tell Jack I thought we were both crazy."[21]

Then Poindexter recalled a similar experience he had had some years earlier. Someone had recommended that he buy a recording of a Bartok quartet, but upon playing it, he had become "so incensed" – to his ear, it sounded like cats screeching – that he almost broke the record. His sister, Helen, a trained musician, urged him not to give up on Bartok, but to first try one of the composer's earlier works and to "keep listening until you hear music." Persevering, Poindexter began to find "even the dissonances . . . interesting." He had passed "some kind of a milestone."[22]

Bolstered by his Bartok experience, he decided to give the Goodnough painting a chance. He hung it, and he bought more

---

20   Ibid., 2.

21   Ibid., 2–3.

22   Ibid., 3–4.

paintings, by artists like Franz Kline and Willem de Kooning. "I had to find out," he wrote. And yet, though he found the artists "interesting and intelligent," he still didn't get it. Then one morning, "it happened." His latest acquisition, a Milton Resnick acquired three months earlier, suddenly made sense:

> I was seeing what Resnick must have seen when he decided the painting was finished. It was a strong vivid thing of beauty. Now it had form and its colors harmonized. Black smudges and careless brushstrokes became balanced elements. . . . It was Bartok all over again.[23]

Soon all of his paintings began to cohere, and George Poindexter continued to collect. And he became a passionate advocate for the new painting, whether he was addressing a hall filled with food chemists or donating his collection to the people of Montana. He felt strongly that it was "only by becoming familiar" with the works themselves, indeed, through "continual and determined" exposure, "that one is able to understand." "No one," he asserted, "can become familiar for you." This powerfully held belief would drive all of his efforts in his native state; it was a theme from which he would never stray. As he told Michael Kennedy's wife, Pete, he was "very much interested in exposing more people to, 'something they know nothing about'" and from "which I have gained so much pleasure."[24]

> *"What my gallery is about is an interest in art and what's going on that I personally can have my heart in. And I'm interested in promoting the artists. And I'm interested in the financial end only to keep going. . . ."*
>
> – Elinor Poindexter[25]

In George Poindexter's tale of his conversion and the beginnings

---

23   Ibid., 4–5.

24   Ibid., 5–6; George Poindexter, letter to Mrs. Michael Kennedy, October 6, 1960, MHSM.

25   Elinor Poindexter interview, OHC, AAA.

of the Poindexter collection of modern American paintings, he left out a central player. He did not mention his wife, Elinor Fuller Poindexter, nor did he allude to the Poindexter Gallery, which Elinor directed and where certain of the artists in the Poindexter collection showed their work. This omission is mysterious, but certainly, in the long view, just as George is the hero of this story, Elinor must be seen as its heroine.

Elinor Fuller was born in Montreal and grew up on Staten Island. Her first exposure to the visual arts came in an art history course at Manhattan's Finch College and through a painter sister, with whom she traveled to Paris. In the 1930s, she first worked in the art world at the Weyhe Gallery, where she assisted Carl Zigrosser, gallery director from 1919 to 1940 (Zigrosser later served as the first curator of prints and drawings at the Philadelphia Museum of Art). Elinor enjoyed the work "so much that I . . . probably had a kind of nostalgia for art galleries." But marriage to George Poindexter intervened, and she left the city for suburban Connecticut, where she raised her three children, Joseph, Leslie, and Christie.[26]

By her own account, Elinor reentered the gallery world in 1953, after her kids had departed for college. George came home one day from a class with Jack Tworkov and told Elinor that Tworkov's dealer, Charles Egan, needed help, "actual help and financial help." The Egan Gallery had been an important outpost of the Abstract Expressionist movement, featuring, for a time, Willem de Kooning, Tworkov, Esteban Vincente, Milton Resnick, Robert Rauschenberg, and Phillip Guston, and it had given Franz Kline his first all-abstract show in 1950. Egan needed help because he drank too much and had what historian Carl Chiarenza calls a "casual business attitude." Unhappy artists were fleeing the gallery; de Kooning, Kline, and Guston, for example, had abandoned Egan for businesslike Sidney Janis.[27]

Ellie, as she came to be known, did step in at Egan, and she found the work congenial. As her daughter Christie Dennis remembers, one of Ellie's first shows at Egan was a 1954 exhibition of Aaron Siskind's abstract photographs. "Siskind was quite a cut-up & threw ice cubes skittering across the floor," writes Dennis. "I was amazed to see

---

26   Ibid.

27   Ibid.; Carl Chiarenza, *Aaron Siskind: Pleasures and Terrors* (Boston: Little, Brown in association with Center for Creative Photography, 1982), 259n.31. See also April Kingsley, *The Turning Point: The Abstract Expressionists and the Transformation of American Art*, 365.

my mother, quite a proper lady, join in dancing on them." By 1955, despite the Poindexters' help, Egan was forced to close his doors – things had become "kind of impossible" – and that same year, Ellie opened her Poindexter Gallery in the Egan space, "since I was paying the rent," at 46 East 57th Street, and then moved a year later to 21 West 56th Street, where she stayed for fourteen years. Ellie would close the gallery in the late 1970s, after George's death, but she continued to deal from her apartment, by appointment, for many years, until her death in 1994.[28]

The Poindexter Gallery would quickly become a significant New York exhibition space, offering dozens of artists exposure, support, and sales of their work. Over the years, Ellie and her assistant gallery director, Harold "Hal" Fondren, refused to follow a single fashion; instead, as Ellie put it, "I went . . . just by if I was interested in people's . . . slides, going to studios and gradually building a group." As interviewer Paul Cummings noted, when he spoke to Ellie in 1970, "you have such great variety . . . figurative painters and abstract and sculpture . . . an enormous range."[29]

As she started out, Ellie needed to add new artists to her stable, since many of the first-generation Abstract Expressionists had left Egan for other dealers. Miriam Schapiro, who was working in the Abstract Expressionist mode during the 1950s (she was later a central figure in both the Feminist and Pattern and Decoration art movements), recalls one of Ellie's recruitment tactics. Ellie would venture into the Cedar Tavern, the social epicenter for the painters, and join a band of young artists, asking to be "a fly on the wall." One night, she sat with Schapiro and her husband, Paul Brach, together with painters Joan Mitchell and Mike Goldberg, and the next morning, Schapiro recalls, "I was excited to get a phone call from Ellie," inviting her to participate in a group show at the Poindexter. Such invitations represented important breaks for young artists, and Ellie, says Schapiro, built some high-quality shows through her sleuthing.[30]

In addition to looking at slides, visiting studios, and socializing with emerging artists, Ellie found artists through referrals from their peers and by visiting museums and galleries. She saw a painting by

---

28   Christie Dennis, letter to author, August 20, 2001; Elinor Poindexter interview, OHC, AAA.

29   Elinor Poindexter interview, OHC, AAA.

30   Miriam Schapiro, interview by author, September 8, 2001.

Richard Diebenkorn, for example, at the Guggenheim's 1954 "Younger American Painters" exhibition. She learned more about the West Coast painter "from my other artists" and finally, through the assistance of Franz Kline, reached him by phone. Diebenkorn replied, "Why, sure," to her invitation and he appeared in the Poindexter's first show, "Ten Americans," in 1955. Ellie gave the talented Californian his first New York solo show the following year. And upon Diebenkorn's advice, Ellie brought his friends, painter James Weeks and sculptor Paul Harris, into the gallery. Harris, who had attended graduate school with Diebenkorn at the University of New Mexico, had had his first experience with the Poindexter Gallery as a reviewer for *Art News,* but his big break came in 1958 when he received a phone call from Ellie. She asked point blank, "Would you like to have a show next week? Dick says I've got to show your work."[31]

Besides Ellie's own contacts in the art world, her assistant director, Hal Fondren (the first gallery assistant had been painter Budd Hopkins) brought to the gallery important connections to both the painters and poets of the New York School. Born and raised in Canton, Ohio, Fondren had served as a bombardier in Great Britain during World War II. Upon his return to the States, Fondren enrolled as an English major at Harvard, where he roomed with Frank O'Hara, who would soon emerge as a central figure in the New York School of poets and as an important critic and curator.

According to O'Hara biographer Brad Gooch, Fondren and O'Hara, "shirking the required courses," took numerous art history classes together. Fondren remembered that they "were afraid to take any courses for credit in that department because all the people were eager beaver future museum directors." "Such an attitude," Gooch writes, "was ironic for Fondren who became a director of the Poindexter Gallery, and O'Hara would make his mark as a curator of the Museum of Modern Art." Fondren also was to meet future New York School poets, John Ashbery and Kenneth Koch, at Harvard.[32]

When Fondren and O'Hara moved to New York, they shared an apartment on East Forty-ninth Street. By all accounts a superb

---

31   Elinor Poindexter interview, OHC, AAA; Paul Harris, interview by author, August 30, 2001.

32   Brad Gooch, *City Poet: The Life and Times of Frank O'Hara* (New York: Knopf, 1993) 145.

chef (he had learned to cook for his siblings after his father died suddenly and his mother had to work long hours), Hal provided a "steadying and domestic influence" in the O'Hara-Fondren household. Eventually, however, he found O'Hara's untidiness and heavy drinking intolerable. "It was sort of a disaster scene," he told Gooch. The friends parted company but remained close friends until O'Hara's untimely death in 1966.[33]

Because "Hal had been a roommate of Frank O'Hara's," writes Poindexter daughter Christie Dennis, he "was no doubt responsible for bringing Frank, John Ashbery, occasionally Merce Cunningham [choreographer and partner of composer John Cage] and others in the arts into the gallery."[34] Both O'Hara and John Ashbery reviewed occasional shows at the Poindexter[35] and wrote poems about or collaborated with Poindexter artists, especially Mike Goldberg (see O'Hara's "Why I Am Not a Painter")[36] and Nell Blaine (who painted two portraits of O'Hara and created the costumes for Ashbery's play, *The Heroes;* Ashbery, in turn, wrote the introduction to *Nell Blaine Sketchbook* [New York: The Arts Publisher, 1986]).

Before coming to the Poindexter, Hal had worked for Eleanor Ward's Stable Gallery on West 58th Street, where he achieved some notoriety, according to his brother Darl, for discovering Joan Mitchell, offering the talented young painter her second show in New York. There he also met Mitchell's lover, Mike Goldberg, who was to join the Poindexter Gallery in 1956. Joan Mitchell, with whom Hal remained lifelong friends, was the frequent beneficiary of his hospitality and great cooking – in an undated letter, she wrote, "Hal, oh that dinner . . . you are a dream" – and according to curator Klaus Kertess, she commemorated the "dinners replete with painters' and poets' swirling egos" at Hal's apartment in her painting, *Evenings on*

---

33   Gooch, *City Poet*, 193.

34   Dennis letter.

35   For example, see "Introducing the Sculpture of George Spaventa," in Frank O'Hara, *Art Chronicles, 1954–1966* (New York: George Braziller, 1975), 128–33; and "Joseph Shannon" in John Ashbery, *Reported Sightings: Art Chronicles, 1957–1987*, ed. David Bergman (Cambridge, MA: Harvard University Press, 1991), 287–93.

36   O'Hara, *Collected Poems*, 261–62.

Seventy-third Street (1956–1957).[37]

When he moved to the Poindexter Gallery, Hal's skills as cook and host continued to be important to his work, helping to cement relations with important gallery artists. He would invite them to sumptuous dinners at the eighteenth-floor penthouse apartment, at West 81st Street and Central Park West, he shared with his longtime partner, a successful businessman. "It was the most beautiful place I've ever seen," recalls Phyllis Diebenkorn, with a spectacular view of the park. Of his own dinners at the Fondren apartment, painter Joe Shannon remembers "astonishing food. Hal was a tremendous cook."[38]

Frank O'Hara continued to benefit from Hal's hospitality, and in a 1958 letter written shortly after he had spent a few days at Hal's country home at Fire Island Pines, the poet suggested a collaboration, fueled no doubt by the "lovely time" that weekend:

> Maybe we should start a gallery together . . . what with our
> fierce dominating-male type personalities and our exqui-
> site taste I don't see how we could fail to lose quite a lot of
> money for some nice backer.[39]

Though they never opened a gallery together, the two friends would collaborate in 1965, when the Poindexter Gallery commissioned Frank O'Hara to write the foreword to the first catalog for the Montana Historical Society's Poindexter Collection of Contemporary American Art, created for an exhibition at the brand-new Yellowstone Art Center in Billings, Montana.

> *I have known the Poindexter Collection . . . while*
> *it was being formed. . . . Mr. and Mrs. Poindexter*
> *have chosen to collect the art of their own time*

---

37   Darl Fondren, interview by author, August 21, 2001; Joan Mitchell, letter to Hal Fondren, n.d., Hal Fondren Papers, Collection of Darl B. Fondren (hereafter HFP); Klaus Kertess, *Joan Mitchell* (New York: Harry N. Abrams, 1997), 25. See also Hal Fondren, "Sunday Afternoons with Joan," in *Joan Mitchell: Paintings, 1950–1955* (New York: Robert Miller Gallery, 1998), 13.

38   Phyllis Diebenkorn, interview by author, September 4, 2001; Joseph Shannon, interview by author, September 14, 2001.

39   Frank O'Hara, letter to Hal Fondren, July 19, 1958, HFP.

*and the art which has been close to them in their
daily life, which gives the collection a highly personal flavor. . . . The people of Montana are to be
congratulated on the acquisition of this splendid
group of works of art.*

– Frank O'Hara[40]

While Elinor Poindexter and Hal Fondren worked hard to make
the Poindexter Gallery a success, George Poindexter focused his
energies on getting the Poindexter Collection seen by Montanans.
He continued to give the Montana Historical Society paintings on a
nearly annual basis (he was not averse to taking the tax benefits), and
he urged Michael Kennedy, and the Society directors who followed
him, to exhibit the collection frequently and broadly. Given his belief
that only "continual and determined" exposure could win over viewers to this challenging art, he was quite willing to do whatever it took
for the "widest possible distribution throughout the state."[41]

George hoped that one day a large gallery at the Society would
be devoted to his collection. When that hope was not immediately fulfilled – in the early 1960s, the Society's building was small, its
staff tiny, and its budget less than $200,000[42] – he began encour-
aging the Society to loan his collection freely. He granted his close
Montana friends, Tom and Mary Tavenner, permission to borrow paintings to hang in their Deer Lodge home, and in 1962, he
made sure that a group of twenty-eight works from the Poindexter
Collection hung during homecoming at his alma mater, Montana
State University, Missoula. The collection was borrowed, too, by
Montana State College, Bozeman; painting instructor Bob DeWeese
brought two Poindexter shows to the college, in 1962 and 1964.
And in those early years, Helena's Carroll College, the University
of Saskatchewan, and the Hilltop Gallery in Butte, Montana, also
showed portions of the Poindexter Collection. New York's Whitney
Museum of American Art included the Poindexter Earl Kerkam *Self*

---

40   Frank O'Hara, "The Poindexter Collection," in *The Poindexter Collection of Contemporary American Art* (Billings, MT/Helena, MT: Yellowstone Art Center/Montana Historical
Society, 1965), 5.

41   George Poindexter, *One Man's Journey,* 6; George Poindexter, letter to Michael Kennedy,
March 30, 1964, MHSM.

42   "Special Examination, February 10, 1961, Office of State Examiner," MHSA.

Portrait in a 1964 exhibition, and in 1966, the Washington Gallery of Modern Art launched a Kerkam retrospective, to which the Society loaned a painting. The Society itself introduced the collection with a "Dedication of the Poindexter Collection" show in March 1964.[43]

Meanwhile, the Yellowstone Art Center in Billings was about to open its doors, and George Poindexter, Billings attorney James Haughey (a close friend of the Poindexters), Mike Kennedy, and the Yellowstone's first director, Terry Melton, collaborated to bring the entire Poindexter Collection to the grand opening of Montana's first contemporary art museum. At first, there had been concern that such an opening show would be "too far out and might frighten . . . away" potential Yellowstone supporters. By May 1965, George was delighted to learn that "all the pictures will be shown in Billings."[44]

From the beginning, Mike Kennedy had suggested that the Poindexters fund the printing of a collection catalog ("since . . . Montanans are notoriously naïve . . . on the contemporary modernists, the catalogue is almost as vital as the paintings themselves"), but it was only with the Yellowstone show that George decided to underwrite a modest four-page catalog. Terry Melton wanted something more substantial, and in his words, he "bullied" the Society into "sharing the costs" for the thirty-two-page catalog, with a full-color cover, a number of works reproduced in black and white, and biographies of the artists. Originally, George had wanted New York School poet and critic Barbara Guest to write the catalog's foreword, but when she was unavailable, Hal Fondren's old friend, Frank O'Hara, stepped in.[45]

Jim Haughey asked George, who was traveling with Ellie to the Yellowstone opening, to address the local Rotary club and prepare "the business men . . . for what is probably going to be a startling experience." George sent five new paintings directly to Billings for the opening, including four works by "new color movement" painters Gene Davis, Albert Stadler, Morteza Sazegar, and Ronald Slowinski.

---

43   "Montana Historical Society Museum Poindexter Collection Exhibition History," MHSM.

44   Michael Kennedy, letter to George Poindexter, September 1, 1964, MHSM; George Poindexter, letter to Michael Kennedy, August 24, 1964, MHSM; George Poindexter, letter to Michael Kennedy, May 19, 1965, MHSM.

45   Michael Kennedy, letter to George Poindexter, January 16, 1963, MHSM; Terry Melton, interview by author, August 24, 2001.

And Terry Melton, who felt that the Society was not the proper repository for contemporary art, suggested to the Poindexters that they give works to the Yellowstone instead, "planting a seed" that would lead, a decade later, to a second Poindexter Collection in Montana.[46]

> *In those days the gallery opening was a ritual event. Almost every Tuesday we went to Sidney Janis, Martha Jackson, Leo Castelli, Tibor de Nagy, Betty Parsons, the Stable, Sam Koontz or Poindexter.*
>
> – Waldo Rasmussen[47]

The first gifts to the Montana Historical Society represented both George and Ellie Poindexter's interest in the heroic period of Abstract Expressionism, but as time passed (and prices rose for works by the movement's first generation), George shifted his collecting focus to the "new generation." Likewise, Ellie – feeling that "Abstract Expressionism [had begun] to weaken" – sought fresh work for her gallery, so long as it "was good whether it was representational even." This brought her to post-painterly abstractionists like Al Held and Jules Olitski and Color Field painters like Gene Davis, but it also led her to so-called second-generation Abstract Expressionists like Nell Blaine and Robert DeNiro, who worked figuratively. As literary historian David Lehman has argued, "The Second Generation painters veered by returning to figuration at the very moment when the critic Clement Greenberg, the ayatollah of Abstract Expressionism, declared that painting had to be abstract and 'flat.'" These painters, like the New York School poets, "opted for aesthetic pleasure." Though they never received the critical acclaim or financial reward accorded the first Action Painters or, a bit later, the ascendant Pop artists, they played vital roles in the New York art world of the 1950s and 60s,

---

46   James Haughey, letter to George Poindexter, June 9, 1965, Poindexter Collection Files, Yellowstone Art Museum (hereafter YAM); George Poindexter, letter to Michael Kennedy, June 30, 1965, MHSM; "Names of Pictures Sent," YAM; Melton interview.

47   Waldo Rasmussen, "Frank O'Hara in the Museum," in *Homage to Frank O'Hara,* special issue of *Big Sky* 11/12 (April 1978): 86.

collaborating with poets and painting strong and expressive work.[48]

Robert DeNiro came to the Poindexter Gallery from Egan in 1955, but soon left for the Zabriskie Gallery, though the Poindexters remained loyal supporters (the first DeNiro painting in this exhibition is from 1954 and the most recent from 1979). Nell Blaine, on the other hand, participated in the very first Poindexter group show and never left. Blaine was an extraordinary figure – and one of Ellie's favorite artists. Born in Richmond, Virginia, Blaine moved to New York in 1942, at age twenty, to study with Hans Hoffmann and began to paint abstractly. She quickly immersed herself in the city's art scene. Her loft on West Twenty-first Street, remembers playwright Arnold Weinstein, "was the place." All white – "the first time any of us saw everything painted white" – the Blaine loft was a gathering place for painters, jazz musicians (Nell played drums), and poets. "I maintain," Weinstein said, "that she started the whole New York School."[49]

Early on, Blaine had been championed by Clement Greenberg, who recommended her for inclusion in the 1945 Guggenheim exhibition, *The Women.* Until she traveled to France in 1950, she "saw in terms of an abstract structure," but her experience in France "was like opening a window. Suddenly a lot of sunlight came in."[50] She turned to "greater involvement with subject matter and the perceived world," painting landscapes and still lifes. Her work in *Ten Americans,* the first show at the Poindexter, was *Merry-Go-Round,* which related "completely," writes art historian Martica Sawin, "to an Abstract Expressionist ethos despite the recognizable subject matter." At this stage, Blaine was championed by Thomas Hess, influential editor of *Art News,* and with his critical support and the backing of the Poindexter Gallery, her work began to sell well.[51]

In 1959, Nell departed for Egypt and Greece. While on Mykonos, where she found a "marvelous studio with a . . . view of Delos," she was suddenly stricken by "terrible fatigue," and a

---

48   George Poindexter, letter to Michael Kennedy, Jan. 12, 1962, MHSM; Elinor Poindexter interview, OHC, AAA; David Lehman, *The Last Avant-Garde: The Making of the New York School Poets* (New York: Doubleday, 1998), 3–4.

49   Quoted in Lehman, *The Last Avant-Garde,* 62–63.

50   Quoted in Martica Sawin, *Nell Blaine: Her Art and Life* (New York: Hudson Hills Press, 1998), 38.

51   Sawin, *Nell Blaine,* 47.

vacationing German doctor diagnosed bulbar-spinal polio. Rushed to Athens, she was placed in an iron lung. Eventually she could return to the United States, but for many months, she lay "almost completely paralyzed."[52]

Only the support of her many art world friends – and her own powerful will – kept her spirits up as she slowly regained partial use of her body. The most overwhelming show of support came when Ellie Poindexter, Thomas Hess of *Art News,* and Leslie Katz of *Arts* magazine assembled the exhibition "For Nell Blaine" at the Poindexter Gallery. Seventy-nine artists contributed works, and Nell was able to live on the proceeds for the next few years, while she relearned how to paint. Ellie and George Poindexter revealed the depths of their support when, in 1964, they retrofitted, for the artist and her wheelchair, a guest house on their banana plantation on the Caribbean island of Saint Lucia. Nell and her partner, British painter Dilys Evans, spent nearly a year there, and when they returned to New York in 1965, the Poindexter Gallery launched the exhibition, *Nell Blaine: An Exhibition of Recent Paintings, 1964–1965, Oils, Watercolors & Drawings Done in St. Lucia, England & Yaddo.*[53] With her recovery, Nell continued her success, and her friendship with Ellie, Martica Sawin writes, lasted "well beyond the closing of the Poindexter Gallery."[54]

Like Nell Blaine, Richard Diebenkorn shifted from abstraction to figuration, and like Blaine, he stayed with the Poindexter for many years, from 1955 through 1970. Numerous artists had their first solo New York shows at the Poindexter, as Diebenkorn did, but a number left Ellie, in her telling, for "galleries that have money to guarantee artists." Diebenkorn, according to his widow Phyllis, found in Ellie a nearly ideal dealer, staying with her "maybe five years longer than he should have." According to Phyllis, Ellie did not keep good records and neither she nor Hal (whom Phyllis "adored") were particularly "proactive" in promoting Diebenkorn's career. But because Ellie didn't push, "Dick liked her a lot. She left him alone, which was exactly what he wanted." Diebenkorn also loved the Poindexter

---

52   Quoted in Sawin, *Nell Blaine,* 60, 67, 68.

53   See *Nell Blaine: An Exhibition of Recent Paintings, 1964–1965, Oils, Watercolors & Drawings Done in St. Lucia, England & Yaddo* (New York: Poindexter Gallery, 1965).

54   Sawin, *Nell Blaine,* 47.

Gallery on East 57th Street, "a big brownstone with high ceilings . . . [with] a couple of ample rooms" and plenty of natural light. And in fact, when the gallery moved uptown in 1969, to 24 East 84th Street, Diebenkorn decided to leave the gallery. He had returned to abstraction with his large "Ocean Park" paintings, and, according to Phyllis, the new gallery, low ceilinged and lacking natural light, was simply not appropriate for his large-scale new work.[55]

Diebenkorn, with his increasing national fame and rapidly escalating prices, was one of the Poindexter's most successful artists ("I'm pleased but apprehensive," he confided in Ellie, "about the high-powered interest in my painting"),[56] and his sold-out shows brought major collectors, like Duncan Phillips of the Phillips Collection, Count Giuseppe Panza di Biumo, and Nelson Rockefeller, to the gallery. It must have come as a shock, then, in 1970 when Diebenkorn announced that he was leaving for the aggressive Marlborough Gallery. But the letters Dick and Ellie exchanged at that difficult juncture reveal the strong friendship and professional respect they shared.

"I have given a lot of thought and concern to a difficult decision over the past few weeks," Diebenkorn wrote, "and I called you as soon as I made up my mind. . . . I hope we can remain friends. You said on the phone, 'I'm not mad' but I want it better than that." Ellie responded the next day,

> Now that we seem to be coming to the end of our long business association, I want to tell you how wonderful it has been for me. You are always a joy personally, and handling your beautiful work has been one of the greatest experiences of my life. I don't resent your going where more can be done for you. . . .

And she provided an explanation for the presence of only a single Diebenkorn painting in the Poindexter Collection at the Montana Historical Society, "I'm feeling badly that I didn't . . . buy [your work] extensively as we went along . . . I always thought I could do it later.

---

55   Elinor Poindexter interview, OHC, AAA; Phyllis Diebenkorn interview; Richard Diebenkorn, interview by Susan Larsen, May 1, 2 & 7, 1985 and December 15, 1987, OHC, AAA.

56   Richard Diebenkorn, letter to Elinor Poindexter, April 1960, Poindexter Gallery Records, 1956–(ca. 1978), Archives of American Art, Smithsonian Institution, Washington, D.C.(hereafter PGR, AAA).

Now there is no time left." Diebenkorn and Ellie remained friends until Dick's death in 1993; Ellie's daughter, Christie Dennis, recalls that Diebenkorn's "death distressed her and when she herself was dying . . . she talked of him frequently."[57]

Other artists have noted Ellie's extraordinarily caring attitude toward her artists. Sculptor Paul Harris, perhaps the only Poindexter artist with strong Montana ties (his wife Marguerite "Meme" Kirk comes from an old pioneer family in the Bozeman area), said of her, "She was terribly casual, but with a deep sense of responsibility toward her artists. For a great spirit, I know no one better in my life." And Joe Shannon, who joined the gallery in 1970, recalled Ellie's "absolute generosity and lack of bottom line niggardliness." She invited Shannon and his family to visit the Poindexters' Saint Lucia plantation and often put them up at her Connecticut place. He noted that, in an "administrative way," Ellie and Hal "weren't the most put together," but "if you're going to be hard about that, go to Marlborough."[58]

The case of Gene Davis, the Washington, D.C., Color Field painter, offers another perspective on the Poindexter Gallery. The self-taught Davis was very conscious of promoting his own career, and he worked with Ellie and Hal to achieve specific goals. In May 1964, he asked Ellie for an additional show, in order to establish beyond doubt that he belonged to the first generation of Color Field painters and to cement the notice he had received, from Clement Greenberg, among others, at his first Poindexter show the previous year. George was not certain about "this painter . . . who paints nothing but colored stripes" ("it's beyond me," he wrote Mike Kennedy), but Ellie agreed to the show. In February 1965, Davis wrote to Hal, asking him, "at the risk of boring you with my vanity," to "call the attention of *Time* magazine to my show." A month later, Davis, in a letter to Ellie, praised Hal for his "first-rate" efforts, which had resulted in a review in the newsweekly and a notice in the *New Yorker*. In September 1965, he wrote to request yet another show the following year, and again Ellie complied, collaborating with Hofstra University to mount *Gene Davis: Selected Paintings, 1963–1966*, for which they published a catalog, with an essay by critic Michael Phillips. Though

----

57   Richard Diebenkorn, letter to Elinor Poindexter, January 24, 1971, PGR, AAA; Elinor Poindexter, letter to Richard Diebenkorn, January 25, 1971, PGR, AAA; Dennis letter.

58   Harris interview; Shannon interview.

by 1968 Davis would depart for the Fischbach Gallery, clearly Ellie and Hal had given him maximum exposure, four New York shows in five years, and had helped position him as a central figure in the Color Field movement.[59]

If I could get these pictures shown I feel
that it would help the whole cultural climate.
— George Poindexter[60]

In 1966, the Montana Historical Society launched another large-scale show of their Poindexter Collection, but this one proved ill-fated. The exhibition, sponsored by the Western Association of Art Museums, was to travel to six museums, in Nevada, New Mexico, California, and Washington state. Sadly, through a series of miscommunications, the tour was a disaster. First, the collection traveled uncrated, and some paintings' frames were badly damaged. In addition, both the museum association and the Society thought the other had insured the show. Upon discovering that the collection was traveling uninsured and after reports of damage, the parties agreed to cancel the show midway through its itinerary.[61]

Meanwhile, Michael Kennedy, the man whose "enthusiasm and conviction" had convinced George Poindexter to make his generous gift ("without his encouragement the collection would probably have gone to Honolulu"), stepped down as director of the Montana Historical Society. In late 1966, acting director Bob Morgan reported the tour fiasco to George, concluding, "[A]t any rate we will have the Poindexters back and we only hope we will have a suitable area for exhibition."[62]

Morgan's desire was not to be realized, and as time passed,

59   Gene Davis, letter to Elinor Poindexter, May 11, 1964, PGR, AAA; George Poindexter, letter to Michael Kennedy, September 11, 1963, MHSM; Gene Davis, letter to Hal Fondren, February 18, 1965, PGR, AAA; Gene Davis, letter to Elinor Poindexter, PGR, AAA.

60   George Poindexter, letter to James Haughey, October 9, 1973, YAM.

61   Mrs. J. Glen Liston, Executive Secretary, Western Association of Art Museums, letter to Robert F. Morgan, December 7, 1966, MHSM.

62   George Poindexter, letter to Dr. H. K. Newburn, president, Montana State University, August 28, 1962, MHSM; Robert F. Morgan, letter to George Poindexter, December 19, 1966, MHSM.

George Poindexter grew more and more disenchanted with the Society's handling of his collection. In autumn 1967, he wrote to new Society director Sam Gilluly,

> I am sorry that Mike Kennedy bit off more than he could chew. . . . And I am afraid that even with your new wing you will only have room for a few. . . . I must admit that I was a little disappointed on traveling around the state and finding only one artist who even knew of the existence of the collection.[63]

George went on to propose the division of his collection into thirds, one-third to go to the University of Montana, one-third to the Yellowstone Art Center, and the remainder to stay at the Society, where he hoped a new gallery was being planned that would "accommodate a third of the pictures." George noted that he would not be donating any further works and encouraged Gilluly to meet with his counterparts at the Yellowstone and the university to "work out the mechanics of the plan." A month later, Gilluly reported that his board had discussed the issue and had asked him to express "their deep and profound interest in the Collection," as well as their intent to circulate it more extensively and "their plans to set aside space . . . for permanent display of as many paintings as possible." In 1968, George informed the Society's board that he wished to loan a sizeable group of paintings to the University of Montana, for an undetermined period.[64]

In its new addition, the Society did establish a Poindexter Gallery, but though it hosted several Poindexter shows, in 1970, 1972, and 1973, the gallery was primarily devoted to rotating exhibits by regional artists. George attended the gallery's opening in 1970 and wrote to Gilluly, "I want to tell you how pleased I am. . . . It is a beautiful room." George was now following a different donation strategy, giving nothing new, but each year turning works already loaned into gifts. And the Society continued to make its Poindexter Collection available to other institutions, with at least nine Poindexter shows

---

63   George Poindexter, letter to Sam Gilluly, October 9, 1967, MHSM.

64   Ibid.; Sam Gilluly, letter to George Poindexter, November 29, 1967, MHSM; George Poindexter, letter to Board of Directors, Montana Historical Society, November 1, 1968, MHSM.

being mounted during the late 1960s and early 1970s.[65]

In 1973, after nearly three years' silence, George donated several more works on loan, including the single Jackson Pollock. Having engineered the loan of a group of works to the university, he now wanted to divide the remainder between the Yellowstone and the Society. He wrote to Sam Gilluly that, while he appreciated the Society's efforts, "I would still like more exposure." "After all," he argued, "the paintings aren't doing . . . much good sitting in your storage." Gilluly responded that, though the Society did not show the collection every year, it did have the "largest exposure in the state," with some 150,000 annual visitors. Jim Haughey, representing the Yellowstone's board, pitched in, telling George that the Billings museum would be "delighted to exhibit works from the collection at rather frequent intervals." George wrote Gilluly, "I don't know what Yellowstone can do to improve [exposure] but I can only hope."[66]

Then, in autumn 1973, George suffered a stroke. Ellie wrote to her Montana friend Jean Baucus that George was "so far unable to walk or write." After talking to Ellie, Gilluly wrote Haughey that, given George's condition, "no decision can be made regarding the collection." In January 1974, upon hearing that George was recovering well, Gilluly wrote him that "the majority of the collection has by now been deeded to the Society." In March 1974, Ellie furthered that process, donating an additional twenty-three works on loan. In August, George had another stroke, but he and Ellie wrote Haughey that they definitely wished to divide their collection between the two museums. "Whatever has not been committed to Helena," the Poindexters wrote, "could go to Billings and we will keep donating new works to [the Yellowstone] until a good group is built up."[67]

In early December 1974, Ellie donated five more paintings, and a month later, on January 1, 1975, Everton Gentry "George" Poindexter passed away at Bridgeport, Connecticut, of "complications following a cerebral hemorrhage." In his will, George left to the Society "all my

---

65   George Poindexter, letter to Sam Gilluly, August 11, 1970, MHSM.

66   George Poindexter, letter to Sam Gilluly, September 13, 1973, MHSM; Sam Gilluly, letter to George Poindexter, September 26, 1973, MHSM; James Haughey, letter to George Poindexter, October 1, 1973; YAM; George Poindexter, letter to Sam Gilluly, October 9, 1973, MHSM.

67   Elinor Poindexter, letter to Jean Baucus, November 19, 1973, MHSM; Sam Gilluly, letter to James Haughey, November 19, 1973, MHSM; Sam Gilluly, letter to George Poindexter, January 3, 1974, MHSM; Elinor and George Poindexter, letter to James Haughey, August 19, 1974, YAM.

works of art which may be on loan . . . at the time of my death"; the sole remaining works not already given were an untitled de Kooning and the superb Franz Kline.[68]

We are all so anxious for the paintings to arrive!
                                                        – Donna Forbes[69]

With the death of her husband, Ellie Poindexter wasted no time in carrying out their mutual resolve, to donate new works to the Yellowstone Art Center until "a good group is built up." Now that the Montana Historical Society owned all of its paintings, she started afresh, giving the Yellowstone works that represented her evolving tastes but also others by old favorites, among them Earl Kerkam, Robert DeNiro, James Weeks, and Nell Blaine. In June 1975, James Haughey, who had worked tirelessly to convince the Poindexters to consider the Yellowstone a worthy home for their collection, welcomed the first installment of Ellie's generosity; he was joined by the museum's new director, Donna Forbes, who wrote to Ellie, "What a wonderful gift to the Yellowstone Art Center."[70]

Forbes immediately began planning the Yellowstone's first show of its own Poindexter Collection, writing to the artists and asking them for statements she could use in exhibit labels. The installation, in a gallery with twenty-four poles (the Yellowstone was housed in a renovated county jail), posed serious challenges, but because the ceiling was only slightly higher than seven feet, the large paintings, hung sparsely, remembers Forbes, "almost filled a panel" and "knocked your eyes out."[71]

Public reaction was mixed. "We've come a long way," says Donna Forbes. "In those days, much of the public was puzzled by the Poindexters, but those who were informed loved the work." Curator

---

68   "Everton Poindexter dies in Connecticut," *Dillon* (Montana) *Tribune-Examiner,* January 8, 1975; "Will of Everton Gentry Poindexter," quoted in Freda B. Stolz, Law Offices of Paskus, Gordon & Hyman, letter to Ken Korte, March 18, 1977, MHSM.

69   Donna Forbes, letter to Elinor Poindexter, May 19, 1975, YAM.

70   Elinor and George Poindexter, letter to James Haughey, August 19, 1974, YAM; Donna Forbes, letter to Elinor Poindexter, May 19, 1975, YAM.

71   Donna Forbes, interview by author, August 28, 2001.

Mike Connelly found that "when we displayed the Poindexters without any information, people laughed at them." But when the museum provided "definitions of art terms, personal statements by the artists . . . and educational booklets designed to help people understand the concepts behind the paintings," he "heard a lot less derisive laughter."[72]

From 1975 to 1990, Elinor Poindexter gave the Yellowstone Art Center 146 works of art, many paintings and drawings plus two suites of lithographs by Robert DeNiro, *Anna Christie* and *Moroccan Women,* selected serigraphs from R. B. Kitaj's series *Mahler Becomes Politics, Beisbol,* and a group of lithographs by California artists, including Montana native son, Peter Voulkos. The Yellowstone exhibited the collection regularly, "always when there was a new gift," recalls Forbes, and almost every year, according to both Michael Connolly and Gordon McConnell, former Yellowstone chief curators. In addition, a few paintings from the collection usually hung in the intimate Members Room.[73]

Ellie never traveled to Montana during those years; instead, Forbes and her staff would periodically visit her in New York. She was, in Gordon McConnell's words, "fragile when we knew her." Describing her as "warm and gentle and generous," McConnell added that she "wanted to abide by her husband's wishes. The collection was a legacy she wanted to leave for him." Donna remembers that Ellie, always "friendly and kind," came across as "still vitally interested in her artists" and seemed "very happy that we were taking" her collection. In 1990, when Forbes and two of her curators traveled to New York to select more works for the Yellowstone, they met Hal Fondren, who was still assisting Ellie (Hal "was absolutely devoted to Ellie," recalls Paul Harris).[74]

At the same time that the Yellowstone was cementing its relationship with Ellie, the Montana Historical Society was taking a vastly different approach to its Poindexter Collection than it had in the past. As the Society grew in size, resources, and sophistication, its curators took a closer look at the collection and its storage and

72   Forbes interview; Michael Connelly, interview by author, March 15, 1981. See also Rick Newby, "The Poindexter Collections: Fine Art in Montana," *Montana Eagle,* April 1, 1981, 11.

73   Forbes interview.

74   Gordon McConnell, interview by author, September 4, 2001; Forbes interview; Harris interview.

conservation needs. In 1974, an assessment by a consultant had revealed major problems with a number of the paintings, some the result of "inherent vice" – a problem with many Abstract Expressionist paintings, because of the spontaneity of their creation and the impermanent materials used by the artists (Jackson Pollock, for example, used house paint) – and some from improper storage conditions and what Society curator Patty Dean called, in a 1981 letter to Ellie, the "cavalier manner in which the paintings were often lent in the past."[75]

The museum staff also called back the loan to the University of Montana, discovering to their dismay that no records had been kept of which paintings were lent. Paintings trickled back over several years, and some of the paintings, displayed in public areas, had suffered abuse. More than ever, Dean and chief curator Mike McCourt were determined to protect the collection. Dean had received her M.A. in History Museum Studies at the State University of New York, Cooperstown, where she met a number of conservators working to preserve the "incredible collection of abstract expressionist paintings" in the Empire State Plaza in Albany, which had "suffered terribly from intentional and unintentional vandalism." Well aware of the balance needed between conservation and public exposure, Dean and McCourt undertook an ambitious plan to conserve as many Poindexter works as budget allowed, build a new temperature-controlled vault with welded steel racks and flat storage for extremely large paintings, and launch carefully conceived Poindexter exhibitions aimed at exposing Montanans to the work, while providing context and interpretation. A 1981 show, *Art in This Century, 1943–73,* for example, featured readings of New York School poets and a talk by pioneering Montana collector Jeff Holter (who had met George and Ellie Poindexter in the early 1960s); besides the Poindexters, suites of prints by Roy Lichtenstein and Robert Rauschenberg, donated by Holter, also hung in the show. As scholar Leanne Gilbertson notes in her study of the Society's Poindexter Collection, echoing Mike Connelly, "The Historical Society has found, through experience, that hostility toward the collection diminishes when educational information is emphasized" and the works are placed in art historical context.[76]

---

75   Patricia L. Dean, letter to Elinor Poindexter, September 17, 2001, MHSM.

76   Patricia L. Dean, letter to author, September 1, 2001; Leanne Gilbertson, "The Poindexter Collection: Abstract Expressionism in Montana?," undergraduate thesis, Department of Art, Montana State University, 1995, 14.

Both the Society and the Yellowstone worked with other museums to further expose their Poindexter collections. The Society loaned works to shows featuring single Abstract Expressionists, including Franz Kline and Jackson Pollock, and it collaborated with other Montana art museums, most notably the School of Fine Arts at the University of Montana, which mounted *Selected Works from the George and Elinor Poindexter Collection* in 1987. This exhibition featured a catalog with an essay by David Adams, perhaps the first assessment of works in the collection by an art historian. And in 1998, the Society cooperated with the Denver Art Museum's Nancy Tieken, who curated a major Poindexter show at DAM, featuring twenty-seven paintings and Tieken's ground-breaking essay on the history of the collection and the Poindexter Gallery.[77]

The Yellowstone also loaned Poindexter works to major exhibitions. The most ambitious was a Robert DeNiro, Sr. retrospective mounted by Great Falls, Montana's Paris Gibson Square for the Contemporary Arts. Paris Gibson curator Mark Leach first encountered DeNiro's work at the Yellowstone and, according to Gordon McConnell, "fell in love with it." Through the Yellowstone's staff, he met Ellie Poindexter and, with her help, was able to borrow, besides six of the Yellowstone's DeNiros and one of Ellie's, another thirty DeNiro paintings and drawings. The show traveled to seven museums around the country and was accompanied by a thirty-two-page catalog featuring essays by Leach and DeNiro contemporary, painter and critic Lawrence Campbell. Campbell wrote, "Robert DeNiro . . . was as much a part of the 1950's as anybody else. . . . [He] always was a kind of Abstract Expressionist, using the term in a broad sense to define a liberated style. . . . In my Elysian fields, in my Museum without Walls, I place DeNiro in the leaders of painting today."[78]

As Montana museums began to vigorously expose not only the state's two Poindexter collections, but also to recapitulate the careers of artists heavily represented in the collections – and as the Montana Historical Society radically reinvented its approach to the original

---

77   See David Adams, *Selected Works from the George & Elinor Poindexter Collection* (Helena, MT/Missoula, MT: Montana Historical Society/School of Fine Arts, University of Montana, 1987), and Nancy B. Tieken, *Montana's Best-kept Secret: The Poindexter Collection of Modern American Masters* (Denver, CO: Denver Art Museum, 1999).

78   McConnell interview; Lawrence Campbell, "DeNiro," in Mark Leach, et al, *Robert DeNiro: Expression as Tradition – Modern Classicism Redefined* (Great Falls, MT: Paris Gibson Square for Contemporary Arts, 1986) 22, 24, 25.

collection – Ellie Poindexter could write to Donna Forbes in 1984, "I feel we are all friends again." Ellie and her children went on, in the mid-1980s, to donate several more paintings to the Society, bringing its Poindexter Collection total to ninety-nine works. As proof of this new and friendly atmosphere, in 1987 the Yellowstone borrowed eleven of the Society's Poindexters for *The Poindexter Collection: Artists of the New York School,* and the current exhibition – a true celebration of the Poindexters' generosity and vision – brings together the two collections in the most extensive and important collaboration yet.[79]

Through an amazing range of media . . . twentieth-century Montana artists seem freer than the [state's] writers to expand form, to abstract, to experiment, to demolish.

– Mary Clearman Blew[80]

Elinor Fuller Poindexter passed away on November 6, 1994, at the age of eighty-eight. With her passing, the question must arise: Did she and George, through their generous gifts of the "more advanced manifestations of contemporary art," alter Montana's cultural climate? Montana's climate has certainly changed, and the state is no longer the "cultural desert" George felt his childhood home to be. A network of local art museums has widely dispersed challenging images and heady theories through the hinterlands, and Montana contemporary artists have produced what Mark Stevens, critic and biographer of Willem de Kooning, has called "a serious tradition . . . a tradition that challenges, irritates, goads, and stimulates artists to make their best work."[81]

To what extent, then, did the presence of works by major modernist American painters in two of the state's leading museums

---

79   Elinor Poindexter, letter to Donna Forbes, November 26, 1984, YAM.

80   Mary Clearman Blew, "This Faded Romance: Art and Literature in Twentieth-Century Montana," in *Montana Century: 100 Years in Pictures and Words* (Helena, MT: Falcon Publishing, 1999), 277.

81   Mark Stevens, introduction to Gordon McConnell, *Yellowstone Art Museum: The Montana Collection* (Billings, MT: Yellowstone Art Museum, 1998), 9.

contribute to this cultural shift? Certainly, modernism and abstraction were not new to Montana when de Kooning's *Woman* first arrived at the Society in 1962. In the 1950s, painters like Helen McAuslin of Macleod championed abstraction within the Montana Institute of the Arts, and teachers like Bob DeWeese exposed Montana students to the modernist tradition. Rancher Bill Stockton, educated in Paris, had seen Jackson Pollock's work, but it was in the "bleak, winter landscape" of central Montana that he found "inspiration for countless Avant Garde paintings." (Poindexter artist Paul Harris first saw Stockton's early 1950s Abstract Expressionist "microlandscapes" in summer 2001, during a visit to the Yellowstone Art Museum. Harris, who arrived in New York in 1955 and counted Elaine de Kooning among his close friends, was astounded. "Stockton anticipated a lot of what [Willem] de Kooning was doing," he said, further asserting, "Stockton's paintings are just as strong as early de Kooning, and better than a lot of Pollocks; they have a lot more weight.")[82]

Abstract Expressionism also came directly to Montana in the person of Bozeman native, ceramics revolutionary Peter Voulkos, who visited Black Mountain College and Manhattan in 1953, where he met Jack Tworkov, Vincente Esteban, de Kooning, and Franz Kline. The experience transformed him, recalls sculptor Rudy Autio, Voulkos's co-director of Helena's Archie Bray Foundation for the Ceramic Arts. Abstract Expressionism, Autio says, was "the glove [Pete] had to put his hand into." In 1954, Voulkos left Helena to run the ceramics program at the Los Angeles County Art Institute, where he in turn transformed American ceramic art.[83]

Another Montana artist, Henry Meloy, scion of a Townsend ranching family, had even closer ties to New York and the Abstract Expressionists. He taught painting and drawing at Columbia and, in the summers, returned to Montana to paint, where he was to influence Rudy Autio, among others. He worked both figuratively and abstractly, and in 1951, he was slated for a show of his nonobjective

---

82   Bill Stockton, "Paris 1948 – The End of an Era," in H. G. Merriam, ed., *The Arts in Montana* (Missoula: Mountain Press Publishing, 1977), 7; Harris interview. See also Helen McAuslin, "Why Paint Abstract Pictures?," in *The Arts in Montana*, 164–70.

83   Rudy Autio, interview by author and Chere Jiusto, November 3, 1998, Archie Bray Foundation for the Ceramic Arts Archives, Helena, MT. See also Rick Newby and Chere Jiusto, "'A Beautiful Spirit': Origins of the Archie Bray Foundation for the Ceramic Arts," in *A Ceramic Continuum: Fifty Years of the Archie Bray Influence*, ed. Peter Held (Helena, MT/Seattle, WA: Holter Museum of Art/University of Washington Press, 2001), 33–34.

work at the Egan Gallery, where Franz Kline had had his first show a year earlier and where Ellie Poindexter would work two years later. Sadly, Meloy died suddenly that year, and the show was cancelled. When Donna Forbes told Ellie of this coincidence, Ellie responded, "Egan had a very good eye and though I never saw [Meloy's] work I'm sure it was important."[84]

But despite this homegrown exposure, and the tenacity of the isolated early modernists – "if we were a minority," said Bob DeWeese, "we didn't act like it" – the Poindexter Collections did provide crucial sustenance to the state's progressive artists. For a 1994 show, *Modern Masters*, at the Society, curators Sue Near and Kirby Lambert asked Montana artists for their impressions of the collection's influence. Kalispell sculptor Kate Hunt mentioned Jackson Pollock who, because he spent his early years in Wyoming, might serve as role model for modernist Montanans. His western background, she wrote, "gave him something different," an awareness that "extends to the horizon." Bill Stockton also spoke of Pollock's influence, noting that though he personally had "evolved" into representation, "the themes of the fifties can be seen in my latest landscapes."[85]

Gennie DeWeese, whose late husband Bob had brought the Poindexter Collection to Montana State College in the early 1960s, noted that the influence of Arshile Gorky had led her to abstraction while "Bob was a strong de Kooning person." Bob, she recalled, "brought the little de Kooning *Woman* home over Christmas . . . to hang in our living room (something you could never do now!)." Another Montana artist, Stephen Glueckert, curator at the Art Museum of Missoula, cites the importance of this direct, hands-on exposure made possible by the "cavalier manner in which the paintings were often lent." In 1968, as a student, he had helped transport paintings from the Society's collection to the College of Great Falls. "It was a thrill," he says, "to hold the Franz Kline in my hands." He adds, "I hate to think of it in a romantic sense, but it was a different – and effective – way to share art," a way he felt the Poindexters would

---

84   Gordon McConnell, "Henry Meloy: Record of a Life," in Donna Forbes, Rudy and Lela Autio, and Gordon McConnell, *Henry Meloy: Five Themes: 1945–1951* (Billings, MT: Yellowstone Art Center, 1990), 13; Elinor Poindexter, letter to Donna Forbes, April 2, 1990, YAM.

85   Bob DeWeese, quoted in Gordon McConnell, *Yellowstone Art Museum: The Montana Collection* (Billings, MT: Yellowstone Art Museum, 1998), 35; Kate Hunt, statement, *Modern Masters* exhibit, June 1994, MHSM; Bill Stockton, statement, *Modern Masters* exhibit, May 1994, MHSM.

have approved. [86]

Perhaps the most impassioned response to the curators' query came from Billings abstract painter, Neal Jussila, who first saw the Poindexter Collection in 1962, when Bob DeWeese brought it to Montana State. Besides installing the show, DeWeese circulated George Poindexter's essay, "One Man's Journey through Color – and Space." The essay, Jussila remembers, "helped create in me a means for appreciating art." He studied the exhibit, "essay in hand," for hours on end. Within a year, he had begun to "imagine myself painting abstractly. . . . The need to paint abstractly was like the intense need for a child in a childless marriage." "The gift of the Poindexter Collection," he writes, "opened my eyes to freedom." Jussila, who has taught for many years at Montana State University-Billings, still distributes George Poindexter's essay to his students.[87]

The Poindexter Collections, as curator and painter Gordon McConnell puts it, serve as "an important anchor for the community of contemporary artists." More recent additions to the state's painting community concur. Painter Phoebe Toland, who moved to Montana from Philadelphia, remembers being surprised to find the collection and "really impressed by the quality of the pieces." "It's a stunning collection," she says. "It floored me." Painter Sandra Dal Poggetto, upon her arrival from northern California, wandered into Helena's Holter Museum and was confronted by an "unmistakable Diebenkorn portrait. I was warmed and felt at home" with "paintings of a period so influential to my early development as a painter." The collection, she says, is "fuel for those who aspire to make strong art here in Montana."[88]

---

86 Gennie DeWeese, letter to Susan R. Near, May 28, 1994, MHSM; Patricia L. Dean, letter to author, September 1, 2001; Stephen Glueckert, interview by author, September 8, 2001.

87 Neil Jussila, statement, *Modern Masters* exhibit, June 8, 1994, MHSM.

88 McConnell interview; Phoebe Toland, interview by author, August 24, 2001; Sandra Dal Poggetto, letter to author, August 26, 2001.

> *The [Poindexter] collection . . . represents a cross*
> *section of contemporary American painting. . . .*
> *To be alive at this time and to have an opportunity*
> *to see and understand this important American*
> *contribution is indeed a great privilege.*
>
> – Frank O'Hara[89]

In August 1973, in a conversation with Montanans Jean Baucus and Jeff Holter, Ellie Poindexter said, "The thing with Charlie Russell is he's unique. I mean he was in the history. . . . The history is really what counts." Elinor and George Poindexter, too, were in the history of their time and place. By so deeply and intimately immersing themselves in the lives of the artists they collected, by actively promoting the works of those artists – and by introducing those works to the people of George's native state – they left a remarkable and lasting legacy, a legacy embodied in the two collections that bear their name.[90]

George Poindexter once lamented, "We are better known for our brand [the Square and Compass] than for our art collection and I'm afraid that it will take Montana fifty years to appreciate it." Happily, the current exhibition, and the cultural climate that makes it possible, suggest that Montana's appreciation of George and Ellie's astonishing gifts is, at least a decade early, well underway.[91]

---

89   Frank O'Hara, "The Poindexter Collection," 7.

90   Elinor Poindexter, quoted in Everton Gentry "George" and Elinor Poindexter, Jean Baucus; and Norman Jefferis "Jeff" Holter, transcription of taped conversation, Holter Laboratory, Helena, MT, August 1973, George Poindexter vertical file, Montana Historical Society Library.

91   George Poindexter, quoted in Jean Baucus, "Visit with Mr. and Mrs. George (Everton Gentry) Poindexter, Holter Laboratory, Helena, August 1973," MHSM.

Missionaries for Modernism
Enigmas, Outtakes, and Extrapolations

Originally presented at the opening of the national traveling exhibition, The Most Difficult Journey: The Poindexter Collections of American Modernist Painting, Yellowstone Art Museum, Billings, MT, March 2002.

Before I get started, I want to note that I've changed the title of my talk today from that listed in the invitation. Rather than present a slimmed-down version of my essay, "Missionaries for Modernism: George and Elinor Poindexter and Montana's Poindexter Collections of Postwar American Painting" – which appears in full in the catalog and which you can read at your leisure – I will here offer a few "Enigmas, Outtakes, and Extrapolations," based upon my findings in the more extended and more coherent essay. During this project – which has been, by the way, the most delightful task of research I've ever undertaken; for which my undying thanks to curator Ben Mitchell, the Yellowstone Art Museum, the Montana Historical Society, and the scores of others who helped me in countless ways – I discovered many details that did not fit into the confines of my narrative and many themes that I had neither the time nor the space to explore. So, if my remarks today seem a bit disjunctive, made up of unanswered questions, personal ruminations, suggestive fragments, and giddy speculations, I hope they at least shed a little more light on the generosity and vision of George and Elinor Poindexter and upon the story of their extraordinary collections in Montana museums.

When Ben Mitchell asked me to write an essay about George and Elinor, the Poindexter Gallery in Manhattan, and the history of the Poindexter collections, I somehow felt like I was coming home. My relationship with the collections, and especially the collection belonging to the Montana Historical Society, is a long and personal one. I first encountered the Society's Poindexter collection in the early 1970s, as an undergraduate at the University of Montana. As some of you may remember, during those years works on loan from the Society's Poindexter collection hung in the university's Student

Union and in faculty offices. For me, as an aspiring young poet drawn to literary and visual modernism, the impact of these often-large-scale modernist works was mostly subliminal, but when I learned that the Society in Helena held many more postwar paintings in its Poindexter collection, by such important American artists as Jackson Pollock, Willem de Kooning, Adolph Gottlieb, and Richard Diebenkorn, I arranged a visit to the Society's storage area. I was astounded by the sheer size of the collection and the physical presence of the works themselves. A native Montanan who had traveled very little outside the state, but who was fascinated by the heroic Abstract Expressionists (seen only in reproduction), I was encountering for the first time actual works – in the flesh, as it were – by some of my heroes, along with many other painters whose names I had never encountered. I remember being flummoxed: How on earth did this remarkable collection, apparently so out of place in the basement of the Montana Historical Society, end up in Helena? What quirk of fate brought these works by modernist masters to a museum best known for its fine collection of Charlie Russell art?

In 1980, I went to work in the Society's museum, and in 1981, I wrote an article, published in the *Montana Eagle,* about the Poindexter collections in Helena and here, at the Yellowstone Art Museum, in Billings. I got some of my facts wrong, and I didn't know major parts of the story, but it was a start. As the Society continued to mount exhibitions of its Poindexter collection, I often participated in the openings, reading George Poindexter's essay about how he began collecting this challenging art, and with other Montana poets, reciting works by the New York School poets Frank O'Hara, Kenneth Koch, and John Ashbery who had had close ties to the artists the Poindexters collected. As the years passed, the Society and the Yellowstone, plus other Montana venues like Paris Gibson Square, Holter Museum, and University of Montana, mounted more shows of the two Poindexter collections, and I was lucky enough to see several of them. By the time Ben approached me early last summer, I felt strongly that the Poindexter collections, despite their origin thousands of miles away, were an important part of my Montana heritage, and I was eager to learn more about how they came into existence.

In my research, I quickly learned – not surprisingly – that the Poindexter story was wonderfully complex, nuanced, and rich, much more so than I had at first imagined. I had known since the early 1980s that New York commodity broker Everton Gentry "George" Poindexter came from a politically prominent Montana ranching and mercantile family, from the Dillon area, and that he had first approached the Montana Historical Society in the early 1960s to donate a painting as a memorial to his father, Joseph Boyd Poindexter, a former Montana attorney general and governor of Hawaii Territory. The painting was one of Willem de Kooning's famous and controversial Woman paintings, a startling choice only a few years after the Society had purchased its esteemed Mackay Collection of Charles M. Russell Art. That first gift led to the loan of much of the Poindexters' considerable collection and then to the donation of those works, 99 in number, to the Society. And, of course, ultimately, the Poindexters would donate a second collection of equal size and importance to the Yellowstone Art Museum. I also knew something of George Poindexter's introduction to modern painting, through his own testimony in the essay, "One Man's Journey through Space – and Color." George's essay is a key document in the origin story of these collections [see my discussion of his essay, presented to an audience of food chemists gathered at an Institute of Food Technology convention, in the preceding essay].

Art historian Thomas Crow argues that the "managers of the American economy and state may have seemed weak and directionless in 1939, unprepared as they had been for the Great Depression and the threat from fascism. But in the decade following the end of the war they were brimming with confidence, and among them were a significant number" – and we can certainly count George Poindexter among that number – "eager to signal that recovery through the patronage of demanding abstract art."

Interestingly, in "One Man's Journey," written probably in the late 1950s, George did not mention his wife Elinor or her role in the development of the Poindexter collection, even though she had opened in the Poindexter Gallery in New York in 1955. Clearly, as I note in my catalog essay, "This omission is mysterious, but certainly, in the long view, just as George is the hero of this story, Elinor must be seen as its heroine." Perhaps, in the company of his peers, the food chemists, George wanted to privilege his stance as an aggressive, confident managerial male, unafraid even of those intimidating canvases. I like to think, too, that some of George's tenacity and openness in regard to the avant garde art of his day came from his western origins. Montana's pioneers, as Joseph Kinsey Howard has written, "were not afraid to try new things." On the frontier, this flexible attitude was quite simply a requirement for survival.

Returning to Ellie Poindexter: Until recently, my impression – and I don't believe I was alone in this – had been that, yes, Ellie ran the gallery for many years, but she was somehow secondary, merely supporting her husband in his desire to collect – and then disperse works of art to Montana museums. Donna Forbes and her curatorial staff here at the Yellowstone knew much more about Ellie than most of us did, and in the late 1990s, Nancy Tieken of the Denver Art Museum did some important research on the functioning of the Poindexter Gallery and Ellie's importance in the New York scene. But it was only at the very end of my research, after it was too late to follow up in any detail, that Christie Dennis (the Poindexter daughter upon whom Jackson Pollock had a huge crush) told me her parents, in fact, collected separately, each following his or her own interests. When I began my research, I found, both in talking to Poindexter Gallery artists and in examining the records of the gallery in the Archives in American Art, that in fact, on the New York front, Ellie was the key player, running an important gallery, first introducing many artists who then went on to other galleries, and nurturing over some years the careers of important artists like Richard Diebenkorn and Gene Davis. Sculptor Paul Harris remembers that Ellie "heard the advice and noted the demands of the individuals who had a draw upon her [George included] – yet she knew her direction and she wasn't about to be diverted from it."

Ironically, while George was less than forthcoming about Ellie's role, at least two gallery artists told me that their impression of George was that he was a supportive husband who knew absolutely nothing about art. Phyllis Diebenkorn, in a recent interview, commented – after reading a draft of my essay – that she was stunned that George was involved, in any way, with the collection or the gallery; she remembered him only as a jovial host who mixed a mean drink. While George may not have interacted with some of the gallery artists, he did befriend a number of the first-generation Abstract Expressionists, including Franz Kline, de Kooning, Tworkov, and others. And Christie Dennis tells of the time that the avant garde composers Morton Feldman and John Cage came to the Poindexter home for drinks, and George slyly served them empty martini glasses "complete with olive," her father's response to Cage's piece, *Six Minutes of Silence.*

Clearly, together, George and Elinor Poindexter made a great team, each bringing a distinct sensibility to their joint collection. Without George's passionate commitment to his Montana roots and without Ellie's broad and deep engagement with the art of her time (George was not as comfortable with Post Painterly Abstraction as Ellie was, for example, despite the movement's championing by his friend Clem Greenberg), the two Poindexter collections in Montana would neither exist nor be so richly diverse.

As a poet, I find myself delighted by the connections surrounding another player in the Poindexter Gallery story, Hal Fondren, the gallery's longtime assistant director. I had long been intrigued by the fact that New York School poet and Museum of Modern Art curator Frank O'Hara wrote the foreword to the first Poindexter Collection catalog, published in 1965 for a show at the brand-new Yellowstone Art Center. As I dug into the Poindexter Gallery story and read widely about the scene, I discovered, in a biography of O'Hara, that a certain Harold "Hal" Fondren had been his roommate at Harvard and that the two young literary lions had shared an apartment when they first moved to New York in the late 1940s. At about the time they moved to the city, O'Hara wrote in a poem he titled, "A Note to Hal Fondren," an expression of confidence that the two friends would make a difference in the art of their time:

> Our responsibility
> is continuous. And painful. But it lingers
>
> just above us and scents everything
> like the spoor of a brave animal. We see
> the land and its art without being prodigal
> and are ourselves its necessity and flower.

O'Hara and Fondren remained friends until O'Hara's untimely death in 1966, and it seems safe to assume that the O'Hara-Fondren connection had prompted the Poindexters to choose O'Hara as the introducer of their collection to the people of Montana (though George had initially wanted another New York School poet, Barbara Guest, to write the foreword).

When I spoke to Hal Fondren's brother Darl (Hal died in the late 1990s), Darl graciously sent me copies of the scant papers remaining at his brother's death. Among them were many letters from expatriated Abstract Expressionist painter Joan Mitchell, who was among Hal's best friends and whom he had helped to discover in the early 50s, and a 1958 letter from O'Hara together with the typescripts of two poems O'Hara had written during a stay at Hal's Fire Island Pines summer house. One of the poems was O'Hara's much anthologized poem "A True Account of Talking to the Sun at Fire Island," in which he writes, "Sorry, Sun, I stayed/up late last night talking to Hal." O'Hara's letter captures the flavor of the two men's friendship. O'Hara proposes:

> Maybe we should start a gallery together, what do you think? what with our fierce dominating-male type personalities and our exquisite taste I don't see how we would fail to lose quite a bit of money for some nice backer, and a lot of our favorite artists would flock to us, if only because we'd be a new gallery to flock to. . . . we might be able to have quite a snappy little outfit, don't you think?

Hal and Frank never opened a gallery together, but clearly, as Christie Dennis remembers, Hal was "responsible for bringing Frank, John Ashbery, occasionally Merce Cunningham [choreographer and partner of composer John Cage] and others in the arts into the [Poindexter] gallery." This relationship – and Poindexter Gallery artist Nell Blaine's deep involvement with John Ashbery and other poets, both as collaborator and friend – offers some insight into the rich cross-fertilization among the arts in New York – and at the Poindexter Gallery – during the 1950s and 1960s.

A final note on Hal Fondren: Among his papers was an inventory of the paintings in his personal collection. Hal's collection included works by many of the Poindexter Gallery's artists, including Robert Natkin, Richard Diebenkorn, Milton Resnick, Nell Blaine, Jack Tworkov, and Mike Goldberg, but it also included works by Joan Mitchell, Cy Twombly, Grace Hartigan, Larry Rivers, and Elaine de Kooning. The inventory, organized by room, noted that even Hal's bathroom featured an acrobat by Georges Rouault. Sadly, as Donna Forbes and Gordon McConnell have testified, Hal did not care for or understand the Poindexters' focus on donating their collection to Montana, and his collection was sold at auction upon his death.

Bringing things back to Montana: When we think of the rise of modernism, of an avant garde art, we tend to think of an absolute rupture with the past, a clean break that leaves earlier artistic styles and notions in the proverbial dust. Recent thinking has it, however, that this rupture, this modernist purity, is simply not the case – and in fact obfuscates the more complex reality as new styles and philosophies emerge. Art historians John E. Bowlt and Olga Matich write, with regard to early twentieth-century Russian vanguardist art, "It is becoming increasingly clear that the avant garde did not suddenly 'arrive' . . . but maintained organic connections with the more remote and recent past and then nourished what came thereafter." In Montana, we talk about our own avant garde bursting upon the scene with the arrival at midcentury of modernist teachers in the state's colleges, artists like Bob and Gennie DeWeese, Frances Senska and Jessie Wilber, Isabelle Johnson, and Walter Hook and of lone ranger abstractionists like Bill Stockton of Grass Range and Helen McAuslin of Macleod. And often we hold up Charlie Russell, our own immensely popular "Cowboy Artist" as the exemplar of the past to be broken with.

In actual fact, the break with our western art past came gradually and never completely. And in the 1950s and early 60s, Montanans, because of the relative dearth of cultural resources, tended to see art as art, without intense rivalries among factions. Witness, for example, the Montana Institute of the Arts, which in those early days included hobbyists, western artists, and the early modernists. There was plenty of crossover between the two camps: For example, Terry

Melton, the first director of the Yellowstone Art Center who mounted the first show of Poindexter artists in Billings, went on to direct the C. M. Russell Gallery in Great Falls. In a recent letter, Melton recalls the first exhibition he curated at the Russell Museum. The show placed Russell's art in context, including both American and European works created during the cowboy artist's lifetime. "I wanted to do something other than wall-to-wall Russell," Melton writes.

> Among the pictures borrowed I selected the most homely Picasso available . . . and hung it right next to the most prime Russell in the show. On opening day an old cowboy with legs in parentheses stood in front of the Picasso and the Russell and then the Picasso (I was ten feet away) and he remarked. . . . "well, Charlie holds up with the best of them, don't he?" I knew we were up and running. But alas, the eclectic attitude did not hold.

Now, Charlie Russell was no eclectic himself, though he knew a lot more about painterly technique and the history of painting than he let on. He actively disliked modernism from the Impressionists on, and in 1914, while in London, he toured an exhibition of Futurist painting with one of the Italian artists. In a letter to a New York friend, Russell noted that the Futurist led him "to something in a frame that looked like an enlarged slice of spoilt summer sausig and said this is not disintegration of simultaneousness but dynamic dynamism. . . . Another he showed me as near as I could make from his talk represented the feeling of a bad stomach after a duck lunch an it mighty near turned mine."

Elsewhere he told a reporter, "I can see this show serving a real good purpose. I'd like to shut some of the old cowpunchers up in here when they're drunk and let 'em wake up with these things all round 'em. It'd cure them of drinking sure – if the shock didn't kill 'em." Russell's comments made good copy, and certainly an overt hostility towards modernism is alive and well in this state and elsewhere in the West. This past year, a vandal damaged two abstract paintings in the *New Montana Painting* show curated by Gordon McConnell at the Nicolaysen in Casper, Wyoming, and Montana state legislators recently derided the work of Rudy Autio, among others, saying their grandchildren could draw better.

But, in the early years, as modernists fought to gain a toehold in Montana, it was often the eclectics, arts supporters and collectors open to both the new and the old, who helped move things forward. Branson Stevenson, for example, was a founder of the Archie Bray Foundation in Helena, a hotbed of modernist innovation in the 50s, while also chairing the board of the young C. M. Russell Museum. Branson had his battles with the young Turks, Pete Voulkos and Rudy Autio, but he did not withdraw his support from the Bray. And in the Poindexter story, prominent Montana arts patrons Jean Baucus and Jeff and Joan Holter were among those most welcoming to the Poindexters and their challenging collection. The Holters would donate to the Montana Historical Society both Russell bronzes and suites of prints by Robert Rauschenberg and Roy Lichtenstein, and Joan Holter, whose grandfather, Dr. William Treacy, set a broken leg for Charlie Russell in the 1890s and let the artist recuperate in the family home, has been *the* key supporter of Helena's contemporary art museum, the eponymous Holter. By the late 1960s and certainly in subsequent decades, the divisions between modernists and anti-modernists have seemed to grow deeper and more bitter in Montana, neither side giving much ground. Perhaps in these pluralist days, it is time to look back to those models of eclecticism, from that bowlegged cowboy who appreciated both Russell and Picasso to the evenhanded and passionate individuals who nurtured our state's cultural institutions when they were young and fragile.

In conclusion, I'd like to honor one more hero in the Poindexter story. An eclectic in his own right, Michael Kennedy was the director of the Montana Historical Society whose "enthusiasm and conviction" had convinced George Poindexter to make his generous gift ("without his encouragement," wrote George, "the collection would probably have gone to Honolulu"). George also noted that "Mike Kennedy bit off more than he could chew" in accepting the collection, and of course, that's true. Critics outside the state have implied that Montana doesn't deserve these fabulous collections and can't adequately care for or exhibit them, and critics inside the state voice the opinion that these paintings with their "weird shapes and messy colors" don't belong here, are an affront to true western sensibilities. As you can imagine, it is my feeling that, if Mike Kennedy hadn't overreached, taking on those challenging works when his institution had little exhibition or storage space, a tiny staff, and a modest budget, we wouldn't be here today, celebrating the opening of this magnificent exhibition. And it is my hope that *The Most Difficult Journey: The Poindexter Collections of American Modernist Painting* will lay to rest, at long last, the criticisms from both sides of the debate.

George and Ellie Poindexter sought to affect Montana's cultural climate. Their collections have certainly done this, in ways both direct and subtle, and clearly this gift from a descendant of Montana pioneers has become an integral – and delightfully unexpected – piece of our cultural heritage. George once lamented, "We are better known for our brand [the Square and Compass] than for our art collection and I'm afraid that it will take Montana fifty years to appreciate it." As I conclude in my catalog essay: "Happily, the current exhibition, and the cultural climate that makes it possible, suggest that Montana's appreciation of George and Ellie's astonishing gifts is, at least a decade early, well underway."

I'd like to close with a quotation from the great modernist American poet William Carlos Williams. It is a statement that I think George and Elinor Poindexter would have heartily seconded:

"It's a strange thing about the 'new'. . . . At first it shocks, even repels, . . . but in a few days, or a month, or a year, we rush to it drooling at the mouth, as if it were a fruit, an apple in winter . . ."

The Miriam Sample Collection, 1985–2005

Originally published in *Drumlummon Views,* the Online Journal of Montana Arts & Culture, Fall 2006–Winter 2007. To view this essay, go to the Montana History Portal at www.mtmemory.org

The Miriam Sample Collection, 1985-2005
Miriam Sample & Gordon McConnell
Privately printed, 2005.
Approx. 600 pages (unpaginated).
Hardcover; not for sale.

This is a review of a book that you may well never hold in your hands – unless you happen to visit the library of one of Montana's leading contemporary art museums. Published in an extremely limited edition (rumor has it that there are ten copies), this massive volume, slightly larger than 8.5 x 11 inches, documents one of the most astonishing gifts to the cultural life of Montana.

In its pages Miriam Sample (1920–2008) of Billings offers a visual inventory of her art collection which, for the most part, resides in the storage areas or on the gallery walls of nine Montana cultural institutions, as well as at the Boise Art Museum, Boise, Idaho; the Portland (Oregon) Art Museum; and the Whitney Museum of Western Art in Cody, Wyoming. The nine Montana institutions, which hold the bulk of the collection, are the Archie Bray Foundation for the Ceramic Arts, Helena; Custer County Art Center, Miles City; Hockaday Center for the Arts, Kalispell; Holter Museum of Art, Helena; Missoula Art Museum; Paris Gibson Square Museum of Art, Great Falls; Rocky Mountain College, Billings; the Montana Museum of Art & Culture at the University of Montana–Missoula; and the Yellowstone Art Museum, Billings.

Although these museums have benefited mightily from Miriam Sample's generosity, it is important to point out that her stated intention has been – first and foremost – to aid Montana's contemporary artists, by buying their work outright. The fact that the museums and the viewing public can enjoy these gifts in perpetuity is strictly secondary. In instances like Miriam's purchase of (for the Yellowstone Art Museum) more than seventy works by Bill Stockton towards the end of Bill's life, her largess has made all the difference, in terms of an artist's financial security and the very tangible honoring of a Montana modernist master.

Nevertheless, Miriam's vision does include the preservation of works by Montana's leading modern and contemporary artists, and she writes in her introduction that the "loss of the Charles M. Russell 'Mint Collection' [to the Amon Carter Museum in Texas] demonstrates the need to retain major examples of contemporary work as a legacy for the state and region." This saga of preservation began in 1985 when Miriam teamed up with the curatorial staff of the Yellowstone Art Museum to create a Montana Collection. Using seed money from the Montana Cultural Trust, which Miriam matched, YAM began to build a truly significant regional collection not focused on the past, but on works being created in the present.

While YAM benefited most significantly from Miriam's determination to make a difference, she "began working with other museums to make sure that more and more works of art stayed in our region." While the more than 500 works by seventy-some artists illustrated – in full color – in this book include many by younger artists, much of her focus is on the paintings, drawings, multimedia works, and ceramic art of Montana's pioneering modernists, especially Bill Stockton, Bob and Gennie DeWeese, Henry Meloy, Rudy and Lela Autio, and Frances Senska. Besides donating works by these artists to the various museums, Miriam has supported major exhibitions by Lela Autio (Missoula Art Museum) and Frances Senska and Bob DeWeese (Holter Museum). Often these exhibitions then traveled to other Montana venues. As Miriam writes, "Collaboration can increase the importance of these collected works, deepening and broadening their impact."

The true range of the Miriam Sample Collection extends into the present, and includes important works by such younger (relatively speaking) contemporary artists of the region as sculptors Debbie Butterfield, John Buck, Patrick Zentz, Richard Swanson, James Reineking, Clarice Dreyer, and Brad Rude, ceramic artists Richard Notkin, Beth Lo, Tom Rippon, David Regan, and Akio Takamori, photographers Nina Alexander and David Hanson, and a host of painters and printmakers, among them Anne Appleby, Corky Claremont, Mary Ann Kelly, Theodore Waddell, Sheila Miles, Neil Parsons, Larry

Pirnie, Jerry Rankin, Harold Schlotzhauer, and Dennis Voss.

A motive, certainly, for all this collecting has been to inspire and challenge other collectors and to help to create, in Miriam's words, "a market for Montana's contemporary artists." As the state's various contemporary art auctions and the exhibition of the Missoula Art Museum's permanent collection at the recent grand opening of MAM's marvelously expanded facility (with many labels reading "Promised Gift") attest, both the contemporary art market and the generosity of Montana's collectors are on the upswing.

I know of no other patron, however, who has given more, made more of an impact on the visual artists and visual arts museums of Montana, than Miriam Sample. Curator and painter Gordon McConnell writes in his foreword to *The Miriam Sample Collection*, "Miriam Sample's collection is more than an aggregation of unrelated things. It has a shape and unifying vision, and it demonstrates a rare correspondence between a group of carefully chosen art works and a sophisticated collector."

The next time you visit your local museum, watch for exhibition labels that read "Gift of Miriam Sample." Each time you spot one, think of that single work multiplied 500 times. Perhaps this book is the only way to comprehend the true vastness of Miriam Sample's gift to the people of Montana. If you have an opportunity to look at a copy, seize the moment. You will be astounded, by the sheer scope of the collection and by this patron's vision, passion, and absolute generosity.

Note: The Yellowstone Art Museum mounted the exhibition, *Gifts to Montana: The Legacy of Miriam Sample,* July 1–October 15, 2008.

15 Ceramic Artists

Peace and Riot in a Gesture
Chou, Pang-Ling's Teapot Mutants

Originally published in *Hsiung Shih* magazine, Taipei, Taiwan,
Summer 1989.

The United States has long had a reputation as a place where artists can create unfettered by constricting traditions. And artists from all parts of the world have often traveled to the U.S. in search of a freedom they found elusive at home. Modern master Marcel Duchamp, who spent much of his life in New York because he found the traditions of his native France "indestructible" and overbearing, once spoke of the U.S. as "good terrain for new developments. There's more freedom here, less remnants of the past. . . . [Young artists] can skip all that tradition, more or less, and go more quickly to the real."

Of course, the reverse can be true. Many American artists have had to leave their homeland in order to tap nascent creative energies, discover the freedom within themselves. Witness the vivifying influence that years spent in tradition-laden Europe and Asia have had, for example, on the American writers Gertrude Stein, Ernest Hemingway, H.D. (Hilda Doolittle), Ezra Pound, Djuna Barnes, Gary Snyder, M.F.K. Fisher, Cid Corman, and Harry Mathews.

For Chou, Pang–ling, the brilliant young Chinese ceramic sculptor from Taiwan (Republic of China), the six years she has recently spent studying and working in the United States have indeed proved liberating. In fact, they have transformed her from a student of languages and literature to the emerging international artist she is today. Before coming to America, Chou had received a degree in English from Taipei's Tamkang University and spent a year in the English graduate program at National Taiwan University, but the scholarly life had left her unsatisfied, and she decided to try her luck at creative pursuits.

Always a "quiet loner, precociously eccentric, marching to a different drum," she knew that, somewhere deep within, she possessed an acute artistic sensitivity that needed only nurturing in order to flower. And so, in 1982, she embarked for the United States, hoping to find there a "broader view and creative approach."

Upon her arrival, Chou enrolled in a graduate program in

drama at the University of Georgia. Her plan was to become a play-wright, but she soon discovered that the creative side of the theater was too collaborative and social for her solitary nature, and she turned to translating a contemporary Chinese play into English and studying dramatic history and theory. Still, she was possessed of an inner need to actively create, and in 1984, during her summer vacation home to Taiwan, she decided to explore clay as an expressive medium because, as she says, it seemed "relatively friendly."

She sought out Fong Sheng–kuang, the iconoclastic Taiwanese ceramist whose efforts to "stay free from commercialism and mindless conventions" matched her intentions precisely. During her two months under Fong's tutelage, Chou found clay to be a true friend. Allowed complete freedom to explore the medium as she desired, she quickly chose hand building for its "intrinsic, intimate quality" and concentrated her efforts on form and content rather than technique.

When she returned to Georgia that fall, she continued to work on her thesis in drama, but at the same time, she began taking courses in the University of Georgia's ceramics program. Studying with ceramists Andy Nasisse and Ron Myers (who again offered her total freedom to follow her own path), Chou encountered a "new aesthetic, a new immediacy and energy that stretched what clay could do."

She soon found herself "hopelessly attracted to the serene intimacy, spontaneity and subtle surface effects" of the ancient Japanese raku process, and she gave free rein to her life-long fascination with found objects, especially those made of metal. As a child, Chou had spent many happy hours in her father's hardware store in Changhwa (a city in central Taiwan), surrounded and somehow comforted by thousands of metal things: nails, screws, nuts, bolts, locks, blow torches, wheels, bearings, vices, wrenches, motors, and pumps in infinite varieties.

Whatever the origin of her tender regard for these artifacts of our industrial world, she quickly began incorporating them – as integral elements – into her ceramic pieces, thereby establishing a dynamic tension between her serene raku surfaces and the jagged, bristling energies of her metallic finds. Chou's joining of metal and clay, however, does not simply set up an opposition between a "bad" desacralized Western industrial urbanism and the "good" ancient spiritual traditions of a nature-loving East. Her relationship with found objects is too complex, and personal, for that.

She says, "People don't look at these things anymore or think or care about them. By using them in my work, I make them visible again, allow them a kind of afterlife." Sometimes she likes to take the objects' point of view. "Just when they've given up hope, I surprise them by picking them up and giving them a second chance, a new position in life." This desire to redeem the objects she finds along country roads, at abandoned brickyards, or in recycling centers lends to Chou's project a spiritual, and even political, dimension.

She might agree with Wassily Kandinsky when he writes that "even dead matter is living spirit. . . . Not only the stars, moon, wood, flowers . . . but also a cigarette butt lying in the ash tray, a patient white trouser button looking up from a puddle in the street. . . ." And the American poet Jackson Mac Low speaks to shared concerns when he notes, regarding the found materials in Kurt Schwitters' collages, "by distancing the objects of everyday experience [Schwitters] allows [the viewer] to see them in a strange context and from a new angle, so that whatever has been taken for granted may begin to be questioned and eventually illumined by critical reflection."

With very little training, Chou seemed to know precisely what her sculptures required, and she eschewed everything else as superfluous. She worked intuitively, always attentive to an "inner watching." Coiling, pinching, and beating the porous raku clay body, she improvised the haunting, often humorous forms she began to call, by turns, her "teapot mutants," her "clay people," her "vessel paradoxes."

She pierced her abstracted "teapot" shapes with the metal objects she had collected and impressed into the still-soft clay "calligraphic lines and textures, cryptic images/ numbers or even popmass-banal phrases." With an "indispensable" paring knife, she incised the clay surface, conjuring up further textures, images, patterns. And she added "little clay bits" to the found objects, subtly completing the connections between metal and clay. Her metaphysical, resolutely non-utilitarian teapots – "loaded with metal castoffs, sealed up, denied any working spout, lid or handle and only given abstract formal suggestions of these elements" – seemed to take on a life of their own.

When Chou fires her "teapots" (in a raku kiln, at around 1700 degrees Fahrenheit), her affectionate propensity to anthropomorphize her works, to see them as "people," again comes to the fore. "I like to think about the firing from their perspective," she says. "I imagine it comes as a big surprise; suddenly they're in the hot, hot kiln, and they're wondering, 'What's this we've gotten ourselves into?'"

Chou is fascinated too by the transformations the firing process induces. "The clay," she says, "once so soft and malleable, turns hard, and the strong metal objects grow suddenly fragile; they flake, change their colors; sometimes I'm not sure if they'll even survive. It seems a wondrous marriage: together, the clay and metal go through 'labors and tortures,' thick and thin, hot and cold."

Hardness/softness; strength/fragility; tenderness/cruelty: the notion of paradox plays a central role in Chou's work, and her completed "vessel paradoxes" can be seen as emblems for our modern world, where cultures collide, conflicting values jostle, and sharply contrasting emotional states struggle for precedence. In her work, Orient meets Occident, the secular and the spiritual join hands, and joy cohabits with anguish.

It is Chou's singular gift, notes Hiromi Itabashi, Director of Tokyo's Atelier Hikosen, that she can successfully create, in her small, intimate forms, a space that somehow contains both tension and "a fresh sense of comfort." Paradox often calls forth laughter, and in Chou's "mutants," with their wildly gesticulating metal appendages juxtaposed to tranquil raku surfaces, humor is always an essential element. Chou sees each work as a "light parody" of an "often preposterous world," a "new revelation in which secret, humorous laws of art prevail though nearby lurks an indifferent, wasteful reality." This insistence on the life-affirming properties of humor recalls Marcel Duchamp's wry insight: "when the serious is tinted with humor it makes a nicer color."

As Chou continued her ceramic explorations at the University of Georgia (she officially entered the university's graduate program in ceramics in 1985, having received her M.A. in drama that same year), she found that her "teapot mutants" needed, even demanded, names, titles, captions. And she foraged, as she had for her metal objects, for verbal phrases that captured – allusively, humorously, mysteriously – the visual richness of her clay-and-metal creations. Aided by her sensitivity to literature and languages and trusting to her intuition, she found her titles everywhere: in the magazines, novels, and collections of poems and plays she consumed voraciously; on billboards and road signs; in casual conversations and the lyrics of popular songs.

With her sculptures already a kind of visual poetry, the titles she chose – *Eyes Blinded by 3 Poisons, From Directed Wind-Flow and Golden Wishes, Little Prayer Contemplating Humane Trapping Methods, Hands Tied and Twisted in a System of Faith,* and *Peace and Riot in a Gesture* – served to heighten the poetic charge and, in fact, became inextricable elements of the works they named.

Language, specifically the Chinese characters, also informed and inspired Chou's work in quite another way. She found in the intricate Chinese characters, "highly hieroglyphic in origin and structurally rich," a model for the kind of dynamic verbal/visual expressiveness she sought in her "vessel paradoxes." During her years in Georgia, she maintained her connection to that original inspiration by teaching Chinese calligraphy to American students, and today, she continues, with ink and brush, to "explore" in a carefree way the characters that, in her early years, had endowed her with a "most indispensable aesthetic enlightenment."

By 1987, when Chou received her Master of Fine Arts in ceramics, graduating with distinction, she had, a scant three years after her first introduction to clay, achieved a remarkable artistic maturity in her chosen medium. Public recognition of that maturity soon followed. Her "teapot mutants" began to be shown in American galleries; one of her works received a medal award in the Metro Art International Competition of the Scarsdale (New York) Art Society; and she was awarded a residency in the Arts/Industry Program at the prestigious John Michael Kohler Arts Center in Sheboygan, Wisconsin.

After her four months at the Kohler Arts Center (where she "wrote plays in clay," creating two series of works based on her fascination with the theater), Chou received another signal honor. She was accepted as an artist-in-residence at the Archie Bray Foundation in Helena, Montana, one of America's oldest and most vital independent centers for the ceramic arts. Founded and run by practicing ceramists, the Bray Foundation offers a relaxed, pressure-free atmosphere in which artists can concentrate exclusively on their work.

There, surrounded by fellow potters and makers of ceramic

sculpture from Thailand, Japan, Canada, Finland, and the United States, Chou returned to her " vessel paradoxes," spending the summer, autumn, and winter months of 1988 creating "still more improvised variations" on her favored theme. Chou's stay at the Bray Foundation proved stimulating and highly productive, the capstone of her American experience. Working in her cluttered studio during the quiet, solitary hours between dusk and dawn, she brought her teapots to an ever-greater maturity.

Throughout 1988, public recognition of Chou's work continued to grow. Her "vessel paradoxes" and the theatrical pieces she had produced at the Kohler Arts Center appeared in three one-person shows and in group exhibitions in Montana, Georgia, Illinois, Kansas, Missouri, Tennessee, California, and New York. And her "clay people" won several awards, including a medal in New York's "I.a.C.: International Art Competition" and first place (professional division) in the "Emerald City Classic: International Art Competition" in Wichita, Kansas.

Finally, in early 1989, Chou, Pang-ling brought her American odyssey to an end, returning to Taiwan. In May 1989, however, she will leave her homeland once again, this time for a visit to Japan where she will attend the opening of an exhibition of her work at Tokyo's Masuda Studio. She will also study the raku process in the land of its origin and may opt for a longer stay.

About her desire to learn from other cultures, she says, "I am not specifically a Chinese/Taiwanese artist. At best, my work should be international in spirit. To speak to all human beings is more what I wish." It is this broad humanity which gives Chou's "clay people" their power and resonance. Through their very complexity, their crude sophistication, their tonic humor, and their ability to countenance the extremes of the human condition, they sing for all of us an untranslatable, but universal song. And as the Argentine poet Roberto Juarroz has written: "Everyone needs one/ untranslatable song."

Note: All quotations, unless otherwise attributed, are from interviews conducted by the author with Chou, Pang-ling, Helena, Montana, Winter 1988, or from Chou's MFA thesis, "a thousand hamlets, all lear: Vessel Paradoxes," Department of Art, University of Georgia, Athens, Georgia, 1987.

Rudy Autio
Coming Home to the Figure

Originally published in Liz Gans, Marcia Eidel, & Rick Newby, *Rudy Autio: The Infinite Figure* (Helena: Holter Museum of Art, 2006). See also *Drumlummon Views,* the Online Journal of Montana Arts & Culture, Vol. II, No. 1 (2008). To view this essay, go to the Montana History Portal at www.mtmemory.org

I. The Journey

> *Figures placed to complement each other in gesture like complementary colors.*
>
> – Henry Meloy[1]

Rudy Autio is celebrated for many things: As seminal force in the launching of a modern ceramic tradition that has successfully blurred, even erased, the line between craft and fine art. As founding artist (with Peter Voulkos) of the Archie Bray Foundation for the Ceramic Arts, one of the great centers for ceramic creativity in the world. As creator of significant works of public art in Montana and beyond. And as an influential teacher whose students have carried the torch of ceramic modernism throughout the United States.[2]

These accomplishments, important as they are, often overshadow Rudy's central achievement of the past twenty-five years: the making of large stoneware (and sometimes porcelain) vessels upon which he paints lovely and colorful dreamscapes where women cavort and horses gambol within an impossible, joyous space.

These works of Rudy's maturity, as Montana State University art historian Harvey Hamburgh has written, are "metaphors for elusive happiness. They belong to the realm of the classical, in the sense

---

1 Henry Meloy, *Notes* (Helena, MT: Henry Meloy Educational Trust, n.d.), 8.

2 For more on Rudy Autio's role in the founding of the Archie Bray Foundation, see Rick Newby and Chere Jiusto, "'A Beautiful Spirit': Origins of the Archie Bray Foundation for the Ceramic Arts," and Patricia Failing, "The Archie Bray Foundation: A Legacy Reframed," in *A Ceramic Continuum: Fifty Years of the Archie Bray Influence* (Seattle/Helena, MT: University of Washington Press/Holter Museum of Art, 2001). For more on Rudy's career, see Matthew Kangas, "Rudy Autio," in *Autio: A Retrospective* (Missoula, MT: University of Montana, School of Fine Arts, 1983), and Lela Autio and Lar Autio, compilers, *Rudy Autio: Work 1983–1996* (Missoula, MT: White Swan Press, 1996). See also, for the fullest biography of Rudy to date, Louanna M. Lackey, *Rudy Autio* (Westerville, OH: American Ceramic Society, 2002).

that their easy, seemingly endless linear movements trace an un-complicated world of pleasure that is beyond our grasp, and perhaps exists only in imagination and art." Another Montana art historian, Hipólito Rafael Chacón, seconds this assessment, adding that Rudy's "figures probe the complex relationship between an Arcadian vision of the celebration of sensual beauty and an almost baroque sadness about the transience of life."[3]

The son of Finnish immigrants who settled in the mining me-tropolis of Butte, Montana, Rudy Autio did not come easily to this bittersweet vision. It was only after a series of explorations, encoun-ters, and detours that he found the exact melding of material and im-agery "where I'm at home."[4] Rudy first began to find creative "home" in the late 1970s, as he turned away from the Abstract Expressionist pots he'd been making (he notes that he "never felt that I quite had a handle" on Abstract Expressionism[5]) and the large-scale bronze, con-crete, and steel sculptures to which he had never fully lent his heart.

Rudy had discovered clay under the tutelage of Frances Senska during his undergraduate studies at Montana State College, Bozeman, immediately following World War II. And of course, the encounter with Archie Bray and his fledgling foundation had been central to Rudy's development as a ceramist, especially the early workshops by such international figures as the British potter and thinker Bernard Leach; the Japanese master potter Shoji Hamada; the scholar of Japanese folk art, Soetsu Yanagi; and the Bauhaus-trained potter Marguerite Wildenhain. Rudy meanwhile studied sculpture during graduate school at Washington State University, Pullman, where he worked in many different media (wood, stone, aluminum, steel) and emulated artists like Italian modernist Marino Marini and Mexican muralist Diego Rivera.

After receiving his Master of Fine Arts, Rudy returned to the

---

3   Harvey Hamburgh, *The Poetic Vision: Visual Forms in Five Montana Artists* (Bozeman, MT: The Haynes Fine Arts Gallery, Montana State University, 1995), 6; Hipólito Rafael Chacón, untitled essay in *Rudy Autio: Work 1983–1996*, 53.

4   All quotations by Rudy Autio, unless otherwise noted, are drawn from an interview with the author, April 7, 2006, Missoula, MT.

5   Rudy Autio, interview by LaMar Harrington, October 10 and 12, 1983, Missoula, MT, and Seattle, WA, Oral History Collection, Archives of American Art, Smithsonian Institution, Washington, D.C (hereafter OHC, AAA); see www.aaa.si.edu/collections/oralhistories/tran-scripts/autio83.htm.

Bray (as it became affectionately known) and went to work full-time for the foundation and adjoining brickyard. As an aspiring sculptor, Rudy was not interested in making conventional pots; in fact, he yearned to work with "serious" materials like bronze and steel. Change was in the air, and when Pete Voulkos returned from a visit to Black Mountain College in the summer of 1953, he introduced Rudy to the Abstract Expressionist ethos and energies he had encountered at the avant-garde institution hidden away in the hills of North Carolina.

Soon the two young mavericks "started to do wild sculpture in clay,"[6] thereby launching in Montana a revolution that would forever alter the character of American – and world – ceramics. Simultaneously Rudy was designing and creating large-scale carved-brick murals for clients of Archie Bray's brickyard; almost all of these murals were figurative, depicting Biblical scenes or Montana pioneer life – depending on whether they were for churches in Great Falls and Anaconda, or for secular institutions like banks and schools.

After Rudy left the Bray for a teaching job in the art department at the University of Montana, he alternated between crafting his Abstract Expressionist vessels and fulfilling various commissions for public art, ranging from stained glass windows to tile murals, monumental bronzes to Cor-Ten and stainless-steel abstractions. Despite his evident success, he felt that something was missing. The metal sculptures, he told his biographer Luanna Lackey, were "a hell of a lot of work, and I found [that] something I had wanted to do all my life really wasn't that interesting. By now I recognized the beauty of clay."[7]

At the same time, Rudy found himself weary of abstraction. He'd always been "pretty good at drawing the figure," even as a boy, and he finally asked himself, "Why abandon the figure?" He thought back to his early encounter with Montana (and New York) artist Henry Meloy, who had painted countless studies of nude models and had decorated the pots of his brother, Peter Meloy (a co-founder of the Bray), with marvelous horses based upon T'ang Dynasty models. Rudy thought, too, of his own earlier figurative murals. Even though

---

6   Autio, interview by LaMar Harrington, OHC, AAA.

7   Lackey, *Rudy Autio*, 76.

they were works for hire, he had found working on them, in some way, deeply satisfying. Now, weary of the "same-old, same-old," he was ready to generate figures of his own choosing. He "toyed" for a moment with the idea of becoming a painter, but quickly realized that "it's just not the same" – he needed that third dimension, and the materiality of clay, to realize his vision.

One day in the late 1970s, while teaching a workshop in Apple Valley, California, Rudy "hand-slabbed" a vessel and, while constructing it, began talking to his students about working with the figure. A woman in the audience challenged him, "Why don't you do a figure?" That "scared me to death," Rudy recalls. "Here's this audience watching me. Did I still know how to do a figure on a piece?" He studied the slabs he'd assembled into a vessel and told the participants, "'Well, I can see a head here – maybe I can move the body this way, and have it envelop and go around. . . .'" He admits, "It turned out pretty good. . . . I started to gouge it with my fingers, and reinforce it with trowel lines . . . painted some black line and filled the lines with different colors. . . . It had an energy that really intrigued me."

The Apple Valley workshop – a genuine epiphany – helped to launch what Rudy now calls a "major move" in his evolution. And just a few years later, a reinvigorated Rudy Autio had been discovered. His figural vessels drew increasing critical attention, and galleries in Chicago, New York, and San Francisco were clamoring for the new work. In 1981, he enjoyed another encounter that further cemented his commitment to the new approach. He was contemplating retirement from The University of Montana, and he applied for a National Endowment for the Arts fellowship, in order to travel to Finland. His stay in Helsinki, working at the Arabia Porcelain Factory, was revelatory. Not only was he able to work without interruption after all those years of teaching, but he also had access to new materials (including a lovely Finnish porcelain and commercial glazes of dazzling hues) and he was treated "like a king." At the end of his stay, the factory remodeled its salesroom into a swank gallery appropriate for the Finnish American's farewell exhibition, and he was fêted by fellow artists, collectors, and critics. Rudy Autio had truly come home: to his ancestral homeland, to a passionate investigation of the figure, and to a sense of himself as a painter whose canvases happened to be massively voluptuous stoneware forms that are themselves, as Rafael Chacón has written, "integral sculptural objects. . . . as dynamic as the rich paintings that cover their surfaces."[8]

II. Models and Masters

Lines in the figure are directions to infinity.
— Henry Meloy[9]

It is a commonplace to call Rudy Autio the "Matisse of ceramics," and certainly Rudy has drawn inspiration from the French master. Early in his career, he found both Pablo Picasso and Henri Matisse worthy models, especially for their energy and mastery of line – but ultimately, he preferred Matisse because his paintings contained "a kind of tenderness" that Picasso's lacked. A later encounter with *The Dance (I)*, 1909, at the Museum of Modern Art, New York, cemented Rudy's sense that Matisse was an ideal model for the kind of work he was eager to pursue. He recalls, "I said, 'My god! This guy was doing what I'd like to do now!' . . . the way he invented that line and made it work and work as painting, but also describing the figure. It was just very canny."[10]

Matisse – and Rudy's fellow Montanan Henry Meloy – were not the only models for Rudy's newfound devotion to the figure. He discovered affinities with the simplifications of Egyptian art, with the complex illuminated letters in medieval manuscripts, with Marc Chagall's magically floating figures, and with the woodcuts of modern Japanese printmaker Shiko Munakata. Looking at Munakata's prints, which blend Japanese woodblock print traditions with Western modernist freedoms, helped Rudy resolve thorny compositional issues. In Rudy's view, Munakata "was just as interesting as Matisse," and he admired in Munakata's works "a certain kind of traditional elegance and a formal way of solving figure description . . . a very lyrical kind of line."[11]

He found the same elegance, simplicity, and lyricism in the decorations on Greek black figure vases. Here was an ancient ceramic

---

8   Chacón, in *Rudy Autio: Work 1983–1996*, 50.

9   Meloy, *Notes*, 9.

10   Autio, interview by LaMar Harrington, OHC, AAA.

11   Ibid.

tradition that spoke directly to his enterprise. He has said, "Those lines on those figures are done with such an assurance. . . . They would take a brush, very fine line, and you could see where they started up here at the arm and came down. . . . Came down and described fingers and hands and arms, as it related to the whole." Rudy noted, "I'm sure that the Greek potters, when they were making their pots too, wondered how's this side going to fit with what [they did] on the other side. . . . . They tried to keep a union of things going," just as he wanted to "have these forms relate to parts of figures as they round the pot and [create] a new configuration of shape relationships."[12]

More and more Rudy found himself drawn to older traditions, not just for technical reasons, but in terms of feeling and meaning. He recalls a visit to the National Gallery in Washington, DC, where he saw a "choice" show of Impressionist painters; he then proceeded downstairs, where he encountered an installation of new American art – "Franz Kline and others." His response was that the brash Americans "weren't any kind of match for the Impressionists – they were so ego-centered." He speaks critically of "so much jazz and pizzazz" in contemporary art and admits that he prefers the "calmer side of hard studious art [of earlier centuries]. It was really meaningful – we've lost a lot of that. . . . Maybe it's an extension of violence. We have to have everything *now,* it has to be different, it has to be original, it has to be novel. . . . I admire the old work much more – so much more solid. A place I'd rather be."

Just as he responded more to the tenderness of Matisse than to the sheer force of Picasso, this ceramic revolutionary of the 1950s today finds himself willing to risk "a little sentimentality" and to embrace beauty (for decades a forbidden notion in contemporary art) rather than contribute to the "jazz and pizzazz" – and what he sees as the deficit of meaning – in much twenty-first-century art and life.

III. The Power of Place

> *Man is one of two things: either the hero or the vic-*
> *tim of the accident of his heritage and environment.*
> *– Henry Meloy*[13]

---

12   Ibid.

13   Meloy, *Notes,* 8.

Rudy Autio is truly an international artist, revered as much in Finland and Japan as he is in the United States. At the same time, a universal art often emerges out of the particulars of the local. Rudy's colleague at the University of Montana, painter and printmaker James Todd, has written that we cannot fully understand Rudy's work if we ignore his origins in Butte. A western mining metropolis second to none, Butte was, in Rudy's words:

> a very interesting busy, bustling place. . . . dense with humanity. . . . sort of an oasis between Minneapolis and the Coast; it was the big city! With opera, acting companies, the arts, boxing matches. . . . there were the Italians and the Yugoslavians and the Finlanders and the Jewish people and the Cornishmen, and all kinds of ethnic groups that maintained their own cultural identities in their own little colonies around the city.
>
> [A]ll of the company heads – the ACM [Anaconda Copper Mining Company] heads – were living in the same community, practically next door to the miners. . . . So, they didn't live in New York and clip coupons, but they lived right in the city, in their splendid houses, with servants and everything like that. But the miners were just down the block, a few houses down. It was this kind of mix that made Butte interesting. . . . [M]y background is so entirely unrural that you can't believe it. I never went out riding horses, or farming. . . . city life is what I knew and kind of grew up in – tenements, housing tenements, one right next to another, three- or four-story tenements. No yards, no lawns. It was like living in Brooklyn![14]

Todd notes, "[H]ow appropriate it seems that the claymaker Rudy Autio came from this city where the materials of earth determine the destiny of its citizens" and he adds that, because of this dependency, Butte's citizenry have developed "special characteristics of realism, optimism, fatalism, flexibility and simple dignity," all qualities that Rudy possesses.[15] But even more than that, it seems

---

14   Autio, interview by LaMar Harrington, OHC, AAA.

15   James Todd, "Rudy Autio Retrospective," in *Autio: A Retrospective*, 3.

that Butte's distinctive culture lent Rudy an openness to the broader world, a profound respect for other cultures, and the fondness of
an urbanite for the complex mixing of elements, whether of social
classes, ethnicities, or the rough and the refined (especially evident
in his work). Out of this colorful place, Rudy took inspiration and a
clear understanding that the world was never simple – only endlessly
fascinating.

IV. The Work

> *There could be movement in lines and in shapes*
> *& colors & values. . . . the idea being that move-*
> *ment & life are identical. . . . Life is the thing de-*
> *sired – the thing we wish to bring into being.*
> – Henry Meloy[16]

The grace and vivacity of Rudy Autio's painted figures and the energetic monumentality of his vessels produce a powerful and, at
times, uncanny tension. Rudy speaks of wanting to "make an agree-
able composition of form and surprise and color, dark and light, and
pattern."[17] He certainly achieves this with the vessels and plates and
paintings and prints in this exhibition. His sense of play and improvisation, his marvelous eye for what pleases, are wonderfully present
in each of these works, all created within the last twenty-five years.

But Rudy achieves much more than this. If we look closely at
these floating nudes and their attendant horses (and occasional other beasts), we see scenes that, as often as they suggest "an Arcadian
vision of the celebration of sensual beauty," call up darker themes,
darker tonalities – of melancholia alongside rapture, of unspoken
threats alongside delightful promises, of the inevitability of death
alongside the miracle of fertility. One has the sense that, despite the
gorgeousness of these leisurely and paradisiacal scenes, terror and
loss and sorrow are never far offstage. This is as it should be. This
tension, this sense of the complexity of existence, lends these works
their power to hold us; they possess the qualities of Eros which,
as Guy Davenport has written, is "about things spinning, moving,

---

16   Meloy, *Notes,* 1.

17   Autio, interview by LaMar Harrington, OHC, AAA.

fluttering . . . colliding frequencies of meaning which sometimes dance together . . . and sometimes remain opposed but joined." In Eros, Anne Carson has written, a "simultaneity of pleasure and pain is at issue"; we stagger "under the weight of Eros." In Rudy Autio's tumbling visions, his chases and escapades, we sense the unfolding of desire, in all its fierceness and its tenderness. Horses dance or bare their teeth, women avert their eyes, converse with skulls and doves.[18]

Whether Rudy refers in his titles to classical myths (*Astarte, Electra, Daedalus, Icarus*), to cultural and natural landscapes of Montana (*Magic Horses of Columbia Gardens, Heart Butte Pony, Lady at Kicking Horse Creek, Goodbye to the Girls of Galena Street*), or simply to places or themes, he aims to "evoke a kind of story." (For him, titling – which he sees as an "enriching process" – is collaborative, one that involves friends and family, especially his wife Lela Autio, an exceptional artist in her own right.) The poetry of these titles only serves to reinforce Rudy Autio's stature as a poet of the visible and the tactile, a visionary artist who has emerged out of the American West to bring us meaningful, tender, haunting works, works that speak to our desires and our fears.

---

18   Guy Davenport, "Eros the Bittersweet" [a review of *Eros the Bittersweet* (1986; 1998) by Anne Carson], *Grand Street* (Spring 1987), 185; Anne Carson, *Eros the Bittersweet* (1986; Dalkey Archive, 1998), 4.

To Stave Off Death
Akio Takamori's Life Studies

Originally published in *Ceramics: Art & Perception* (Sydney, Australia), Summer 1992.

The work of ceramic sculptor Akio Takamori is truly cross-cultural. A hybrid of influences and energies, it is impure and lively, touched by traditions but not bound to them, always erotic, sometimes violent, often filled with tenderness and longing.

Japanese by birth and an American resident by choice, Takamori is not willing, as purists demand of Japanese ceramists, to maintain "the grandeur of a traditional style."[1] Instead, having turned aside from the techniques and attitudes he learned during his apprenticeship at a traditional pottery in Fukuoka, Japan, he seeks – in a more Western sense – to express his own struggle with, and delight in, existence.

Official Japanese culture as manifested, for example, in the tea ceremony, with its values of harmony, reverence, purity, and tranquility, Takamori finds "too stoic." Instead, he is attracted to the art of Japanese peasants, describing it as "alive, vivid, straightforward, and with a positive sense of eroticism." He loves naive and folk art from many cultures; these often-anonymous artists, he says, make work that is "healthy, so positive, so powerful." It has a "different sophistication."[2]

During his years of study in the United States (1974 – 1978), at the Kansas City Art institute and the New York College of Ceramics at Alfred University, Takamori confronted another form of orthodoxy, that of the Western abstract tradition. He began with small porcelain figurines, "whimsical and erotic," but he felt pressure from peers and teachers to work bigger, looser, more abstractly, in the style of the day. In his own estimation, he did not find the freedom to do his first mature work until 1978 when he spent time at the Archie Bray Foundation, the renowned center for the ceramic arts situated on the outskirts of Helena, Montana.

---

1   Jean Tessier. "Ceramic Dream of Shigaraki." *Ceramics: Art & Perception*.6 (1991): 50.

2   All quotations from Akio Takamori, unless otherwise noted, are transcribed from interviews with the author, July 1991 and March 1992.

In his mature work, Takamori returned to the human figure; like the peasant and naive artists he admires, he depicted – directly, narratively, and with great sophistication – the most basic of experiences and emotions: birth, sexual desire and sexual union, familial love, ambivalence and anguish, joy and the sorrow that loss brings. And he immersed himself in those visual traditions that truly resonated for him, letting them nourish his work. He drew upon images from his own culture – funky and humorous fishermen's shrines, Shinto fertility shrines with their stone phalluses, *shunga* (the reclining or spring pictures of traditional Japanese erotica), and the popular woodblock prints of Shiko Munakata – and culled inspiration from Greek mythology, Chinese, French, and Spanish cave paintings, Persian miniatures, shamanistic carvings from Canada, Tantric watercolors, and the rich imagery of Christian Europe.

"Intervening in an interconnected world," writes American ethnographer James Clifford, "one is always, to varying degrees, inauthentic: caught between cultures, implicated in others."[3] Never at home, neither American nor Japanese, Akio Takamori is a true cosmopolitan, a citizen of the world, and most clearly himself, inauthentic or, more to the point, authentic in a new way, outside the continuity of a single culture or tradition. As Edward Said has written in trying to define and describe this new cosmopolitanism: "To do as others do, but somehow to stand apart. To tell your story in pieces, as it is."[4] In an essay published in 1987, Takamori expressed his predicament succinctly: "I am fortunate to be an artist who is familiar with both Eastern and Western artistic and philosophical traditions. My art is an attempt to integrate the two, to explore what is best and significant in how these traditions view life, death, and reality."[5]

Takamori is a master draughtsman, and he papers the walls of his studio – situated on Vashon Island in Puget Sound off the Washington coast – with studies for the figures that populate his voluptuous slab-constructed stoneware vessels. His drawings form a kind of visual journal, and in fact, he has recently experimented – to his mind, largely unsuccessfully – with incorporating text into his

---

3   James Clifford. *The Predicament of Culture: Twentieth Century Ethnography, Literature, and Art.* Cambridge and London: Harvard University Press, 1980, 11.

4   Edward Said. *After the Last Sky: Palestinian Lives.* New York: Pantheon, 1986, 150.

5   Akio Takamori (with Peter Ferris). "The Figure Erotic." *Studio Potter.* December 1987: 12.

pieces. His drawings always tell a story, and in telling his story one piece at a time, as it is, Takamori confronts his obsessions, dramatizes his fears, shares his pleasures.

Critically, much has been made of the erotic in Takamori's work – articles about his oeuvre have titles such as "The Battleground of Eros" or "The Figure Erotic" – and it seems true that the encounter between men and women, as lovers and antagonists, mates and adversaries, is his most consistent theme. John Berger calls this kind of persistent obsession a "bias of the imagination" which determines the "gestures and perceptions of artists throughout a life's work, even when their conscious attention is elsewhere."[6]

Always fascinated by the sexual, Takamori grew up in Nobeoka, Japan, the son of a physician who ran a venereal disease clinic for prostitutes and had a library populated with books on Picasso and Brueghel as well as graphically illustrated medical texts, all of which fascinated the young Takamori. In one interview, he recalls discovering in his father's library a copy of *The Key* – one of Junichiro Tanizaki's complex and subtle tales of sexual obsession – illustrated with Shiko Munakata's candid woodblock prints. He took pleasure in one print in particular, that of a woman sprawled on a bed with her husband's eyeglasses casually perched on her bare belly. Takamori loved that image, its freedom from romanticism, its almost clumsy verisimilitude.[7]

"My own first erotic pieces were naive, too romantic," notes Takamori. Like many male artists, he idealized the female form, creating in his early work many images of what he calls "quiet joy." These reclining women are pure objects of male desire: desire for the infinite pleasures of fleshly communion, desire for simple touch or even a return to the womb.

As Takamori has matured, both as a man and an artist, his approach to the erotic has altered greatly. Today, instead of depicting the desire for fusion (his men and women no longer melt into each other), he creates figures whose faces are contorted with anger or express the pain of solitude. He speaks of the space between a man and a woman as a "kind of sacred vessel" and of "powerful differences"

---

6   John Berger. *Keeping a Rendezvous*. New York: Pantheon Books, 1991, 160.

7   See Susan Biskebom. "Akio Takamori." *Artists at Work: Twenty-Five Northwest Glassmakers. Ceramists and Jewelers*. Seattle: Alaska Northwest Books, 1990, 69.

between the sexes. As erotically charged as ever, his current works are closer to emotional reality, harder edged, no longer languorous fantasies.

In 1987, Takamori wrote, "I want viewers to see my figures as open, optimistic, sometimes humorous, expressions of themselves, and they should not be judged too seriously."[8] It has always been difficult to see Takamori's work, with its dualities and contradictions, as simply light-hearted; as early as 1983, Michael McTwigan saw something else in Takamori's figures: "This is seduction as threat, not as pleasure. By uniting, [Takamori's] couples risk losing more than they might gain."[9]

In more recent pieces, Takamori's vision continues to grow in complexity and richness and, if anything, it has taken on a darker tone. The story he tells through these new pieces is that of a more intransigent world, one not so easily grasped or rendered harmless. It is still beautiful, touched by joy and considerable humor, but the optimism is muted, and the issues are of an undeniable seriousness. "[Eros) is a tremendous force to live, to reproduce, and to stave off death," Takamori told follow ceramist, Andy Nasisse, in 1986,[10] but as he acknowledges in *Fallen Angel* (1991), it can also lead to the sorrow of AIDS.

Fallen Angel, a pair of vessels – one a man's bust, the second a man's torso from belly to mid-thigh – examines the modern plague from a unique perspective. Takamori's angel is human and vegetal at the same time, a great tree uprooted, blown over by coastal winds. Eyes downcast, already a part of the earth, his body entwined with dark leaves and chill stems, the angel – in his falling – is not alone: tiny heads inhabit the interior of his torso, populate his cranial cavity: grieving onlookers, loving witnesses, companions in death as well as life.

Another bust and torso, identical in form to *Fallen Angel,* tell a story of beginnings. Takamori's *Youth,* more brightly colored than his angel, is ripe with potentialities. Here, there is little cause for grief. A mother bird and her young fly through the sky-blue interior

---

8   Takamori (with Ferris). "The Figure Erotic," 12.

9   Michael McTwigan. "The Clay Figure." *Ceramic Echoes: Historical References in Contemporary Ceramics.* Kansas City, Missouri: The Nelson-Atkins Museum of Art, 1983, 97.

10   Andy Nasisse. "Battleground of Eros: Akio Takamori." *American Ceramics,* 1986: 32.

of the youth's bowed head, and a nest full of eggs resides inside his torso. His body interlaced by tendrils of a caressing vegetation, *Youth* radiates hope, vivid life, the circle begun again.

"To stave off death": birth and its dislocations are recurrent themes for Takamori, especially since the arrival of his son, Peter and, more recently, daughter Lena. In the face of these new beings, he finds himself continually adjusting and re-evaluating his beliefs and attitudes, gaining greater self-knowledge, not always painlessly. "As a man," he says, "you must locate yourself in the birth of a child. You don't have the instant love that mother and child share; you may feel alienation, even jealousy, and yet you must be supportive." In many of the darkly humorous works Takamori has created on this theme, the male figure watches over the mother and child, always separate, but attentive, envious of their intimacy, his luminous eyes alive with ambivalence: "jealousy, love, and mystery."[11]

Takamori's *Bust of Modern Man* is a wholly different being: an effort, says the sculptor, to express (and expunge) the guilt and rage he felt when he confronted the gulf between the romantic expectations of his youth and the realities of adulthood. With his fixed glare and the interior of his head splintering, as if his brain had just exploded, *Bust* embodies the berserker male, untouchable, inhumane, destructive to self and others: a frighteningly honest and purgative image.

Takamori notes that in his efforts to understand himself as a man, "I must really research women, my mother, my aunts." In watching his wife Vikki with their son Peter, Takamori found himself looking back to his relationship with his own mother. "All of us, men and women," he says, "first find ourselves in a female world, speaking a female language. It's only later that we males separate and enter the male culture of fathers, brothers, uncles." A recent piece entitled *Her Room* might be the result of this realization; inside a woman's head, Takamori has drawn a well-furnished room, and in that room, a na- ked man sits at a table, having returned, perhaps, to his first home.

Takamori's most recent works, those he showed in his February 1992 exhibition at the Garth Clark Gallery in Los Angeles, are each based on stories from Greek mythology: *Leda and the Swan,*

---

11   Nasisse. *American Ceramics*: 32.

Ulysses and Nausicaa, Eros and Psyche, Daphne, even a *Medea Vase.* Beautifully crafted, classically erotic, these works express a new calm, a new tenderness. Less intense and complex, more unconditionally loving, these new pieces may indicate that Takamori's more violent works of the past two years have resolved certain inner struggles. Since completing his Greek series, Takamori has allowed himself a fallow time, a time away from his studio and his work, a time for traveling and teaching workshops: further evidence that he is undergoing an inward shift, a sea change. No doubt, in the coming months, Akio Takamori will emerge revitalized from his time of quietude, producing new and ever more surprising expressions of his particular "bias of the imagination."

Out of the Box
The Graphic Art of Akio Takamori

A version of this article first appeared in *American Ceramics,*
New York, NY, Spring 2002.

Even if he had never set pen to paper or carving tool to wood, Akio Takamori could lay claim, with absolute justification, to the title "graphic artist." The Japanese-born ceramic sculptor, best known for his eroticized envelope vessels and his more recent explorations of memory in the form of two-thirds-lifesize figures, has always drawn on clay. Critics speak of his "fluid calligraphic brush," his "fresh vision and spontaneous brushwork," his "extraordinary graphic sense." However, apart from these drawings on clay, Takamori has brought forth a parallel body of graphic art, works on paper (including drawings, etchings, lithographs, wood engravings, and silkscreen prints) that play with, recast, and extend the themes, images, and obsessions evident in his ceramic work.

Like many artists who do not regularly work on paper, Takamori has created most of his prints at the invitation of printmaking studios, whether at the Sun Valley Center for the Arts, Lawrence Lithography Workshop, Anderson Ranch, or the Armstrong-Prior Workshop in Phoenix, Arizona. And with the help of the studios' master printers, Takamori has succeeded in elaborating a small but vivid and refreshingly candid body of images in intaglio and lithography. Recently, stimulated to address the challenges afforded by the various print media and the qualities of different papers – and eager to further extend his means of expression – Takamori has begun working "more proactively," in his words, seeking out opportunities to fashion engravings, etchings, and monoprints with master printers with whom he has previously worked, particularly John Armstrong at Armstrong-Prior.

Takamori has drawn since he was a child. His first drawings, he recalls, were of people and houses (domestic images very unlike the soldiers, tanks, and battleships his more militaristic brother liked to draw), and in his father's library, he first encountered the artists who would most profoundly influence his graphic style: Shiko Munakata and Pablo Picasso. While Picasso and, to a lesser extent,

Matisse, influenced him with their freedom and economy of line, it was the mixture of modernist sophistication, psychological acumen, and folklike innocence in Munakata's prints that touched Takamori most deeply. "I totally did not have eyes towards our own traditional art or *Ukiyo-e*," he recalls, but in Munakata's work, he found a Japaneseness that took into account the lessons of European modernism, a Japaneseness that did not "turn me off" with its refinement and rigid stylization. (The flatness, simplified line, and vibrant blocks of color in modernist painting come, in part, of course, from the Japanese woodblock prints that artists like Degas, Van Gogh, Toulouse-Lautrec, and Gauguin first saw – and were influenced by – in the nineteenth century, with the reopening of trade relations between Japan and the West. And Munakata, in turn, was deeply influenced, in the early twentieth century, by an encounter with a reproduction of Van Gogh's *Sunflowers*.)

Throughout his career, Takamori has been drawn to naive art, the folk arts of many cultures, and even the depictions, again first seen in his father's library, of Netherlandish peasant weddings and fairs, in the paintings of Pieter Bruegel the Elder. And he has always been interested, not in high art, but in "breaking out of the stylized, traditional line." He finds folk art "alive, vivid, straightforward, and with a positive sense of eroticism." A peculiarly Japanese expression of this folk freshness can be found in the *Otsu-e* prints (made with stencils and hand-decorated with brush and ink), produced for the tourist trade by anonymous artists in the town of Otsu. These bold prints depict wrestling gods, hilarious demons, playful monkeys, and boisterous folk heroes, and they often illustrate, with great good humor, moral lessons. They possess, as Takamori puts it, "a different sophistication."

Ironically, in order to enter a Japanese art school, Takamori had to study classical European drawing, in the most rigid academic style. He took private lessons, drawing with pencil "still lifes and plaster European figures." But by the time he had entered the first stage of his artistic maturity, during a residency at the Archie Bray Foundation in 1978 (just after receiving his MFA from Alfred University), he was drawing furiously in a style that combined the deft line of Picasso with the boldness and humor of the *Otsu-e* artists and the psychologically charged dynamism of Munakata. He lined his studio with images (on inexpensive paper) of embracing lovers, scenes from Buddhist tradition (Buddha's birth, the appearance of the goddess Kwannon to a man), bodies intertwined with (and metamorphosing into) trees and serpents and other human bodies, and erotic tableaux watched over by scores of tiny disembodied human heads, clearly sentient, amused and compassionate, but sometimes judging human folly with ruthless glee.

These drawings were not ends in themselves; they represented, in the most traditional sense, studies. "I draw to develop and prepare," says Takamori, and he notes that his drawing on the "clay surface has been my final work." And as part of his process, especially for his envelope vessels, he cut his drawings apart to use them as tracings, allowing him to transfer his images, exactly as he envisioned them, to the clay surface. With true modesty, he notes that only those "really interested in the artist" would want to see the drawings; "most people may rather skip that and see the final. . . ." Just in the past year Takamori has begun creating drawings that he sees as truly final in their own right; these images, in ink and gesso on Japanese paper, reflect a new thematic direction in his work, an effort to take into account the impact on Japanese culture, in very human terms, of the American occupation immediately following World War II. This is a theme he is also developing in his ceramic work, seen most recently at an exhibition of his figures – Japanese villagers interacting with American GIs – at the Frank Lloyd Gallery in Los Angeles.

Takamori has been making prints since 1982. In that year, the Sun Valley Center for the Arts invited him to create a suite of silkscreen prints that included *Male Dog* and *Female Dog,* a pair of mysterious half animal/half human figures, and since the late 1980s, he has worked regularly with master printers. Often, as in his sculptural work, his print imagery plays with issues of gender, race, sexuality, religion, and memory.

In the 1993 lithograph, *Fertile Tree,* a male and a female figure share the limbs of a tree, curved away from each other, scarcely touching, but each alert to the other's physical presence. In another lithograph, *Western Paradise* (1996), he conflates the Buddhist notion of a joyous heaven, watched over by Buddha himself and his bodhisattvas, with a more earthly vision of a guilt-free eroticism. The recumbent figure in this print seems female though, in Mahayana or Pure Land Buddhism, women cannot enter the Western Paradise until they attain a masculine state through rebirth.

Takamori's prints with religious themes often turn the expected on its head, bending gender, tracing the edges of the transgressive. In his *Annunciation* (1996), for example, a male figure, his erect penis seemingly holding up the world, is visited by an angel, bearing the impossible news that the man will soon give birth to the child of God. And in the monoprint *Saint* (1989), based on a painting by the self-destructive, Rimbaud-like Japanese artist Kaita Murayama, a haloed male figure urinates into a pond, while tiny human heads watch from the surrounding trees (and cascade down the stream of urine). Here, as in many of his works on clay, Takamori offers images that ask us to accept, even celebrate, the body and its functions – and he pokes gentle fun at the complexes we have about the bodily. "There's no reason to be shy or uptight about these things," says Takamori. "They're simply there."

A tribute to Picasso and his many graphic works on the same subject, Takamori's monoprint, *Artist and Muse* (1996), presents a delighted, relaxed artist contemplating a female figure who might be some voluptuous Neolithic fertility goddess. And in another telling monoprint, *Self-portrait with Icarus* (1996), Takamori's monumental head, with quizzical, worried expression, fills more than half the picture plane, while the tiny golden figure of daring (and foolish) Icarus tumbles out of the pitch-black sky. Is the artist, with his provocative images and highly charged innocence, tempting the gods?

Takamori has long been intrigued by chine collé, the process wherein a thin piece of Chinese rice paper is adhered, with glue, to a heavier sheet and then the pair of sheets are run through the press, creating a single sheet with distinctive colors and textural effects. The resulting hybrid paper, says Takamori, "is almost like a clay surface," and many of his wood engravings, monoprints, and lithographs feature chine collé, lending them richer, more integral color and texture than they might otherwise have had. And as he has grown more interested in the qualities of printmaking unique to the discipline, Takamori has begun to move away from the straightforward printing of images on a sheet of paper.

In 2000, with his most recent etchings and engravings created at Armstrong-Prior, Takamori has begun "moving outside the box."

In a series of three untitled engravings (with chine collé), he found himself inspired by a set of adult sex toys (made of paper) he had discovered in a Japanese bookstore. These simple paper cutouts of men with erect penises and naked (and anatomically correct) women led Takamori to create his own cutouts, not as directly sexual, but clearly erotic, which he then affixed (with a single dab of glue) to the surfaces of his prints. His male and female figures, crouching, their hands outstretched as if snared in the bonds of Eros, float in a gravity-free space, adrift on the currents of their own desire.

Another print Takamori made in 2000, the etching *Box,* plays with the notion of three dimensions without actually erupting off the surface of the paper. *Box* is a witty instruction manual that teaches the viewer to assemble a vividly colored box in which a series of human figures crouch, huddle, or crawl. At the same time, it suggests, with its clearly delineated structure and friendly arrows, a map out of the labyrinth, a way to rescue these abject captives from their pink and yellow prison of Eros.

In creating his ceramic sculptures, by melding three-dimensional form and the art of drawing (as Edward Lebow comments, "his forms are half drawn and half shaped"), Akio Takamori has proven himself a master graphic artist. But with his works on paper, he continues to add further dimensions to that mastery, revealing himself as an endlessly inventive, provocative, and ultimately wise commentator on the human condition. Junichiro Tanizaki once called Shiko Munakata, "an impertinent artist who gouges the universe." The same could be said of Akio Takamori.

Robert Harrison's Architecture of Space

Originally published in Glen R. Brown & Rick Newby, *Robert Harrison: The Architecture of Space* (Helena, MT: Drumlummon Institute/Holter Museum of Art, 2009). This essay draws upon four earlier articles on the work of Robert Harrison: "Robert Harrison: Shrines for Potters," published in *American Ceramics* (New York, NY), Autumn 1991; "Rooms within Rooms: The Installations of Robert Harrison, 1991–1992," first published in the catalog to the Robert Harrison exhibition, *Architecture without Walls,* University of South Australia Art Museum, September–October, 1992, and reprinted, in slightly different form, in *Ceramics: Art & Perception* (Sydney, Australia), Winter 1992–93; "Robert Harrison: Spirited Variations," published in *Ceramic Review* (London, United Kingdom), Spring 2000; and "Earthly Visions, Celestial Alignments," published in the catalog accompanying *Robert Harrison: A Mid-career Retrospective,* at the Jundt Art Museum, Gonzaga University, 2001.

Spirals and archways, chimneys and Xs carved in earth, still lifes and colonnades, profane icons and spiritual spaces: ceramic artist Robert Harrison of Helena, Montana, has created an impressive body of sculptural work spread over four continents. The range and depth of his accomplishment extends from site-specific sculptures to large-scale gallery installations to stand-alone wall pieces and screens.

Working with Clay (and Other Things)

Harrison began his career as a ceramic artist in the early 1970s under the tutelage of Robert Archambeau at the University of Manitoba. Initially attracted to the roughly elegant traditions of Japanese pottery as transmitted by his teacher, the Canadian-born Harrison found himself fascinated, too, by American and European painters and sculptors (Stella, Rauschenberg, Oldenberg), by Robert Smithson's heady theories and spiral jetties, and by the possibilities of postmodern architecture. As the years progressed, he was profoundly influenced, during European travels, by Neolithic standing stones and eloquent fragments of Roman temples, stadia, and aqueducts. The works of contemporary earth artists (Andy Goldsworthy, Nancy Holt, Richard Long) grew increasingly important to his approach, as did the eccentric structures built by Barcelona visionary Antonio

Gaudí. Harrison's eclectic tastes were to lead him far from his pottery roots, and halfway back again.

When he entered the University of Denver's graduate program in ceramics in 1979, Harrison was ready to step outside the tradition of vessel making and to begin to explore other possibilities in his ceramic work. Today, Harrison sees his move from pottery to sculpture as a natural evolution, but at the time, he recalls, it was difficult, even painful. "I've always loved clay as a material, and I love the traditional forms," he says. "When I first began making sculpture, especially when I incorporated non-ceramic objects, it felt like I was somehow betraying my family." His sense of loyalty, however, couldn't still his exploratory urge, and his artistic excursions have led him to use, besides raw clay and fired ceramic artifacts (manufactured bricks, shards from other artists' pots, commercial vases, teacups, and tiles), such disparate materials as galvanized culvert pipe, granite capitals from discarded columns (and other architectural fragments), red volcanic rock, wooden beams and poles, Styrofoam, concrete, and aluminum-wrapped television cable.

At the same time, Harrison retains his allegiance to ceramics (he is a past president of the board of directors for the Archie Bray Foundation for the Ceramic Arts, and past president of the board of the National Council on Education for the Ceramic Arts [NCECA]), and some of his most recent works are all clay, a return to roots, however temporary, that delights and surprises him.

Aligning the Stars

Harrison finds himself drawn to spiritually resonant sites and spaces, and his gallery installations echo and honor the cathedrals, ruins of Roman temples, and Celtic megaliths he visits during frequent European travels. His installations, which manipulate space in powerful ways, might be called the reliquaries of a private religion, and the relics they contain – despite their undeniably personal nature – somehow speak eloquently to many who visit them. Like a handful of other contemporary ceramic artists – interestingly, this group includes Louis Katz, Rebecca Hutchinson, Richard Swanson, and Richard Notkin, all of whom live at least part-time in Harrison's current hometown, Helena, Montana – Harrison has made the installation an integral part of his work. During the past thirty years, his installations have been featured at Alberta College of Art Gallery, Calgary; the Banff Centre School of Fine Arts, Alberta; Holter Museum of Art, Helena; the University of South Australia Art Museum, Adelaide; and Gonzaga University, Spokane, Washington.

Usually developed at the instigation of gallery directors, Harrison's installations – despite their obvious connection to his outdoor pieces – allow the sculptor to exercise a side of his nature impossible to fully indulge in those works of his situated out-of-doors. "When I'm working outside," notes Harrison, "nature always surprises – and delights – me, the effects of moisture and extremes of temperature on my materials, the look of the work depending upon the angle and intensity of the sunlight. Indoors, I get a different kind of pleasure; I can control all the elements, especially the lighting, and instill a sense of heightened drama, an almost magical or spiritual atmosphere."

Raised in a non-religious home, Harrison finds himself drawn to spiritually resonant sites and spaces. "I see my installations," says Harrison, "as sanctuaries. When you enter them, I want you to enter another dimension." Harrison's installations, especially those in recent years, imbue secular spaces with a sense of the sacred.

Always fascinated by architecture and strongly influenced by "the earth art and other large-scale work being done at the time," Harrison began to move away from traditional pottery during the last years of his schooling and created his first installation for his MFA exhibition at the University of Denver's School of Art Gallery in 1981.

This shift in his work, he says, was "startling" to himself and his potter colleagues. Until then, the only large-scale work he had done was an exercise in his first sculpture class. Using bricks, he built an eight-foot tall, circular, silo-like structure in which he lit a fire, "as if it were a kiln." It was, he recalls, "an eccentric structure that stood on its own," the first evidence of his transition from pot making to the creation of nonfunctional, but spiritually charged architectural works.

Harrison's MFA installation was also closely tied to the act of firing, and it introduced what has been a key image for Harrison throughout his career: the X or cross form. Small by the standards of his current work, eight to ten feet square, this first installation was

Japanese in feeling and drew its strength from the simplicity of its design. Set inside a square wooden frame, two to three feet in height, and surrounded by 500 pounds of loose sawdust, the exoskeleton of Harrison's hollow X was constructed of commercially made soft or insulating bricks. Harrison then filled the X-shaped chamber with bright yellow overlapping bags of "Cedar Heights Airfloated Clay, quality since 1924." "About clay, but abstracted," the MFA installation, notes Harrison, could be interpreted as a kiln, with the sawdust as a fuel source, ready for a "conceptual firing."

In 1982, Harrison was teaching ceramics at Gonzaga University, Spokane, Washington, and as an assistant professor and head of the ceramics program, he was granted a one-man show in the university's Ad Gallery. The installation he created for this exhibition was entitled *Four-X Transposed* and was based on a set of four silkscreen prints Harrison had just completed. With *Four-X Transposed,* moving away from works which simply referred to the processes of making ceramics, Harrison took on more ambitious themes. The original suite of prints, *Four-X,* introduced Harrison's concern with the struggle between nature and technology, placing loose, sumi-like Xs over highly mechanical grids. The installation that followed took up the same theme, reflecting Harrison's basic optimism that "nature is still able to override technology."

For the installation, he created an eight-foot square grid, again very mechanistic, out of extruded clay; oxidation fired, it had a flawless, neutral surface, "no variations or accidents allowed." Three feet above it, Harrison suspended by ropes a four-foot square clay X, also extruded; pit-fired, the X had a mottled black and white earthy surface, "very organic and natural," a handmade look in contrast to the machined surface of the grid. Here, for the first time, lighting played an important role in a Harrison work, allowing him to control precisely the shape and intensity of the shadow cast by the X.

Critic Lucy Lippard has noted that she finds it "interesting that an X across the earth has been a favorite motif for male earth artists," adding that, though these Xs can be perceived as "anti-ecological" and "domineering," "it is the attitude . . ., the artist's sensitivity . . . that determines the effect of the imagery." While Harrison himself has observed that "the X . . . always seemed masculine to me, very male. . . ." and a number of his outdoor Xs might be seen as aggressively male marks scarring the earth, his use of the X in *Four-X Transposed* seems profoundly life-affirming and "female," values he has attributed to images like the circle and the spiral, both of which appear often in his later work.

As a clear affirmation of the natural world (and as a personal icon), *Four-X Transposed* gave Harrison his first insight into the spiritual impact his work might have on others. Gonzaga University is a Jesuit institution, and Harrison found that many of his priestly fellow faculty members returned again and again to his installation as they might to a shrine. "They loved it," Harrison notes. "The cross, after all, is an X. It was so abstract and secular, not identifiably Christian, and yet they could identify with its spiritual qualities."

It was only with *Art/Architecture,* a 1992 one-person exhibition at the Holter Museum of Art in Helena, that Harrison broke through to a new and more refined understanding of the possibilities an installation offers, both in terms of controlling the viewer's experience of the gallery space and of giving up control, accepting the viewer as collaborator.

"Finally, it dawned on me," says Harrison, "that I could, through my orchestration of light and space, force viewers to see things in a certain way and, at the same time, encourage them to participate more fully, on a perceptual level, in the creation of this little world, or of many parallel worlds."

Harrison's first "room within a room," *Art/Architecture* consisted of two rows of columns marching down a ramp in the museum's Bair Gallery. At the head of the colonnade stood an arch formed of papier-maché-covered Styrofoam (colored by ceramic oxides, yet another tribute to Harrison's pottery roots) and set upon a pair of gleaming steel, gold-dusted columns. The piece culminated visually in an "earthnest" or altar of reddish volcanic rock topped with cast ceramic shells and bathed in light. Over the nest, Harrison had suspended a pair of wooden window frames that might have come from a cathedral, suggesting the presence of a wall, of a "transparent" room set within the gallery. Another, simpler frame – further substantiating the illusion of a room within a room – hung off to the side, lending a slight asymmetry, and its shadow, to the piece. On the walls on either side of the colonnade, Harrison affixed large images of works of art and architecture that had somehow inspired him, from

Warhol's *Marilyn* to a magnificent Iranian mosque (source for the papier-maché capitals on his columns). Viewers found themselves guided, by the lighting and Harrison's columns, down the ramp and through the archway, stopping perhaps to meditate at the "earthnest" and then moving on to the room's periphery to ponder the artist's favorite images.

Like Harrison's *A Potter's Shrine* at the Archie Bray Foundation, *Art/Architecture* was an ideal site for meditation or communion, more clearly a sanctuary or sanctified space (for a religion both comfortingly familiar and inextricably alien) than any of his earlier installations, and yet it invited widely varying interpretations. Was it the playhouse of a wise and eccentric child? A place for assignations, the passing of notes and furtive kisses? An educational display at a perverse county fair? A folly in a garden? Or a "reliquary not of saints' bones," as French theorist Roland Barthes has written, "but of [the artist's] pleasures"? The work's ambiguity, its "transparency," as Harrison likes to call it, cried out for analogies; as Barthes writes, "Metaphor is the only way of naming the unnamable."

Unnamable, transparent, playfully indifferent to the conventional – with its references to wide-ranging cultures and artistic traditions, its quirky, pastel colors, and offbeat materials (Styrofoam, steel culvert pipe, gold leaf) – *Art/Architecture* proved amenable to collaborations with other art forms, and during its tenure at the museum, it hosted a jazz concert and a poetry reading among its columns, lending a unique quality, congenial and spiritual, to the performances.

Less coherent as a unified image than his earlier works, more complex and susceptible to multiple interpretations, *Art/Architecture* was the first work in a series Harrison calls "Architecture without Walls," in which walls are sketched on the air, in a kind of architectural mime. The second is the piece he created at the University of South Australia Art Museum, where – he said immediately before departing for Australia and New Zealand in late July – he hoped to "redefine and refine my concepts, make use of new materials (preferably something I can't find anywhere else in the world), and improvise a distinctive space, something intimate, magical, and playful." With each new installation, Robert Harrison sows yet another of his small and sacred worlds: a fictive space that invites participation by all who cross its (imaginary) threshold, a refuge – not always comforting – from the world, large and profane, in which we reside each day.

Another example of Harrison's mastery of the installation was the centerpiece (and center point), *Celestial Alignments,* to his 2001 Gonzaga retrospective, which incorporated Harrison's usual mix of materials. Surrounded by four spiraling wooden columns and dramatically lit from above, the central "stack" – at nine and a half feet tall – stretched to the heavens. The stack, with its ziggurat crown of cut steel, was constructed of culvert pipe and enshrouded in galvanized wire fencing. The shroud, in turn, was wrapped with television cable sheathed in pliable aluminum and filled with multi-colored shards of locally manufactured tile, a tribute to ceramics and to hard-working western farmers who pile rocks in the corners of their stony fields.

To enter that sacred space, the viewer passed down a narrow corridor (birth canal, passageway to a burial chamber) and through *Celestial Archway,* a Styrofoam arch that alluded, in its decoration, to Van Gogh's *Starry Night* and, in its form, to the weightier, earthbound arches Harrison has erected across North America and in Australia, Europe, and China.

Conversing with a Site: Arches and Stacks

In 1980, while working at the Omaha Brickworks, Harrison created his first site-specific sculpture, carving an "X" into a clay hillside at the brickworks. He was fascinated by the notion that the Nebraska weather would be his collaborator, each storm subtly or violently altering his handiwork, but at the same time, he began to consider the possibility of constructing something more permanent, a shrine, an instant ruin, a provocative folly.

Another old brickyard would offer Harrison his first opportunity to leave just such a permanent mark. Between 1983 and 1985, Harrison spent his time working at the Archie Bray Foundation, formerly the Western Clay Manufacturing Company, on the outskirts of Helena. There he found plentiful space, materials for the asking, and institutional, financial, and moral support for new, more ambitious works.

Harrison built his first semi-permanent piece – entitled *Tile-X*

– on the grounds of the Bray brickyard in 1984. (He had earlier created another hillside "X" – *Montana X* – on a piece of property belonging to Robert "Irish" Flynn, a University of Manitoba professor of ceramics and Archie Bray alumnus who has recently retired to Helena.) A pyramid-like structure built of discarded ceramic drain tile manufactured at the Bray brickyard and bound together with metal strapping, *Tile-X* is situated on a north-south axis, extends twenty-five feet along each axis, and stands twenty-two feet high. *Tile-X* is tall and broad enough to compete visually with the brickyard buildings nearby, and it echoes – in abstract form – the brooding face of Mount Helena directly to the south.

Tile-X was a breakthrough piece for Harrison; by its very size and scale, it gave him the confidence to attempt still larger projects, to hone his construction skills, to indulge his fantasies. One of Harrison's dreams was to build a monument to the potters and ceramic sculptors who were his comrades at the Bray, and in the spring of 1985, he began to construct *A Potter's Shrine.*

As a clear turning point in Harrison's work, *A Potter's Shrine* presented a number of daunting challenges. Harrison was incorporating new forms (the shrine's brickwork floor was to be a Celtic cross – a kind of "X" – placed within a circle). He had to learn the art of laying bricks, not just for the complex floor (which features the cross set in a herringbone pattern), but for the walls and archways as well. And he had to overcome many logistical difficulties, foremost among them, the unpredictable Montana weather and a chronic shortage of time to devote to the project.

Despite the obstacles, Harrison brought his project brilliantly to completion. Both social and spiritual space, *A Potter's Shrine* truly resonates with its site. In its brickwork, it echoes the original studio buildings built in the early 1950s by Rudy Autio, Peter Voulkos, and other Bray pioneers, and it mimics – in its circular form (and acoustical qualities) – the brickyard's crumbling, but elegant beehive kilns, constructed before 1916. As unofficial curator of the shrine, Harrison asked Bray residents to contribute to what he saw more and more as a collaboration, and many Bray residents – past and present – have complied, placing (imperfect) examples of their works on the shrine's walls, ledges, benches, and floor. Finally, the Bray's board asked Harrison to place Rudy Autio's bust of Archie Bray – founder of the foundation and its guardian angel – within the shrine. Deeply honored by the request, Harrison placed the bust, sculpted by Autio in the early 1950s, facing west, "at eye level in a position where [Bray] could oversee 'future developments.'"

Since that beginning in the mid-1980s, Robert Harrison has created nearly seventy site-specific works. A 1988 work, also at the Bray, established Harrison's emerging vocabulary. Entitled *Aruina*, this row of five unruly brick columns stands at the northwestern corner of the Bray grounds. Connected by tile-and-brick covered arches, the columns of *Aruina* frame the nearby Scratchgravel Hills and, with considerable wit, play with the conventions of classical architecture. *Aruina* is made up of modern industrial materials – concrete, stout cardboard tubes (the interior architecture of the columns themselves), and bricks from the adjoining brickyard. Shards from discarded polychrome sculptures by Japanese artist Michio Sugiyama – embedded in the spiraling patterns of brickwork – add touches of energy and color.

With *Aruina* as starting place, Harrison began to elaborate and improvise. Though he created other colonnades (his *Cullumned Spiral* [1989] at the Kohler Sculpture Park in Wisconsin and *Black Mountain Colonnade* [1994] on his own property are prime examples), he turned increasingly to a simplified vocabulary: the arch, the column, and the buttress.

In 1995, at his alma mater, the University of Manitoba, Harrison and a group of students fashioned a work – *Red River Passage* – that marked, in his view, the epitome of his efforts to mix and match shapes, textures, and colors. In this work, by some species of alchemy, Harrison brought together seamlessly (while retaining a pleasurable tension) an arch cast of stabilized adobe and covered with tiles, a brick column, and a curving buttress (almost a wall) of galvanized metal. Perhaps it is the paved area, set with manufactured cobblestone bricks, that unites the work – and gives it its social dimension, allowing visitors a zone of peace, a place for meditation or repose.

Other particularly significant Harrison archways include *Penland Arch* (1994; Penland School, North Carolina) and *Medaltarch* (1999; Medalta International Artists in Residence Program for the Ceramic Arts, Medicine Hat, Alberta). Unlike the siteworks Harrison has built in the American West, where the landscape is austere (and

Harrison responds with rich, saturated colors), *Penland Arch* is black and white, an elegant Yin/Yang symbol carved out of the vegetal chaos of a dense North Carolina forest. *Medaltarch,* too, contributes something new to Harrison's oeuvre: a tiny brick building with its own columns – a crypt, a shrine – supports one end of the arch, underscoring the uncanny sense that humans have dwelt here.

In Fall 2008, Harrison created his most recent archway, *Fuping Gate,* in Fuping, China, at the behest of "entrepreneur, ceramic magazine editor and publisher, and ceramic enthusiast" Dr. I-Chi Hsu, co-founder of the Fuping Pottery Art Village complex; the complex will eventually feature museums devoted to the world's many ceramic traditions. In *Fuping Gate,* Harrison utilized locally made brick and ornamental glazed roof tile (including "three-dimensional dragons, flowers, and chickens") picked from the "boneyard" of a Fuping brick factory. The elegant brickwork of the final archway contrasts dramatically with the wildly colored tiles cascading down its flanks.

The summer of 1999 brought Harrison to another stage in his art. Invited to participate in the "Creating the Yellow Brick Road" symposium and conference hosted by the University of Wolverhampton, England, he spent eight days crafting a new brick-centered body of work. Having previously used fired brick and tile almost exclusively, Harrison found himself facing the prospect – challenge and opportunity – of working solely with wet brick clay. Improvising freely (unlike his usual mode of carefully planning every detail of a work) and using only one material (rather than his usual collage of found materials), Harrison turned first to his familiar vocabulary of the 1990s, creating *Ironbridge Archway.* After completing the arch – and finding himself fascinated by the "ubiquitous British chimney" – he moved into new territory, designing and constructing his own brick chimney stack, based on the "elaborate [and] organic" Tudor chimneys of Hampton Court Palace south of London (and to a degree, on the stack forms of American ceramists Peter Voulkos and David Shaner). Harrison's *Chimney Stack #1* – for him, the most seminal work of the symposium – quickly spawned *Chimney Stacks Royal Pair.* In turn, these works led him, in the coming year, to devote much of his energy to exploring the chimney form, a form that – like Celtic standing stones and Roman architectural fragments – manifested, for Harrison, a singular presence and power (and the opportunity for infinite and inventive variation). Since his time in England, Harrison has built stacks in Denver, Colorado; on the Bray grounds (utilizing bricks and ceramic pipe found onsite); and in Lancashire, Great Britain, and Oslo, Norway (among many others, including most recently (early 2007), Shuli, Taiwan).

In Denver, as part of a "Big Mud" project sponsored by NCECA, Harrison contributed two chimney stacks he called *Chimney Stacks Pair*. Again, working with wet brick clay, he crafted his own bricks, faceting them with a knife. As with his Welsh stacks, the new *Pair* was built in two parts – a broad, muscular base and a slender, more graceful chimney. Harrison constructed the sturdy, stair-stepped bottom out of his customized bricks and then mold-formed the articulated chimneys. Suggesting movement but never moving, *Chimney Stacks Pair* – reminiscent, rhythmically, of Brancusi's *Endless Column* – honors the ancient traditions of brickmaking and chimney-building and lends a spirited presence to its sober brick-paved setting.

On (and Off) the Wall

Perhaps the least known aspect of Harrison's *oeuvre* is what might be called his wall-work, his "scarcely still lifes." These collages of ceramic fragments, plaster, paint, wood, and gold leaf emerged out of Harrison's experience as a resident at the Kohler Arts Center in Wisconsin. There, working with the Kohler porcelain clay body (intended for bathroom fixtures), he cast from his own molds pots, figures, and natural objects (leaves, shells) that he then shattered and reassembled, setting his shards into beds of plaster and containing them in found window frames.

Harrison soon began building custom frames, breaking his complex images into odd shapes. Referring to the histories of architecture, ceramics, painting, and sculpture, both western and eastern (witness such titles as *Rococo Teacup Icon, The Three Graces: Chinese Memories, T'ang Meets Yuan,* and *The Birth of Venus DeMilo*), these works fulfilled Harrison's desire to create small-scale, highly personal relics/icons that might lend spirit to rooms and galleries. The high point, and most complex manifestation, of this body of work is *Broadwater Divider: Starry Night Revisited,* a screen that giddily expresses, and meditates upon, Harrison's love affair with art history (and especially its celestial visionaries), as well as his delight in collage and the purely kitsch aspects of ceramics. In these wall works, Harrison's early austerity and classical/modernist rigor have transmogrified into celebrations of vertiginous movement, glittering surface, and postmodern playfulness (see his *Palladian Dream: Rococo Reality* for a clear expression of this tension between the two strains in Harrison's sensibility).

Ambition and Evolution

Robert Harrison has – following the lead of such mentors and heroes as Peter Voulkos and Rudy Autio – skillfully and unselfconsciously brought trends from contemporary "fine" arts into the often-ghettoized "craft" of ceramics, successfully blurring and rendering meaningless such false distinctions. In thirty years' sustained work, this exceptional artist has made a truly significant contribution to the health of ceramic arts today.

Note: All quotes by Robert Harrison are drawn from a series of interviews with Rick Newby conducted between 1990 and 2008.

Beth Lo

Taking Stock of Familial Relationships

Originally published as cover story, *American Craft* (New York, NY), June/July 1999.

Nearly a dozen years ago, ceramist Beth Lo made a radical break in her work. Or, perhaps more accurately, life made the break for her. She had just begun her first teaching job, stepping into the position long held by legendary ceramic sculptor Rudy Autio at the University of Montana. And she was pregnant with her son Tai. Until that point, her ceramic work had been vessel oriented – lovely and subtle bowls, conical almost-New Wave vases, quirkily animated cruets and cups – and she had depended on "shape and pattern and form"[1] to deploy a witty and playful abstraction all her own.

Alert to profound personal changes, Lo turned to drawing, because it's so "quick and direct." As she drew and translated her drawings into porcelain and mixed-media sculptures, figures and stories emerged. These new works – "more literal, narrative, and figurative" than her earlier vessels – dealt with issues that arose directly out of her lived experience. More than that, they became an extended meditation on the "enormity of birth"; on the powerful bonds between mother and child; on her struggles to be a "good" parent and to shape a "good" child; on her own mother and father and her emerging empathy for them as parents and as Chinese Americans; and on her own Chineseness. She found herself inspired by the visceral and psychological energies of Frida Kahlo's paintings and by the mother-and-child studies of Mary Cassatt, who had worked with easily sentimental imagery "without being cloying in any way."

More and more, after having struggled in her youth with her place outside the cultural mainstream, Lo embraced her roots, "reaching back to the things I loved about being Chinese and bringing them forward into the work." The sounds of the language, the formal elegance of Chinese characters, the delicacy of origami, the pleasures of playing mahjongg: these cultural artifacts – passionately remembered from childhood – fed her new work.

---

1   AII quotations from Beth Lo are drawn from an interview with the author, Missoula, MT, January 19, 1999.

Lo's drawings of mother and child and her sculptural tributes to her parents radiate a quietly spiritual quality, partaking as they do of relatively pure emotions: tenderness, wonder, joy, sorrow. In particular, a series of giant hands – drawn on gypsum wallboard (popularly known as Sheetrock) – speak movingly of bereavement. Created soon after her father's death, these articulate and anguished hands cradle origami birds, smaller hands (hands of the grieving child?), sets of fingerprints, and implements that pierce: tacks, staples, nails.

In sharp contrast, many of Lo's more recent works – particularly, her "good children" vases, plates, and figures – are charged with humor and ambivalence. It is a kind of compassionate ambivalence that takes stock of familial relationships and life changes that are seldom simple, rarely pure. In these "good children" works, Lo explores her role as parent – as one who must teach "correct behavior" – with considerable irony, laughing at the societal expectations that surround child-rearing. But because Lo is the daughter of Chinese immigrants, her take on these issues grows increasingly complex, richly nuanced, carrying the import of her works far beyond the merely personal or confessional.

On the necks of her porcelain "Good Children" vases, Lo transcribes in her own calligraphy admonitions with which her mother might have chided her. Don't steal; don't lie; honor your parents; don't scold others; brush your teeth every day; study; wash your face and hands. These mundane strictures, brushed in black ink and drawn from Confucian tradition or "old folk wisdom," are – for those who do not read Chinese – a primarily formal, decorative, even exotic element. And yet, in their legible dignity, they set up a tension between the slightly Western, gently transgressive, and faintly diabolical children and what Rey Chow has called the "conservative assertions of Confucian culture."[2] The children – whose look derives from Chinese socialist-realist paintings – deploy across the vases and plates in almost comic-book fashion, washing dishes, drinking tea, picking up their rooms. They are nearly "cute," Lo's word. "I'm interested in 'cute,'" Lo says, "because it is one of contemporary art's last taboos and because cuteness has such broad appeal, plays such a role in popular culture in both the East and West."

---

2   Rey Chow, *Woman and Chinese Modernity: The Politics of Reading between West and East* (Minneapolis: University of Minnesota Press, 1991), 61.

Lo's transcultural stance took a profound turn in 1995 when she traveled to China. On a visit to the Shaanxi History Museum in Xi'an, she encountered an exhibition of T'ang Dynasty figurines depicting women. "They spoke to me," she said. "They had an air of sophistication that was very modern." Reading more about the period (618-907 A.D.) only deepened her fascination with these figurines, usually made to be buried with the dead. "During the T'ang Dynasty, women had more influence and control over their lives than at any other historical time except for maybe under Communism," Lo says. The only woman emperor of China – the ruthless and capable Empress Wu Zetian – reigned during the T'ang, and women took an active part in court life, rode horseback, and even wore men's clothes.[3] Lo was also struck by the freedom T'ang women had to display their femininity; they contrived elaborate hairdos – to each of which a poetic name was given – devoted much time to makeup, and wore gowns with plunging necklines.[4] "It must have been a fun time to be alive," says Lo. "If you look really hard at them, you can see that freedom." And to honor those freedom-loving women, Lo began to sculpt her own "T'ang" figurines.

In preparation for working on these coil-built figures, Lo asked her mother for more traditional sayings that embodied radically unrealistic expectations or were so mundane as to be laughable. These sayings she penned on the torsos of her figures, saving the most poetic or absurd for their titles: "Save Up to Buy a House," "Take the Smallest Pear," "Rally One's Forces After a Defeat" (this figure is modeled after a Han Dynasty work). Lo's white porcelain figures stand generally less than two feet high and rest on unglazed terra cotta pedestals. Each is as individual as the T'ang Dynasty figurines Lo saw in Xi'an, and yet, unlike their models, Lo's haunting figures do not appear contented, or pleasure-loving, or comfortable in their freedom. Washes of color – typical of T'ang Dynasty ware and, in Lo's private iconography, emblematic of tears – drip down their torsos. There is a sense of movement toward lives more fully lived, but at the cost of great struggle. These good daughters (and sons) are not in the least diabolical. Their fight to leap to freedom – beyond the strictures

---

3   Li Wei and Yan Xinzhi, *Women of the Tang Dynasty* (Kowloon/ Xi'an: Pacific Century Publishers/ Shaanxi History Museum, 1995), 3.

4   Li Wei and Yan Xinzhi, *Women of the Tang Dynasty*, 8, 17, 21.

of Confucian culture, of parental demands – leaves them stunned, weary, agitated. They are not triumphant, only steadfast.

As her son edges toward independence, Lo turns her thoughts to letting go: letting go of her expectations of her son, of her need to have him need her, of her desire for control. "It is a kind of grieving," she says, and in a new series of mixed media works – "little altars that say goodbye" – she works out her grief in increasingly formal and mysterious ways.

In no way literal and rarely narrative, Lo's altars hark back to her giant hands, both in their elegiac mood and in their use of gypsum wallboard. Scored and folded into distinctive shapes, the wallboard becomes, in Lo's hands, a startlingly expressive medium. The very beautiful "Envelope" (1998), for example, echoes the red envelopes stuffed with money with which elders reward "good" children on Chinese New Year. "Envelope" also recalls the oversized envelopes sold in Chinese grocery stores that contain funerary papers. Strips of multi-colored funerary papers decorate the envelope's exterior, while more admonitions – in Lo's delicate calligraphy – peek out of the interior. Hands painted red and strangely elegant upholstery tacks float above the Chinese characters. Another wallboard work, "Untitled" (1998) – "a shrine, an altar, a farewell," says Lo – haunts with its violently sliced funerary papers, its mysterious porcelain tubes, its Plexiglas shelf upon which colored epoxy pools (like tears), its splashes of bright red and yellow and the somber gray of the gently curving gypsum board itself.

These altars are not easily read. More spiritual than playful, more richly poetic than anything Lo has yet created, they represent the culmination of a dozen years' work. They are, in Beth Lo's words, "open-ended," and they may well lead this gifted artist to make new leaps, in heretofore unimagined directions, where she will continue to explore the mundane and the daily in ways that touch us all.

Bobby Silverman
Object, Still Life, Installation

Originally published in *Ceramics: Art & Perception,* Sydney, Australia, September 2000.

Paraphrasing Paul Klee, Bobby Silverman spells out his artistic credo, "Art does not reproduce what we see; it makes us see." Silverman speaks also of his desire to transform a space (with the interplay of light and beautiful objects, saturated color and compelling pattern), while inducing in the gallery-goer "a dream-like state," a feeling the "opposite of angst."[1] A recent Silverman installation, *Beyond Memory,* at Farrell/Pollack Fine Art in Brooklyn, New York, fulfils the artist's desires and offers a fresh vision, conceptually stimulating, visually ravishing, and emphatically pleasurable.

In 1998, Silverman began to develop this new vision while in residence at the European Ceramics Work Centre (EKWC) in 's-Hertogenbosch, The Netherlands. During his stay at this remarkable incubator for innovation in the ceramic arts, he not only had plenty of free time, the opportunity to rub shoulders with painters, sculptors and industrial designers, and access to cutting-edge technologies (he used computer modelling to design new forms before throwing them on the wheel), he also found himself, perhaps most importantly, taken seriously – as ceramic artist – by artists in other media and "never [having] to deal with the tired art versus craft issues." In this "refreshing and liberating" atmosphere, Silverman took his already sophisticated approach and pushed it into new zones, where the barriers between art and craft dissolve.[2]

Although he had already been creating nesting or stacking groups of plates, bowls, and vases before he traveled to the EKWC, while there he refined the work, concentrating on his approach to glazing. In particular, he began using European commercial glazes that, in Silverman's words, "enable the eye to penetrate below the

1   All quotes from Bobby Silverman are drawn from interviews with the author, Helena, MT, and Baton Rouge, LA, December 1999, April and May 2000.

2   For critical perspectives on Silverman's new work created at the EKWC, see Xavier Toubes and Edward Lebow, "Bobby Silverman" (s'Hertogenbosch, The Netherlands: European Ceramics Work Centre, 1998); "Bobby Silverman" in *Ceramics Monthly* 47:6 (June/July/ August 1999), 48-49; and D. Eric Bookhardt, "Bobby Silverman: Objects Of Pure Perception" in *American Craft* 59:3 (June/July 1999), 50-53. Quotes from *Ceramics Monthly,* 49.

surface" and make possible "a fusion of form and surface that allows the work to more closely represent the natural world. . . ."[3] At the EKWC, Silverman also loosened, as Edward Lebow points out, the "symmetry" of his groups of vessels, "animating the layered members of his nested forms with shifts in proportion and scale."[4]

At the same time that he was making subtle adjustments in color and form, Silverman took an audacious step in presenting his new work. At the conclusion of his EKWC stay, he exhibited his nests and stacks as a unified installation, as an array of interrelated objects rather than as individual works of art. And by setting the installation afloat on a softly luminous concrete floor rather than on conventional pedestals, he forced the viewer into an unaccustomed, even startling, relationship with his self-described "still lifes."

"Recontextualising the vessel," Silverman calls his effort to render the familiar unfamiliar, to place his vessels outside their usual circumstances, far from kitchen cupboards, china cabinets, or dinner tables. This "enstrangement," as Russian formalist Viktor Shklovsky has called it – to present an object "as if it were perceived for the first time" – is a time-honoured modernist strategy and, in Silverman's hands, it allows, in Roman Jakobson's phrase, the "irrational structures" of the art work to "once again disturb us. . . ."[5]

With his exhibition at Farrell/Pollack Fine Art, Silverman takes even further his notion of an installation made up of clusters of pots lusciously glazed and elegantly deployed across a floor. As he worked to complete this "recontextualization," Silverman thought often of a meditation by poet Rainer Maria Rilke on the paintings of Paul Cezanne. In describing Cezanne's painting process, in which the great Frenchman "represented apples, onions and oranges purely by means of color," Rilke spoke of "the scales of an infinitely responsive conscience . . . which so incorruptibly reduced a reality to its color content that it resumed a new existence in a beyond of color, without any previous memories."[6] Naming his installation *Beyond Memory*, in homage to Rilke and Cezanne, Silverman sought to bring, not just

---

3   Bobby Silverman, *Ceramics Monthly*, 49.

4   Toubes and Lebow, "Bobby Silverman."

5   Viktor Shklovsky, *Theory of Prose* (1929; Elmwood Park, IL: Dalkey Archive Press, 1990), 6; Roman Jakobson, *My Futurist Years* (New York: Marsilio Publishers, 1997), 189.

6   Rainer Maria Rilke, *Letters on Cezanne* (New York: Fromm International, 1985), 65.

a similar obsession with color, but a kindred spirit of responsiveness and beauty – transcendent and earthly – to his new work.

Silverman has long been inspired by the richness and complexity of nature – and particularly of the plant world. He sees *Beyond Memory* as a kind of water garden (certain assemblages of pots are set on polished steel squares, suggesting the glint and glimmer of a pond's surface) and his porcelain bowls and vases – in rich whites, yellows, blues, blacks, and celadons – can be seen as ravishing blooms, outgrowths of an exotic efflorescence of the imagination. And, like a formal garden, *Beyond Memory* holds us with its complex form, with its "symmetries and repetitions and variations and completions. . . ."[7]

Silverman created *Beyond Memory* while on leave from Louisiana State University, Baton Rouge. As he worked in his Montana studio, he observed the changing effects – over the course of days and months – as slanting light from south-facing windows illuminated his already radiant pots. As summer progressed into autumn, he came to relish a certain angle of light that caught his still lifes at their most luminous. And in installing his work at Farrell/Pollack, he worked with New York theatrical lighting designer, Bill Bradford, to replicate, as closely as possible, just that angle and degree of intensity (with the attendant shadows and highlights) that had so pleased him during his Montana sojourn.

In addition to "directing" the lighting for his installation, Silverman also controlled, to a considerable degree, the viewer's perspective on the exhibition by closing off the entrance to the gallery. That the work was situated on the floor – and therefore vulnerable to clumsy feet – was a factor, but not the primary one, in this decision. By making gallery-goers view *Beyond Memory* from the room's threshold, Silverman wanted to force them to see the installation as a whole – as a complex and elegant garden – even as they admired particular stacks and nests. Perhaps for the first time, even more so than in his EKWC show, Silverman pushed beyond the solitary object, and even the still life, into the realm of installation art, where the work "comprises not just a group of discrete art objects to be viewed

---

7   Charles W. Moore, William J. Mitchell, and William Turnbull, Jr., *The Poetics of Gardens* (Cambridge, Mass.: The MIT Press, 1995), 158.

as individual works of art but an entire ensemble or environment."[8]

Certainly, Silverman was inspired here (and in his notions about lighting) by masters of the installation, Robert Irwin and James Turrell, who – in the words of critic Ronald Onorato – tailor "the physical space to affect the mental space of those involved." The two artists – obsessed with human perception and cognition – play with and control every aspect of an installation, from entrance to exit, and every stimulus the visitor receives, including (especially) light. By so manipulating the environment, both Irwin and Turrell seek to heighten "a reflexive awareness of our senses – optic, haptic, spatial – as we become enmeshed in how rather than what we see."[9]

As a maker of objects, however, Silverman remains concerned with what we see. He has, he admits, a personal sense of beauty, one that can be defined "in classical terms: refinement, elegance and perfection."[10] Silverman's relationship, sensual and spiritual, to beautiful objects, as D. Eric Bookhardt has noted, springs from childhood visits to his grandparents' apartment in New York, where the domestic objects – carpets, ceramic vases, and antique furniture brought from Russia – suggested "a foreign country. . . another, much older time. Symbolic, rather than... strictly functional," these objects – both distinctly Other and familiarly familial – took on mythic weight for the young boy.[11]

This fascination with the exotic and the ancient brought Silverman to Asian ceramic traditions and, more particularly – for their marvelous "fusion of form and surface" – to the elegant monochrome pots of China's Sung, Ming, and Ch'ing eras and those of Korea's Koryo dynasties. His own monochrome pots – the nesting bowls topped with plump vases, his slender carved vase forms, his stacking blue teabowls – echo in their purity and sensuality this tradition, one that has given humans visual and tactile pleasure for millennia.

Silverman's garden of pure forms and seductive colours – of

---

8   Robert Atkins, *Artspeak: A Guide to Contemporary Ideas, Movements, and Buzzwords* (New York: Abbeville Press, 1990), 90.

9   Ronald J. Onorato, "Being There: Context, Perception, and Art in the Conditional Tense." in *Individuals: A Selected History of Contemporary Art, 1945-1986,* edited by Howard Singerman (New York: Abbeville Press, 1986), 197, 199, 200.

10   Bobby Silverman, unpublished artist's statement, 1999.

11   Bookhardt, "Objects of Pure Perception," 50.

objects that, though flower-like, are apparently intended for use in eating and drinking – recalls yet another tradition, this one European: the "table-top" tradition of late 17th- and 18th-century Germany and France, in which finely crafted ceramic figures and clusters of figures – which were also tureens, cups, or baskets – graced the tables of the wealthy and powerful. These figures – modeled at Meissen and Nymphenburg – were used, in the words of Philip Rawson, "only in a nominal sense, being set out together to be seen, not scraped with knife and fork." They had a ceremonial function, but that function, writes Rawson, was "still related, however fanciful the iconography, to food and to the containing of food."[12]

By melding elements of pre-modern traditions with modernist and postmodernist art practices, Bobby Silverman has succeeded in sidestepping the "tired art versus craft issues." Taking his work into a "beyond of color, without any previous memories," he transforms, with his dream garden, both the exhibition space and our ideas about the real. While retaining a powerful and intimate link to the lived universe, to the pleasures of gardens and the sensual acts of eating and drinking, his latest work is not simply about gustatory rituals or the natural world; in profound and startling ways, it makes us see all things anew.

---

12   Philip Rawson, *Ceramics* (Philadelphia: University of Pennsylvania Press, 1984), 199, 200.

Things of the Spirit
Jason Walker's Interrogation of Technology

Originally published in *Ceramic Excellence: Fellowships at the Archie Bray Foundation, 2002–2003* (Helena, MT: Archie Bray Foundation for the Ceramic Arts, March 2003); reprinted, in slightly different form, in *Ceramics: Art and Perception*, Sydney, Australia, March 2004.

For Idaho native Jason Walker, his two-year stint at the Archie Bray Foundation has been a kind of coming home. Born and raised in Pocatello, Jason finds the wide-open spaces of Montana, and the equally wide-open Bray community of artists, congenial and welcoming. "This has been the perfect place," he says, "to cultivate my transition from teaching to setting out on my own, as a studio potter." And in receiving the Taunt Fellowship for his second year, Jason has found his Bray experience greatly enhanced. "Getting the Taunt means I don't have to find a job," he notes. "I have more time to experiment, more time in the studio – and that's what the fellowship's designed to do."

Growing up in southeastern Idaho, Jason came to love the surrounding natural world. From a young age, he "pushed out into the wild," hiking, backpacking, biking, crosscountry skiing, and snowboarding. At the same time, he was exposed to technology at its most rarefied. His father worked as a technician at the top-secret Idaho National Engineering Laboratory, built in 1949 for the construction, testing, and operating of nuclear reactors. And Jason quickly came to associate technology with danger, secrecy, and the forbidden ("we could never visit my father at work").

It was years later, during his time in northern California, immediately after graduate school at Penn State, that Jason began to combine his love for nature and his questioning of technology in the drawings that are integral to his ceramic work. He was teaching at Napa Valley College and living directly across from the Napa River. "That poor river," he says. "You couldn't swim in it; it was pretty foul." The immediacy of the polluted river, the density of population (after the relative emptiness of the Rocky Mountain West), the relentless traffic, and the proximity of Silicon Valley pushed him to an ongoing questioning: "how do mechanical devices alter our relations to the world?" He was reading the writings of Neil Postman, especially his *Technopoly: The Surrender of Culture to Technology*, and "wondering about the future of humanity." It was, in his words, "a fruitful but lonely" time.

Out of this time of searching came Jason's distinctive take – darkly ironic, beautifully rendered, and unsettlingly thoughtful – on the American dream. He creates his drawings with black underglaze, wielding a long-bristled watercolor brush, on every surface of his porcelain plates, bowls, covered jars, and boxes. Birds and satellites (flying things represent, for him as they do in many shamanic cultures, things of the spirit), power plants and light bulbs, pipes and plugs, insects and wildly proliferating leaves mingle in his tableaux. Signs warn us that we're never secure, that we're perpetually under surveillance. "Danger," reads one. "Wilderness is a state of mind with economic potential."

Jason insists that his work is more "sociological than political" – he does admit to being a Luddite "at heart" (the original Luddites, in early 19th century Britain, destroyed the newfangled machines that put skilled craftspeople out of work) – but his works, beautifully handcrafted, with their ambivalence and urgency and clear intelligence, do what the best of political art must do: draw us in, challenge our preconceptions, keep us aware – and therefore truly human.

Jason Walker's greatest strength may lie in his masterful deployment of drawings across three-dimensional surfaces. In talking about a 1997 study trip to Japan, he notes that the experience confirmed his desire to bring together the Japanese passion for the object, to be looked *at,* and Western illusionist perspective, to be looked *into.* During his time at the Bray, he has taken to applying, to his wheel-thrown pots, handles and spouts – slipcast light bulbs, plumbing joints, electrical plugs, and gauges – that echo the obsessive images in his drawings, rendering ever more seamless his integration of two- and three-dimensional space.

Whatever Jason Walker embarks upon after his Bray residency, he will doubtless persist in unsettling us, with witty and powerful works that quietly question the ever-increasing gap between man-made and natural, between technologically driven "disembodied activity" and the inescapable "pain of mortality."

The Bird-People of Adrian Arleo

Originally published in *American Craft,* New York, NY,
December 2006/January 2007.

Nearly a decade ago, ceramic sculptor Adrian Arleo happened upon
– in an exhibition of Egyptian art in Phoenix, Arizona – an arresting
image. The tiny figure, half human, half bird, stood at most eight
inches tall. Carved of wood and painted white, the little bird-person possessed, in Arleo's words, an "endearing" quality. Like much
Egyptian art, it stood rigidly erect, and its face offered little expression, but despite this, it "felt whimsical."[1] Arleo loved the scale of the
work, and the image lingered in her mind for years. The exhibition
labels failed to identify the intriguing creature, and she hoped to
learn more.

Then in 2005, during a visit to the Guggenheim Hermitage
Museum at the Venetian Resort-Hotel in Las Vegas, she encountered
another Egyptian show. This one, "small but very good," included a
miniature black stone sarcophagus and, at its side, another bird-person, this one truly tiny at one-and-a-half inches. It stood resting its
little hands on the sarcophagus, seeming to caress the burnished
stone. It was, says Arleo, "so tiny and so powerful," offering up "more
emotion and gesture" than most Egyptian figures.

The Hermitage's labels noted that this creature is known as Ba
and that it represents the personality or soul of an individual – his
or her non-physical aspects. The Ba lives on, in the tomb of the deceased, after the physical body expires, and it possesses the uncanny
ability to leave the body and then return. Because it moves regularly
between the underworld and the world of the living, the Ba traditionally appeared as a bird with a human head.

Arleo had combined human and bird imagery in earlier works,
often to suggest fragility and vulnerability and the impermanence of
life. In her encounter with the two Egyptian Bas, she felt a powerful
sense of recognition; "they seemed so familiar." For her, these frail
bird-people underscored – with their whimsicality and tenderness

---

1   All quotations by Adrian Arleo, unless otherwise noted, are drawn from a telephone
interview with the author, June 8, 2006.

– the resilience of the human spirit. She especially responded to the "strange" bringing together of the Bas' wings, their human forearms, and their "expressive little hands." Birds and hands have been key images for Arleo in recent years, even before she encountered the Phoenix Ba. But it was not until she began her own Ba series that the melding of human and avian qualities reached such a marvelous apotheosis.

As she began creating her own bird-people, she was already known for her haunting clay sculptures that suggest mythologies of transformation and metamorphosis. Most often, her figures have been metaphors for interdependence among species, celebrations of our closeness to profound natural rhythms. Her wasps' nests may host human figures (*Wasp Nest – Three Figures*); the flesh of her men, women, and infants is literally honey-combed (*Honey-Child Baby*); a pair of birds builds their nest on a young girl's folded hands (*Nest Arms*); more hands – hundreds of them – lovingly encase a horse or a crouching woman (*Horse of 1,000 Hands*).

From her home and studio below Lolo Pass in Montana, on the verge of a great wilderness, Arleo has long been drawn to "movement, sensuality and . . . the figure."[2] But she is not simply another figurative sculptor, content with mimesis. Rather she seeks to embody, with her complex images and startling juxtapositions, truths about our richly conflicted existence in the material world. There is a quietness, sometimes serene, sometimes melancholy, in the faces of her humans. In older works, their eyes are often closed or downcast. Perhaps this reflects her desire to capture inward states of feeling and cognition. She notes, too, in an artist's statement, that her faces sometimes lack specificity because a "work of art can tap more deeply into us when it has no specific feature, and so resonates as an archetype."[3]

Over the course of time, though, she has turned away from this absence of the particular. As she notes, "The eyes, when I was starting out, were undefined; they have since evolved from being closed, to being downward turned, to being open and forthrightly gazing."[4]

---

2   Adrian Arleo, "Body Language" in *The Figure in Clay*, ed. Suzanne J. E. Tourtillott (New York: Lark Books, 2005), 18.

3   Adrian Arleo, artist's statement for September 2004 exhibition, Synderman-Works Gallery, Philadelphia.

4   Arleo, "Body Language," *The Figure in Clay*, 21.

And with her new forthright bird-people, Arleo finds herself crafting faces with truly distinctive qualities. Just as the Egyptian Ba is the embodiment of personality, so these new figures – both in face and body – radiate character.

Always a student of art history, Arleo models each face as distinct from the next. Some are tranquil or pensive (*Ba as Raven; Shy Ba*), others appear aloof (*Dove Ba*), and still others seem bemused or slightly alarmed (*Two Owl Bas*). For the face of *Dove Ba*, for example, she has combined elements from a statue of the Buddha and a fifteenth-century portrait of the Virgin Mary. Occasionally her Bas flock together, as in *Girl with Many Bas* (this is a band of female Bas, unusual thus far in the series); sometimes her Bas watch over the vulnerable, as with *Ba for Conan*, in which a black Ba protects the infant human at his feet.

It has been said that hands express character, and in the case of Adrian Arleo's Bas, this is certainly the case. One Ba underscores a point with a sweep of the hand; another folds his hands across his belly (as a sign of contentment or self-protection?); yet another seems on the verge of making a small but significant gesture. These delicate (and articulate) hands assert an undeniable connection to the human.

In almost every instance, despite their apparent seriousness, her little bird-people elicit a smile or a chuckle. This quality of humor, absent from much of Arleo's work (in which important themes are treated with appropriate gravity), may be what Arleo identified as "endearing" about that first Egyptian Ba. In fact, when she looks at the Bas in her studio, she sees 'slightly eerie" works of art that are, at the same time, "like having a pet." A sense of delight, of play and wit, inevitably lingers after we encounter an Arleo Ba.

For this remarkable sculptor, the discovery of an ancient emblem of the Egyptian belief in immortality has led her to create some of her most memorable works, these small figures that seem preternaturally alive, loveable and eerie, melancholy but good company, downright humorous and spiritually resonant.

Teapots Against the Darkness
The Achievement of Richard Notkin

Originally published in *Richard Notkin* (Davis, CA: John Natsoulas Press, 2008). Portions of this essay earlier appeared, in somewhat different form, in *Kerameiki Techni* (Athens, Greece), April 2002, and *Sculpture* (Washington, DC), June 2000.

"the opposite of History, creator of ruins,
out of your ruins, you have made creations."
– Octavio Paz, tr. Eliot Weinberger

Here, in the twenty-first century, when every day brings reports of fresh horrors, when violence and hatred appear to have triumphed over compassion and tolerance, ceramic sculptor Richard Notkin devotes his time to the making of teapots (and other meticulously crafted works of ceramic art). But Notkin's teapots do not evade reality, and they are not intended to help us escape into a perfected dream world, far from the harshness of politics and terror (as were the expressive, playful, marvelously wrought Yixing teapots – designed for the delectation of Ming and Qing dynasty literati – that have inspired and influenced Notkin since 1983). Instead, Notkin's teapots ask us to look more closely at the world in which we live and, upon reflection, to act with greater wisdom.

In fact, a 2001 Notkin teapot, begun well before the events of September 11, affords the viewer no escape. It chillingly recapitulates our very human failure to learn from the past. Entitled *20th Century Solutions Teapot (Variation #1)*, this teapot – which seems scarcely a teapot except in name, and because it possesses spout, lid, handle – is a miniaturized tableau of near-total destruction: an image of ruins that might be the remains of the World Trade Center, but is instead modeled on photos of bombed-out German cities after World War II. In the days following September 11, concerned that the imagery of his new teapot was "too painful," Notkin thought of abandoning it, but has since concluded that the message of *20th Century Solutions* is more urgent than ever, as we enter the new century with "the technologies of *Star Wars* and the emotional maturity of cavemen."

This impulse to create an art that challenges, confronts, lampoons, and mourns the "seeds of human conflict and our many follies" is nothing new for Richard Notkin. He likes to joke, "I once thought I might make the teapot that saved the world," and yet this desire is more than a joke. Though he knows that no work of art can save the world, he believes that art is "the light that combats the darkness." "Imagine," he says, "a world without art. What would keep us going?"

Like his avowed models, the Goya of the *Disasters of War* etchings and the Picasso of *Guernica,* Notkin seeks to make a difference through powerful imagery. And astonishingly, the teapot form has proven a near-perfect vehicle for his complex and increasingly universal expression. It has held his attention since 1976, and between 1983 and 1994, he dedicated nearly all of his artistic effort to fashioning a series of remarkable teapots – slipcast but each unique – that represents one of the most sustained and committed bodies of work in contemporary world ceramics. Notkin continues to add to this series, but since 1994, he has divided his time equally between the making of teapots and larger scale, more purely sculptural work.

Though they draw explicitly on those articulate Yixing teapots, Notkin's own works are absolutely western and modernist. (Notkin has been instrumental in introducing western ceramists to the 500-year-old Yixing tradition – and in bringing western modernism to the potters of Yixing; see Marvin Sweet's *The Yixing Effect: Echoes of the Chinese Scholar* [Beijing: Foreign Languages Press, 2006] for a full discussion of this cross-cultural inspiration.) Many of Notkin's teapots incorporate elements of his personal iconography: nuclear power plant cooling towers, chess boards and gambling dice, H-bomb mushroom clouds, human skulls and brains, light bulbs, fire hydrants, stacked wooden crates, pyramids, oil barrels, peanuts in the shell. Each teapot is a beautifully coherent assemblage of a particular set of these icons. Improbable combinations, radical shifts in scale (a mushroom cloud atop a human skull), and sardonic humor (both in imagery and in their titles; witness, for example, *Pyramidal Skull Teapot: Military Intelligence I*) recall the strategies of disjunction and defamiliarization deployed in the political photomontages of John Heartfield and Hannah Hoch and by Dali, Magritte, and other Surrealist painters.

Always drawn to the "small, tight, and precious," Notkin

achieves intensities of meaning and emotional power by rendering each element, no matter how tiny, in exquisite detail. As literary scholar Susan Stewart writes, creating miniature objects, "emblematic of craft and discipline," multiplies the labor, but it also multiplies the "significance of the whole object." And Gaston Bachelard has said, "[V]alues become condensed and enriched in miniature."

Another subset of Notkin's teapots, less playful and ironic (and more relevant than ever in the context of September 11 and ongoing war in the Middle East), is made up of his variations on the human heart. Rendered life-size and in exact anatomical detail, Notkin's heart teapot series is still evolving in the form of new variations and currently numbers about 55 pieces. The largest grouping within the Yixing Series, the works in the heart series take on issues of conflict, globally, regionally, and within each human heart. Through judicious use of glaze and lustres (unusual within the Yixing Series, where most teapots are constructed, unglazed, from a super dense and finely textured red clay that reveals every detail), Notkin makes of the heart an eloquent object.

More unitary than Notkin's assembled teapots. these compelling works, without taking sides, lament particular conflicts or disasters – *Salvador, Beirut, Sharpeville, Hiroshima* – and honor their victims. Or they address more universal themes. *Heart Teapot: Ironclad,* for example, with its impregnable surface, confronts the armoring of the human soul – against compassion, tolerance, simple love – that makes war possible; the *Pre-New World Order II* teapot, with its camouflage cladding, similarly challenges the militaristic turn of mind. The chain-bound *Hostage I* teapot, while it may have arisen out of some specific hostage situation, speaks to the sense of entrapment or captivity many feel in their daily lives. The *Mace* teapots turn the heart into a weapon, studded and ominous. And yet despite their avowed subjects, these teapots somehow engender a sense of hope. They are – after all the conflict, suffering, and denial – pulsing human hearts, beautiful in their form and susceptible to redemption.

Not always working small, Richard Notkin has turned in recent years to the creation of larger works that – in their imagery, scale, and sober color range – proclaim a seriousness of intent that galvanizes and unsettles the viewer. The tile mural, *Passages* (1999; now owned by the Portland Art Museum), depicts in black, white, and infinite shades of gray the mushroom cloud of a nuclear explosion (specifically a test in the Crossroads series at Bikini Atoll shortly after World War II). At nine and one half feet wide by almost seven feet high, *The Gift* captures the eye – and then holds it, with the discovery that each three-inch square tile (there are 1,106 of them set in 28 staggered courses) depicts a different image, each of which is a beautifully realized composition in its own right: shattered masonry, frontal and side views of a human skull, brain and heart tissue, ears, dice, and crates, all fragments of that Notkin iconography in development since 1981.

Another large Notkin work, *Legacy,* is made up of 1,000 individual human ears, ranging in length from three-quarters of an inch to two feet. When exhibited, these ears sprawl atop one another, attentive to the discords and harmonies of a millennial world. This assemblage of resonating ears – formed from 27 different molds in 50 different stoneware clays and sandblasted, tumbled, or polished to resemble timeworn river stones – attains a powerful presence, at once monumental and intimate, evocative of human receptivity and of an all-too-common failure to listen. They recall most forcefully the piles of shoes, glasses, and gold fillings found in Nazi concentration camps following World War II.

The recent Notkin tile mural, *All Nations Have Their Moment of Foolishness* (2006; now held by Sacramento's Crocker Museum), offers the viewer a tightly cropped portrait of George W. Bush (glowering or dumbfounded). Made up of 344 separate unglazed earthenware tiles fired in sawdust-filled saggars, *All Nations* is strangely moving, somehow both compassionate and accusatory. As Notkin has written, "The image was chosen not to ridicule, but to capture some essence of the man. This particular image of Mr. Bush impressed me for its lack of expression or emotion." The array of tiles in *All Nations* includes fresh additions to the Notkin inventory of images, especially a hooded figure from Abu Ghraib.

In these dark times, Richard Notkin's belief in the redemptive power of art, embodied both in his profoundly refined yet populist teapots and his equally affecting larger works, seems essential. So long as we continue to pulverize frail humans and great buildings into dust, we will need the heart-full visions of this extraordinary artist.

Tom Rippon's Postmodern Marionettes

Originally published as cover story, *American Craft*, New York, NY, February/March 2000.

There is something fable-like, almost legendary, about the story of Tom Rippon's emergence as a truly distinctive American ceramic sculptor. Born in Sacramento, California, in 1954, Rippon lost his beloved mother at the age of nine. "My sister and I raised each other,"[1] he recalls, and from a young age, he learned to rely on his own wits, leaving the family home by the time he turned sixteen. At the same time, Rippon found himself the beneficiary of extraordinary kindnesses from family members and mentors, who sensed in the boy not only need, but exceptional talent.

Clay came early into Tom Rippon's life, in the person of an aunt, Ruth Rippon. Educated at the California College of Arts and Crafts, Ruth is a ceramic sculptor whose distinguished career includes thirty years of teaching (1956–1987) at California State University, Sacramento. Though her work lies within the tradition of classical humanism, certain of her sculptural tableaux project a surreal atmosphere, perhaps a seminal influence on Tom's later work. From age six onward, the future sculptor received encouragement – and clay – from his doting aunt. At first, Ruth did all the glazing and firing of her nephew's work, but soon she taught him the range of skills he needed to realize his own ceramic visions.

Other childhood influences included a "little Mexican marionette" acquired on a family trip to Tijuana. Rippon loved the fact that the figure, with its articulated joints, moved at his command. Movement and the figure have always fascinated him, and his earliest aspiration was to be a film animator. He conjured up his own cartoon characters and created flipbooks that brought them leaping to life. Like many boys, he built plastic models, but instead of cars or planes, he chose figures to construct – pop culture icons like Godzilla.

By the time he entered high school, Tom was helping his art teacher to fire kilns and even co-teaching night classes, in exchange

---

1   All quotes from Tom Rippon are drawn from an interview with the author, Missoula, Montana, November 17, 1999.

for materials and a key to the school building. At sixteen, the prod-
igy began to exhibit his sculptures – "simple little constructions
based on sea anemone forms" – at the Candy Store Gallery in
Folsom, outside Sacramento.

At the Candy Store, the talented teenager was in excellent
company, showing with the likes of Robert Arneson, Clayton
Bailey, Sandra Shannonhouse, and David Gilhooly, prominent fig-
ures in the vital Northern California Funk clay scene. The Candy
Store also exhibited California Funk painters Roy DeForest and
Maija and David Zack, together with leading members of the Hairy
Who group from Chicago.

Robert Arneson, the ringleader and acknowledged master
of the Funk movement, soon took Tom Rippon under his protec-
tion. When Arneson invited him to informally pursue his ceramics
education at the University of California, Davis, Rippon jumped at
the chance. In the late 1960s and early 1970s, Arneson ran the Davis
clay program as a "loose, unstructured teaching environment."[2] Tom
Rippon's arrangement at Davis must have been the loosest, most unstructured of all. Arneson provided him with a "little place to work,
a corner in a hallway," and hired the teenager to take care of his four
sons. Never enrolling in the university, Rippon stayed at Davis for
four years. "Those were different times," says Rippon of the early
1970s. "An arrangement like that could never happen today. But I
learned so much."

"Bob Arneson," Rippon remembers, "could cut you like a knife
with a few words. That's all it took to get you working and thinking."
Telling Rippon that he had fallen into a creative rut, Arneson soon
had his apprentice exploring new forms, including his first human
figures, "very small and abstract." "I was so young I didn't know how
to think critically. Bob taught me what art's all about – conceptually."
And crucially, the elder ceramist introduced Rippon to the possibilities and pleasures of using art historical references in his work.

One day, Arneson told Rippon, "Your time is up," and the
young ceramist left Davis behind. He continued to develop his own
sculptural vocabulary, focusing more and more on playful explorations of the human figure. His work brought him increasing national

---

2   Garth Clark, *American Ceramics: 1876 to the Present,* revised edition (London:
Booth-Clibborn Editions, 1987), 121.

notice, and in 1975, at the age of twenty-one, he had his first solo exhibition – at Helen Drutt Gallery, Philadelphia.

In the mid-1970s, during a lecture tour of the Midwest – with his friend Richard Notkin, whom he'd met at UC Davis – Rippon found himself at the Art Institute of Chicago. Invited to accept a teaching post there, he revealed that he had never received an undergraduate degree. Despite his lack of credentials, the School of the Art Institute of Chicago offered him a place in its Master of Fine Arts program, together with a teaching assistantship. Rippon took the offer, and in 1979, he was awarded his MFA.

"I went to the Art Institute as much for the Chicago experience as for the school itself," Rippon confesses. At the Candy Store Gallery in Folsom, he'd been introduced to the hard-edged paintings of the Hairy Who group, Chicago Imagists like Karl Wirsum, Jim Nutt, and Gladys Nilsson. "I loved their work," he said, "the starkness, the intense colors, the rough subject matter, frightening and sexual." Many of those qualities entered Rippon's work, but he would use them to his own ends and "much more subtly."

After leaving the Art Institute, Rippon did brief teaching stints at Montana State University, Bozeman, and California State University, Sacramento, before spending most of the 1980s teaching ceramics at Tennessee Technological Institute, Cookeville, and University of Nevada, Reno. In 1989, he took a teaching position at the University of Montana, Missoula, where he remains today. From 1990–1996, he served as the chair of the UM Department of Art.

By the mid-1980s, Rippon had arrived at the sculptural approach he continues today. Although he had studied under the master of Funk, his work – like that of several other Arneson students, including Notkin and Richard Shaw – partakes more of the "fetish finish" style that emerged in Los Angeles during the early 1960s and of the 1970s Super-Object movement, with its obsessive craftsmanship, appropriation of surrealist and Dadaist strategies, and trompe l'oeil effects. From a young age, Rippon has boldly experimented with his materials, never worrying too much about ceramic conventions. Rather than working with wet clay, he finds that he can achieve the effects he desires by manipulating dry clay, treating it as if it were wood, grinding, carving, and sanding it to achieve a satin-smooth surface. His works are assemblages, the various parts joined together with steel rods and pins. His dancing figures, though articulated, only imply movement; he prefers, as he says, to "control the dance." Color is central to Rippon's work, and through experimentation, he has come upon techniques that render his colors particularly vivid. As a teenager, he applied low-fire lusters to his work without first glazing the porcelain. Without the clear glaze, he did not get the "oil-slick" look characteristic of lusters, but instead, happily, he achieved what Nancy Bless has called "an unusual silky iridescence that coheres his color range." He also applies to his surfaces "impure" colorants like acrylics, colored pencils, and pigmented epoxies.[3]

And in choosing his subject matter and his forms, too, Tom Rippon has followed his own path. Again, unlike the Funk artists, he found his subjects not in the public realm of savage satire and political statement, but by working poetically, out of the resonant material of daily life. Marionettes, cartoons, pop culture: All influence and inform the sculptural explorations of his maturity. All these populist influences render his work, despite its sophisticated allusiveness, approachable, even seductive. And then, after he brings the viewer close – to savor the tasty colors of his lusters, the goofy postures and tendril-like limbs of his goddesses and brides, the off-kilter charm of his tableaux – he springs the trap of meaning. What is Domestic Mourning? And why does it look so cheerful? Why are the figures of his Unseen Ballet dressed entirely in black, gray, and white, the garb of grief? Why do his teapot lids take on the form of women's heads, flamboyant and coquettish? What about the recurrence of gameboards and fragments of Italian architecture? And is there something to these obsessions with sports figures and musicians and the objects of domesticity? As with the best poems, the questions posed by these segmented constructions of porcelain and steel pins have many answers – and no definitive answer.

Provisional, open-ended, rambunctious, Tom Rippon's constructions hark back to certain tradition-shattering experiments by early modernists. Following Robert Arneson's advice, Rippon found – and continues to make brilliant use of – the art-historical images that most durably inflame his imagination: Giorgio De Chirico's paintings from his Mannequins series, images like *The Disquieting*

---

3   Nancy Bless, *Tom Rippon: A Poet's Game* (Sheboygan, WI: John Michael Kohler Arts Center, 1993), 2.

Muses, Hector and Andromache, and *The Seer* (Rippon's *The Seer* of 1987 is a direct homage); the biomorphic forms that populate paintings by Dali, Miro, and Tanguy; the eroticized dolls of surrealist Hans Bellmer; and the marionettes of Bauhaus master Oskar Schlemmer (Rippon's *Unseen Ballet* series represents an unabashed tribute to the costumes for Schlemmer's *Triadic Ballet*).

The fascination of early modernists for the mannequin, the marionette, the robot, the doll represented – at the start of the twentieth century – a deeply ambivalent response to the ever-increasing influence of science and technology on the human enterprise. This fascination was alternately Utopian and pessimistic. The Russian constructivist El Lissitzsky designed a geometric "New Man," happily reconstructing, in Peter Conrad's words, man's "soft, padded, lazy body, reducing it to efficient angles."[4] In his urban dreamscapes, peopled by his mute mannequins, De Chirico admitted to painting "the melancholy of beautiful autumn days, afternoons in Italian cities." De Chirico's melancholy, argues Guy Davenport, was a common response to a "new world born in the dynamo and the internal combustion engine, but [out of which the early modernists] did not know what kind of soul" might emerge.[5]

Today, at the start of a new millennium, Tom Rippon's marionettes reflect less anxiety than their modernist predecessors. And they are scarcely melancholy. Despite the dire history of the recently departed century and the challenges of his own life, Tom Rippon stands on the side of the optimists. Perhaps he believes, with Heinrich von Kleist – the German Romantic whose 1810 essay, *On the Marionette Theatre,* profoundly influenced Oskar Schlemmer and Hans Bellmer – that "we shall find [grace] at its purest in a body that is entirely devoid of consciousness or which possesses it in an infinite degree; that is, in the marionette or the god."[6]

Tom Rippon's perpetually dancing figures and animated still

---

4   Peter Conrad, *Modern Times, Modern Places: How Life and Art Were Transformed in a Century of Revolution, Innovation and Radical Change* (New York: Alfred A. Knopf, 1998), 402.

5   Guy Davenport, *Objects on a Table: Harmonious Disarray in Art and Literature* (Washington, DC: Counterpoint, 1998), 85, 95.

6   Heinrich von Kleist, 'On the Marionette Theatre," in *What Is Dance?: Readings in Theory and Criticism,* edited by Roger Copeland and Marshall Cohen (London: Oxford University Press, 1983), 184.

lifes, watched over by a benevolent creator, embody his cartoonish but nuanced, private but welcoming, joyous but grieving – and ultimately grace-filled vision of the world.

A Folk Spirit
The "Punch'ong" Pots of George McCauley

Originally published in *Ceramics: Art & Perception* (Sydney, Australia), September 2000

A native of the American South, George McCauley has long been drawn to the "unconscious and deep in the bone"[1] freedom of spirit of his native region's folk artists and to the notion of outsider art. And like many outsider artists, McCauley refuses to acknowledge academic distinctions between art forms – he makes pots and ceramic sculpture, he crafts furniture of wood and hammered tin, he works with the simplest of vessel forms and he embellishes his Gothic sculptures with "fantastic extravagance."[2] "I have," he says, "a multiplicity of things inside me."[3]

But this unclassifiable artist is no *naif*. As Peter Voulkos notes, "George McCauley has an intuitive approach. . . . Although casual in expression, his work is refined in execution."[4] Educated at the University of South Carolina (BFA, 1970) and the University of Georgia (MFA, 1978), McCauley brings a knowledge of world ceramic traditions – and a love of folk arts from many cultures – to his expressive pots and sculpture.

A central figure in his development was ceramist Ron Meyers, who was his teacher at both South Carolina and Georgia. "Ron's devotion to making pots – his work ethic – has always inspired me," says McCauley. Of McCauley, Meyers notes, "George has been a close friend for many years. I have always admired his commitment to his art while never losing his sense of humor."[5] More than anything else, McCauley and Meyers share a playful approach. "I'm not telling a story, as such, with my work," says McCauley. "I'm expressing a personal feeling as viscerally and freely as I can."

This emphasis on the intuitive, on spontaneity and working

---

1   Guy Davenport, "Appalachian Gothic," *New York Times,* September 29, 1968.

2   Peter Held, "George McCauley," *Ceramics Monthly,* January 1997, 44.

3   All quotations by George McCauley from two interviews with author, Helena, MT, Aug/November 1999.

4   Peter Voulkos, telephone interview with author, September 1999.

5   Ron Meyers, telephone interview with author, September 1999.

from the gut, comes as much from McCauley's contact with the ceramic abstract expressionist tradition (as embodied in the person and work of Peter Voulkos) as it does from his appreciation for folk art and artists. McCauley first encountered Voulkos when the ceramic revolutionary presented a workshop at the University of Georgia in the late 1970s. McCauley was instantly fascinated by the immediacy of Voulkos' innovative approach.

In 1998, those influences – the radical freedom of a Western avant-garde and the casualness of folk pottery – came together for McCauley in a singularly satisfying way. McCauley had come to Montana in 1993 as a resident artist at the Archie Bray Foundation for the Ceramic Arts, and when he left the Bray in 1995, he stayed in Helena, as part of the mountain town's vibrant ceramics community, maintaining a close relationship with the foundation. In 1997, he met and befriended three Korean ceramists – Lee Hun-Chung, Kim Jeoung-Beom and Chin Yi-Cheol – who had come to the Bray as visiting artists. At the end of their stay, Lee and Kim invited McCauley to Korea, to work alongside them in their studio.

"I have always been drawn to Asian work," McCauley recalls. "And in graduate school, all of us read Soetsu Yanagi's *Unknown Craftsman,* which eloquently championed the easy-going naturalness . . . and endless beauty of Korean wares."[6]

In Kwachon, just south of Seoul, in a small space carved out of Lee's studio, McCauley set to work with the materials at hand. He hesitated to continue simply to make the extravagantly modeled and brightly colored sculptural candlesticks, sconces, and covered jars that had marked his Montana years (though he did create a handful of these works during his Korean stay, but without his characteristic blue, purple, and green barium glazes), nor was he inspired to replicate contemporary Korean production pottery, "precise and pretty."

Instead, he took as his starting point the Punch'ong pots of Korea's Yi Dynasty (1392 – 1910) that had so inspired Soetsu Yanagi – and had had, since the 16th century, such a profound influence on the aesthetics of Japanese teaware. These Punch'ong pots are characterized by "austere simplicity, total absence of artificiality, natural

---

6   See Soetsu Yanagi, *The Unknown Craftsman: A Japanese Insight into Beauty* (Tokyo: Kodansha International Limited, 1972), 122-123.

tranquility"; at the same time, they are rife with imperfections: "glaze shrinkage due to insufficient firing, careless decoration, hasty if solid potting that results in asymmetry, warped rims and crazed glazes."[7]

"I loved the sense of freedom in those pots," McCauley says. And he set out, not to replicate the Punch'ong ware, but to honor a pottery tradition that, in Yanagi's words, arose as a "natural outcome of the untrammeled state of mind . . . a state of mind of just being or 'thusness' which is not yet confined in any preconception." In Yanagi's view, the imperfections of the Punch'ong pots derived from this lack of preconceptions: "They live in a world where accuracy and inaccuracy are not yet differentiated."[8]

The Punch'ong potters threw their pots on uneven, crudely crafted wheels. "The Koreans do not make such wheels because they like unevenness and dislike evenness," wrote Yanagi. "They just make their wheels in that happy-go-lucky way."[9] For some years, McCauley had taken his pots off the wheel and distorted them by hand in order to approximate the delightful asymmetry of his folk models. In Korea, this approach worked well as he sought to match, and even go beyond, the unevenness of the original Punch'ong pots. "I wanted my pots to be round and not round. I just worked. I didn't try to make every pot a good pot."

Working with a local earthenware clay, white slip, and clear glaze, rubbing iron oxide into the clay for a touch of color – and leaving fingerprints and drips as they happened – McCauley made many pots during his two-and-a-half month stay in Korea. He fired this body of work in a gas reduction kiln in Kwachon. And out of the kiln came crude, whimsical teabowls, teapots, jars, and vases that seemed to allude as much to the face jugs of McCauley's native American Southeast as they did to their Korean models. Like the Punch'ong pots, they felt "relaxed, natural, and tranquil."[10]

In solidarity with the ingenuity and improvisatory talents of folk artists everywhere, McCauley scavenged Kwachon for non-ceramic materials to complete the presentation of his postmodern

---

7   Goro Akaboshi and Heiichiro Nakamaru, *Five Centuries of Korean Ceramics: Pottery and Porcelain of the Yi Dynasty* (New York, Tokyo, and Kyoto: Weatherhill/Tankosha, 1975), 11-12.

8   Soetsu Yanagi, *Two Essays* (Helena, MT: Archie Bray Foundation for the Ceramic Arts, 1952; 1983), 14.

9   Ibid.

10   Akaboshi and Nakamaru, *Five Centuries of Korean Ceramics*, 11.

Punch'ong pots. Using cast-off wood cut with a blunt saw blade, he built rough stands for his teabowls and teapots, splitting sections of cheap green garden hose to stretch over the wooden bases to add color and texture. He studded the stands with brass nails, and out of rusted wire he fashioned handles for them. Now they were ready for exhibition.

Before travelling to Korea that year, McCauley had sent slides of his work to Woo Byung-Tal, director of Seoul's Tho Art Space and, at the end of his stay, Woo hosted a solo exhibition of McCauley's Korean output. In early July, the George McCauley show, *Souvenirs: Made in Korea,* opened to a warm reception. Woo recalls McCauley's approach as "play expressed with direct thinking rather than result of planning," an "attitude . . . close with Punch'ong." And when he saw some of the pots, he said he "felt the power and the sense of closeness" to "Korean traditional expression."[11]

McCauley had also been invited to present workshops at seven Korean universities, and during these one-day events, he showed slides, demonstrated his throwing and hand-building techniques, and answered questions from crowds as large as 200. "I was treated like a king," he says.

Perhaps McCauley's "souvenirs" intrigued Koreans because they hark back to a tradition that – in its birthplace – barely survives today. (Working alongside McCauley in the Kwachon studio, Lee and Kim crafted figurative sculpture and installations as consciously sophisticated and conceptually driven as McCauley's pots were crude and intuitive. "My pots are closer to the Japanese teaware that was inspired by the Punch'ong tradition than they are to modern Korean pots," notes McCauley.)

Since returning to Montana, George McCauley has continued with this work. Besides his sculptures writhing with nudes and animals and occult symbols from many cultures – suggestive and humorous – his tables and chairs and sconces made of galvanized roof flashing and wood rescued from demolished train trestles, and a line of painterly and tender majolica-like pitchers and plates, teapots and bud vases, McCauley continues to explore the possibilities of the Punch'ong tradition. In 1999, at the Archie Bray Foundation,

---

11   Woo, Byung-Tak, email to author, January 2000.

he fired – with Ron Meyers – a wood kiln full of teabowls and jars. Again, he relied on his own intuition and the most rudimentary of materials. Again, he achieved pots of singular simplicity, darker in tone and less tranquil than those he made in Kwachon, but still exemplary re-imaginings by a mature Western artist of a great ceramic folk tradition.

The Arts of Slipcasting and Jitterbugging
Richard Swanson's Dancing Teapots

Originally published in *Ceramics: Art & Perception*, Sydney, Australia, March 2002.

Flow is important to Montana sculptor Richard Swanson, and so are the relationships among forms. It is no surprise, then, that Swanson should be drawn to the flowing forms found in dance, ancient and modern. He works in clay and with a variety of other materials (mattress ticking, window screen, baling twine, straw, peat moss, barbed wire, sheet aluminum, steel, bronze, cardboard) – and he has created a number of his non-ceramic forms specifically to be danced with or among. These works are generally human scale, and some of them move, suspended from ceilings or ducking and bobbing as their materials flex. Others, while remaining perfectly still, imply movement. None, however, are more expressive of joyful motion than his sculptural teapots fashioned from an iron-red clay.

In the 1970s, Richard Swanson began his career as a studio potter, and even today, he produces a line of plates, jars, cups, bowls, and other vessels that provide the foundation for all his artistic endeavors. From the beginning, his pots have sported his favorite creatures: leaping fishes, soaring birds, cavorting human figures. These forms, simplified and made animate through the quickness of his drawing, reflect his fascination both with the material world and with cultures whose relationships with nature seem much more "intimate and joyful" than our own. Swanson admits to an "envy and nostalgia" for that closeness. His own works, and his sculptural teapots in particular, champion an intimacy, with the shrinking natural world and the ever-recurring sensuality of bodies in motion, that we can still savor, despite the challenges of our sped-up, over-stimulated, hyperreal 21st-century existence.

Swanson's slipcast, limited-edition teapots, now twelve in number – the first created in 1991, the latest from 2001 – are graceful, but also irrepressibly playful. They share with Swanson's totem creatures, birds and fishes, a "fluidity of shape" that is antic, nearly goofy, in its joyousness. They are rounded, voluptuous, the absolute opposites of Swanson's elegant barbed-wire sculptures, with their intimations of threat and danger. They are closer in spirit to Netsuke carvings of laughing Buddhas or Mixtec terra cottas of couples happily copulating than they are to the grave (and immobile) statuary of classical Western tradition. These "folk" sculptures by a sophisticated artist of the postmodern era possess an archaic and uncontainable liveliness. As Guy Davenport writes, "The archaic is one of the great inventions of the twentieth century." Just as the Renaissance looked back to Hellenistic Rome for its inspiration, argues Davenport, we have "looked back to a deeper past" in which we imagine we "see the very beginnings of civilization."

Pablo Picasso was one modern who found kindred spirits among ancient African sculptors and the Neolithic cave painters of Spain and France. In turn, Richard Swanson has been drawn to Picasso's ceramic work. Indeed, among Swanson's earliest sculptural explorations are works distinctly reminiscent of Picasso's seductive female figures and lively animal forms. Soon, however, Swanson found his own path into the archaic, resonating to "Inuit carvings, Pre-Columbian ceramics, African sculpture [and] to some extent Japanese netsuke carvings and Yixing teapots. . . ." He admired the "concise vocabulary of these pieces, their use of everyday life as subject matter, their compact forms, and their straightforward but unique way of relating figurative elements."

As he developed his own vocabulary, Swanson sought the perfect clay body, or the perfect combination of clay and glaze. In creating a group of one-of-a-kind sculptures – figurative works with titles like *Birth, Vortex,* and *Goat Rider* that were clear precursors, in approach and theme, to the teapots – he worked with a white clay body to which he applied terra sigillata, resulting in a rich red-brown surface. In works like *Seated Lovers,* he achieved a surface that mimicked stone, by applying terra sigillata mixed with copper to the bisqued piece and firing it in sawdust. While these works proved successful, even powerful, Swanson still wasn't satisfied; he wanted to achieve what he was coming to admire in Yixing ware: a purity of material, where no decoration beyond the sculptor's modeling is necessary. And then Swanson's good friend, Richard Notkin – the Helena-based sculptor who has been instrumental in introducing western ceramists to the Yixing ware of China – shared with Swanson a clay body he had "come up with" for his own slipcast work. This clay mixture, super dense and finely textured, with a rich red coloration derived from its high iron content, proved ideal for Swanson's teapots. "It's really sensuous and burnishes beautifully," he notes, and "it needs no surface decoration."

Swanson first encountered the notion of sculptural pots as limited editions in his study of Picasso's ceramics, and for his teapots, he found slipcasting to work beautifully, allowing him to create editions of up to twenty-two (the more complex pieces, like *Fish Rider,* have as few as twelve in an edition). Swanson first sketches his ideas for a teapot and then allows the details to "evolve from the clay." There is, he says, something about "designing for multiples that makes you hone down to essentials." Far from simple, his plaster molds can include up to thirteen ingeniously interconnecting pieces. After he removes the pieces from the mold, he assembles them "a little bit wet," applying slip to the joints and smoothing the surface. When the teapot is bone dry, he sands it with a fine mesh screen (used in perfa taping) and fires it to Cone 08. After bisquing, he smooths the surface again, this time with 200 mesh sandpaper. He fires the pot a second time, to Cone 5, and completes the final burnishing with emery cloth, creating the satin-smooth surface that is these pots' signature. Swanson pays close attention to how he stacks his teapots in the kiln; he fires them alongside glazed pots – this lends them a sheen from the vaporizing glaze – but he doesn't want too much sheen. "I'm not looking for a glazed effect, just a 'color blush,'" he says.

Swanson began the series, in 1991, with *Elephant Rider.* The elephant, in his view, is an "amazing, simple form," and he followed his languorous elephant and rider with the harder-charging *Elephant Runner* the following year. These pots, with animals and humans melding into singular forms, led in 1993 to a purely human work, *Sitting Pretty.* In this playful teapot, a delighted woman sits astride the shoulders of her kneeling male partner. In another 1993 teapot, a similarly kneeling figure triumphantly holds aloft his *Proud Catch,* one of Swanson's beloved fish. A pair of fish take a male figure for a joy ride – a kind of water dance – in *Fish Rider,* 1993. Swanson returned to the purely human with the rollicking *Jitterbug,* 1995, his first teapot to directly acknowledge the importance of dance to his overall enterprise (his first collaboration with dancers, *Building Bridges,* had come the year before, and 1995 saw him collaborate on three separate dance/sculpture works). Perhaps Swanson's most beautifully realized teapot, *Bird in Hand,* 1995, features not a full human body, but a pair of graceful hands. While one hand cradles the bird, the other caresses its outstretched wing, forming a delicate and lovely arch. More robust are Swanson's *She* and *He* teapots, 1995 (a voluptuous pair of *He* and *She* tea bowls accompany them), as is *Mermaid & Dolphin* from 1996. *High Stepping,* 1997, features a single exuberant dancer (with a gold ring through her belly button, the only non-ceramic element in the series), while a recent work, *Leaping Lady,* 2001, is a variation on *Sitting Pretty,* with a female figure balanced across the lap of her kneeling partner (a fancy dance move? a tender interlude in the midst of gymnastic lovemaking?). Another 2001 teapot, *Proud Catch II,* combines the graceful introspection of *Bird in Hand* with the triumphant spirit of the original *Proud Catch.*

Dancers and frolicsome fish, elephants and dolphins, cavorting lovers and birds at rest: Richard Swanson's sculptural teapots link us to our animal natures, the joys of movement, and some of the world's most vital traditions, archaic and otherwise. Like Yixing teapots and ceramic bottles from the Moche culture of Peru, they tell stories and invite touch, effortlessly embodying the unquenchable human imagination at play.

Rituals of Perception
Chris Staley's Spiritual Modernism

Originally published in *Ceramics: Art & Perception,* Sydney, Australia, December 2002.

There is something uncanny – both haunting and calming – about the works of American ceramist Chris Staley. They are unambiguously pots: plates, bowls, cups, covered jars. And yet they possess an intensity, a kind of aura, that suggests, not just the rituals of eating and drinking, but rituals of another sort entirely. At the same time, these objects are not in the recent tradition of the "pedestal pot" (the vessel that yearns to transcend its humble origins of kitchen and table). No, by their modest scale alone, the pots in Staley's elegantly balanced tableaux stand in solidarity with their useful brethren. Their effect is to lull us, lure us, into reverie, into a remarkable openness to the world, all senses alert.

In 1936, the German-Jewish thinker Walter Benjamin, in a famous formulation, defined the aura of a work of art as "an extraordinary weave of space and time: the unique appearance of a distance, however close it may be." Benjamin went on to say that the "earliest works of art originated in the service of a ritual" and that it was of "decisive importance" that a work "never entirely separates from its ritual function." Benjamin then lamented, perhaps prematurely, the "decay" of the aura – the total disconnect from art's ritual origins – in our "Age of Mechanical Reproduction."[1]

The French phenomenologist Gaston Bachelard specified that the "cosmic image," the work of art, "is immediate." He added, "The communication between the dreamer and his world is very close in reverie; it has no 'distance'. . . ."[2] This paradox, that the auras of certain works of art create a distance and yet bring us into an immediate intimacy with the world, expresses precisely the quality that emanates from Staley's subtle, highly charged works.

---

1   Walter Benjamin, "The Work of Art in the Age of Mechanical Reproduction," *Illuminations,* tr. Harry Zohn (New York: Schocken, 1968), 222–224. For the passages quoted here, I have relied on the translations in John McCole, *Walter Benjamin and the Antinomies of Tradition* (Ithaca and London: Cornell University Press, 1993), 4, 5.

2   Gaston Bachelard, *The Poetics of Reverie: Childhood, Language, and the Cosmos,* tr. Dennis Russell (Boston: Beacon Press, 1969), 17.

Staley is, in fact, a champion of functional pottery, and yet he knows that, most likely, his elegant arrays of teabowls and plates and boxes will not be used. Still, he wants them to serve a crucial function, "as a conduit," he says, "to our tactile being, and thus helping us to feel alive." With these pots that can be mistaken for works of "fine" art, Staley brings the "kitchen into the gallery" and thereby tempts gallery-goers to reach out and touch.[3] To do so brings into question what the Mexican poet Octavio Paz calls the "religion of art." "We look at the work of art," writes Paz, "but we do not touch it. . . . Being made *by* human hands, the craft object is made *for* human hands: we can not only see it but caress it with our fingers."[4]

Staley's most recent pots, in their tranquility and strength and seductive beauty, might be compared to those crafted by Japanese, Korean, and T'ang Dynasty masters, but while he acknowledges a "spiritual kinship" with Asian ceramists, Staley insists on a different lineage. Decrying postmodernism's strategies of appropriation, simulation, and irony (which suggest, to him, the exhaustion of hope), Staley sees himself in the modernist tradition of Kasimir Malevich, Constantin Brancusi, Mark Rothko, and Joseph Beuys, idealists who believed, as Staley puts it, in a "visual language that would alter how we relate to the world." Staley admires in these artists their simplified forms, their spiritual aspirations, their desire to, in the words of Malevich's friend, Roman Jakobson, "discover meaningful elements directly in pictorial space" and to place, in Beuys's phrase, "the dignity of nature . . . into the center of immediate personal experience."[5]

A deeply thoughtful artist and teacher, Staley takes ideas seriously. It is his belief that "pots are enhanced if [the artist's] decisions are based on . . . philosophical reflections. . . . when the artist has such convictions, these, in essence, are 'fired' into the pots."[6] And while he has been called a "romantic – perhaps even a sentimental throwback," with an "an outlook closer to Bernard Leach's faded view

---

3   All quotations by Chris Staley, unless otherwise noted, are drawn from a series of interviews with the author, summer/autumn 2001.

4   Octavio Paz, "Use and Contemplation," in *In Praise of Hands: Contemporary Crafts of the World* (Greenwich, CT: New York Graphic Society, 1974), 18, 21.

5   Roman Jakobson and Krystyna Pomorska, *Dialogues* (Cambridge, MA: MIT Press, 1983), 9; Joseph Beuys, *Early Drawings* (New York: W. W. Norton, 1992), back cover.

6   Chris Staley, "The Challenge of Making Pots at a University," *Ceramics Monthly* (February 1996): 57

of ceramics as a noble human cause," it seems more accurate to link Staley's thought and intention to recent thinking about perception, 21st-century life, and the role of art.[7]

Staley believes, with many others, that in modern times vision has become our overwhelmingly dominant sense, with the result that "we are literally losing touch with the very world we live in." French theorist Guy Debord notes that sight, "the most abstract of the senses," has today been elevated to the "special place once occupied by touch." Roland Barthes tells us that, in medieval times, the "most refined sense . . . the one that established the richest contact with the world, was hearing: sight came in only third place, after touch."[8] While the causes of this change in the hierarchy of the senses are debatable (the rise of the printed book and mass literacy, shifts in theology, etc.), it seems clear that, in Staley's words, "our sensory paradigms" have altered radically. Staley is particularly concerned that the move away from "our awareness of touch has far greater implications than our society gives it."

The phenomenologist Maurice Merleau-Ponty believed that, in fact, "synaestheitic perception," the blending of the senses, "is the rule, and we are unaware of it only because scientific knowledge shifts the center of gravity of experience." David Abram, in his recent book, *The Spell of the Sensuous,* notes further that this "intertwining of sensory modalities seems unusual to us only to the extent that we have become estranged from our direct experience."[9] And in opposition to this pervasive estrangement, Staley hopes, through his pots that invite caress, to activate the already existing blending of senses, particularly sight and touch. He seeks to achieve this through several strategies: keeping his work to an intimate scale ("when things get to be the size of your torso, you tend to look at them versus touch them"); replacing light-reflective glazes with those that absorb light, thereby luring the viewer closer; using quieter colors, "with more connection to skin and earth" (his most recent work, seen at Gallery

---

7   Ed Lebow, *Christopher Staley* (Wichita, KS: Wichita Center for the Arts, 1999), 2.

8   Guy Debord, *The Society of the Spectacle,* tr. Donald Nicholson-Smith (New York: Zone Books, 1994), 17; Roland Barthes, *Sade/Fourier/Loyola,* tr. Richard Miller (New York: Hill and Wang, 1976), 65. See also Martin Jay, *Downcast Eyes: The Denigration of Vision in Twentieth-Century French Thought* (Berkeley: University of California, 1993).

9   Maurice Merleau-Ponty, *Phenomenology of Perception,* tr. Colin Smith (London: Routledge & Kegan Paul, 1962), 229; David Abram, *The Spell of the Sensuous: Perception and Language in a More-Than-Human World* (New York: Vintage Books, 1996), 60.

Materia, Scottsdale, Arizona, March 2002, employs only blacks and a range of whites); and creating fruitful tensions among rectangles and circles, refinement and roughness, form and formlessness, random marks and what he calls "the sublime."[10]

Though it is true that Staley's works are imbued with ideas, they are also records in clay of his own lived experience, moving from his aggressively energized early vessels ("unconsciously sexually charged") to the anguished works of the early 1990s ("clay as viscera . . . transformation of structure to entropy"), reflecting key personal losses, to his current work, which embodies the mature artist's more contemplative spirit ("trying to make work that reflects slow time").

The works in Staley's most recent exhibition suggest a subtle, but important, new shift in his work. Perhaps this shift, to a darker, less tranquil tonality, reflects recent historical events: the eruption of terrorist horror, seemingly unresolvable conflicts in the Middle East, threats to civil liberties. Plates and cups are pocked with constellations, and ceramic "stones" lie in bowls, reminders of the greater cosmos, beyond the strictly human. But one work in particular draws the eye and hand and heart: a squat, powerful stoneware "box," made entirely of black clay, with a mysterious, vaguely threatening object on its top, a kind of shuttlecock with one end raggedly cut and seeming almost to explode. This box – a talisman from some forgotten ritual? – seems to gather to itself all the light in the world. Or is it all the darkness? Its density brings disquiet, certainly – and awe at the leaps of imagination and skill that have led Chris Staley to create this extraordinary, uncategorizable, and absolutely riveting work of art, this strange and compelling "pot" that takes into account the evils of this world, just as his plates and cups and bowls, his stones and stars, remind us of the pleasures of fully living, our senses wide awake.

---

10   Quoted in Judy Donaldson, "Chris Staley: Significance of Touch," *Ceramics Monthly* (May 2001): 69.

How Many Worlds?
The Ceramic Art of Stephen Braun

Originally published in Janet Peoples, David Peoples, &
Rick Newby, *Stephen Braun: Cause & Effect* (Davis, CA: John
Natsoulas Press, 2007). This essay subsequently appeared in
Ceramics: Art & Perception, Sydney, Australia (No. 78), 2009.

Sculptor Stephen Braun seeks to create a piercing visual language, one that motivates us, if not to act, then to think differently. Out of the human figure and an ever-evolving inventory of icons, Braun constructs allegories that reflect fiercely held concerns. We often respond first to the wry humor and fiery wit of these articulate tableaux. Their sly titles, too, lead us to chuckle at uncomfortable truths: *Talkin' Trash, Just One More Little Bite, Race to the Top, My Car Thing, Collateral Damage, Freedom-lovin' Patriot, Tele Prompted.*

Braun's themes may be familiar – environmental degradation; excessive consumption; tragedies of war; alienation from any semblance of the real – but his works somehow render these tropes both fresh and urgent. His totemic sculptures possess uncanny presence; they haunt and prod us. They are not jokes, though they may appear jocular. Instead, they touch us in some deeper place.

Braun's icons, which swarm about his figures like nettlesome insects, derive from many different realms: forms of transportation (automobiles, airplanes, boats), human anatomy (penises and sperm cells, uteruses and ovaries), the natural world (fishes and stones, the planets, and especially the earth itself), sources of energy (the oil barrel, the atomic symbol), various media (especially television and the Internet); an array of toxins ("arsenic, dioxin, and the host of chlorine combinations"), and every consumer product imaginable.

Braun works in what he calls the "bastardized American raku technique" developed by Paul Soldner in the 1960s. Traditional Japanese raku has been used since the 16th century to produce wares for the tea ceremony. These hand-built raku wares, redolent of contentment and calm, embody an aesthetic that aims at "elimination of movement, decoration and variation of form." Central to the American version, with its emphasis on improvisation, is post-firing reduction. This dramatic process involves removing the red-hot ceramic object from the kiln and placing it in a sealable chamber (say, a metal trashcan with a tight-fitting lid), together with combustible materials (straw, in Braun's case).

In Braun's works, the resulting effects include well-smoked surfaces and muted colors, lending his works a quiet, restful quality akin to that found in the Japanese raku wares. Because he has often worked so large (the torsos of some of his pieces are life-size), Braun's raku process can involve considerable risk. Wearing asbestos gloves and protective garb, he has only seconds to shift the unwieldy pieces to the reduction chamber (before the gloves burn through and he sustains major burns). The quiet surfaces of Stephen Braun's raku figures, together with this element of danger fired into the works (and the seriousness of his themes), lend them a provocative tension, between tenderness and rage, between compassion and blame.

Trained as an anthropologist at The University of Montana (where he also studied under ceramic revolutionary Rudy Autio and mixed-media sculptor Ken Little), Braun believes that each culture defines its reality through the construct of language. With his sculptures, he aims to "break culture down" and offer unadulterated "hyper-perceptions." As a young artist, in an effort to shatter his own cultural projections, he fasted and deprived himself of sleep for days (in a kind of vision quest). Making his home on cattle and sheep ranches in southcentral Montana, at the foot of the Crazy Mountains (a "powerful spot"), he came to see the natural world as "primary" and began to incorporate animal imagery, especially deer, bears, and coyotes, into the imagined worlds of his monoprints and sculptures. While serving as visiting artist at Eastern Montana College (today, Montana State University–Billings), he connected with Crow and Northern Cheyenne students who shared his evolving perceptions about the primacy of nature and the destructive qualities of the dominant consumer culture.

Like other socially conscious artists of the 20th and 21st centuries, Braun employs distortion, disjunction, and defamiliarization to challenge the constructs our culture offers us. His powerful expressions bring to mind the works of German Expressionists George Grosz, Otto Dix, and Max Beckmann; John Heartfield, the master of political photomontage; the California Funk ceramists; and postmodern sloganeers like Barbara Kruger.

Braun's giant *Enviroman,* at over eight feet tall, towers above our expectations. At the same time, *Enviroman* seems all too familiar, a kind of Everyman, not unlike the *Elck* or Everyman – with his greed and vanity – castigated by medieval and early Renaissance moralists. In Pieter Bruegel the Elder's 1558 drawing entitled *Elck,* Bruegel's Everyman seeks himself (in vain) in the detritus of the world he inhabits. Like Braun's male and female figures in *Talkin' Trash,* he loses his essential self in a welter of things.

The comparison with the great Netherlandish painters of the fifteenth and sixteenth centuries is more apposite than it might seem. Stephen Braun acknowledges few influences, but he speaks freely of Hieronymus Bosch as a seminal influence on his artistic vision. Best known for his triptych *The Garden of Earthly Delights* (which features an utterly compelling vision of Hell), Bosch presented his contemporaries with moral lessons that, through the extremity of his vision, still move, trouble, and fascinate us.

Vasari, in his *Lives of the Painters,* noted that both Bosch and Bruegel had their own modes of defamiliarization, rendering "fantasies, bizarre things, dreams, and imaginations" in an effort to shake the complacency of foolish sinners. Certainly, some of Braun's figures dwell in a hell of their own making. In a work like *On Board,* six human heads project from a car, seemingly unable or unwilling to extricate themselves from this death trap, its surface ominously charred and emblazoned with crosses. And in his several *Tired* pieces, humans struggle desperately to avoid being entombed by rubber tires. As in Bosch's hell, Braun seems to say, the punishment must fit the sin – and then some.

Not unlike those of the stylized figures of Bruegel and Bosch, the heads, and especially the faces, of Braun's Everyman and Everywoman are somehow unsettling, even heart-breaking. By simplifying their features and rendering them bald and, for the most part, expressionless, Braun makes these creatures both like and unlike us – they seem marionettes or mannequins upon whom we can project our greatest fears and desires. And yet, unlike many of the early modernists (like Fernand Leger, who in 1923 was pleased to see technological man becoming a "mechanism like everything else"), Braun sees this dehumanization as a terrible loss. His figures' faces reflect a spiritual emptiness that still manages to retain vestiges of compassion, valor, and a capacity for love.

Those Braun works that focus on war, and specifically the current Iraq conflagration, seem the most accusatory, the least willing to acknowledge that Everyman is simply lost, merely a fool. These raw works, whether they acknowledge the tragedy of *Collateral Damage* or the vicious patriotism of the torturers of Abu Ghraib, do not raise questions; they simply assert the monstrousness of an ongoing evil. Like the best photomontages of John Heartfield (think of his *Pan-German* [1933], with brownshirt Julius Streicher standing proudly astride a bloodied victim of Nazi street violence), Braun's war tableaux hold us, without mercy, to account.

Art historian Peter Selz, in his recent study, *Art of Engagement: Visual Politics in California and Beyond,* anatomizes a rich tradition of socially and politically engaged art in the American West. Selz writes of Robert Arneson, "How can an outsider, a craftsman who works in the humble medium of clay, a man who lives 'out there'. . . find his way in the art world?" Selz goes on to suggest that just such "outsider" qualities served Arneson well and, in fact, allowed him the freedom to "achieve work full of personal iconography that also deals with politically charged issues like the catastrophe of nuclear annihilation or the absurdity of overindulgence."

Curator Susan Landauer, in an essay she contributed to Selz's book, notes that "conditions in the West . . . were conducive to a far greater range of artistic expression" than in the market-driven New York art world. Moreover, Landauer continues, artists in the West tended to be closely allied with the New Left and embraced a "far more inclusive approach that combined an intense personalism with an uncompromising critique of society."

Stephen Braun certainly stands in this tradition, and it can be argued that his critique of consumer culture and corporate dominance arises out of his education and life in Montana. Because of the state's colonialist history, Montanans on the Left, in the words of poet Kenneth Rexroth, "had no nerves, no illusions, and . . . were curiously urban – but urbanites of a city which was gone." Montana history, as the late historian K. Ross Toole wrote, "has been brief, explosive, frenetic, and often tragic. The economic picture has often been one of exploitation, overexpansion, boom, and bust." Now making his home north of Whitefish, Montana, Braun speaks of his adoptive state and much of the West as a "Third World economy."

The exploitation of natural resources – and attendant overconsumption of consumer goods – remains a persistent theme in Braun's work. In an interview, he asks, "Is it ethically responsible that, just because you have wealth, you spend it by consuming things?" His *How Many Worlds?* pieces articulate another uncomfortable question: How many planets would it take to sustain humankind if all humans consumed goods (and natural resources) at the same rate as Americans do? The answer, of course, is many too many. With their high-end emblems – Rolls Royces, Rolex watches – and unending battles for resources, the figures in these apocalyptic visions threaten to annihilate us all. The man in Braun's *Just One More Little Bite*, his suit emblazoned by symbols of excess, cannot stop eviscerating the planet. For him (for us?), there seems to be no turning back.

Despite the humor and wit in Stephen Braun's work, there is also melancholy. Like Hieronymus Bosch, he is a pessimist who persists in the effort to awaken his fellow humans to their/our collective follies. This struggle in the face of enormous odds adds another dimension to his work, a spiritual energy that cannot help but move us. In the presence of these works literally wrested from the fire, it is difficult to remain unscathed. Stephen Braun says, "I am not trying to tell people what to think or what to do, but instead to present a snapshot of culture as I see it."

These snapshots, captivating and unsettling as they are, do not let us rest easy. And yet, through their spiritual force, they suggest that we are all in this together. In so doing, without in any way assuaging our guilt, they confer upon us a species of forgiveness. Powerful and tender, the sculptures of Stephen Braun speak both to our sadly fallible humanity and to our best selves. They ask us to choose, between a blissed-out media-induced blindness and a painful, but exhilarating consciousness of our impact upon this Earth.

Rebecca Hutchinson
The Gesture of Place

Originally published in *American Craft*, New York, NY, April/
May 2007.

Within the marvelously pluralist landscape of contemporary ceramics, Rebecca Hutchinson is one self-defined ceramic artist whose work
crosses more boundaries than most. Her elegant and mysterious biomorphic forms – constructed of handmade paper brushed with a slur-
ry of porcelain paperclay or woven of paperclay-coated sisal thread
– straddle the divides between ceramic and textile arts, between sculpture and the vessel, between the ephemeral and the timeless, between
ecological concerns and the purely aesthetic. By remaining committed
to the (multiple) traditions of ceramics and yet determined to follow
her own aesthetic path wherever it may lead, Rebecca Hutchinson
brings a fresh perspective to our discussions of the clay arts – and what
their role might be in an increasingly de-naturalized world.

A professor of Artisanry/Ceramics at the University of
Massachusetts–Dartmouth, Hutchinson is, as she likes to say, "of
the tribe" of Environmental artists, but she feels especially close to
those (like Patrick Dougherty, Michael Singer, and Roy Staab) whose
works share with her ruggedly refined forms an exceptional sensitivity to site, natural materials, and what she calls the "gesture of place"[1]
(she disavows any affinity with the massive and domineering earth
works of Robert Smithson, Michael Heizer, and Nancy Holt).

Dividing her time between Massachusetts and Montana –
and as the daughter of a medical technologist and a psychologist –
Hutchinson finds herself deeply concerned about the links between
the human and the non-human, with what she calls "total ecosys-
tem function, specifically looking at dynamics of species survival
and site activity individually as they function in the parameters of
place." This has led her to turn away, despite her training as a potter, from the fetishization of the well-crafted object so prevalent in
recent ceramic arts. Rather, she writes, "[m]y interest in ecology has
taken me to understand species structure and organism growth on

---

1   All quotations from Rebecca Hutchinson are drawn, unless otherwise noted, from interviews with the author, Helena, Montana, July 2005 and August 2006.

all environmental levels."[2]

This truly holistic approach leads to complex and delicate structures that most resemble spiders' webs, the nests of birds, or massed floral forms. Moreover, Hutchinson's earth-centered works partake in what critics Yve-Alain Bois and Rosalind Krauss call the tradition of the "formless," a subset of modernism that explores the abject, the tactile, and the entropic ("a degradation that leads to a continually increasing state of disorder and of nondifferentiation within matter"[3]). Entropy appears most strikingly in Rebecca's outdoor sculptures, especially her ambitious series, *Ten Sites, Ten Situations: Site Works in Rural America,* where the effects of weather over time invariably deconstruct her fragile structures. This recognition that all life is ephemeral can also be seen in her gallery works, which exist only in the spaces for which they are created, and only for the time of the exhibition.

Hutchinson sees a clear connection between her own work and that of her Environmental-artist peers, engaged – as they passionately are – in articulating concern for increasingly threatened natural systems, and the vast canvases of nineteenth-century painters like Thomas Moran and Alfred Bierstadt, who sought to capture the sublimity of the Rocky Mountains and, in so doing, helped to create the movement to preserve prime examples of the American Sublime (like Yellowstone and Yosemite National Parks).

Three recent solo exhibitions embody Hutchinson's vision for an art that speaks of the strength *and* fragility of the natural world and of our profound connectedness to all things. At the same time, the groups of works in these shows can function purely as gallery environments that engage visitors on many levels – as affecting abstractions, as bodies in space, as elegant objects for contemplation. Like the multiples of Eva Hesse (think of her suspended works, *Contingent* and *Right After,* both 1969, which she described as "paintings as sculpture"[4]), Hutchinson's post-Minimalist objects bear an uncanny and uncontainable charge – of emotion, spirit, and intelligence. In each of three recent exhibitions – her 2006 installation at

---

2   Rebecca Hutchinson, unpublished artist's statement, 2005.

3   Yve-Alain Bois and Rosalind E. Krauss, *Formless: A User's Guide* (Cambridge, MA: MIT Press, 1997), 14.

4   Quoted in Robert Pincus-Witten and Linda Shearer, *Eva Hesse: A Memorial Exhibition* (New York: Solomon R. Guggenheim Museum, 1972), unpaginated.

Manchester Craftsmen's Guild of Pittsburgh; the 2005 installation, *Communal Condition,* at Washington State University, Pullman; and her 2004 New England Artist Awards exhibit at the Society of Arts and Crafts, Boston – Hutchinson has refined and extended her repertoire of forms and processes.

Made of literally thousands of florets assembled out of rolled handmade paper sheets coated with porcelain paperclay and then pegged together with twigs, Hutchinson intended the works in Pittsburgh to be viewed from multiple vantages – more so than any of her previous installations. It took her a full year to assemble the florets, and eleven days to install these graceful floral forms. It is only when the viewer walks underneath them and looks upward that their true expansiveness – the multiplicity of their parts – becomes evident. While abundance might be said to be the theme of this show, the installation in Washington State celebrated, in Hutchinson's view, gravity and, more particularly, the "gentleness of gravity." These webbed objects, each different from the next, suspended from branches found locally, seem to drip and pull, terminating in "intimate sacs" that recall the sensual curves of swallows' nests. Spare and angular, these long-stemmed works – Asian in feeling – are unique in Hutchinson's oeuvre. The show at Boston's Society of Arts and Crafts offered Hutchinson the opportunity to orchestrate an intimate space. Unlike the larger galleries in Pittsburgh and Pullman, SAC offered a bay window in the historic structure, where she installed five skirted bell forms ("very feminine," says Hutchinson), with 100 florets to each stem. This time Hutchinson wove the florets with sisal thread and again coated them with her signature paperclay, achieving a feeling of openness furthered by the absence of color. During the past half-decade, Hutchinson has limited her palette to white. (Although these woven works seem far distant from what we generally think of ceramic objects, they can be seen as standing within the continuum of clay arts; as critic Glen Brown writes, we can "read in these elegant woven forms a suggestion of the memory inherent in the ceramic tradition – a popular speculation about the first fired pot is that it was a mud-covered basket accidentally hardened in a fire."[5])

---

5   Glen R. Brown, "Memory Serves: Time, Space and the Ceramic Installation," *Critical Ceramics,* March 10, 2001; http://criticalceramics.org/articles/nceca01/memory2.htm

With each of her singular installations, Rebecca Hutchinson transforms space, captures our imaginations, and asks us to contemplate, not just her arresting forms, but the natural phenomena to which they allude: the outrageous fecundity of flowers, the nurturance of nests, the strength and delicacy of spiders' webs, the temporality of all existence, especially our own. By refusing to create works that have a future, she challenges us to share her concern about, and care for, the lovely, evanescent, and enduring natural world.

Ceramic Globalism

Gritty and Un-housebroken
Origins, Reception, and Dispersion of Funk Ceramics

Originally published in Peter Held, John Natsoulas, and Rick Newby, *Humor, Irony and Wit: Ceramic Funk from the Sixties and Beyond* (Tempe, AZ: Arizona State University Art Museum, Ceramics Research Center, 2004).

In the early 1960s, critic Donald Phelps championed the "Muck School," a strain in contemporary art that acknowledged, celebrated, and cracked jokes about the less-than-genteel dimensions of American culture. Phelps was characterizing a new species of taboo-shattering comedy best represented by Lenny Bruce, who played "a game of Russian roulette with absurdity, realism, and his audience's feelings," and by the comics in *Mad* magazine, where any given panel was a "tapestry of uncontrollably screaming figures, demolished kitchenware, pools and rivulets of indescribable fluid. . . ." This brand of "gritty, un-housebroken, garbage-happy" art, rich in humor and the detritus of American consumer culture, found some of its most passionate and lasting expressions in the works of the Funk clay artists who first emerged in the mid-1960s in Northern California.

With roots in Dada, Surrealism, and the Beat ethos of the 1950s, the Funk ceramists shared aesthetic predilections with parallel movements, including the cooler Pop artists, the California Assemblagists (with whom they overlapped most significantly), Neo-Dadaists like Robert Rauschenberg and Jasper Johns, and the unruly Chicago Imagists. But arising out of the counterculture of 1960s Northern California, and more specifically the Bay Area – with, in the words of painter R. B. Kitaj, its "tough, radical, pacifist, anarchist strain" and, perhaps more importantly, its isolation from East Coast artistic arbiters (San Francisco, noted poet Kenneth Rexroth, "was very much a backwater town") – Funk possessed a raw and antic spirit that jolted the art establishment.

California sculptors like George Herms and Wallace Berman, founders with Ed Kienholz of the California Assemblage movement and precursors to the Funk ceramists, had strong ties with the Beat Generation poets who populated San Francisco's North Beach and

Western Addition in the 1950s. Berman, for example, published the journal *Semina,* which brought together his own images (and those of collagist Jess and photographer and curator Walter Hopps) with poems by Beat luminaries Allen Ginsberg, Michael McClure, David Meltzer, and Philip Lamantia. Today the journal, as William Wilson puts it, "resonates an aura that combines the magical delicacy of Joseph Cornell with the moral fervor of Ed Kienholz." George Herms, too, consorted with Ginsberg as well as Lawrence Ferlinghetti, owner of legendary City Lights Books in North Beach, and Beat novelist Jack Kerouac. This fertile mix also included North Beach coffeehouses and jazz haunts like the hungry i, the Cellar, Vesuvio's, and the Co-existence Bagel Shop and alternative art spaces like the King Ubu, East-West, and Batman galleries.

Bruce Conner, one of the most remarkable and enigmatic of Bay Area artists – draftsman, filmmaker, painter, assemblagist, performance artist, and photographer – introduced elements from Beat poetry, Asian philosophies, jazz, Dada, drug culture, and the collages of Kurt Schwitters – leavened with a powerful dose of Cold War dread – into his wildly diverse works. Brought to San Francisco by fellow Kansan and Beat poet Michael McClure, Conner bridged the worlds of the Beats and the first explosions of the hippy movement in the Bay Area (he grew famous for the light shows he masterminded at the Avalon ballroom). "Sinister, fetishistic reflections on consumerism and the destructive powers of time," writes *Los Angeles Times* critic Kristine McKenna, Conner's works "incorporated decorative fragments, tattered scraps of memorabilia, mass-produced goods and erotic imagery," all of which would appear in the equally outrageous works of the Funk ceramists.

Funk has never been an exclusively ceramic movement. There are, after all, Funk painters (Roy DeForest, William T. Wiley, Joan Brown, Jay DeFeo), unclassifiable multi-talents like Conner, and Funk sculptors like Robert Hudson who work in numerous media other than clay (just as many of the Funk ceramists work variously, in bronze, aluminum, copper, found materials, etc.). But clay has been a central material for the movement, and especially – naturally enough – for those Funk artists associated with Robert Arneson and his MFA program at the University of California Davis.

As Arneson developed his own aesthetic, he found himself rebelling against several traditions: first, against – in the words of Signe Mayfield – the diminished "place of ceramics in the hierarchies of the art world," and second, against the influence of his two principal mentors, Antonio Prieto (representing the well-made pot) and Peter Voulkos (the purely abstract expressionist vessel). Arneson's rebellion against the belittling of ceramics led him to insist, following Voulkos's lead, on clay as a wholly suitable material for "serious" sculpture, and his rebellion against his two ceramic fathers led him to an exploration of subject matter and to a playful and irreverent predilection for art historical reference (an "attitude," writes Victoria Powers, "that accepts all art history as available material").

Arneson's focus on subject matter, which allowed the expression of social commentary and broad humor, had its roots in a return to figuration among Bay Area painters like Richard Diebenkorn, David Parks, and James Weeks. This turn to representation, seconded by the emerging Neo-Dadists and Pop artists, enacted a liberation from the "new academy" embodied in first-generation Abstract Expressionism. As curator Susan Landauer has recently noted, as late as 1963, prominent New York critic Hilton Kramer could be astonished by the "audacity" of Richard Diebenkorn's still life, *Knife in a Glass*, and wonder whether he shouldn't "shudder at such naked esthetic atavism."

Among East Coast critics, this discomfort with a Californian fascination with the real only deepened in the encounter with the excessive, brash, and crude imagery of the Funk artists. Hilton Kramer again – in a famous encounter with Robert Arneson's work during the 1981 Whitney Museum exhibition, *Ceramic Sculpture: Six Artists* – wrote in a *New York Times* review that Arneson's sculptures were "dominated by a gruesome combination of bluster, facetiousness and exhibitionism." These qualities, Kramer asserted, placed a "fatal limit on what [Arneson's] gifts allow him to accomplish, or even to conceive."

Stung and emboldened by Kramer's harsh critique, Arneson responded with *California Artist,* a *tour-de-force* self-portrait that celebrates, with lavish color and considerable wit, the laid-back

California lifestyle and what Kramer called in the same review the "general cultural impoverishment" of the California art scene. Despite this work of defiance, notes Steven A. Nash in his catalog essay to the 1993 exhibition, *Arneson and Politics,* Arneson took to heart Kramer's criticisms, and his works until his death manifested "greater moral and political commitment," especially his late sculptures on the themes of nuclear war and racism.

Some New York critics have done useful work in sorting out which artists exemplify the true Funk worldview (though, in fact, many of the artists under the Funk heading still bridle at the label). Donald Kuspit, writing in a 1994 catalog essay about Viola Frey, noted that the "funk point is to use raw physicality to show the human turned inside out to show the endemic emotional crudity beneath the polite, slick social surface." Frey's plates were too refined and subtle – and not populist enough – argued Kuspit, to constitute Funk works.

Not surprisingly, West Coast critics have generally been more sympathetic to the aims and accomplishments of the Funk artists, perhaps because they better understand the culture out of which the movement emerged. Christopher Knight, writing in the *Los Angeles Times,* opined in 1993, "If the Funk attitude, in its many variations, often seemed to trivialize ceramics in a not unworthy effort to deflate the pious rhetoric that had congealed around it, Funk's irreverence also spoke of a new anxiety toward the precarious status of the work of art in the contemporary world."

The poet Gary Snyder has written that, out of the self-conscious Bohemia, North Beach – because of the "deeply dug-in and committed thinkers and artists of the era" – came "pulse after pulse . . . from the fifties forward that touched the lives of people around the world." The same might be said of the energies, ideas, and aesthetic emanating from TB-9 on the UC Davis campus, where Funk ceramics had its inception and where Robert Arneson and his many collaborators, both students and fellow faculty, elaborated and extended the original notion, what Jonathan Fineberg has characterized as a "startling offensiveness" that "raises everyone's emotions to maximum poignancy, prompting serious thought on [a given] subject." In his catalog essay for the first (1967) exhibition of Funk work, curator Peter Selz noted, "Funk art . . . is largely a matter of attitude," and from its epicenter at Davis, the Funk attitude has dispersed throughout the world.

Australian Margaret Dodd, for example, returned to her homeland after studying with Arneson, introducing a variant she called "Skangaroovian Funk" which Janet Mansfield recently testified has "deeply changed the face of Australian ceramics." After his stint with Arneson, Briton Sean Henry returned to the United Kingdom where he brings an expressive freedom linked to Funk both to his clay work and his polychrome figurative bronzes. And of course, Arneson's protégées are myriad Stateside, carrying the Funk message to every corner of the land, whether to the wilds of Montana (where, ironically enough, Arneson students John Buck, Debbie Butterfield, Richard Notkin, and Tom Rippon bring a very unFunklike refinement of technique to their sophisticated works), to Oregon (where David Gilhooly works his madcap magic), to Funk's birthplace, California (where the purest, though still diverse, expressions of Funkitude emerge, from the studios of Clayton Bailey, Richard Shaw, Peter Vandenberge, and Erik Gronborg).

Out of the isolation, ambition, and creative fervor of Arneson and his cohort erupted a distinctively American brand of critical art, humorous and lacerating, a courageous, principled, and often plain goofy response to the darkest corners of American culture. Long may it thrive.

Wrested from the Earth
The Recombinant Poetics of Stephen De Staebler

Originally published in the exhibition catalog *Stephen De Staebler* (Chicago: Zolla/Lieberman Gallery, 2008). Portions of this essay first appeared in *American Craft,* New York, NY, October/ November 2004. For a more extensive examination of Stephen De Staebler's life and work, see my monographic essay in *Matter + Spirit: Stephen De Staebler* (San Francisco: Fine Arts Museums of San Francisco/University of California Press, 2012), together with major essays by Dore Ashton and Timothy Anglin Burgard.

> *From scraps of mountains I have concocted men.*
> – René Char

When visitors – critics, collectors, curators, artists – wander the grounds of sculptor Stephen De Staebler's home and studio in the Berkeley Hills, they are struck by the sense that they have stumbled upon the ruins of an archaic world. Figure columns line the pool's perimeter, armless and headless torsos abound, landscape forms sprawl, and out of slopes and bushes emerge half-buried fragments – thighbones, ribcages, shins, and delicately formed feet – from failed figures (fired as early as 1962 and as recently as 2007).

De Staebler has said that, if he hadn't turned to sculpture, he might have pursued a career in archaeology, and surely this personal boneyard symbolizes a passion for artifacts wrested from the earth. His mode of working, too, suggests a profound connection between processes of erosion and the entropic decline of the human body. As art historian Glenn Adamson notes in his recent study, *Thinking Through Craft:*

> De Staebler did not employ traditional wheel or coil building techniques, but he also refused to use . . . armatures. . . . Instead he worked huge solid slabs into shape by pushing and pulling [them] with his entire body. His works were devoid of any conspicuous marks of the hand, bearing instead evidence of an insistent but non-demonstrative physical interaction. Even De Staebler's working method amounted to an analogy between the internal

forces and mass of his own body, and the "natural limitations" of the clay body.

This embodied metaphor, linking earth and the human, has long given De Staebler's work its singular resonance. Ever since he built his Berkeley Hills home, in the early 1980s, he has embraced the notion of recombination, that is, of taking fragments from earlier unsuccessful works and re-using them, resurrecting their forms to make molds for new bronze works. And now, at mid-point in his seventh decade, he has taken this process to its logical endpoint: using the actual remnants from various periods to assemble entirely new "transgenic" works, which include no freshly built and fired parts. This method of collage, which assembles fragments made by the artist's own hand (never quoting from the work of others), has led to the extraordinary works in this exhibition (with four exceptions, the *Figure Columns* XXXI, XL, XLII, and XLIV [2005–2006], from an earlier series).

Like his *Figure Columns,* these new works possess a presence very nearly sacred in feeling. Constructed of fired clay and pigment, they resemble nothing so much as relics found at the site of some hitherto undiscovered city, perhaps in Egypt, Sumeria, or the Yucatan, and yet, despite their apparent antiquity, they speak of a shared humanity that spans cultures and eras. Both tender and tough, these fragmentary figures offer evidence of a sensibility that understands both the inevitability of physical death and the unquenchability of the human spirit. They resemble the colossi that ornament Egyptian tombs, but on an intimate scale. Like those great figures, De Staebler's effigies cast a spell both disquieting and oddly soothing. Each work seems the still point in a zone of preternatural quiet.

If anything, these latest figures are more disquieting than De Staebler's previous work, and less calming. They feel more fragmentary, as if collected and assembled by a forensic archaeologist determined to solve an ancient crime. Perhaps the most haunting work in this exhibition, *Thorax Figure,* feels somehow monstrous, offering to our eyes evidence of great violence, the trace of conflict with no easy resolution.

As De Staebler further reduces his means, shrinking his focus from the full figure to the leg alone, his works have grown ever more poignant, more suggestive, more fully human. In this exhibition, the several *Leg* works (*Leg with Flared Thigh, Leg with Fractured Shin, Two Found Legs, Leg with White Knee,* and especially *Leg with Split Knee*) stand almost at the vanishing point, startlingly delicate tributes to human fragility and resilience.

His work may appear timeless, but Stephen De Staebler stands in a profoundly modernist tradition, one in which artists have explored and recontextualized, shattered and reassembled their materials in new, powerful, and often unsettling ways. The branches of this tradition most closely aligned with De Staebler are the California Funk and Assemblage movements. But unlike many of the Funk and Assemblage artists, De Staebler is drawn, not to savage satire, direct political commentary, or raucous wit (like Robert Arneson or Ed Kienholz), but to the deepest elements of human experience: loss and rebirth, entropy and energy, grief and healing. His works possess an unmistakable *gravitas,* even at their most graceful and celebratory.

Despite his self-described "ornery individualistic approach," De Staebler has acknowledged numerous debts, not only to his mentor Peter Voulkos, but also to the rugged bluffs of his native Indiana, to the frontality of Egyptian sculpture, and especially to Alberto Giacometti, for whose somber works he continues to avow a deep affinity.

"Only that which does not cease to hurt remains in memory," wrote Friedrich Nietzsche in *The Genealogy of Morals.* To be in the presence of Stephen De Staebler's recombinant figures – his shattered shinbones, split torsos, and flared thighs, his monstrous thorax – is to participate in a profound remembrance, to dwell in the pain of mortality and, simultaneously, to experience the power of this American master's healing art.

Geometrical Codes/Material Bodies
Twenty-first Century Clay and the Hyperreal

Originally published in the exhibition catalog, Rick Newby & Dana Plautz, *The New Utilitarian: Examining Our Place on the Motherboard of Ceramics* (National Council on Education for the Ceramic Arts, 2006), accompanying the invitational exhibition of the same name at the 2006 NCECA Annual Conference, Ronna and Eric Hoffman Gallery of Contemporary Art, Lewis & Clark College, Portland, OR.

I.

Men imagine every once in a while that they have discovered the truth, and that nothing should exist outside of it.

– Alberto Savinio

A few months back, in a small contemporary art museum in the Northern Rockies, my wife and I witnessed a lecture on "New Media and the Visual Arts" by a young video artist whose own works reveal prodigious talent, a predilection for gratuitous violence, and a gleefully juvenile desire to shock. What was striking about this gentleman's presentation was not the samples he proffered as exemplary of new media (mostly modest short videos strong on narrative and surprisingly unadventurous in their use of digital technologies), but the certainty with which he expressed his belief in the absolute primacy of art created with those technologies. He sneered at works in "obsolete" media (whether paint or bronze, stone or ink, glass or clay), fiercely dismissing object-based art in its entirety.

With horrified fascination, I listened as he spoke yearningly, rapturously of the time when we will "leave behind our bodies." A true believer transfixed by possibility, he saw the emerging digital world in spiritual terms, as a paradise of flows and memes, of perfect pixels and the last ragged vestiges of the real replaced by the hyperreal (defined by French theorist Jean Baudrillard as "the product of an irradiating synthesis of combinatory models in a hyperspace without atmosphere").[1]

The current exhibition, *The New Utilitarian: Examining Our Place on the Motherboard of Ceramics*, takes a look at the meeting (some would say collision), of digital technologies and the ceramic arts. Despite its dynamism and diversity, the community of contemporary ceramics has long been deeply conflicted about advanced technology in general. Certainly the modern studio potter tradition arose out of a desire, in tune with the tenets of the Arts and Craft movement and the western discovery of profound Asian ceramic traditions, to bring back "hand" work – as a reaction against the deadening homogeneity and poor quality of manufactured wares. One of the artists in this exhibition, Garth Johnson, notes, "There are still ceramic artists who look at a slab roller with distrust, not to mention an electric kiln controller or CAD router."[2] At the same time, the computer (and all its ancillary tools) and the World Wide Web have profoundly penetrated our culture. The ironies become glaring when ceramists condemn the dehumanizing effects of industrial processes and new technologies – using as their electronic soapbox the Clayart listserv (http://www.acers.org/cic/clayart/) sponsored by the American Ceramic Society.

Whether they hark back to the insights of the Arts and Crafts visionaries or speak to current anxieties about the loss of haptic experience (the way we experience the world, as bodies in space – not just visually, but with all of our senses), thoughtful ceramists remain for the most part deeply committed to the profound materiality of the ceramic object. At the same time, they find accommodations to, experiment with, and in some cases embrace the digital realm.

The New Utilitarian showcases diverse and stimulating responses to the inescapable presence of new media. Some of the thirteen featured artists critique or interrogate technology. Others acknowledge the ubiquity of the new technologies, crafting out of the detritus of digital culture new metaphors for twenty-first century existence. Still others matter-of-factly turn to digital tools for the creation of their works, designing and in some cases fabricating their objects without direct intervention by the human hand. In general,

---

1   Jean Baudrillard, "The Precession of Simulacra," *Simulations*, trans. Paul Foss, Paul Patton, and Philip Beitchman (New York: Semiotexte, 1983), 3.

2   All quotes from artists in the exhibition, unless otherwise noted, are drawn from their statements in this catalog.

there is little evidence of digital messianism (as embodied by that callow young video artist).

Instead, these ceramists appear calm in the face of radical change, eager to try out new tools, but not overmastered by an insurgent faith.

II

Technology without ideas is nothing. Ideas without the appropriate technology are futile.
                                                    – Richard Notkin

Some artists in *The New Utilitarian* are more comfortable with digital tools than others. Bennett Bean, best known for his complex, gorgeously gilded vessels that allude variously to jewelry designs, Mimbres pots, and the geometric abstractions of painter Larry Poons, first used the computer when he wanted to design rugs. Adobe Photoshop allowed him to "duplicate endlessly complex things over and over, with no labor except a little punch." He adds, "Art is the way you make ideas appear in the world, and the computer is a great tool to do that. Everyone thinks art is about handmaking, but it's no more that than when you're making a novel by typing it. . . . basically it's ideas we're talking about."[3]

Most recently, Bean has designed the pure forms of the ceramic knives in this exhibition using the three-dimensional imaging program, Rhino, and then having the knives fabricated by a Computerized Numerically Controlled [CNC] machine tool. The hand did play a role in the design process, Bean admits. He could not draw the knife he envisioned on the computer; he had to first build the prototype by hand and then scan it. The hand, in a sense, did the imagining. Bean collaborated with jewelers Barbara Heinrich and Caroline Streep to create the knives' sumptuously glittering handles.

Sally Brogden too designs her works on the computer, and a computer-directed tool mills the foam forms out of which she fashions her plaster molds. From these molds emerge her minimalist clay objects, machined and sleek and yet, perhaps because of their

---

3   "Interview: Bennett Bean," Pat Malarcher, interviewer, www.bennettbean.com/articles/ surfacedesign98/surfacedesign.htm; originally published in *Surface Design Journal* 22:3 (Spring 1998).

rich surfaces, invoking what Brogden calls the "memory of touch." In writing about Brodgen's "entirely ambiguous forms," Stephanie Bowman notes the affinities with the work of minimalist Donald Judd and applies art historian Rosalind Krauss's appraisal of Judd to Brogden, that the "illusory power of [the] work is not pictorial illusion but lived illusion."[4] Like the best abstract art in any media, these elegantly pure forms, through some manner of alchemy, awaken all of our senses.

Like others in this exhibition, Gary Carlos uses ceramic tile to create wall murals. His *Dessertification* is, on one level, a visual joke (conflating *desert* with *dessert)* and, on another, a deadly serious critique of the role new technologies play in the ongoing and ever-hastening destruction of natural landscapes. Carlos plays with the pixelation that a wall of tiles can suggest, layering complexity into the image. As he notes, "From up close, [*Dessertification*] resembles a 'false-color' satellite image of an American agricultural region, but from a distance they reveal a pixelated image of two children eagerly reaching for a plate of donuts."

Richard Notkin is best known for his exquisitely crafted small-scale teapots inspired by the Yixing teaware tradition of China. Notkin's teapots offer a critique of technology (or more accurately humanity) that is difficult to refute. Our technologies, his work asserts, grow ever more powerful at the same time that our emotional maturity remains appallingly stunted. Like Carlos, Notkin creates large-scale tile murals that offer, close up and far away, wildly different images. Like the painter Chuck Close (in his portraits composed of rigorous grids, the "pixels" of which are fashioned by hand), Notkin crafts his murals out of small images (in this case tiles), each of which is a beautifully realized composition in its own right. For example, the Notkin work in this exhibition, *Four Tiles (After Michelangelo),* represents just a tiny fraction of the individuated tiles that will make up the mural tentatively entitled *Progress.* From a distance, *Progress* will offer the image of a mushroom cloud while, close up, the cloud will dissolve into more than a thousand tiles (and separate images). Another Notkin mural, *The Gift,* is owned by the

---

4   Stephanie Bowman, "Sally Brogden's Connections," *Ceramics: Art & Perception* 41 (2000), 13.

Portland Art Museum and is currently on exhibit in the museum's Decorative Arts Gallery.

Jeff Irwin is another tile muralist. Irwin uses the computer and laser print transfer processes to create the images that enliven his tiles. These narrative works, reminiscent of German expressionist prints, vividly address environmental concerns. Dense with visual information, works like *Thirst* and *Layered Landscape* – in addition to their ostensible content – seem to echo, and comment on, the dizzying onslaught of information we face from the Internet and other new media (as Baudrillard has fretted, "Doesn't information kill education?").[5]

Garth Johnson has fashioned another kind of mural with his array of plates, *Moon Magic: The Future Is Not as Good as It Used to Be.* As its title explicitly states, this wonderfully loopy work celebrates past visions of the future that, in their fond depiction here, look downright cozy and quaint compared to our hyper present. Odd as it may seem, Johnson's edgy work and ideas (see his web log, *Extreme Craft,* http://extremecraft.blogspot.com, for a further sampling) reveal – at the same time that they critique, with exquisite irony, conspicuous consumption and mass taste – a profound nostalgia for a simpler age.

Steven Montgomery depicts forms of technology – corroding, timeworn machinery – for which we may harbor a surprising nostalgia. His *Disjunction #2,* an image drawn no doubt from his youth in Detroit, represents an engine block sundered by what appear to be natural forces. Montgomery is dedicated to recording the impact of time on the supposedly impregnable artifacts of our industrial culture. He seeks to make each piece, through painstaking effort, appear as if "it just emerged out of the East River after a few decades or was newly extracted from ground zero."[6] Instead of Roman columns, German castles, or Native American tipi rings, Montgomery's ruins are composed of the detritus of our industrial past, rendered ever more poignant as American industry dwindles

---

5   "Cybersphere 9: Philosophy: [Jean] Baudrillard on the New Technologies, an interview with Claude Thibaut," www.uta.edu/english/apt/collab/texts/newtech.html.

6   "Steven Montgomery: Sculpting Time," Pravin Sathe, interviewer, *NY Arts Magazine,* 9:7/8 (July/August 2004), http://nyartsmagazine.com/pages/nyam_document.php?nid=43&did=281.

in the face of global forces.

British-born Margaret Realica creates her own remarkable technological artifacts. These works, constructed of porcelain but also of Plexiglas, plastic tubing, and electrical parts, celebrate the inventiveness that technology can engender. Coolly playful, Realica's tuners, turbines, and water devices might suggest some Rube Goldberg experiment except that they are infinitely more elegant than some hastily assembled, purely functional assemblage of parts. They possess a mysterious rightness, an aura of efficiency and intricate utility. Far from their inspiration in the humble teapot, Realica's objects exist in a utopian future, evidence of a science-based creativity that embraces pleasure.

Like Margaret Realica, Steven Thurston is fascinated and inspired by the sciences. He uses many materials (poplar, castable refractory mix, Rayite Machinable Media, bee's wax, and found hardware) in his allegorical works – and like Realica, he is clearly not looking backward to a crafty paradise, where advanced technology is never welcome. As he says, "I [have] willingly embraced . . . new forms of technologies to find a balance between traditional craft and industrial practice." Whether they echo eighteenth-century architecture, atomic particles, or cellular structures, his creations seek to analyze the "relationship between an object and the process required to generate that object." This lends to his magical structures a sense that they have been wrested from an alternative universe, one where "unknown forms" seem slightly familiar because they resemble other forms we know well – and yet they possess a truly bracing strangeness.

Seattle-based Charles Krafft is known for his wit, and certainly his *SPONETM Sentry Series* is evidence of his darkly playful and complex sensibility. But in their sheer beauty and because of the unsettling presence of human remains (crematory ash) in the bone china formula Krafft has borrowed from Josiah Spode, the series' shovels recall us to their memorial purpose. Whether he is simultaneously exploring the histories of weaponry and porcelain (as with his *Porcelain War Museum Project*) or, as here, the rituals, ancient and modern, of death, Krafft's humor and irony scarcely mask his deeper purpose: to comment on central human issues and, while he is at it, to subvert what he refers to as "all the Bernard Leachian sanctimony that seemed to go with studio potting."[7]

As Paul McMullan notes, he is a true citizen of the technological present, and his work reflects a fascination with pop culture (echoing the concerns of the pioneering Pop and Funk artists as well as those of postmodern avatars like Jeff Koons). They also evince a willingness to engage what he terms "this culture of mass imagery and propaganda . . . this bombardment of information." His assembled works, collaged out of "forms derived from handmade and hobbyshop moulds,"[8] offer us witty perspectives on the disquieting ways in which the hyperreal invades our conscious minds.

A native of Hong Kong, Ho, Sin-ying offers an immensely sophisticated meditation on contemporaneity with her objects that yoke ancient ceramic forms with computer decal transfers and the ones and zeroes of binary code. The cyber text deployed across her blue-and-white porcelain vessels is an insistent notation, as rigorous in its beauty as any human alphabet. Ho speaks of her "ongoing observations of the old and the new in terms of communication, language, aesthetics, technology, identity, economy and power." This ambitious inventory clearly informs every detail of her articulate work, and from her perspective as the resident of three different countries (Hong Kong, Canada, and the United States) and participant in two languages (Cantonese and English), she affords us a truly global perspective, one in which "many nationalities and cultures . . . merge together and evolve into an unknown." In her sure hands, the unknown, this *Gibberish,* results in wholly fresh works of art, among the most unexpected in this exhibition.

With her haunting *TWomb,* the Korean-born artist Nina Jun may have created the most successful, and philosophically satisfying, melding of the real and the virtual in *The New Utilitarian.* This birth/death nest/mound – which echoes Samuel Beckett's memorable phrase, "[giving] birth astride a grave" – combines shards of "inert" ceramic with video imagery dancing with virtual life. This apparent contradiction, that the digital represents living, pulsing energy while the shards symbolize the end of life, suggests that our knee-jerk suspicions. may not be borne out by experience. Perhaps the parallel (or

---

7   Charles Krafft, "The Devil's Hobby Hut," *Studio Potter* 27:2 (June 1999), 40.

8   Peter J. Barr, "Paul McMullan: In the Fullness of Time," *Ceramics: Art & Perception* 57 (2004), 30.

shadow) universe made up of pixels does not *necessarily* take us away from genuine lived existence.Underscoring this apparent paradox, critic Donald Kuspit asserts in a provocative recent essay,

> Digital representation is supposedly more emotionally remote and intellectual than painted representation. But this is not necessarily so. The intensification of optical quality that digitalization brings with it more than compensates for the loss of the haptic dimension, all the more so because the digitalized sensation is in constant optical motion, generating an intimacy and vividness all its own. . . . the geometrical code is more substantial than the material body.[9]

Whether or not we are convinced by Kuspit's startling thesis, the works by the thirteen artists in this exhibition provide powerful arguments for the importance of, and infinite possibilities for, extending the ceramic arts via digital media. Further, *The New Utilitarian* suggests that bringing together the virtual with the ancient medium of clay will lead to ever more assured and fully realized expressions. Without becoming true believers in new media, ceramists will doubtless continue to use the full array of digital tools and to exploit the tensions, contradictions, and ambivalences that this collision between new and old – between the virtual and the material – fruitfully engenders.

---

9   Donald Kuspit, "The Matrix of Sensations," *artnet Magazine,* August 5, 2005, http://www.artnet.com/magazineus/features/kuspit/kuspit8-5-05.asp.

The Aesthetics of Disappearance
Ceramic Perforation in a Postmodern Age

Originally published in Emily Galusha & Rick Newby,
*Perforation: Tony Marsh, Jeffrey Mongrain, Mary Roehm, Marit
Tingleff, Xavier Toubes* (Minneapolis, MN: Northern Clay Center,
2005).

*To pierce, punch, or bore a hole or holes in; penetrate. To pass into or
through something:* The act of perforation has played – since ancient
times, in many cultures – a role in the creation of works made of clay.
And yet, despite its long history, ceramic perforation takes on new
meanings, new tonalities, a fresh vibrancy in this first decade of the
twenty-first century.

As evidenced by the works of the five ceramic artists in this
exhibition, perforation clearly remains an important strategy in the
world of postmodern ceramics, driven by new (or revived) interest
in such themes as ornament (condemned to oblivion by high modernism), dematerialization of the object, technology as boon *and*
threat, the utilitarian versus the use-free, and the polarities of light/
shade, positive/negative, presence/absence, inside/outside.

Mary Roehm, Xavier Toubes, Jeffrey Mongrain, Marit
Tingleff, and Tony Marsh each bring maturity, intelligence, and
exceptional craftsmanship to their perforated works, but their approaches are radically different one from the other, emerging out
of differing contexts, reflecting strikingly distinct sensibilities.
Perforation is only one of a number of strategies these artists em-
ploy, but it clearly represents a central concern – in some cases, a
full-blown obsession – for each of them.

For millennia, traditional ceramists most often made their holes for
purely practical purposes. In the Korean ceramic tradition, for example, potters fashioned the crocks called *onggi* from a clay body
that contained grains of sand and other impurities. In the firing, the
impurities vaporized, leaving behind tiny holes that allowed the vessels to breathe. This rendered the rustic "life-breathing" *onggi* jars
perfect for storing fermented foods like bean paste, soy sauce, and

kimchi. Some Southwestern American Indian cultures pierced ceramic disks, crafted from potsherds, with a single hole in the center and used them as spindle whorls. Larger disks discovered at archaeological digs in Oklahoma and Arizona have as many as ten perforations; these may have been used as strainers or jar covers (again allowing for ventilation).

Early Egyptian potters drilled a hole four millimeters in diameter through the shoulders of their *amphorae* (wine jars). These holes may have allowed the gases produced by fermentation to escape, but more likely, they allowed a merchant to treat his clients to a taste of the wine without breaking the vessel's seal. The client would draw wine through the hole, using a hollow reed as pipette.

Other ancient clay workers perforated their vessels for mysterious, most likely spiritual or ceremonial, reasons – often related to death and the afterlife. In one American Southwest tradition, the Mimbres people created funerary pots with holes in their bottoms. Such a "spirit hole," writes potter and scholar Rina Swentzell of the Santa Clara Pueblo, "is the place through which the breath flows." These pots were often "placed over the head of the buried person, for it was known that when people died their breath left their body." Through the pierced pot, the deceased's breath "rolled back up into the clouds."[1] In Bronze Age Germany, the perforations in funerary vessels (which held the ashes of cremated loved ones) allowed family members to periodically place offerings of animal bones or meat inside the urns.

By the mid-twentieth century, as modernism emerged in the ceramic world, clay artists aimed to break free of the craft label and elevate their work to the level of fine art. Revolutionaries like Peter Voulkos explored various strategies – including perforation – in their search for a new vocabulary. As early as 1956, borrowing equally from the Japanese *Haniwa* tradition and Abstract Expressionism, Voulkos created his *Rocking Pot*, in Karen Tsujimoto's words, "an upside-down vessel with crudely carved holes [that] sits on two rockers, its simple form pierced by crescent-shaped shards." The *Rocking Pot*, asserts Tsujimoto, "ruptured all connections to utilitarian pottery,

---

1   Rina Swentzell, "Walk Carefully in the World: Mimbres and the Pueblo Tradition," *Studio Potter* 28:1 (1999), 51.

literally and figuratively overturning the pot form."[2] Voulkos and such peers and students as Paul Soldner and Peter Callas ripped, tore, and pierced their work with unprecedented fierceness, always in the service of greater expressivity, and to establish clay as a medium equal to bronze, stone, and wood for the making of sculpture.

In recent years, in what Garth Clark has called this "boundary-less world of postmodernism," many clay artists besides those featured in this exhibition have turned to perforation as one technique among the dazzling array available to them.[3] Lawson Oyekan creates trunk-like vessels of stoneware that reference the giant anthills of his native Nigeria; pierced with countless holes, his many-eyed totems seem to watch over us, quietly attentive. German artist Barbara Schmidt creates – out of porcelain and wire – elegant ceramic lace, bridging the boundaries between clay and textiles. American ceramist Jimmy Clark makes pit-fired storage jars that often have "spirit holes" inspired by the Mimbres tradition.

Canadian Jim Thomson produces "corrosive, assaulting" work that alludes to such functional perforated forms as colanders, sieves, drain covers, and filtration screens. According to writer Mick Wilson, Henry Pim's perforated fragments suggest "filters and other various broken grids and lattices," and "the skin of the palm and fingertips is set to itching by seeing the edge[s] of those perforated holes." In Norwegian ceramist Sidsel Hanum's streamlined minimalist forms, the perforations "provide associations," writes Frank Falch, "with the opportunities inherent in clay . . . with its contrasting soft vulnerability and its ultimate hardened state."[4]

Perforations in ceramic vessels challenge – play with, even mock – our assumptions about ceramics as simply utilitarian craft. Danish editor Jorunn Veiteberg has written, "Does the production of utility objects and the creation of works of art represent two distinct spaces with different rankings in the cultural hierarchy, or do

---

2   Karen Tsujimoto, "Peter Voulkos: The Wood-fired Work," in Rose Slivka and Karen Tsujimoto, *The Art of Peter Voulkos* (Tokyo/Oakland: Kodansha International/The Oakland Museum, 1995), 100

3   Garth Clark, "Meaning and Memory: The Roots of Postmodern Ceramics, 1960–1980," introduction, Mark Del Vecchio, *Postmodern Ceramics* (New York: Thames & Hudson, 2001), 23.

4   Glenn Allison, "Fire at Both Ends: Recent Work of Jim Thomson," *Ceramics: Art & Perception* (Sydney) 52 (2003), 26; Mick Wilson, "Henry Pim: Grids Conduits Bodies," *Ceramics: Art & Perception* 50 (2002), 43, 44; Frank Falch, "Sidsel Hanum's Ceramic Minimalism," *Ceramics: Art & Perception* 38 (1999), 65.

. . . 'thinking objects' [by artists working in media traditionally associated with the crafts] allow for other points of view?"[5] The works by the five artists in this exhibition are certainly "thinking objects" riddled with contradictions, rich in ideas, steeped in metaphorical significance, and often quite simply beautiful. They most certainly blur the boundaries between craft and art and, by their sheer presence (linked to an equal urge for absence), move us far beyond the old dichotomies.

Mary Roehm: The Space Between

In speaking of her pierced bowls, cups, cylinders, and columns (some as tall as six feet), Mary Roehm prefers to use the term "punctuation" rather than "puncture." She sees her punctuations – and the visual rhythms they engender – as a way to "strengthen the form without changing the form." She adds, "It's so active. It activates the piece." Like scarifications on a human body, her piercings render the familiar unfamiliar, generating what early Russian modernist Viktor Shklovsky called "enstrangement" whereby we encounter an object "as if it were perceived for the first time."[6]

This activation, this enstrangement, in her view, happens because the punctuation challenges the "viewer to consider volume and space in a different way." Critic Nancy Princenthal, in a 2001 essay, notes that Roehm's "ruptures are . . . obstacles to received ideas, causing interest in what ordinarily is unmarked, purely latent emptiness, but refusing the usual, complementary definition of solid form."[7]

Roehm's most recent work, including the pieces in this exhibition, she finds more cerebral – situated somewhere between the analytic and the intuitive – than her previous work (which was "born of a potter's perspective"). As she works with perforations and oppositions, juxtaposing white and black porcelains (the black is based upon a clay body she first encountered at Shigaraki, Japan), she talks of our desire to see things in simplistic black and white and about

---

5   Jorunn Veiteberg, "Scandinavia," in the special section "Shapes of Things to Come," *Crafts* (London) 181 (2003), 24–25.

6   Viktor Shklovsky, *Theory of Prose* (1929; Elmwood Park, IL: Dalkey Archive Press, 1990), 6.

7   All quotations from the artists in this exhibition are drawn, unless otherwise noted, from phone and email interviews with the author conducted in spring 2005; Nancy Princenthal, "Mary Roehm: Emptiness Deferred," in *Mary Roehm* (Philadelphia: The Works Gallery, 2001), 1

how, with her elegant "split" cylinders and still lives with alternating black and white vessels, she tries to show "the space between . . . where we should live." About respecting difference and understanding that "both perspectives can be right," these works, in the words of Shigaraki ceramist Shiro Otani, "are full of tension, but also exude a certain warmheartedness." The aura that surrounds them, he adds, affords "a moment of relief from the turbulence and complexity of modern life. . . . Stillness is what I feel."[8]

A long-time professor of ceramics at State University of New York–New Paltz, Roehm travels frequently to Japan and calls a number of Japanese ceramic artists friends, but still, she notes, her work resides somewhere between East and West. She is drawn to the western modernist tradition, but finds it limited and seeks to "make it richer" through a variety of strategies, including perforation ("tear it, open it, alter it," she says). Likewise, though she "respects and loves" Japanese and Chinese ceramics, she really sees herself taking the grand Asian porcelain tradition and "challenging or contradicting" it.

Never content with mere technical mastery (she is celebrated for her extraordinary throwing ability), Roehm continually seeks to challenge her materials, to "go to the extreme to find restraint." By drawing upon, and playing with, multiple traditions, she achieves remarkable works that bristle with punctuations, capturing our attention and bringing us to think anew about volume and emptiness, presence and the somehow comforting absence of certainty.

Jeffrey Mongrain: Re-igniting the Common

As a young man, Jeffrey Mongrain briefly attended seminary, but ultimately decided against becoming a Jesuit priest. The decision to turn away from his vocation did not foreclose an interest in the spiritual, and today, Mongrain creates many of his most powerful works for religious spaces. In recent years, he has completed site-specific installations in Christus Church, Cologne, Germany; the Cathedral of St. John the Divine, New York; La Scala Santa, Rome; and Corpus Christi Church, Baltimore. Most recently, he has accepted a commission to

---

8   Quoted in *Mary Roehm: Sense & Sensibility* (New York: Dalchi Gallery, 2002), unpaginated.

install a work in the Basilica of St. Mary in Minneapolis. As Janet Koplos has noted in *Art in America,* visiting a Jeffrey Mongrain exhibition, because of his work's "inward concentration and spiritual aura," can feel "like making stops on a pilgrimage."[9]

A native Minnesotan (born in International Falls) and today teaching at Hunter College, New York City, Mongrain works with many materials, ranging from clay, wax, stone, glass, and iron to water and sewing thread. He is drawn to strong reductive visual forms, and the minimalist "icons" he fashions are often freighted with personal significances that he translates – by mysterious means – into universal metaphors.

For Mongrain, as with the other artists in this exhibition, perforation is one of many strategies. He chooses to pierce his ceramic bells, pillows, haloes, and disks because the holes set up a "visual vibration, a visual twinkle," and like Mary Roehm, he likes, in his words, to "re-ignite the identity of a common object." Somehow, his perforations generate the illusion of motion; his bells especially seem to move, or are about to move, or must surely move should we turn our eyes away.

During the eight years he spent teaching at the Glasgow (Scotland) School of Art, Mongrain developed a deep appreciation both for visually rich Gothic interior spaces (where he would site his installations) and for the remarkable statuary and other memorials Europeans have long created to honor their dead. He was especially taken with the medieval crypt sculptures known as *gisants* he found in Great Britain. As Glen R. Brown has written in *Sculpture,* "Despite the naturalism and life-size scale of these *gisants,* their function as memorials . . . render[s] them less surrogate presences than eternal reminders of the absence of the deceased."[10] Mongrain's "gently abstracted" *Pillow with Drain* and *Halo Hollow* likewise speak to us of human absence, even if nonspecific (we can provide our own losses), and his bells seem to toll out memories, fragments of a past irrevocably lost.

Another kind of loss is memorialized in Mongrain's recent *Pierced Moose and Branch,* in which multiple piercings acknowledge the impact global warming has had on the vegetation that no longer

---

9   Janet Koplos, "Jeffrey Mongrain at Perimeter [Gallery]," *Art in America* (July 2002), 98.

10   Glen R. Brown, "Jeffrey Mongrain: Invocations of Absence," *Sculpture* 20:5 (June 2001), 14.

sustains this great North Woods creature. Mongrain collected the leafless branch – from which this branch was cast in an amber red resin – in northern Minnesota.

Not all of Mongrain's sculptures are about leave-taking or sorrow. Another recent work, created specifically for this show, speaks of an absence reimagined as presence. This work, *Atrial Septal Defect EKG: 1st Open Heart Surgery, Sept. 2, 1952; Sound Wave Series,* commemorates the world's first successful open heart surgery to repair a 12-millimeter hole in the heart of a five-year-old girl; the surgery was conducted at the University of Minnesota in the early 1950s. A celebration of the possibility of redemption or reclamation, this polished black disk, with its ripples replicating the sound waves of the young girl's heartbeat, reminds us that every loss need not be irrevocable.

Visual as well as aural phenomena fascinate Mongrain, and with his *E-Peephole: Iris of Dr. John Daugman,* he interrogates the concern for personal security that obsesses our contemporary culture. This white ceramic disk, modeled on the peephole in an apartment door, shows us the iris of a visitor, and not just any visitor, but that of the inventor of the technology that allows positive identification of human beings by scanning their irises. There is something unsettling – "ghost-like," Mongrain says – about contemplating this ever-present, unblinking eye.

Whether he is celebrating the irrepressibility of hope, worrying about a kind of ocular omniscience, memorializing losses, or underscoring absence with visual vibrations, Jeffrey Mongrain reorients us – in each work, using perforation precisely as appropriate – to the world, its heartbreaks and benevolent spirits, its terrors and piercing joys.

Xavier Toubes: Poet of the Material World

Born in A Coruna, Galicia, Spain, Xavier Toubes is a genuinely international artist. Educated in London and at New York State College of Ceramics at Alfred University, he taught for a decade at the University of North Carolina. He then spent the 1990s as Artistic Director of the European Ceramics Work Centre (EKWC) in the Netherlands, where he established himself as a remarkable visionary in the field of ceramics.

Toubes' vision was a response to modernism, not as pure reaction (as in the case of much postmodernist art practice), but rather in the spirit of possibility. He saw the Work Centre as a place of research and experimentation, where the "tremendous potentiality" of ceramics could be realized. This meant exploring the ceramic traditions of every culture, making available any and all materials to the resident artists, providing the latest technological tools, and introducing artists from other realms to the clay arts. (Today, Toubes serves as professor of art in the School of the Art Institute of Chicago.)

Critic Polly Ullrich has written that, in Toubes' view, "ceramics . . . pose a convincing alternative to a contemporary art community still in thrall to the practices of Conceptualism and the dematerialization of the art object." In addition, he wanted to further liberate ceramics from its craft roots; he sought particularly to "wrench the identity of ceramics away from . . . the requirements that [it] be small in scale, non-vertical, symmetrical and of a certain thickness."[11]

Certainly, in his own art practice, Toubes has succeeded in achieving these goals. His often large-scale and vertical works reflect his concerns with materiality (especially his desire for surfaces that are "very much worked"), his pursuit of beauty (which often involves an "unfinished quality"), and his drive to take a stand as a "maker of things." Toubes' involvement with perforation has extended throughout his career. Early on, he started making holes in many of his pieces, but it was never an issue, something to which he devoted much thought. It came naturally, perhaps as a reflection of his urge to convey meaning through the much-worked "skin" of his objects.

He acknowledges that his perforations speak to the tension between inside and outside and make the viewer "spatially and intellectually aware of the interior" as part of the vessel. Critic Vincent McGourty expresses this quality in Toubes' work, "By multiple piercing of the vessel there is an attempt . . . to drain off the fixity of what we accept as the identity of vesselhood. . . . The flow is paradoxically both ways because the holes allow us to access the inner space of the vessel, which at the same time they render void."[12]

The works by Xavier Toubes in this exhibition are more

---

11   Polly Ullrich, "Xavier Toubes," *American Craft* (June/July 2001), 65.

12   Vincent McGourty, "Xavier Toubes: New Worlds – New Vessels," *Ceramics: Art & Perception* 44 (2001), 14

sculptural than vessel oriented. These expressive forms, variously made of porcelain and stoneware, are rendered further articulate by their bubbled, blasted, pierced surfaces. Coiling and pinching the clay, Toubes works rapidly, often on several pieces at once, some of them as tall as seven feet. And he directs much of his attention to their skins, manipulating the surfaces by hand and various tools, applying glazes and lusters, subjecting them to acids, sandblasting them. He tries to keep his efforts "fresh or innocent," always experimenting.

Although the perforations in his sculptures may allude to the dematerialization of the art object or the "aesthetics of disappearance" championed by poststructuralists, Xavier Toubes' densely worked and profoundly present sculptures, inescapable in their solidity, lend *gravitas* to our ongoing engagement with the physicality of existence.

Marit Tingleff: The Space Inside

Norwegian ceramist Marit Tingleff created her first perforated piece in 1988. She was worried about the holes in the ozone layer, and she had always been attracted to "beautiful old porcelain dishes with perforations." She made her piece as a metaphor for ozone loss and as a tribute to perforation in the porcelain tradition.

She soon found herself adding perforations to other works. She had long been fascinated by the theme of "doubling," and the titles of her work reflect this concern: *Dark Double; Object with Double Bottom; Double-walled, Fast Bowl; Double Black and White.* She began by asking herself fundamental questions: "What is a volume? How can I explain a thickness in the wall? How can I get air and light into a massive material [like] clay? Why do I, who works in this three-dimensional material, paint the ornaments instead of model them?"

This questioning led Tingleff to further perforation. She was not "so interested in the perforation in itself, but how the holes or the piercing arise when I am modeling the walls – or the surface. Maybe what I find most interesting: how the perforation can let me (you) inside the wall, to a hidden space, the volume of the wall."

Edmund de Waal writes that Tingleff makes "'uneasy objects' with hidden volumes, false bases and strange pierced openings that confuse the eye and hand."[13] Tingleff notes that it has "never been my intention to disorient the viewer, but to surprise or invite the viewer to discover some new strange landscapes." She is most interested in the "shadow the piercing makes and how the holes make it possible for the viewer to touch the inside of the body (quite sensual!)."

This interrogation and exploration of three-dimensional vessels – and especially Tingleff's interest in modeling her decoration, building it into the work, as well as applying it as glaze – lends a seductively tactile quality to her work. As a painter, Tingleff works with slips to achieve a sense of depth to the surfaces of her monumental platters. "I paint," she says, "layer onto layer, wash off, add something new, dig into details – the space within the one-dimensional surface, the colour lying behind the colours."[14] In this, she is influenced by abstract painters like Asger Jorn, Cy Twombly, Gerhard Richter, and Mark Rothko, but equally by Thorvald Bindesboll (1846–1908), the first Danish modernist architect and a prolific ceramist whose work remains a touchstone for her.

Today, perforation has become essential to certain of Tingleff's works. When she decided, for example, to make a series of ceramic clouds, she wondered, "Can the heavy clay give an expression of air and light?" In her experiments, she quickly discovered that "without piercing, these shells [of the cloud forms] were without life, just stiff and ugly; with holes the air could flow and the space inside became alive." Indeed, Marit Tingleff's wonderfully expressive organic forms, with their great depth and marvelous sensual surfaces (and interiors), gently pierced to allow in the air and light, offer every evidence of being very much alive.

Tony Marsh: Like a Veil

In a conversation with fellow ceramist Kurt Weiser and independent curator Jo Lauria, Tony Marsh addressed his practice of perforation in relation to the dematerialization of the art object. He said, "I remove as much as possible of the forms but instead of making them

---

13   Edmund de Waal, "Marit Tingleff and Martin Bodilsen Kaldahl: Galleri Norby, Copenhagen," *Ceramic Review* (United Kingdom) 201 (2003), 57.

14   Quoted in de Waal, 57.

less, this seems to add a strange and interesting dimension to them."[15] This apparent paradox underscores the power and persistence of the ceramic object even when an artist like Marsh pushes the clay to the verge of dematerialization. In the face of willed oblivion, it somehow asserts its obdurate materiality.

Tony Marsh, perhaps more than any other artist in this exhibition, has pushed the limits of perforation furthest. For many years, he perforated his vessels fiercely, punching "absolutely as many" holes as possible, always aiming to render the boundaries between presence and absence ever thinner (since 2002, he has turned to new, non-perforated bodies of work). He loved the process of subtraction. It brought him into an "engagement with light," a rare thing for a ceramic artist, and it was rife with risk. Because he had to work quickly, with absolute attention, he felt a total engagement. He made the walls of his earthenware objects thinner and thinner, his holes smaller and closer together. He drilled each hole individually, when the clay was leather-hard, and because his walls were so thin and the holes so close together, he lost nearly half of the objects he started. Although he never counted, he believes many of his objects have "six, eight, ten thousand holes."

As a young potter, Marsh spent three years at the Shimaoka Pottery in Mashiko, Japan. Halfway through his stay, he was invited to assist the workshop's master potter, Tatsuzo Shimaoka, a National Living Treasure of Japan. It was not an easy year and a half. The master was strict and unbending, but Marsh grew to deeply admire him as a "clear reflection of his culture" and his work as a kind of encoding of that particular place and time. Marsh found himself challenging many things in the Japanese tradition, but upon his return to the States, he realized that he, too, must be of his own time and place, not just copying Japanese pots.

In many ways, Marsh's work developed in opposition to the Japanese tradition. His way of working, rapidly, with absolute attention, was most definitely "not about meditation." And the work itself, with all its perforations, did not even pretend to be about utility. Though pieces by this quintessentially American artist have often been mistaken for the work of a European modernist, their quiet

---

15   Jo Lauria, "Dialogues in Clay: A Conversation between Tony Marsh and Kurt Weiser," *Ceramics: Art & Perception* 50 (2002), 11.

restraint, as Marsh is quick to point out, reflects a deep connection to Asian ceramics.

As Marsh further refined his perforated vessels and objects, they did seem almost to disappear. "Like a veil," they let light pass through, generating shadows within and without. Marsh further enhanced the otherworldliness of these objects by slowly applying four coats of a white vitreous engobe to their surfaces. The engobe (between a clay and a glaze) softened the edges of the perforations and allowed the light to bounce around inside and then pass back out, generating a subtle, uncanny glow.

No longer considering himself a potter, Marsh aims rather to honor potters with his work. He speaks of pottery as a "very old, strange, abstract expression somewhere between culture and nature." "Some pots," he says, "are just as powerful as any art object." Today a professor at California State University, Long Beach, Tony Marsh continues to create elemental forms that, like the pots they honor, afford us immense visual and tactile pleasure and speak eloquently to our shared humanity. At the same time, like the works of the other artists in this exhibition, his perforated forms bring fresh light and air to a rich and ancient tradition.

Jerry Bennett and Bean Finneran
Pushing the Limits

First appeared in the exhibition catalog, *Provocative Clay*, ed. Lena Vigna (John Michael Kohler Arts Center, 2010 [digital version]/2022 [print version]).

In this time we call the postmodern, the ceramic arts have grown increasingly, even wildly, diverse. Since the 1950s, gallery-goers have often encountered handcrafted pots of undoubted utility alongside adventurous ceramic sculptural works that (more-or-less comfortably) straddle craft and fine art traditions.

The American artists Jerry Bennett and Bean Finneran – and their works featured in *Pushing the Limits* at the John Michael Kohler Arts Center – stand at the sculptural end of this continuum. And yet their "seed jars" and "cones," "rings" and "cores" challenge our notions of what ceramic sculpture should be. By their apparent fragility, they leave us musing: How are these structures built? What do they signify? How do these artists achieve their startling effects, of near transparency, of apparent randomness that still achieves a pleasing order, of lightness in the face of an obdurate gravity?

At opposite ends of the North American continent (Bennett in Philadelphia and Finneran on San Francisco Bay), the two artists explore natural and cultural forms in ways that are kindred and yet radically dissimilar. Each creates his or her work by assembling multiple objects. One sees himself firmly within the ancient and honorable tradition of the ceramic arts, while the other avows that she is simply a contemporary sculptor who happens to use clay. One, stripping almost all color from his work, seeks the perfect shade of white; the other saturates her stacks of "curves" with impossibly vibrant colors. Their mutual achievement is to refresh the art of clay, bringing to this most mutable of materials qualities of whimsicality, inventiveness, and an undeniable sense of play, together with an almost spiritual aura – lovingly built into the works through untold hours of patient labor.

Vessel shapes. Gridded structures that allude to open-weave textiles, chain-link fences, the skeletons of buildings under construction, the box trusses of suspension bridges. Plant-like tendrils with plenty of gesture: Jerry Bennett's seed jars and baskets are hybrid creatures, referring both to the burgeoning natural world and to the ingenious artifacts humans have always left in their wake.

Bennett's sculptures derive their peculiar delicacy (and strength) from the porcelanous paper clay the artist uses in their construction. Bennett is a key figure in what he terms the "exploding" field of paper clay (he was an honored guest at the 2005 First International Paper Clay Symposium in Kesckmét, Hungary, and he has led paper clay workshops at Philadelphia's Clay Studio and the International Ceramic Studio in Hungary).

Paper clay, simply put, is clay mixed with paper fibers, rendering it extraordinarily strong, even when wet. As sculptor Valerie Lyle puts it, paper clay offers "the multiple benefits of greenware strength, moisture wicking for fast even drying, and wet on dry applications." Writing in *Ceramic Review,* Felicity Aylieff notes that paper clay has "had a phenomenal impact on the development of ceramics in recent years, significantly broadening the scope of the 'achievable' in clay and providing opportunities to create work of considerable scale, strength and complexity."[1] Bennett especially values the ability of paper clay to resist warping and its strength prior to firing, allowing him to move his delicate structures to the kiln without breakage.

Another American sculptor who regularly uses paper clay, Rebecca Hutchinson, points out that clay strengthened by adding cellulose (whether it is paper or straw or other plant fibers) is nothing new. For millennia, humans have built enduring structures of earthen bricks fortified with cellulose – think of the numerous vernacular building traditions based on adobe (a Spanish word derived from the Arabic), from Asia to North Africa to the Americas.[2] Jerry Bennett has managed to make this ancient and earthy material his own, weaving improbably ethereal structures that seem to radiate (or gather) light. (In addition to his work in ceramics, Jerry Bennett is a weaver, and his gridded structures could just as easily derive from

---

1   Valerie G. Lyle, "Figurative Sculpture in Paper Clay" (MFA Thesis, Department of Art and Design, East Tennessee State University, 2001), 22; Felicity Aylieff, "Working with Paperclay and Other Additives," *Ceramic Review* 189 (May–June 2001), 56.

2   Rebecca Hutchinson, interview with the author, Helena, Montana, July 2005.

textile weaving traditions as from architectural models or the outlines of African seed jars.)

Like the contemporary ceramic artists who punch or drill
holes in their vessels and other forms in an effort to counter the solidity of clay,[3] Bennett hopes – by painstakingly building his jars of
thin coils ("about the thickness of a soda straw") – to truly push the
limits, rendering his works translucent, or better yet, to make them
nearly vanish, leaving behind only a glimmer of texture and a hint of
structure. In this impossible pursuit of simplicity and transparency,
Bennett has, in recent years, radically reduced his palette, moving
almost exclusively to white (he notes that "this heightens the interest
of the surface").[4]

Bennett avows a lifelong interest in patterning; "it's built into
me," he says. Paper clay allows him to explore "very thin, highly textured surfaces in the intricately assembled vessel forms." He adds that
his thin coils, "through their repetition . . . form a pattern which
not only envelops the surface but also defines the line and structure
of the forms."[5] This integration of means infuses these delightfully
eccentric and antic works with barely controlled energies; they seem
about to topple, or lift off, or reach out and touch us.

Aiming to create "more than just a vessel," Bennett sees each
of his seed jars as a metaphor for the importance of protecting genetic quality, a crucial issue in this time of ongoing threats to the
biosphere and destruction of species. The tendrils that animate each
piece, reaching out to the light (or to passersby), invoke plant forms
and, for the artist, the agglomerations of tiny creatures that make up
coral reefs (threatened in much of the world). This ecological concern underlies all of Bennett's work, infusing his airy forms with a
marvelous liveliness and, at the same time, a sense of the fragility of
our earthly existence (Bennett expresses the fear that we humans –
and our technology – will "destroy it all").

Jerry Bennett's works in *Pushing the Limits* claim our attention,
and our affection, by celebrating complexity and diversity and by

---

3   See Rick Newby, "The Aesthetics of Disappearance: Ceramic Perforation in a Postmodern
Age" in *Perforation: Tony Marsh, Jeffrey Mongrain, Mary Roehm, Marit Tingleff, Xavier Toubes*
(Minneapolis, MN: Northern Clay Center, 2005).

4   All quotations from Jerry Bennett and Bean Finneran are drawn, unless otherwise noted,
from phone and email interviews with the author conducted in June–July 2005.

5   Jerry Bennett Pottery website, "Artist's Statement," www.jerrybennett.net/pages/11/.

being quite simply beautiful – exotic (and richly spiritual) forms that seem to have emerged unbidden into the light. *Philadelphia Inquirer* critic Victoria Donohoe recently wondered, "Might [Bennett's] next step be to spiritualize things a bit" so that his "art can be seen as the vehicle for something other than glamorous surface?" With this extraordinary body of work, Jerry Bennett has achieved just such a spiritualization, but without disguising what Donohoe has praised as the "unmistakable buoyancy . . . energy – and . . . idiosyncrasy" that have been his trademarks.[6]

Bean Finneran makes her home on the verge of a salt marsh in Marin County, just north of San Francisco. Infatuated by her surroundings, by powerful tidal forces and extravagant sea creatures, this sculptor has found a manner of working that celebrates the natural wonders she witnesses every day and, at the same time, places her on the cutting edge of ceramic sculpture. Having first worked in clay as a production jewelry maker – and coming from a background in the performing arts – Finneran brings to her sculpture an approach inspired less by ceramic vessel traditions and more by late-twentieth century vanguard sculpture movements, especially post-Minimalism. Unlike Jerry Bennett, who sees himself firmly ensconced within ceramic tradition (and his work as a meditation on traditional forms), Finneran is, in her own estimation, simply a sculptor who works with a material that serves beautifully to enact her vision.

Like Jerry Bennett, Finneran favors repetition and assembling works out of multiples. In her case, all of the works in this exhibition are built of "curves," curved rods of fired clay that she colors vividly with acrylic stains. Even though, within a single work, the curves are similar in size and identical in color, Finneran rolls the pieces by hand, rendering them unique, just as every blade of grass or snowflake is unique.

Finneran eschews the mechanical production of her multiples because she wants the "action of the hand" to be evident. "It's insane,

---

6   Victoria Donohoe, *Philadelphia Inquirer,* March 20, 2005, quoted in Jerry Bennett Pottery website, "Reviews," www.jerrybennett.net/pages/11/.

I know," she says of her laborious process, but then she speaks of her commitment to a slow and thoughtful transformation of materials and space. Like the artist Allan McCollum, instead of creating – in the words of art historian Rosalind Krauss – an "endlessly proliferating series of increasingly meaningless signs," Finneran's one-of-a-kind multiples "seem instead to have the character of something absolutely unique."[7]

In an essay on Ann Hamilton (a sculptor Finneran admires), the critic Rebecca Solnit writes, "Making art is in some ways a gesture against [the] speed and fragmentation of production, a restoration of the full process from imagination to execution, of the relationship between mind and hands."[8] Finneran speaks of a corresponding desire to infuse her work with a sense of time, of fully lived experience that can never be successfully mimicked by industrial processes. Like Jackie Winsor and other post-Minimalists, she is acutely aware that, as Bruce Kurtz has expressed it, her investment of long hours in meditative labor allows the "resulting form" to visually re-enact "the slow process of its becoming."[9]

Alongside her jewelry and sculpture careers, Finneran has participated as a performer (since the early 1970s) in one of North America's finest cutting-edge theater companies, Soon 3 Theatre of San Francisco. The brainchild of her husband, Alan Finneran, Soon 3 presented works of non-narrative visual theater throughout the world. As Martin Esslin, the biographer of Bertolt Brecht, has written, Soon 3's works are "brilliantly choreographed as a sequence of stylized movements which are clearly part of a work-process and yet have the emotional force and awe-inspiring power of a religious rite." Critic and scholar Theodore Shank has noted that, in Soon 3's works, there is

> no pre-existing concept from which the performance grows, no idea to be investigated or illustrated. Instead [Alan Finneran] makes intuitive decisions about the objects, performers, and tasks to be incorporated and

---

7   Rosalind E. Krauss, "X Marks the Spot," in Krauss and Yve-Alain Bois, *Formless: A User's Guide* (New York: Zone Books, 1999), 219.

8   Rebecca Solnit, "The Making: Landscapes of Emergency," *As Eve Said to the Serpent: On Landscape, Gender, and Art* (Athens: University of Georgia Press, 2001), 166.

9   Bruce D. Kurtz, "Post-Minimalism," in *Contemporary Art 1965–1990* (Englewood Cliffs, NJ: Prentice Hall, 1992), 136.

organizes them into an animated composition. . . . one may project on [these works] a metaphor for our physical world. . . .[10]

From her theater work, Bean Finneran draws into her sculptural forays a love for process, considerable comfort with improvisation, a predilection for dramatic staging, and a profound sense of play.

Critic Maria Porges has spoken of Finneran's "performative" art,[11] and given the artist's long association with Soon 3, it is no surprise that a key stage in Finneran's creative process is the installation of the works themselves. She prefers working with a large crew (as if they were a circus putting up the big top). The team creates each cone or ring from scratch, as it were, piling up the curves one by one, interweaving them in a form specific to that site and that moment. And then when Finneran and her team take the show down, they store away the hundreds and thousands of curves until they can be assembled again – in another space, in other combinations. Although she is "not trying to copy nature," Finneran loves the endless transformations of the natural world. "Things in nature are always changing," she says, and she aspires to capture that quality, of birth and death and rebirth, in her cylinders and cones that critics compare variously to sea anemones, eccentric topiaries, and coral reefs.[12]

Finneran is careful to point out that her work does not contain "some big message"; she is instead simply trying to "deal with beauty." Of course, in today's often cynical and jaded art world, to "deal with beauty" is a revolutionary act, and in the presence of Finneran's astonishing cones and rings, we are struck by their preternatural playfulness, the sheer high spirits of these creatures that speak to our desire, too often forgotten, to experience again the transient but indelible richness of the phenomenal world.

---

10   Martin Esslin, quoted in Soon 3 Theatre program, no date; Theodore Shank, "California Cool: Soon 3/Hellmuth-Reynolds/Snake Theater," *Performing Arts Journal* 4:3 (1980), 74.

11   Maria Porges, "Bean Finneran's Performative Art," *Ceramics: Art & Perception* 57 (2004), 12–14.

12   See Porges, "Bean Finneran's Performative Art"; Teri Cohn, "Bean Finneran at Mills College Art Museum," *Artweek* 36:3 (April 2005), 17; Colin Berry, "'Subtraction & Addition' at the Museum of Craft & Folk Art," *Artweek* 35:6 (July/August 2004), 17.

At the same time that they "push the limits" of the ceramic arts – by embracing new materials and new approaches – Bean Finneran and Jerry Bennett remind us that the transformative power of the human eye and mind and hand can still surprise, can still bring unalloyed pleasure, and can lead us beyond the purely human, stimulating a profound reconnection with the spirits of nature.

Lawson Oyekan
Healing Powers

Originally appeared in Emily Galusha & Rick Newby, *New Works: Lawson Oyekan: Solstice Lip Series, Minneapolis* (Minneapolis, MN: Northern Clay Center, 2006).

Every human, Lawson Oyekan says, has a "fundamental capacity to be the cause of significant change."[1] Certainly through his own richly textured vessels and cylinders, this singular sculptor aims to encourage transformations of the spirit. Many of his earlier clay works, often towering abstractions of the human form, represented a fierce, yet philosophical – and even tender – response to the hurts life throws our way.

Now, with his new body of work created at the Northern Clay Center, Oyekan achieves what he calls a "choreography of colors, forms, and light" that marks a turning away from pain into the fullness of healing. He does not believe that "artists create their best work out of pain." Rather, he sees "wonderful things" emerging out of the "overlap of many positive experiences." Not about lamentation or defiance (as he suggests his earlier works were), these new slab-built cylinders – perforated, incised with numerals and other symbols that dance, decorated with colors Oyekan encountered in Minneapolis – acknowledge and celebrate a "coming up for air" by an artist who once fought to keep from being "buried alive by circumstances." A quiet joy emanates from these roughhewn cylinders, a kind of aura or subsonic pulse that washes away our preconceptions and leaves us, however modestly, transformed and enlivened.

In 1990, Princeton University scholar and theologian Cornel West asserted that a "new kind of cultural worker is in the making, associated with a new politics of difference." A major intellectual force in the rise of multicultural and postcolonial studies, West went on to characterize the "distinctive features of the new cultural politics of difference":

---

1   All quotations by Lawson Oyekan, unless otherwise noted, are drawn from interviews with the author, April 13 and May 1, 2006, Helena, MT and Minneapolis, MN.

> to trash the monolithic and homogenous in the name of
> diversity, multiplicity and heterogeneity; to reject the ab-
> stract, general and universal in light of the concrete, specif-
> ic and particular; and to historicize, contextualize and plu-
> ralize by highlighting the contingent, provisional, variable,
> tentative, shifting and changing.[2]

In the subsequent decade and a half since West made his pronounce-
ment, the cause of multiculturalism has been alternately celebrated and vilified, but West's words resonate today when we consider
Lawson Oyekan, whose powerful works can only be understood and
fully appreciated by examining the genuinely multicultural qualities
they embody.

Born in South London, but raised in Nigeria, Lawson Oyekan
received his arts education at London schools and resides in the
British capital today, while creating much of his work in a studio
in Denmark. A true citizen of the world, he brings an exceptional
breadth of experience and knowledge to his totemic sculptures. This
complex admixture includes cutting-edge art theories and Yoruba
drumming traditions, the surface qualities of West African termite
mounds and a scientist's knowledge of clay chemistry, a determination to heal in the face of entrenched racism and a sense of magic as
the mastery of skills, in whichever field one engages.

At first glance, Oyekan's work is often seen as purely African.
In a review of a Lawson Oyekan show at the Garth Clark gallery,
New York Times critic Ken Johnson went so far as to ask, "Is geography destiny?" and then answered in the affirmative, "[Oyekan's]
towering clay vessels could have been made by an African tribal artist." Later, Johnson acknowledged that the "sophisticatedly modern"
works also owed something to Minimalism and, in their "ambitious
scale and rugged finish," to the monumental sculpture of ceramic
Abstract Expressionist Peter Voulkos. As critic Matthew Kangas has
properly noted, "It is part of Oyekan's power as an artist that the cultural references in his work point in many directions rather than just

---

2   Cornel West, "The New Cultural Politics of Difference," in *Out There: Marginalization
and Contemporary Cultures* (Cambridge: MIT Press, 1990), 19.

specifically making narrow national references."[3]

Other critics fail to acknowledge the complexities of Oyekan's work, preferring to see him – and his powerful forms – as purely exotic, primitive (as "tribal" *Other* rather than as a fellow citizen in an increasingly globalized universe). Oyekan speaks of such critics as belonging to the "lemon" category. In an artist's statement, he notes that, in British vernacular, "'lemon' is an expression for an unintelligent, narrow-minded person . . . a type of shallow man confirmed as more educated than the thick or the brain dead type."[4] In opposition to this "lemon" stance, he insists on the true complexity – and singularity – of his life experience, and therefore of the work itself.

The problem, as Oyekan sees it, is that "lemon" critical approaches do "not even attempt to engage the work." Indeed, in his words, this species of "lemon" elitism

> enhances a desperate inward consolidation through jealously crafted and guarded opportunities, personalized to subjugate, to dominate, to dismember, to cannibalize, and to eliminate. I have been fascinated to see the sort of racism inherent in elite structures of art criticism – particularly in relation to the ceramic arts, which are often relegated to the category of "crafts," and to artists whose work is dismissed as only the expression of a particular culture. . . .[5]

Lawson Oyekan came to this postcolonial critique – of crude *and* subtle forms of racism and Eurocentric thinking – through painful personal experience. When, at the age of twenty-two, he returned to London from Nigeria to attend art school, he came, he recalls, as a "positive African." Instead of encountering similarly positive attitudes in his host country, he found instead bewildering close-mindedness and outright racism. Today, he sees himself as British, but in the 1980s, "there were all kinds of social circumstances that I queried. . . . As a person I felt that there was some element of darkness, or rather blindness, in society. . . . The relationship with people of other

3   Ken Johnson, "Art in Review: Lawson Oyekan," *New York Times,* May 2, 2003; Matthew Kangas, "Lawson Oyekan," *Sculpture* 22:9 (November 2003), 72.

4   Lawson Oyekan, "We Evolve 'Good,'" in *Lawson Oyekan and the spirit of nature* (Baltimore: Maryland Institute College of Art, 2004); see www.mica.edu/lawson_oyekan/iframe.html

5   Ibid.

colors or ethnic background was such an ugliness. . . Most people's instinct was just to hate."

"Horrified by the kind of human landscape I was living in," he asked himself, "Why choose to be destructive?" And in defiance of the blindness and ugliness, he began constructing a series of tall vessel forms he entitled collectively *Trial with Light*. In their "size and volume and closed space," these works approximated the human form. Oyekan began piercing their walls. He perforated his vessels not for purely formal reasons, but to signify. But what might the holes in the walls of his voids mean?

We can speculate, and we can certainly find his perforations pleasing – they generate a richly worked surface, together with the dense and mysterious calligraphic marks that he incises into the clay (Andrea Pollan has compared these to the private and playful symbols generated by the Swiss painter Paul Klee; Lisa Tamiris Becker calls them a "kind of cryptic drawing in the tradition of Cy Twombly or Lucio Fontana"; and Janet Koplos speaks of the "'aliveness' of their surfaces."[6]). Perhaps more accurately, as British ceramist Clare Twomey writes, his "visual linguistics of surface has [sic] developed as a part abstract interpretation and part written text in Yoruba – the written language of Nigeria."[7] By his own testimony, he means his perforations to suggest the "sharp jabs of experience" which, though they might cause pain, also let in a healing light.

He also refers to his perforations as "eyes." To Oyekan, the eye represents both vulnerability and uncommon strength. During his late childhood, as he told Andrea Pollan while in residence at the Maryland Institute College of Art,

> [h]e watched a cheetah resting in the afternoon sun and became mesmerized by how many flies the animal tolerated on the delicate tissue of its eyeballs before its tail swatted them away. This formative encounter provoked his interest

---

6   Andrea Pollan, "Crucibles of Transformation," in *Lawson Oyekan and the spirit of nature* (Baltimore: Maryland Institute College of Art, 2004) – see www.mica.edu/lawson_oyekan/iframe.html; Lisa Tamiris Becker, "Because the Earth is 1/3 Dirt: Toward Paradaeza." in *Because the Earth is 1/3 Dirt* (Boulder: University of Colorado/CU Art Museum, 2004); Janet Koplos, "Lawson Oyekan at Garth Clark/Long Island City – New York," *Art in America*, November 2003.

7   Clare Twomey, "Lawson Oyekan: The Spirit of Nature," *Ceramics: Art & Perception* 60 (2005), 24.

in just what an entity can endure and where that point of balance is between fragility and strength, between acceptance and refusal.[8]

Within the multiple traditions of ceramic art, Lawson Oyekan sees himself as most drawn to the sculptural and conceptual, and his experience in Great Britain only deepened his desire to create works that were conceptually, emotionally, and spiritually enriched by a rigorous inquiry into his own experiences – painful and positive – as a person who straddles several worlds. In this search for a personal approach, he found that the dominant British ceramic aesthetic simply did not afford enough latitude for his investigations. He has said, "I was more interested in the thinking of ideas and the tasks of developing forms from these sources rather than learning to make pots like Lucy Rie, Hans Coper, or Bernard Leach, whose collective interests appeared to seek gratification in Zen Buddhism."[9]

Trained as a scientist and having worked as a sculptor in other materials before he engaged clay, Oyekan found that ceramics was a field in which he had a great deal to learn. At the same time, he notes, "It was like joining a cult of mysticism" rather than approaching things from a scientific perspective. Firmly committed to following his own path, he refused to meekly accept even the most basic ceramic truisms – for example, that one should always wrap one's work to prevent it drying out. He turned instead to his Nigerian background for inspiration, finding in the termite mounds of West Africa a way of working with the earth that made perfect sense. He did not replicate the broad-based triangular forms the termites constructed, but rather sought to formulate a clay body that mimicked the one the termites used, which never cracked – even though perpetually exposed to the elements.

He says, "I wanted to work as freely with the clay as the termites did." On a 1986 trip to Nigeria, he gathered clay samples from termite mounds and brought them to England, where he was able to "work out scientifically why the termite mounds never cracked." With the help of the "brilliant" ceramic technologist Nigel Wood at

---

8   Pollan, "Crucibles" – see www.mica.edu/lawson_oyekan/iframe.html

9   Lawson Oyekan, quoted in Pollan, "Crucibles" – see www.mica.edu/lawson_oyekan/iframe.html

the Royal College of Art, Oyekan was able to take the refined clay used by British potters and "toughen it up a bit," thereby generating a recipe that closely replicated the termites' own tough clay body. From that point on, he never covered his works with plastic, "whether the weather was warm or cold," letting them dry naturally.

This independence of mind, which extends from the technical to the aesthetic, moral, and spiritual, has resulted in works that dwell in a region that truly straddles cultures – and can be seen as both universal and strikingly individual. As Clare Twomey has argued, "It is the combination of his direct method of making, the complexity of content, [and] contemplated starting points that makes Oyekan's work unobtainable yet lucid." Unlike more traditional ceramic works (what he calls "lazy pots"), Oyekan's structures demand that the viewer spend time in contemplation of the unfamiliar. These works are not pretty; they are not instantly decipherable; they *are* powerfully physical reminders that the human spirit remains indefatigable. They force us, Andrea Pollan writes, to confront the "issue of cultural otherness," and "it is the viewer's unfolding interaction with the work that begins to make this secret agenda detectable and intriguingly subversive."[10]

Neither here nor there, neither British nor Nigerian (or perhaps both), Lawson Oyekan nevertheless believes in the power of place. Much that he has learned has come out of the specificity of places – sounds and colors and qualities of light – and his work almost always refers, even if obliquely, to the place(s) where he creates it. It seems clear that this concern for *placing* his work represents a kind of honoring of the local, what he calls the "beautiful character of the place," whether it is Seoul or Stuttgart, Baltimore or Minneapolis. This concern appears to tie Oyekan to two quite different traditions: first, that of the site-specific sculpture movement that emerged out of Conceptual Art in the 1960s and 70s, and second, the complex aesthetics of Yoruba drumming. As one African drummer has told ethnomusicologist John Chernoff, "Every place . . . has its own rhythms

---

10   Twomey, "Lawson Oyekan," 25; Pollan, "Crucibles" – see www.mica.edu/lawson_
oyekan/iframe.html

which give it character; going there, one must find a rhythm that fits, and improvise on it."[11] Oyekan will spend hours, even days, in an exhibition space and in the surrounding community – as he has done at the Northern Clay Center and in Minneapolis – to soak up sense impressions distinctive to that place, before embarking on a new body of work consciously crafted for that locale.

In Oyekan's view, to improvise upon the rhythms of a place can mean an actual engagement with sound. Perhaps more than most contemporary ceramic artists, he is alert to the acoustic, recording in his works the "memory of a place by its acoustic presence . . . the acoustic energy generated by that space." In speaking of his own way of working, he draws an analogy to "how a tapdancer – without listening to a particular jazz number or any kind of music" – explores a given space's acoustic contours. As he says, "In physics, it is clearly explained that any object in space generates a sound. . . . I create these sculptural forms . . . and in the Danish landscape [where his studio is situated], the way the wind rushes past them creates an audible sound."

Of course, in the space of a gallery, Oyekan's works do not generate actual sounds; rather, they bear latent within them acoustic potential to which the artist has been attentive. "These are," Oyekan notes, "the sort of magical qualities that are locked into the composition, the quiet quality that appeals." A given work "bears that quality [of sound] in its quietness, in the gallery," and he encourages visitors to "through their imagination access the sound qualities."

In speaking of the importance of sound in his work, especially in terms of healing, he offers memories of his Nigerian youth, recalling that traditionally the Yoruba people are woken by drums. The "drummers hint at all kinds of things to be done," but they also offer best wishes: that "you wake up well today . . . that you enjoy good sunshine today . . . that your animals not go missing today." This deep engagement with sound, of course, is only "part of the composition." "All these things are totally mixed," Oyekan adds – and it seems clear that he is correct. In the personal mythology his works embody, Oyekan's passion for science and his disinterest in the Asian-inspired clay traditions of Great Britain play as great a

---

11   John Miller Chernoff, *African Rhythm and African Sensibility: Aesthetics and Social Action in African Musical Idioms* (Chicago: University of Chicago Press, 1981), 155.

role as his love for Yoruba drumming and his fascination with the surfaces of termite mounds.

Like the German artist Joseph Beuys, Lawson Oyekan can be seen as a modern (or postmodern) shaman. Just as Oyekan explores the possibilities of healing through his work, Beuys believed that "[a]rt is a genuinely human medium for revolutionary change in the sense of completing the transformation from a sick world to a healthy one."[12] In Oyekan's expression, knowledge, especially of a highly specialized kind, can be expressed as "magic." His sense of magic – that "quality of mystery that still exists" – comes, at least in part, from an uncle who was a great horseman and who, because of his immense skill, was considered a magician by his Yoruba peers. Lawson Oyekan is just such a magician. By developing his own remarkable set of skills, by refusing victimhood, and indeed by defying the forces of ugliness and hatred, Lawson Oyekan has followed a path that leads not only to his own healing, but to remarkable works of art that speak of endurance and dignity in the face of the "essential inconstancies in human nature."[13] It is beautiful and moving to witness such an enterprise, one that speaks unashamedly of hope at a time when constant news of horrors and sorrows, corruption and cupidity, wear away at our nerves and our spirits.

---

12   Quoted in Greg Masters, "Joseph Beuys: Past the Affable," *Artarchive*, http://artchive. com/artchive/B/beuys.html

13   . Oyekan, "We Evolve 'Good.'"

The Yixing Effect
Echoes of the Chinese Scholar

Originally published as the preface to Marvin Sweet, *The Yixing Effect: Echoes of the Chinese Scholar* (Beijing, PRC: Foreign Languages Press, 2006)

In 1950, when the British potter Bernard Leach declared in *Craft Horizons* that he saw little potential in American ceramics because its practitioners lacked a "cultural taproot," American ceramists responded predictably. Bauhaus-trained, adoptive American Marguerite Wildenhain riposted in her "Potter's Dissent," "It ought to be clear that American potters cannot possibly grow roots by imitating Sung pottery or by copying the way of life of the rural population of Japan." Out in Montana, Frances Senska, the legendary teacher of Peter Voulkos and Rudy Autio, had her own retort. "We came from so many different places, and could give our own spin to whatever we were doing," she said. "[In America] you can select any tradition you want and follow it, or make up your own as you go along."

Through the second half of the twentieth century, as American ceramics developed its own voice – truly eclectic and wildly diverse, drawing from all world ceramic traditions – one of the traditions that American artists found particularly congenial was that of Yixing, China. Yixing is one of three principal Chinese pottery centers whose artisans have, for hundreds of years, produced tea ware of surpassing beauty, ingenuity, and grace. The very first teapot, in fact, was designed in Yixing.

As is their custom, contemporary American artists have not so much imitated or copied the Yixing pots, but rather have drawn inspiration from them, finding in these diminutive works a kindred concern for the natural world, refined craftsmanship, and objects that are both utilitarian and – as Richard Notkin puts it – "powerful works of art."

Like the impact of twentieth-century translations of Chinese and Japanese poems by Ezra Pound, Amy Lowell and Florence Ayscough, and Arthur Waley on modern American poetic practice, Asian ceramics in general have had a profound effect on artists in the West. But as Marvin Sweet – together with essayist William Sargent, an authority on Asian export art – clearly demonstrate in this marvelous book, Yixing ware has had a special resonance for Western ceramists.

Illustrated with more than 150 images, *The Yixing Effect: Echoes of the Chinese Scholar* offers the reader (and viewer) many riches: a concise and thoughtful history of the scholar tradition in China, tracing its philosophical underpinnings and the scholars' ties to the Yixing potters; an illuminating essay on the influence of Yixing ware in earlier centuries in Europe and America; and an insightful overview of the many ways American artists have worked with, played with, and elaborated upon the Yixing tradition.

With *The Yixing Effect*, the authors have produced an exemplary work of scholarship that will surely serve as one of the definitive sources on its subject for many years to come.

Painters, Printmakers, & A Few Non-ceramic Sculptors

Like a Prayer
The Prints and Paintings of Anne Appleby

Originally published in Rick Newby, *Anne Appleby: Recent Work* (Helena: Holter Museum of Art, 1998).

Walk into a gallery filled with Anne Appleby's art, and you may underestimate the power of the apparently monochromatic paintings and prints. And then, before you can turn away, they begin to work on you. They start to glow, to awaken your senses. You realize that, though each panel is a single color, there is dimension to these colors: twenty to forty layers of underpainting add richness and depth (yes, these flat works project a sense of space) and the feeling of something living. And you read the titles – *Kinnikinnick, Sweet Pine, Sage* – and you think: "Maybe these reductive paintings, these square panels, can tell me something about how things grow and die and decay and are born again, about the spirits of plants, and about our place on earth." And of course, you are right.

Anne Appleby is an abstract painter with a crucial, even decisive, difference. Though she studied at the University of Montana and San Francisco Art Institute (where she received a Master of Fine Arts degree in 1989), the other key influences on her work, and on the ways she views the world, come from far outside the contemporary visual arts scene – from the teachings of an Ojibway holy man and from the creek bottoms, meadows, and hillsides of her home country near Jefferson City, Montana.

It began almost as if by fate, this difference. In the late 1970s, in Helena, Montana, Appleby first met Eddie Barbeau, the Ojibway holy man. Her apprenticeship with Barbeau lasted fifteen years. Barbeau taught her many things about Indian culture and religion, but she values most the lesson she learned the day he asked her to paint a bear on a shield. Fresh out of art school, Appleby painted a perfect rendering of a bear. Barbeau made her start again; he was after "the way a bear's energy or spirit would feel, its essence," not its outward aspect. That lesson was crucial for Appleby; thereafter she sought to portray, not appearances, but the essences of things, making it easy for her to move into an abstraction that remained profoundly grounded in the natural world.

In graduate school, Appleby started to paint series of large monochromatic panels around natural elements: fire, the extinction of songbirds, water, the four directions of Indian tradition. But an accident brought her directly to the body of work she continues to explore today. While setting up a tipi on her place in Montana one year, the tipi's poles fell on her head, giving her a concussion. For several months, she couldn't stand long enough to make large paintings, and out of necessity, she turned to working with small square panels. At the same time, because of her injury, she studied the medicinal uses of the plants that grew nearby.

Soon absorbed by the life cycles of plants and seduced by the complexities of the modernist grid, she began to paint, panel after panel, color after color, the sequence of a given plant's existence: from root to new shoot to new leaf to mature leaf to seed to decaying seed to the frosting of the leaf to the decaying of the entire plant. Sometimes she painted other elements – Sun, August, even the Four Directions – but generally her work explored, and continues to explore, with endless patience and subtlety and exactitude, the flora of her Montana valley: Mountain Ash, Aspen, Willow, Wild Rose.

Anne Appleby participates today fully in the contemporary art world, and yet her work stands to one side of that world. Where much contemporary art is fueled by arcane theories and ironic, even cynical, strategies, she aims to "bring people back into the body, help them dwell in their senses." Her paintings are beautiful, in a very old-fashioned way, and she admits that her work may have more to do with the Romantic movement – with its emphasis on spirit over appearance – than with modernism. Like the abstractionists whose works most resemble hers – painters like Brice Marden and Agnes Martin – she is concerned about meta-issues of paint and painting, and at the same time, her paintings refer directly to the rhythms, scents, sounds, and sights of the natural world.

Fiercely at home at the center of the four directions, Anne Appleby is a painter whose luminous, bittersweet panels speak of the vastness and intimacy of the cycles of growth and decay, presence and absence, death and birth.

Beckoned Into Landscape
The Paintings of Dale Livezey

Published in Rick Newby, *Dale Livezey: Paintings* (Reno, NV: Stremmel Gallery, 2007); an earlier version appeared in Peter Held and Rick Newby, *Open Country: The Landscapes of Dale Livezey* (Helena, MT: Holter Museum of Art, 2001).

"At dusk, things take on a light-life/ of their own: greens glow, whites/ shine, browns grow black. . . ," writes poet Eamon Grennan.

Montana painter Dale Livezey is a poet of dusk and of daybreak. He has always been drawn to the swiftly changing light, the intensities of color, that come at sunset (and at dawn). He nurtures an obsession with the play of shadow in folds of landscape (in the depths of gullies, at the verge of forests, along unruly clusters of willows) – and he delights in the moody changeability of these magic times between night and day. There is a contemplative, almost prayerful quality to Livezey's dramatic and serene evocations of real (and wholly imagined) places at their most striking.

These landscapes (for nearly all of Livezey's production is landscape, with the occasional still life and rare portrait) capture western hillsides and mountain slopes, deep forest and sweep of open country, creeks and high lakes, coulees and river valleys, and the ever-present vastness of the Montana sky. They speak of place, but even more of perception – and of perception attached to feeling. They are, in the best sense, emotional landscapes; they call up – through an alchemy of pigment, compositional rightness, and painterly skill – emotions that reside in every beholder.

Almost entirely self-taught, Dale Livezey has schooled himself in the western landscape, immersing his vision in both the sharply etched beauties of the Rocky Mountain Front (at the ravishing margin between mountain and prairie) and in the more modest pleasures of central Montana, where tablelands afford the greatest drama, and a simple coulee can hold your eye for hours.

But Livezey has also taken as his principal teachers two American artists, Maynard Dixon and Wolf Kahn, a pair of painters – mavericks like Livezey – who internalized the lessons of modernism while never rejecting the rendering, however simplified and intensified, of the visible world of landscape. In Dixon, Livezey discovered a painter of nearly Cubist landscapes who felt powerfully that the West "is spiritually important to America." And in Kahn, he found a daring colorist who, in the words of art historian Meyer Schapiro, "makes the abstraction and the representation at the same time."

Following his mentors' leads, Dale Livezey has turned away from the conventional rendering of a detailed realism in favor of a dynamic and simplified vocabulary of planes and cubic forms (in the mode of Dixon) and a palette that sometimes stretches into heightened, "untrue" colors that express a truer reality (as with Wolf Kahn).

Unlike many painters of the West, Livezey is not interested in narrative. Rather than tell a story, he hopes to afford viewers emotions akin to those they might feel in front of a landscape on the Rocky Mountain Front, say, or at the foot of a tableland on the Montana prairie. He rarely includes any trace of the human in his paintings, "or even an animal," because these traces of living beings suggest narratives that can distract from the purely visual impact. In fact, he recently said, "I have found that I'm more attracted to abstract painting than to representational work. The artist is not trying to tell you anything. The viewer is completely free. Personally, when I'm out in a beautiful place in nature, I feel a similar freedom."

But unlike abstractions, Livezey's paintings do speak directly to our memories of places and the feelings that these particular places evoke. He adds that he hopes those who view his paintings are "comforted by the non-narrative quality and beckoned into the painting. This beckoning aspect is something that a landscape can offer that few abstract paintings can."

Working exclusively in oils (except for the rare block print), Livezey paints full time, but at a pace that meets the demands of his imagination. His is not a swift expressionist brush seeking an effect of spontaneity; rather he prefers to work slowly, searching through many sessions – wet paint applied to dry, night after night – to achieve a surface enlivened and deepened by highly charged layers of underpainting.

This approach, developed over thirty years, enables Livezey to create paintings that are emotionally and spiritually resonant, somehow right, even when they depict places that exist only in the painter's imagination (a surprising number of Livezey's landscapes cannot be found in the real world).

Of this role of invention in his paintings, Livezey recently said,

> My paintings are more and more fictional landscapes. I find it more liberating to paint landscapes out of my head than being chained to documentation. In the painting process, I can establish a dialog with the painting as it is being created. I start with only a rough idea of what the painting will eventually be. As elements take shape, they demand other elements for a "proper" balance both in composition and color – and I respond. This process can be time consuming, but very rewarding. I think, for abstract painters this process is very similar.

Montana fiction writer Peter Fromm, the covers of whose books are often graced by Livezey paintings, says of the quality of "rightness" in the artist's work: "Oftentimes I'll work for weeks, months, just trying to fix a story in a place, a very particular place – nothing that blows your ideas of landscape out the door, just something so everyday that it takes a second glance to realize its incredible beauty. Then I'll happen upon one of Dale's paintings and realize that the place has been there all along, perfectly realized on his canvases. He does it to me every time."

A. B. Guthrie's *The Big Sky* is a landmark in the literature of westward expansion, and Guthrie's phrase still resonates with many westerners. It is no accident then that, when the 1947 novel was re-issued in 1992, the publishers chose a Dale Livezey sky painting, *Evening Glow,* as the appropriate cover image. And when the collection of literary essays, *Writing Montana,* was published in 1996, it is small wonder that the Montana Center for the Book selected a Livezey landscape, *Ridge over Smith Creek,* for the cover, as clearly embodying "the endurance, the realism, the various forms of terse eloquence" that characterize, in the words of critic William Bevis, the best of Montana literature.

The fruit of deep commitment by an artist for whom the act of painting landscape is a spiritual practice, the paintings in this exhibition call forth our dreams and our memories – of landscapes we have loved or imagined we might. This exhibition proves Dale Livezey to be a singular painter of the American West, a true voice of this spiritually important place.

Painting Air at Large Scale
Michael Haykin's *Intimate Terrain*

Originally published in Michael Haykin & Rick Newby, *Intimate Terrain: The Paintings of Michael Haykin* (Helena, MT: Holter Museum of Art, 2003).

Since 1995, when he first visited the Montana Artists Refuge in the old mining town of Basin, Michael Haykin has spent his summers painting – with passion, discipline, and an eye for the real – a semi-arid, harshly beautiful landscape he finds endlessly compelling. And since building a new home and studio in the foothills of Montana's Elkhorn Mountains, Haykin has devoted his eye and hand to "wandering around this little canyon" and attempting to capture – "every single day" – its elusive, subtly ravishing reality. Working from field sketches to more fully realized drawings to color studies, he has, over the course of a year, created the suite of large-scale, multi-paneled paintings he has titled *Intimate Terrain*. Seductive and complex, the paintings of *Intimate Terrain* offer a fresh, darkly luminous vision of the American West.

For the past seven summers in Montana, Haykin has painted literally hundreds of landscapes, most small scale, depicting his favorite places. Always working in the field (*en plein air)* and with dispatch (he often completed two small canvases in a day), he developed a working method and visual vocabulary that led logically to the paintings of *Intimate Terrain*. There exist, however, crucial differences between his small landscapes and the new work. First, of course, there is the question of scale (Haykin made a sudden leap from paintings as small as 1 x 2 feet to multi-panel works stretching to 10 x 12 feet). And because of their sheer size, the *Intimate Terrain* paintings could not be completed in a single session out-of-doors, but rather took up to a month each to finish indoors, working from sketches and photographs. Haykin's small paintings were always single panels whereas the new works are composed of multiple panels (as few as three and as many as nine). And whereas the small works always offer traditional perspective, the *Intimate Terrain* paintings – with the boundaries between panels never quite matching – challenge our expectations, offering the modernist pleasures of disjunction and multiple perspectives (reminiscent of Cubist strategies).

During his studies at the University of Virginia in Charlottesville, Haykin came under the influence of noted landscape painter Richard Crozier, co-author of *Inventing the Landscape* and a celebrated American New Realist. But Haykin is not exclusively a landscapist (or a realist). He also paints what he calls his "small room series," figurative works that explore the "border area between dream and actual time," and an ongoing group of portraits, "faces that are magnified, flattened . . . existing in the moment between communications and expression – 'proof of the soul.'" But surely it is in his landscape work, and most dramatically with the monumental paintings of *Intimate Terrain,* that Michael Haykin will leave his mark: as the interpreter of both the "soul" of a beloved landscape and the experience of vision itself: the interplay, primal and complex, between one gifted painter's eye and the forms he selects from his chosen landscape: *Boulders. Creek. Blizzardsticks. Burn. Road. Fire. Treelight.*

Just as in his portraits, where he is interested in affording the viewer a "glimpse beneath the surface of the face, deeper than musculature," Haykin is also after something more than surface when he creates his landscapes. He aims, instead, at capturing the shimmer between himself and the object(s) of his gaze. "Sometimes," he says, "I end up painting air. But it's not just air; it's more fleeting than that. In the changing moment, I try to hold the image long enough to paint, but without freezing it." Haykin's approach results in paintings that are powerfully composed of substantial forms, offering significant detail, and yet distinctly out of focus. Rather than replicate the haze conjured by heat or dust, this effect of "shimmer" mimics the way we actually see, as our eyes move quickly from subject to subject, blurring the boundaries of things.

While Haykin's landscapes can be linked with the vibratory works of George Seurat and other Postimpressionists and with the atmospheric landscapes of fellow Montanans Russell Chatham, Richard Pence, and Dale Livezey, his use of color calls to mind another of his influences, the Color Field abstractionist Morris Louis. Known for his "Veils" of transparent acrylic paint and his later "Unfurleds," on which he poured stains of more opaque, intense color, Louis had a "magical ability," in Haykin's words, to layer one color on top of another and yet keep each layer "pure and glowing." Though Haykin works with oils instead of acrylics, he achieves similar effects by applying many extremely thin layers of paint. In a painting like *Creek,* for example, Haykin's pure colors for sky and water, leaf and cloud glow with an almost hyperreal radiance.

Though Michael Haykin is far from an abstract painter (in his rendering of objects, there is little "distortion, manipulation, or interpretation"), his paintings in *Intimate Terrain* have much in common with works by a band of Montana abstractionists who, like Haykin, are concerned more with essences of the natural world (what Haykin calls the "essential qualities that exist beneath . . . the surface of human experience and the atmosphere of landscape") than with simple representation. These painters, Anne Appleby and Sandra Dal Poggetto among them, often work with multiple panels (see Appleby's luminous minimalist celebrations of wild plants and places) or the modernist grid (see Dal Poggetto's recent *In Situ* paintings, which incorporate grid structures and the actual feathers of upland game birds). Like these artists, Haykin, painter of air, aims to draw the viewer's keen attention to the forces and images of the natural world (water, fire, tree, stone) he finds so arresting.

In *Intimate Terrain*, Michael Haykin's use of the multi-panel format, of the slightly off-kilter grid, represents his most fruitful innovation. Like the groundbreaking Cubists, he uses the disjunctions of multiple perspectives, in the words of another post-Cubist, David Hockney, to approximate "how we actually see . . . not all at once but rather in discrete, separate glimpses which we then build up into our continuous experience of the world." Because each masterfully composed painting in *Intimate Terrain* cannot be, in Hockney's phrase, captured in "one frozen look," the eye finds much of interest as it moves over the subtly broken surface. It is a pleasurable but unsettling journey, rich with discoveries. Before *Blizzardsticks* or *Boulders,* we are held for long moments, by discontinuities, by sheer scale, by intensities of color and feeling, and, oddly enough in these dark times, by beauty. Art historian Rosalind Krauss has argued that the grid "is what art looks like when it turns its back on nature." In Michael Haykin's capable hands, the grid – through some delightful alchemy – brings us closer to the realities of vision and to a surer sense of our place in the natural world.

Illustrations for a Text That Does Not Exist
Doug Turman's Watercolor World

Originally published in *Drumlummon Views,* the Online Journal of Montana Arts & Culture (Helena, MT): Spring/Summer 2006. To view this essay, go to the Montana History Portal at www.mtmemory.org

> *Many watercolors and all sorts of other*
> *things. Most of it inside me, deep inside, but*
> *I'm so full that it keeps bubbling up.*
> – Paul Klee, upon departing Tunisia, 1914

Trout of astonishing colors, classical figures of the whitest marble, Islamic star charts, geographers imagining new continents, Renaissance maps, fragments of Dante written in a gorgeous cursive, 1920s aeroplanes, mid-century Italian postage stamps, western landscapes populated by cacti, quotations from paintings by Paul Klee, Henri Matisse, and Charlie Russell, portraits of a weeping Meriwether Lewis, green peas, and footprints leading nowhere: What do these seemingly disparate images have in common? They all leap from the brush of prolific and prodigious watercolorist Doug Turman (who also happens to be an accomplished printmaker and painter in oils and acrylic).

One small Turman watercolor will include several of the images listed above (or others from Turman's vast repertoire). Turman works this swarm of images into a composition that seems to tell – begins to tell – stops in the middle of – a lovely and humorous story. The story line may not be readily apparent, but somehow this doesn't matter. Like Persian miniatures torn from the pages of the narratives they illustrated, or like Kurt Schwitters' self-sufficient collages, Turman's watercolors lead vibrant and very full lives, separate from any text.

Like the best modernist art, they are infinite, suggestive rather than explicit. And like the Persian miniatures Turman has studied passionately, they form "perfect patterns," brilliantly colored and harmonious. They are rich in allusion, but it is an allusiveness that is more playful than laden with meaning. These watercolors take us on delightful journeys, suggesting that their creator is a seasoned traveler who cannot help but share the sights he has encountered along the way.

Though this is true, Doug Turman is a peculiar sort of traveler. By his own admission, he's "never been anywhere" – though a recent sojourn in Great Britain, Germany, and Italy suggests otherwise. Raised in Missoula, Montana, in a family that might serve as model for a Norman Rockwell painting – "my father was the mayor, we had a dog" – he did leave the West for a few years, attending undergraduate school at Ohio's Oberlin College and spending some time in the museum world, working at the Phillips Collection in Washington, DC.

But for the bulk of his adult life, Turman has lived and painted in the American West, in Arizona and Montana. "I do my traveling through my work," he says, and with a wry grin, he allows as how he may be one of the few artists (if not the only one) who has work on all seven continents – he's even placed a watercolor at the South Pole Station in Antarctica.

And it is in his watercolors that Turman does his most adventurous traveling. These (usually) small and magical works somehow make visible a vast and richly textured universe, one that we recognize instantly as home. It is a dream home, to be sure – our best and most yearned-for habitation, where pleasure reigns and we are safe from sorrow.

Following the example of Matisse, Turman consciously – and no doubt out of a deep need – refuses in his art the negative, the ugly, the very real sadness that afflicts every life. His work has been accused of being escapist, "too rosy," merely decorative. But, he counters, why not celebrate pleasure, the beautiful – so that the artist offers the viewer, as Matisse said, "an art of balance, purity and serenity, devoid of troubling or depressing subject matter"? Just as Matisse was out of step with the other great modernists, because of his insistence on rendering the voluptuousness of life, so Doug Turman is a maverick, following his own joyous and quirky path.

Turman is no stranger to sorrow. His first-born son died in his arms, only three days after birth, of a rare genetic disorder, and that tragedy was, in Turman's words, "in some ways, both the best and the worst thing that ever happened to me." He found strength in the act of painting and in the steadfast love of family and friends, and though he suffered from clinical depression for a time – and through a divorce – his work continued to celebrate beauty, a beauty "tempered by grief." Reassured that his belief that art should instill pleasure was not skin deep, was in fact something fundamental to his nature, he entered the discipline of painting even more rigorously, pushing himself technically, extending his insights into ever more articulate series of paintings.

The notion of the series is integral to Turman's work, and many of the watercolors he's created are linked – by repeated images, shared size, and reiterated themes. He began his first major series, "Love Letters," in the mid-1980s, and with more than seventy watercolors completed, the series continues to grow. His "Trout Dreams" series stands complete at thirty-nine paintings, each containing at least one trout – amid ceaseless streams, mysterious earths, spirals of constellations. Other Turman series include "Conversations with Paul," an homage to Paul Klee, "master of the small painting," and "The Geographer," a tribute to a geographer friend who – like the artist – unifies the world "by human logic and optics, by the light and color of artifice, by decorative arrangement."

Sometimes working with obsessive precision and sometimes with extreme looseness and daring, Doug Turman is a master of his chosen medium. It is only through his playful and densely textured sensibility that he creates works – these miniature fables, histories, and romances – that we can read "almost as we read a text." Every Turman "Love Letter" or "Trout Dream," every "Conversation with Paul" or session with "The Geographer," takes us to another place, where things form a perfect pattern, and we can escape – joyous as carefree travelers – from the "troubling or depressing subject matter" of our daily lives.

Two Print Portfolios
by Peter Rutledge Koch & Griff Williams

Hard Words

Originally published in Maggie Mudd, Pat Williams, Rick
Newby, & Griff Williams, *Hard Words: Digital/Typographic Prints
by Peter Koch and Griff Williams* (Missoula, MT: University
Galleries, University of Montana–Missoula, 2000). This essay
was later included in Peter Rutledge Koch, et al, *Hard Words:
Memory and Death in the Wild West* (Berkeley/Palo Alto:
Editions Koch/Stanford University Libraries, 2017).

In that treasury of Montana lore, *Frontier Omnibus* (1962), in the introductory note to excerpts from the 1869–1870 journal of Danish immigrant Peter Koch, another Koch (Elers, bibliophile, novelist, and author of the recently published *Forty Years a Forester*) wondered what it must have been like for his progenitor – who was just then establishing the first trading post in what is today Fergus County – "a young university man of gentle up-bringing thrown in with the hard-bitten crew of wolfers and woodcutters with whom he spent his first winter in Montana."

In early May 1870, the laconic Peter noted, "Hauling wood. Living on catfish." A few days later, he wrote, "Very hot and nothing to eat." Hard words for a hard land.

Today's Peter Koch – another bookman in the family line – has turned his hand on occasion, since the early 1990s, from the crafting of extraordinary books – austere books, books of an urgent refinement, books that are, in Robert Bringhurst's words, among the "twentieth century's . . . most accomplished attempts to do justice to ancient Greek tradition" – to the making of typographic prints. These small-scale prints, combining single words set in wooden type – "broke," "froze," "hard" – with photoengravings scavenged from small Montana newspapers, bring together Koch's deep Montana roots, his love of the found object (the discarded image), and his mastery of typographic design.

And now, with *Hard Words,* a collaboration with fellow Montana expatriate and master of the digital Iris print, Griff Williams (while Koch is the master of that archaic and arcane technology, the letterpress), these intimate, handcrafted prints are transformed, in scale, with saturated color, by their sheer, intractable presence.

And still, they bring us back to that hard Montana existence, where words are precious and carefully chosen; they speak in a laconic expression as eloquent as that of Koch's beloved Pre-Socratics. "All things come in their season," wrote Herakleitos in Guy Davenport's translation (published in 1990 by Peter Koch in an edition of elemental simplicity).

In Montana, it is always the season for Peter Koch's and Griff Williams's startling and seductive *Hard Words*.

Nature Morte

Originally published in Mary Evellyn Sorrell, Rick Newby, Griff Williams, & Peter Rutledge Koch, *Nature Morte: Peter Rutledge Koch* (Helena, MT: Holter Museum of Art, 2004). This essay was later included in Peter Rutledge Koch, et al, *Hard Words: Memory and Death in the Wild West* (Berkeley/Palo Alto: Editions Koch/ Stanford University Libraries, 2017).

". . . the fear of death from civilization": A profound melancholy pervades the images in *Nature Morte*, master letterpress printer Peter Koch's second foray into the realm of the digital Iris print – and a profoundly bitter irony arises from the juxtaposition of these images with the blocky words with which Koch chooses to caption them (and even more so, with the forward-looking, grandiloquently expansionist entries from the journals of Lewis and Clark that float across the picture plane).

With these somber works, Peter Koch gives us an irreverent antidote to the boosterism – and even sheer silliness – that has surrounded much of the celebratory afflatus that has thus far surfaced on the occasion of the two-hundredth anniversary of the grand expedition to open the American West.

As scion of a prominent Montana pioneering family, Koch brings an insider's perspective to his critique of Westward Expansion, and as a literary outlaw, he offers a decidedly postmodern take on issues of colonialism, environmental degradation, and racism. Quoting Kafka, Koch asks, "If the [text] we are reading doesn't wake us up with a blow on the head, what are we reading it for?"

Nature Morte partakes of a tradition in Montana arts that critic Ken Egan, Jr., characterizes as producing "visions of cataclysm," narratives that recount "promising beginnings and disastrous endings." Many of these works, Egan argues in his study, *Hope and Dread in Montana Literature,* leave us feeling helpless in the face of historical forces beyond our control. This strain of nostalgic catastrophism has long been a powerful theme for Montana's visual artists, from George Catlin's early lament that the region's native peoples were "fast travelling to the shades of their fathers," to Charlie Russell's fury over "trails plowed under," to photographer L. A. Huffman's urgent effort to capture "This Last West" before it vanished irrevocably.

In Peter Koch's "visions of cataclysm," we are offered something quite different, not hopelessness, but a provisional hope based on a clear-eyed critical stance toward the accepted wisdoms. Koch insists – and I think rightly – on the purgative effects of works like the somberly witty prints in *Nature Morte.* Like an "axe for the frozen sea inside us" (again quoting Kafka), these heartrending (and angry) images ask us to ponder the nature of our beautiful but threatened place in this world. Like Koch's uncle, Elers, we are driven to ask the most difficult questions: "Is it possible that it was all a ghastly mistake, like plowing up the good buffalo sod of the dry prairies?"

Paul Harris
Our Desperations, Our Delights

Previously unpublished. Written in response to the publication of *Paul Harris: Black & White Drawings & Prints, 1938–2006* (Bolinas, CA: Wrongtree Press, 2007). Paul Harris (1928-2018) was the only artist associated with New York's Poindexter Gallery with strong ties to Montana (see "Missionaries for Modernism: New York's Poindexter Gallery and Montana's Poindexter Collections" elsewhere in this volume).

> *A collection of beautiful forms is not enough.*
> *Forms must cry out about loneliness,*
> *our desperations, our delights.*
>
> – Paul Harris, 1999

At the verge of the Pacific Ocean, in the secretive hamlet of Bolinas on the northern California coast, from his spare wooden house set high on the bluffs, the singular American artist, Paul Harris, invents "out of necessity" remarkable images and forms. Still lifes, luminous and joyful, in pastel, crayon, and acrylic. Sculptures simultaneously witty and grave ("unapologetic fetishes," Bill Berkson calls them, "surrogates for the figures and objects of memory and dream, or for the pinpoint flashes of meaning in everyday life").

And from the confines of the artist's tiny drawing studio arise perhaps the most constant of his endeavors: drawings in black and white and subtle shades of gray: portrayals of the human – figure or physiognomy – direct, without equivocation or subterfuge. The drawings (and prints) gathered in *Paul Harris: Black & White Drawings & Prints, 1938–2006* are the products of this constancy, the outcomes of a steadfast dedication to the art of drawing.

Like another American master, R. B. Kitaj, Harris believes in the centrality of the act of drawing – as separate from and equal to his other artistic endeavors. These sixty-four magisterial works span the decades between 1938 and 2005, and they range from the wildly gestural to economical works – spare as that wooden house – that convey an unquenchable engagement with the stuff of life, with both elemental forces and ordinary circumstances.

The spirit of Eros presides over a number of these works,

infinitely more so than it does over Harris's sculptures and still lifes. Bill Berkson observes, "The two genders rarely appear together in [Harris's sculpture]," but here, particularly in his two series of *Paradise Variations* (as lithographs and in pencil on acetate), he confronts and celebrates human sexuality. Harris's fabric, wood, and bronze sculptures and his magnificently colorful drawings bespeak a generous sensuality (echoing the writings of Colette, one of his literary touchstones), but in *Paradise Variations,* his men and women – their forms simplified, cropped, anonymous – commingle with insistent grace and total abandon. They seem, at least in the moment, purely sexual beings. These nakedly erotic works are astonishing; they have the power to stir and trouble us. As the poet and classical scholar Anne Carson writes of Eros, "Beauty spins and the mind moves. . . . A simultaneity of pleasure and pain is at issue."

As many have noted in writing about the corpus of Paul Harris's work, he is a poet of the radiant quotidian, of the magic of the ordinary: His works (and the drawings and prints in this volume are no exception) have a habit of gently intruding upon our attention; they challenge and enrich our perceptions; they help us live more intensely. In describing her experience with one of Harris's sculptures, Phyllis Diebenkorn writes, "We have lived with many contemporary works of art . . . but none have been so insistent on being part of life, on changing the very meaning of our environment, as Paul's sculpture."

Like another of his literary heroes, Franz Kafka, Harris works with great subtlety. The insistence of his works on our attention comes quietly, gently, at the edge of consciousness, but with unmistakable power. The poet Christopher Middleton calls Kafka's narrative voice "transparent, ever-inquiring, tenderly comical, ferociously paradoxical." In his remarkable portraits in this volume, Paul Harris achieves a similar complexity of tone. These humans – some nameless, others bearing only their given names (Emily, Bill, Sergio, Katie, Ida) – bear all the signs, in their marvelous faces, of having lived deeply. They "cry out about loneliness, our desperations, our delights." They often seem austere, as still as Harris's still lifes, unashamedly melancholy, but their melancholy has been, as Guy Davenport writes of Kafka, "stripped . . . of those elements that would quickly soften into kitsch." With these richly individuated character studies – sculptural, monumental, and at the same moment, profoundly intimate – Paul Harris allows his sitters their dignity. And in consequence, we come to feel that we know these faces, that we have always known them.

Because, in his own phrase, he invents out of necessity, with images and forms generated by his unconscious or from "concentrated yearning or desire," Paul Harris has always followed his own rigorous, joyous path. Critics have made efforts to pigeonhole him, and he has been variously included in discussions of the Pop, Funk, Pattern-and-Decoration, and Bay Area Figurative movements. But he has never succumbed to the seductions of the *zeitgeist*. Rather, he has created a body of work – tenderly comical, ferociously paradoxical, ever-inquiring, and transparent – that will outlast every trend and movement. His images linger, unparalleled, unforgettable, in the consciousnesses of those fortunate enough to encounter them. And the publication of this lovely book makes it possible for many more eyes to enjoy just such an indelible encounter.

Long Lines of Dancing Letters
The Japanese Drawings of Patricia Forsberg

Originally published in Rick Newby, *Long Lines of Dancing Letters: The Japanese Drawings of Patricia Forsberg* (Helena: Drumlummon Institute, 2008). See also *Drumlummon Views,* the Online Journal of Montana Arts & Culture, Vol. II, No. 1 (2008). To view this essay, go to the Montana History Portal at www.mtmemory.org

> *We struggle to locate ourselves in a tangle of histo-*
> *ries. . . . There are more things in modernity than*
> *are dreamed of by our economics and sociology.*
> — James Clifford, *On the Edges*
> *of Anthropology,* 2003

> *[O]ne's sight changes: you see things with an eye*
> *more Japanese, you feel color differently. The*
> *Japanese draw quickly, very quickly, like a light-*
> *ning flash, because their nerves are finer, their*
> *feeling simpler.*
> — Vincent Van Gogh, letter to
> Theo van Gogh, Arles, June 5, 1888

Browsing a stack of books I own but haven't read, I come upon this quotation from *A Guide to the Gardens of Kyoto:* "It is not the materials in isolation that form a garden but the fragments in relation. . . ." Montana artist Patricia Forsberg's Japanese drawings, or more properly, her mixed-media works – crafted out of ink and gouache and fragments of splendid Japanese papers – resonate with this characterization of classic Japanese gardens (and by extension, Japanese design in general). Like Van Gogh, who found his Japan in the south of France, and like the French theorist Roland Barthes, who saw in Japan a paradigmatic Empire of Signs ("The author has never, in any sense, photographed Japan," writes Barthes; rather, "Japan has starred him with any number of 'flashes' or better still . . . a situation of writing"), Patricia Forsberg finds in Japanese culture a kind of aesthetic paradise where, ideally at least, the literary and visual arts meld into daily life in ways that are meaningful, spiritually resonant, and quite simply lovely.

Perhaps more so than their compatriots elsewhere, given their proximity to the Pacific, artists in the American West have long been drawn to Asia and its arts. Think of the Pacific Northwest abstractionists Morris Graves and Mark Tobey, and their adoption of elements from Chinese and Japanese painting. Or of the profound impact on western ceramic artists of such Japanese potters and thinkers as Shoji Hamada and Soetsu Yanagi (especially their visits in 1952 to the Chouinard Art Institute in Los Angeles and Montana's Archie Bray Foundation).

In Montana, of course, Townsend ranch kid (and Columbia University art instructor) Henry Meloy painted T'ang Dynasty horses on his brother Peter's pots, and Rudy Autio looked as much to Japanese sources (Hamada, Yanagi, and especially the printmaker Shiko Munakata) as he did to Matisse and the Greek figure vase tradition. Beth Lo has explored both the ceramic traditions of her Chinese heritage and the rich contradictions that surround her experience as a Chinese American. Richard Notkin, Richard Swanson, Eric Van Eimeren, and other Montana ceramists have embraced aspects of the Yixing teapot aesthetic, rendering their own improvisations upon this wonderfully expressive Chinese tradition. Artist and scholar Marvin Sweet has named Helena the epicenter in the U.S. of what he calls the "Yixing Effect" (see Sweet's book by the same name, published by Beijing's Foreign Languages Press and serving as the catalog to a major 2006 exhibition – mounted by Helena's Holter Museum of Art – of both traditional Chinese and contemporary American "Yixing" pots).

All of which is to say that Patricia Forsberg is not alone in her explorations of Asian aesthetic principles, cultural values, and spiritual traditions. At the same time, her series of drawings, created over more than ten years and numbering in excess of 200 intimate works, stands as one of the most engaging, masterful, and achingly lyrical engagements by an artist of the American West with a specifically Asian culture. Just as Provence became Van Gogh's Japan ("it is a beautiful Japanese dream," he wrote of the Provencal countryside), Patricia has found her Japan within the confines of an artist's studio.

Created in the late 20th and early 21st centuries, Patricia's elegantly sensual and often melancholy "Japanese" works echo the ancient tradition – in both Chinese and Japanese cultures – of the seamless bringing together of painting and poetry. And Patricia's drawings/collages honor (and borrow from) the blossoming of the first truly homegrown Japanese culture, more than one thousand years ago, created primarily by women artists, and especially by women writers.

Behind all of Forsberg's Japanese works hovers the extraordinary world of Japan's Heian era (794–1185 AD). At least since Arthur Waley translated Lady Murasaki's six-volume *The Tale of Genji* (published ca. 1015 AD and considered to be the first psychological novel in world literature) in 1921–1923, women artists in the West have looked to the period and especially to the Japanese court's exceptionally talented female writers as models and inspirations.

Virginia Woolf famously reviewed the first volume of Waley's translation of *Genji* in 1925 and expressed her envy of a time and circumstance when, instead of focusing on war and politics, a culture could dwell almost entirely within the aesthetic dimension. While Europeans of the Dark Ages "burst rudely and hoarsely into crude spasms of song," Woolf wrote, "the Lady Murasaki was looking out into her garden, and noticing how 'among the leaves were white flowers with petals half unfolded like lips of people smiling at their own thoughts.'" Of course, this era of relative tranquility and luxurious introspection was temporary, only to be followed by centuries of civil war and brutal rule by warlords.

In the grand tradition of American self-invention, Patricia Forsberg has seized upon the aestheticism of the Heian court as a part of her own cultural ancestry. Kakuzo Okakura has written in his *Book of Tea* that this is not "aestheticism in the ordinary acceptance of the term, for it expresses conjointly with ethics and religion our [the Japanese] whole point of view about man and nature." As Ivan Morris writes in his classic study, *The World of the Shining Prince: Court Life in Ancient Japan*, the Heian era

> will always be remembered for the way in which its people
> pursued that cult of beauty in art and in nature which has
> played so important a part in Japan's cultural history. . . .
> The "rule of taste" applied not only to the formal arts but
> to nearly every aspect of the lives of the upper classes in

the capital. It was central to Heian Buddhism, making . . .
religion into an art and art into a religion. . . .

The immense leisure enjoyed by members of the upper class allowed them to indulge in a minute cultivation of
taste. Their sophisticated aesthetic code applied even to the
smallest details, such as the exact shade of the blossom to
which one attached a letter or the precise nuance of scent
that one would use for a particular occasion.

Morris adds, "Finally, the aesthetic cult . . . provided the framework
in which the "good people" not only expressed but even experienced
their emotions. . . . Even when Murasaki's characters are plunged
into the most agonizing grief . . . they express their emotions in ele-
gantly-turned poems of thirty-one syllables."

Freed by servants of all domestic duties, the women of the
court, imperial consorts and ladies-in-waiting, lived together in the
palace, where they whiled away their leisure playing games, reading,
practicing calligraphy and music, entertaining male visitors, and in
many cases, writing poems, tales, and memoirs. While Japanese men
of the time wrote their works in Chinese (the official language of the
time, just as Latin was in the West), the women were free to write in
the Japanese vernacular. Using the *kana* phonetic script, they could,
in Ivan Morris's words, "record the native Japanese language, the language that was actually spoken, in a direct, simple fashion that was
impossible in . . . pure Chinese."

Because of their leisure, their access to this strong, vivid language, and their genius, the women of the Heian court have left us an
unparalleled record. Among the important works are Lady Murasaki's
diary and her masterpiece, *The Tale of Genji,* Sei Shonagon's witty
and richly observed *Pillow Book,* Lady Sarashina's melancholy *As I
Crossed a Bridge of Dreams,* and the poems of Ono no Komachi and
Izumi Shikibu, available in English in *The Ink Dark Moon,* beautifully
translated by poet Jane Hirshfield with Mariko Aratani. (Many of the
titles of Patricia's drawings are drawn from Komachi's and Shikibu's
verses, and when she exhibits the work, she couples each drawing
with the complete poem that inspired it.) As Hirshfield writes in her
introduction, these "court attendants must surely have been the most
illustrious company of women writers ever to share a set of roofs."

Their literary works have clearly served as sources and inspirations in Patricia's re-imagining and transfiguration of Heian culture, but it is more difficult to trace her influences from Japanese visual arts. Certainly, her drawings partake of the "Japanese genius," in the words of art historian Jack Hillier, "for the expressive line, for pattern and design, the representation of natural objects as a means to an end, not an end in itself." For Japanese printmakers and painters, the making of art, "like poetry," notes Hillier, was "the 'spontaneous overflow of powerful feelings' and took its origin from 'emotion recollected in tranquility.'"

This quality of restraint, which yet contains undercurrents of intense emotion, is evident in Patricia's drawings, where we find ourselves in the midst of moments of repose colored by melancholy, outright grief, fleeting joy, and occasionally an antic humor. Some event has just transpired or is anticipated: the arrival or departure of a loved one, the change of seasons, an ongoing solitude for which there is no respite ("Call It Loneliness, That Deep, Beautiful Color," as one of her drawings is titled).

Perhaps the closest source for Patricia's drawings might be woodcuts created in the 1600s to illustrate a later edition of *The Tale of Genji* (examples can be seen in Edward Seidensticker's 1976 translation of the novel). These marvelous prints depict life within the palace, a world made ever more interior by screens within screens behind fences within walls. Even when these men and women venture outside, the omnipresent fog seems to tame and contain them; this is a profoundly inward-looking universe. As Sei Shonagon wrote in her *Pillow Book*,

> [W]e women generally stay hidden behind our screens or curtains. It is delightfully quiet there. . . . In the winter one sometimes catches the sound of a woman gently stirring the embers in her brazier. . . . On other occasions one may hear several voices reciting Chinese or Japanese poems.
> . . . Bright green bamboo blinds are a delight, especially when beneath them one can make out the many layers of a woman's clothes emerging from under brilliantly coloured curtains of state."

The sense of enclosure so central to Patricia's Japanese works resonates with these words, and the women we see in her drawings might be said to be, if not delighted, at least content within the comforting embrace of a familiar room. Some appear to be truly insouciant, happy to nap for a lazy moment or a long afternoon; others curl into themselves, radiating grief; some confront the viewer frankly, with their sexuality or their boredom; still others huddle against cold or loss. Although a few appear to be Japanese, most of these women seem ancestrally European and profoundly modern in spirit. Their sheer nakedness would have marked them as *other* in the Heian world. Lady Murasaki and her cohorts wore clothing that was, in Ivan Morris's words,

> immensely elaborate and cumbersome, consisting *inter alia* of a heavy outer costume and a set of unlined silk robes (twelve was the standard number). . . . So that their fastidious blending of patterns and colours might be properly admired, women wore the robes in such a way that each sleeve was longer as it came closer to the skin.

And in fact, the naked female form was considered anything but beautiful in Heian culture. Lady Murasaki, at the sight of a pair of maids whose clothes had been stolen during the night, wrote: "Unforgettably horrible is the naked body. It really does not have the slightest charm."

Female experience has long been central to Patricia Forsberg's artistic enterprise, and so too has her affectionate and insightful exploration/appropriation of other cultures. Witness, for example, her works of the 1980s, when she immersed herself in another culture obsessed with beauty, that of Renaissance Italy. For those who know her Renaissance-inspired paintings, with their wild patterns, vivid colors, and madcap humor, Patricia's Japanese drawings seem models of restraint and calm. But her concerns remain much the same; in 1985, she spoke of the essential elements with which she sought to imbue her work. Her paintings would be "patterned, symbolic, private and masked, humorous, dramatic, energetic, and alive." The Renaissance paintings were, for the most part, interiors (like the Japanese drawings) – and in 1985, she wrote of the tension in that earlier work between the "pursuit of freedom, choice, and space" and the "inevitable taming and containment of the environment, animals, and our lives."

That tension between freedom and containment, this modernity of spirit – the absolute nakedness of the work – is what takes Patricia Forsberg's Japanese drawings far beyond mere imitation or even heartfelt tribute. In their exploration of the interior life of women today, these drawings are, quite simply, marvelous expressions of one artist's allusive imagination, speaking across centuries and cultures with restrained feeling, quiet power, and a riveting sense of beauty all their own.

Montana Improvisations
Jim Todd's Jazz Wood Engravings

Originally published in Yvonne Seng, James Todd, & Rick Newby, *Jazz Icons: Wood Engravings, Woodcuts & Paintings by James Gilbert Todd, Jr.* (Helena, MT: Holter Museum of Art, 2012).

Painter and printmaker Jim Todd is a true Montana original. While many of his peers paint iconic Montana landscapes, indulge in nostalgic celebrations of pioneer culture, or partake in abstract expressions (that often relate to our vast landscape), Todd participates in a different tradition, one that is resolutely urban (a cosmopolitan urbanism rooted in the Montana experience) and politically engaged. This self-created tradition includes such fierce forbears as early twentieth-century German satirists (Georg Grosz, John Heartfield), Mexican muralists (Diego Rivera, José Orozco), and a wide-ranging roster of other socially committed artists (Käthe Kollwitz, Hannah Höch, Ben Shahn).

Some of Todd's most powerful works reflect what critic Ralph Shikes calls the "indignant eye" – think of Todd's chilling portrait of Chile's General Pinochet and his generals, *Guardians of the Southern Hemisphere,* or his nightmarish pair of hand-painted woodcuts, *Las Vegas by Night/Tijuana by Day* – but it can be argued that his most personal work resides in his series of portraits, primarily wood engravings, of jazz artists – a series that stretches from the mid-1960s to the present.

In the grand mythos of the American West, the words "Montana" and "jazz" are seldom linked. And yet this music – which arose in New Orleans out of the collision between African and European musical forms – did find its way to Montana early in the twentieth century, and it continued to flourish well into mid-century, especially in urban centers like Great Falls, Butte, and Helena. Of course today, a small but vital jazz scene can be found in many Montana cities and towns.

Jim Todd, as he notes in his essay in this catalog, encountered jazz as a young man in Great Falls, where he was enraptured by this wonderfully improvisatory music in local joints like the legendary Ozark Club and through recordings. As recent research on the Ozark

Club (visit the Ozark Club exhibit at The History Museum in Great Falls) and black culture more generally (note the Montana Historical Society's recent project, *Uncovering Black History in Montana*) shows, African American contributions to Montana's rich cultural mix have been significant and lasting.

During his distinguished career, Jim Todd has made the conjunction of social history and the visual arts a primary focus for both his artmaking and his teaching (he taught humanities and art for thirty years at The University of Montana, including a decade as chair of the Department of Art). Jazz, that hybridized, purely American music, became Todd's perfect subject, given his passion for social justice and his lifelong love for the music itself. Jazz has been called the "sound of surprise," embodying a radical freedom, and the history of jazz is inextricably linked with the black struggle in America for equal rights and basic human dignity.

As historian Joachim Berendt writes, "Almost all great jazz musicians have felt the connection between their playing styles and the times in which they live." Both black and white, the jazz players Todd has chosen as his subjects, several of whom came to public attention in the late 1950s and early 1960s, are particularly linked to the Civil Rights movement and to the fight for recognition of jazz as a universal music.

Think of bassist and composer Charles Mingus' *Fables of Faubus* (1959), an enraged protest against the Arkansas governor who called out the National Guard to prevent integration in Little Rock's schools, and his *Meditations on Integration* (1964). Think, too, of bass clarinetist and flutist Eric Dolphy, who became a *cause célèbre* among his fellow musicians because he died alone and uncared-for in a German jail, a veritable exile from the country he loved because he could not find sufficient work stateside. As saxophonist Archie Shepp wrote of Dolphy, "He died in the tradition of the black artist – *i.e.*, relatively unknown, certainly having been forced all too often to accept work far below his enormous capabilities." Pianist Thelonious Monk, like Dolphy, Mingus, and Charlie Parker (another Todd subject), was a singular innovator, bringing to the jazz tradition a new harmonic freedom coupled with horn-like phrasing, "anchored," as Berendt writes, "in a strong blues feeling and saturated with a mocking, burlesque sense of humor" (qualities not unlike those in Todd's more satiric works; see, for example, the woodcut, *Hitler in Combat,* or the acrylic painting, *Aryan Spook).*

Another area of social concern for Todd is the role of women in jazz. His portraits of jazz women celebrate the role women have played as preeminent vocalists in the form. Singers like Bessie Smith, Ella Fitzgerald, Billie Holiday, and Anita O'Day have literally been the voice of jazz since the beginning. But it is only slowly that, within this male-dominated music, women have begun to perform in other roles; Todd's portraits of pianists Marian McPartland and Jutta Hipp acknowledge some of the first women to break the gender barrier.

Two other Todd portraits record the enormous change in women's status within jazz in the last forty years. The Japanese-American pianist Toshiko Akiyoshi has broken all the barriers to become the leader of her own big band and a major jazz composer. Perhaps even more impressive, Carla Bley has been a force in jazz since the early 1960s. A founder in 1965 of the Jazz Composers Orchestra, a big band intended to further avant-garde composition and performance, Bley has since the mid-1970s led her own big band and generated some of the most distinctive (and humor-filled) compositions in modern jazz, reminiscent of the work of Kurt Weill. Bley pioneered the notion of independent artist-owned record labels, with her WATT Records, and she founded the late and lamented New Music Distribution Services, which made creative improvised music available to a wider audience, helping to further recognition that jazz is one of the world's great classical musics.

There is no question about Jim Todd's command of the art (and craft) of wood engraving. In the catalog to his 2002 retrospective at the Missoula Art Museum, the renowned British wood engraver Simon Brett wrote that, not only is Todd a master of the medium, but a genuine innovator, breaking the "stereotypes of size and content with which wood engraving is too often associated." By working larger than the norm, Todd increases the impact of his prints, and upon joining the Society of Wood Engravers, he dazzled the British members with the size and "modernity" of prints like his *Mulligan and Monk* (which measures 14 x 11 inches and graced the poster for the Society of Wood Engravers' 1995 75th anniversary exhibition at Oxford's Ashmolean Museum).

What is it about Jim Todd's jazz engravings that renders them so captivating, more so even than his portrait series honoring print-makers (Rembrandt, Jacques Callot, Picasso, Hannah Höch, José Posada) or world changers (Galileo, Charles Darwin, Gandhi)? There is something profoundly grave and dense about these images of jazzmen and -women, a bodying forth of lives devoted to exuberant and soulful creativity in the face of very real obstacles: of racism, sexism, and plain old philistinism. This sense of lived experience, hard earned and always passionate, may well come from Jim Todd's early love of jazz, his personal engagement as a young jazz drummer, his sense of a vast world opening up on the fleet notes of Louis Armstrong's trumpet (whom he might have heard at the Great Falls Civic Center, ca. 1950).

No matter the origin of the power of these astonishing portraits, we are fortunate to see them all together, in a single exhibition, to be haunted and moved by their uncompromising dignity, their quiet sorrow, their joy.

Gordon McConnell
The Past That Was

Originally published in Marci Rae McDade and Rick Newby, *West of True: Jane Waggoner Deschner & Gordon McConnell* (Fallon, NV: Churchill Arts Council, 2014).

> *Thriving on physical sensation, wedded to violence, dominated by the need for domination, and imprisoned by its own heroic code, the Western appeals finally beyond all these to whatever it is the high-up hills betoken.*
>
> – Jane Tompkins, *West of Everything: The Inner Life of Westerns*[1]

Montana painter Gordon McConnell, in his haunting new exhibition, *West of Everything: New and Selected Paintings,* recapitulates real and imagined scenes from the classics of Western film. Such scenes have been McConnell's chosen imagery for the past thirty-odd years, but in his most recent work, something fundamental begins to change. From the start, McConnell's work has been intellectually challenging and rendered with considerable wit, embodying a corrosive vision. In the recent work, the changes are subtle and emotionally powerful. There is a mournful or retrospective quality, a sense that this work is no longer primarily playful or satiric, but rather constitutes an extended elegy for a lost time and place, a western culture that, however flawed, deserves if not our respect, at least our affection.

"At first," McConnell has written, "I had a subversive or satirical intention. The early work was intentionally crude and also tended toward darkness and expressionistic violence." And then in recent years, he found his attitudes and his approach changing. He writes:

> [M]y intentions have become more constructive, and my inclination is to honor the heritage of the West, the cinema, and the tradition of the great painters – Remington and Russell, yes, but also Manet and Sargent, Pollock and

---

1   Jane Tompkins, *West of Everything: The Inner Life of Westerns* (Oxford & New York: Oxford University Press, 1992), 5.

de Kooning, Kiefer and Richter.[2]

It can be argued that this more constructive intention has grown increasingly intense and personal in the past two years, as Gordon McConnell has dealt with major life changes, in particular the death of his father, James Gordon "J. G." McConnell. Like many native-born westerners who seem thoroughly urban, Gordon McConnell has startlingly direct and deep connections to the fabled West of cowboys, cattle drives, and Indian wars.

His father, J. G., was born in 1918 near Pampa, Texas, and as a boy and young man, the elder McConnell helped tend his family's herd of Herefords. J. G.'s obituary notes, "He grew up on the frontier stories of his great uncle and aunt, Henry and Fanny Lovett, and attended the funeral of Charles Goodnight [1836–1929]. His uncle, Skinny Adams, was a range boss on the JA Ranch,"[3] Goodnight's legendary ranch in the Texas Panhandle.

Charlie Goodnight, of course, was one of the principal cowmen who drove wild Texas longhorns north in the great cattle drives following the Civil War, and he is reputed to be the model for Larry McMurtry's character Woodrow F. Call in the Pulitzer Prize–winning *Lonesome Dove* – in the CBS *Lonesome Dove* miniseries, Tommy Lee Jones plays the grizzled Captain Call. J. G.'s great-uncle Henry Lovett had been an early-day buffalo hunter, woodcutter, ranch hand, and then successful rancher.

J. G McConnell farmed and ranched in eastern Colorado until 1959 (Gordon McConnell was born in 1950), but conflicts with other family members caused him to leave the land and undertake a new career as a science teacher. Gordon recalls that his father retained a great love for the mythic West (what Gordon has dubbed the "Phantom Empire") and that he watched the Encore Westerns channel "obsessively."[4] His passion for Western film was contagious, and Gordon – with considerable tenderness – remembers one evening

---

2   Gordon McConnell, "Paintings 2006: A Portfolio." *Drumlummon Views: The Online Journal of Montana Arts & Culture*, Vol. 1, No. 3, Fall/Winter 2006–2007; https://www.mtmemory.org/nodes/view/91842?keywords=Drumlummon%20Views&type=all&highlights=WyJkcn-VtbHVtbW9uIiwidwidmlld3MiXQ==&lsk=83893f8a889b51974e915fe328e377ac

3   "James Gordon 'J. G.' McConnell Sr.," *Amarillo* (TX) *Globe-News*, February 12, 2013; http://amarillo.com/obituaries/2013-02-11/james-gordon-jg-mcconnell-sr

4   All quotations from Gordon McConnell, unless otherwise noted, are drawn from a phone interview with the author, October 31, 2013.

coming home from school and his father sitting him down and re-galing him with a blow-by-blow account of the plot of *My Darling Clementine,* John Ford's 1946 masterwork that starred Henry Fonda, Linda Darnell, Victor Mature, and Walter Brennan. *My Darling Clementine* remains one of Gordon's touchstones, and recastings of its images appear frequently in his works.

Gordon believes that his father felt the loss of the agricultural life acutely and that watching Western films reconnected him, how-ever partially, to that deeply meaningful portion of his existence. The literary critic Leslie Fiedler, in his famous essay, "Montana; or the End of Jean-Jacques Rousseau," opined that the Montana cowboys he witnessed exiting movie theaters after viewing Western films firm-ly believed that the "authentic hero is the man who herds cattle."[5] Wallace Stegner, expressing a desire to "bury" the mythic cowboy, wrote: "But I know I can't. He is a faster gun than I am. He is too at-tractive to the daydreaming imagination."[6] Pablo Neruda, the Nobel Prize–winning Chilean poet, wrote:

> . . . in films where bullets fly on the wind,
> I am left in envy of the cowboys,
> left admiring even the horses.[7]

Gordon McConnell, by internalizing his father's love for Westerns and recognizing his own sense of loss over a lack of con-nection to the "authentic," agricultural, mythic West, understands better than most that these films touch something elemental in the American psyche. It is easy enough to treat the Western film iron-ically, but Gordon McConnell, through these utterly compelling paintings, gives us a twice-imagined past, riddled with contradic-tions, rich in complex feeling (sorrow, dread, tenderness), stark *and* opulent – a place Out Where the Black Winds Blow. This may not be an entirely inviting place, but Gordon McConnell leaves us con-vinced that it is absolutely *real.*

---

5   Leslie Fiedler, "Montana, or the End of Jean-Jacques Rousseau," *An End to Innocence: Essays on Culture and Politics* (Boston: The Beacon Press, 1955), 136.

6   Wallace Stegner, *The American West as Living Space* (Ann Arbor: The University of Michigan Press), 79.

7   Pablo Neruda, "We Are Many," *Pablo Neruda: Selected Poems,* ed. Nathaniel Tarn (Bos-ton: Houghton Mifflin/Seymour Lawrence, 1990), 363.

> *Staged twentieth century Hollywood history, in
> endless iterations, is as real as the nineteenth cen-
> tury blood and thunder epic of conquest and con-
> flict that inspired it.*
>
> – Gordon McConnell[8]

If Gordon McConnell's personal lineage includes buffalo hunt-
ers and range bosses, his artistic genealogy possesses its own trajectory. McConnell can be said to belong, at least by inclination,
to the Pictures Generation, a group of artists who emerged in the
1970s and 1980s in reaction against the dictates of Minimalism and
Conceptualism, where the specific object reigned supreme (painting was unthinkable) or the aesthetic work dematerialized altogether into pure idea. The Pictures Generation represented, as the critic
Hal Foster has written, a "Return to the Real." In Foster's words, this
"trajectory of art since 1960 was committed to realism and/or illu-
sionism: some pop art, most superrealism (also known as photoreal-
ism), some appropriation art."[9] The Pictures Generation artists took
as their subject matter the unstoppable flow of images from mass
media: television, film, magazines, and pop music, and they emerged
from two centers, New York City and the California Institute of the
Arts (CalArts) in Valencia.

After receiving his B.A. in Studio Art in 1972 from Baylor
University, McConnell spent a semester at CalArts where he studied
with John Baldessari, a mentor and model for the Pictures Generation
through his extensive use of all manner of appropriated imagery.
McConnell didn't immediately connect with Baldessari's approach,
but he would not forget the older artist's imaginative recapitulations
of found photographs. Before and after graduate school in art history
at the University of Colorado, McConnell worked in Texas where he
encountered the work of artists like Vernon Fisher, Bob "Daddy-O"
Wade, and Ed Blackburn, all of whom were working with found
western imagery. Blackburn's reuse of cowboy film publicity stills

---

8   Gordon McConnell, "Statement"; http://gordonmcconnellstudio.com/html/statement.
html

9   Hal Foster, *The Return of the Real* (Cambridge: MIT Press, 1996), 128.

particularly drew McConnell's interest. While in Boulder, he redis-covered the movies of John Ford and began to develop his own style. His viewing of Ford's *Stagecoach* was revelatory:

> The print was battered, the images de-resolved, flickering and stuttering. Details of the coach, horses and characters dissolved in abstract shadows as the searing glare of the Arizona desert spilled into the auditorium. Still, the com-pelling story and performances, dynamic action set-piec-es and powerful cinematic compositions came through. In its ruined state the old film seemed like a relic of an actual frontier.[10]

While he admired the work of such Pictures Generation artists as Robert Longo (Longo's sculptural *Seven Seals for Missouri Breaks* was an inspiration), he was also drawn to the work of the German artist Gerhard Richter, especially Richter's photo-pictures of the mid-1960s. Like Richter, McConnell was temperamentally drawn to black-and-white imagery, sharing the German master's "sense of re-straint and natural affinity for a *grisaille* palette."[11]

But it was not until McConnell moved to Montana in 1982 to assume the position of curator at the Yellowstone Art Center (now the Yellowstone Art Museum) that he found his own voice. His ar-rival in Billings "brought [him] into intimate contact with some of the most storied places of the historic West and also gave [him] the opportunity to study the paintings of two of the most influential cod-ifiers of western imagery, Frederic Remington and Charlie Russell." He came to understand both the impact Remington and Russell (and other western illustrators) had had upon filmic depictions of the ear-ly West and the crucial ways in which film, "in its temporal, techno-logical, and theatrical mediation," differed from painting.[12]

McConnell met fellow Montana artists with whom he shared the challenges and joys of forging a personal visual language. From rancher/painter/sculptor Theodore Waddell, who had studied with

---

10   McConnell, "Statement."

11   Dietmar Elger, *Gerhard Richter: A Life in Painting* (Chicago: The University of Chicago Press, 2002), 125.

12   Gordon McConnell, "Curriculum Vitae"; http://gordonmcconnellstudio.com/html/cv-gm.html

pioneering Montana modernist Isabelle Johnson, he learned to "create forms with the brush" and to cultivate "accidental effects." Together with fellow curator Christopher Warner (now at the Otis College of Art & Design, Los Angeles), he learned to paint as he went along. Like many artists of their generation, McConnell and Warner had received very little technical training in the art of painting, and so they "invented ways to paint things."

Today, having invented his own way to paint, Gordon McConnell is a master of his medium. Like many of the artists of his generation, he began by using appropriated imagery to create satirical effects, but as he has come to better understand his own ties to the mythic West and to the role that Western film has played in connecting westerners to their origins, he has eschewed a cool, critical stance for one more heartfelt and appreciative of tradition. But his remains a dark vision, full of melancholy and danger, with paintings like *Afterimage: Burnt Shadows; 10,000 Ways to Die;* and *Black Shapes Stenciled Across the Road* reminding us of mortality and the attendant grief, of the inevitable losses that works of art can help us to bear.

To Restore a Wealth That Is Wild

Sandra Dal Poggetto's Immersive Art

Originally published in *High Desert Journal,* Winter 2022; https://
www.highdesertjournal.org/issue-33-content/newby-a-wealth-
that-is-wild This essay also appeared in the catalog, *Sandra Dal
Poggetto: Immersive Landscapes* (Bozeman, MT: Echo Arts, 2022).

Montana-based painter and writer Sandra Dal Poggetto speaks of
key experiences in her youth, ones that have led her on a profound
journey of rediscovery – enabled by her art practice and her passionate embrace of hunting. A lifelong Westerner, she grew up in
the town of Sonoma in Northern California's wine country. She describes that childhood:

> Manzanita, chamisa, and oak surrounded my home. The
> mild Mediterranean climate of the coastal California hills
> invited outdoor play, and I accepted the invitation with
> pleasure. Often I saw blacktail deer tracks in the powdered
> soil, or jackrabbits, and heard the call of quail during quiet
> morning and evening hours. The smooth, taut skin of the
> manzanita I caressed. I pinched and ran my nails down the
> slender, flexible chamisa branch so that I could hold the
> stubby needles in my palm.
>
> Within the concentrations of chamisa was a network
> of animal tunnels aglow with a diffused light. Through
> these I would crawl until I came to the wide trunk of a live
> oak whose coarse, gray limbs I would climb and, through
> the deep green of small, waxy leaves, look out over the val-
> ley. The slopes of chaparral, I knew, were shaped by fire,
> and the valley below was favored with river water.[1]

This full-bodied embrace of landscape ended for Dal Poggetto
in adolescence. She writes, "The power of postwar commercial
America – promoted by pervasive television, magazines, and radio – sucked me into a virtual world devoid of nature. Hello, Andy

---

1   Sandra Dal Poggetto, "Duccio in the Eye of the Hunt: Modern Connections between the
Chase and Art," *Gray's Sporting Journal* (1996), 21:6.

Warhol."[2] For Dal Poggetto, though, this change came with sudden and painful clarity.

She recalls walking in Jack London State Park near her home one day. "I wandered off the path and knelt down in the dry grass. Gradually, I sensed that a sheet of glass was separating me from everything around me: the trees, the grass, the brush. I felt alienated, separated from something that I loved."[3]

Dal Poggetto began to look for a way back from that alienation, not consciously perhaps, but with determination. She turned to the study of art, attending the University of California, Davis, where she encountered a faculty comprised of such prominent figures in the Assemblage, Funk, and Bay Area Figuration movements as Robert Arneson, William T. Wiley, Manuel Neri, and Wayne Thiebaud. Though Thiebaud would influence her through his passion and seriousness, her most important teachers were Neri, whose blending of classical traditions with the gestural approach of Abstract Expressionism resonated with the young artist, and the painter Cornelia Schulz, whose ideas and shaped canvases – where, writes critic Julia Couzens, "reasoned geometry pushes against seduction's looping pull"[4] – left an imprint.

An art-historical journey to Italy deepened this newfound passion for painting and drawing. Being of Italian heritage and having grown up where many Italian immigrants had settled, Dal Poggetto felt a natural affinity for things Italian, and during her UC Davis summer abroad (and on later visits to Italy), she became entranced with Etruscan funerary art and the frescoes of early Renaissance masters, particularly Giotto.

She became a voracious student of art history. The artists whose works she found most congenial ranged from the anonymous Greek figure-vase painters to Delacroix and Goya, Degas and Matisse, Mark Rothko and Cy Twombly, Emily Carr and Joan Mitchell, Philip Guston and Susan Rothenberg, and her favorite out

---

2   Sandra Dal Poggetto, "Primal Colors," Center for Humans and Nature website, Chicago. Retrieved from: https://www.humansandnature.org/hunting-sandra-dal-poggetto

3   Sandra Dal Poggetto, interview by Brandon Reintjes, *Sandra Dal Poggetto: Meditations on the Field* (Missoula: Montana Museum of Art & Culture, 2014), 11. Retrieved from: https://www.blurb.com/books/5518565-sandra-dal-poggetto-meditations-on-the- field

4   Julia Couzens, "Cornelia Schulz and Carrie Lederer @ Patricia Sweetow," *Squarecylinder*, November 29, 2017. Retrieved from: https://www.squarecylinder.com/2017/11/cornelia-schulz-and-carrie-lederer-patr icia-sweetow

of the Bay Area tradition, Richard Diebenkorn. Paul Cezanne, perhaps more than any other painter, was for her always "at the center." She loved his ability to capture the "incredible tension that is life," but she was equally delighted that he spent so much time in the countryside, losing himself in his preferred places. She saw this practice not only as artistic discipline, but as a strategy for "extending his childhood," remaining ever in touch with the natural world – one of her own life goals.[5]

Now irretrievably committed to the life of an artist, she would begin to find early recognition for her own work. After graduating from UC Davis in 1975 and completing an MFA at San Francisco State University in 1982, she had her first solo exhibition at San Francisco's Dana Reich Gallery in 1985. The reception for this early work was markedly enthusiastic. Widely published critic Jerome Tarshis wrote, "Of all the first shows I remember seeing . . . the one that most knocked me out was Sandra Dal Poggetto's. . . . Her newer work is reminiscent of cave and Egyptian wall painting in its emphasis on outline and its earthy colors. . . . her work suggests she is on her way to the kind of mastery that could easily put her on the covers of art magazines."[6] Another critic lauded her "images of elliptical birds darting above a vast, achingly bare landscape" and the "disturbing and subtly drawn contrast between radiant landscape and . . . struggling, shapeless human forms."[7]

Dal Poggetto notes, "I now see that painting has been a conduit back to that unalienated relation with the natural world,"[8] but it took more than an art practice to recover the pure joy in nature she had experienced as a child. When she met her husband, writer and conservationist Brian Kahn, he introduced her to the discipline and pleasures of hunting. She quickly became a convert, for more complex reasons perhaps than the average novice. Hunting became a second, essential conduit out of alienation. She writes:

---

5   Sandra Dal Poggetto, conversation with the author, Helena, MT, September 4, 2019.

6   Jerome Tarshis, "Jerome's Unknowns," *San Francisco FOCUS* (July 1985), 27.

7   Kate Regan, "Shimmering Rays and a Troubled Lyricism," *San Francisco Chronicle* (February 2, 1985), 75

8   Sandra Dal Poggetto, "Hidden in the Wide Open," a talk at the Buffalo Bill Center of the West (BBCW), Cody, WY, on the occasion of the acquisition of her work, *American Fork No. 4*, by the Whitney Western Art Museum , November 11, 2014. Retrieved from: https://centerofthewest.org/2014/11/04/sandra-dal-poggetto-hidden-wide-open/

> Through hunting, I experience the sensation of a place. My body becomes more permeable; my senses simultaneously relax and intensify.
>
> I become vividly conscious of the swell of a hillside, the shape of a meadow, the color and texture of wildrye, the snap of a twig under hoof, the chittering alarm of a squirrel, the chill and density of cold air. A breeze at my back, whoosh of thrush, flick of a tail. There are no words. I respond to these cues with caution, delicacy, discernment, patience, and then action.[9]

Then, in the late 1980s, her husband Brian took the job of executive director of the Montana Nature Conservancy, and they moved to Helena. For a contemporary artist hoping to find a congenial local art scene, this may not have been an ideal move. At that time, Montana had a few small museums dedicated to modern and contemporary art, but almost no private galleries – commercial or otherwise – that ventured beyond the traditions of Western art and straight landscape. On the other hand, and more importantly Dal Poggetto had literally reversed the ratio of humans to landscape. From densely populated Northern California, she had come to a place of vast spaces sparsely populated by people but unimaginably alive with plants and animals. Though from an art-world perspective she did find it lonely, here she met and conversed with conservationists, archaeologists, and geologists whose rich knowledge of her new home only added to her determination to express in her art a deeper connectedness to the natural world. She became aware of the rich pictographic art created by Indigenous people throughout the region. She grew fascinated by the fossil remains embedded in the stones of the Rocky Mountain Front. She was drawn to remnants of almost lost ecosystems.

In her early paintings, Dal Poggetto posited a critique of technological man. Though she is wonderfully skilled at the art of drawing (*Indigenous,* 1987), she soon turned to simplified forms to represent the human. Happening upon Henry Dreyfuss's *Symbol Sourcebook:*

---

9   Sandra Dal Poggetto, "Wildtime," *Basalt* (2015), 10:1. Retrieved from: https://www.eou.edu/basalt/basalt-volume-10-number-1/featured-artist-sandra- dal-poggetto/

An Authoritative Guide to International Graphic Symbols, she began using these stylized symbols in place of more realistic depictions. In the section on "Accommodations and Travel," she found the touching "Lost Child" symbol, often posted in airports, which would appear in several early 1990s works (*Latitude*, 1991).

Here, too, we see her newfound fascination with fossils, and, in the case of *Latitude*, the delicate fishes embedded in the Green River Formation. Her *Understory* (1993) utilizes a version of the beloved PBS "Everyman P-Head" (albeit with a bigger nose; "I like big noses,"[10] she notes). This drawing suggests that underlying the barely animate P-Head still stands the swirling, vividly alive phenomenal world. Just as her humans were becoming more formulaic, her investigations of landscape grew richer and ever more nuanced.

Her *Botanical Writings* series of the mid-90s continued to erode the human presence in her work. Another new series, *Meditations on Hunting* (after the essay by Spanish philosopher José Ortega y Gasset), marked her turn to full abstraction. She says, "Through abstraction, I really could include more, not less . . . of my full experience" in the landscape. And yet, she wasn't entirely satisfied. In her view, these works remained "quite formal, composing visual elements of shape, color, texture, value" and were therefore "too general in feeling" – not wild enough.[11]

Then, at the start of the 21st century, "an important thing" happened. While visiting New York's Metropolitan Museum of Art, Dal Poggetto wandered into the Pre-Columbian galleries, where she found herself confronted by stunning feather works created by the Wari culture of Peru. Remarkably modern in feeling (though they date from before the Spanish conquest), these cotton or leather panels – with rows of feathers attached in abstract designs of elegant simplicity – were "mesmerizing" to Dal Poggetto, and they felt "instantly familiar."[12]

"I understood," she says, "that these were feathers from birds that were hunted by people in a very particular place, in a very particular landscape."[13] She quickly realized that, by using the feathers of

---

10   Sandra Dal Poggetto, conversation with the author, Helena, MT, November 3, 2021.

11   Sandra Dal Poggetto, "Hidden in the Wide Open," BBCW, 2014.

12   Ibid.

13   Ibid.

the game birds she harvested back home, she could create her own feather works – not as imitations of the ancient Wari masterpieces but instead paying homage to her own particular place and the birds who dwell there. At first, she created these works with feathers only, using thread to attach the tail feathers of wild turkey, blue grouse, pheasant, and ruffed grouse to handmade paper in her own elegant patterns (*The Stillwater*, 2005).

Soon, Dal Poggetto wanted to expand the field, combining the feathers with marks of her own making (*Breed No. 7*, 2012). Creating the feather works led her deeper into the world of Montana's mountains and high plains and away from the formality still evident in the early *Meditations on Hunting*. Instead of imposing the modernist grid on these new hybrid works, she upended the usual order of things. She told critic Mark Stevens in 2002: "I didn't like the idea of imposing the grid on the feather. So I reversed it. . . . The feather dictates the organization of the space. The feather is an uncompromising structure, so the painting is determined by its shape."[14] Stevens, co-author (with his wife, Annalyn Swan) of the Pulitzer-winning biography *de Kooning: An American Master* and the recent *Francis Bacon: Revelations*, adds: "The feathers themselves were already full of internal grids, lyrical geometric forms and repeating patterns. (Few things in this world have the beautiful rigor of a pheasant feather.) But they were not strict rectangles, so Dal Poggetto organized the shapes in her grids to reflect their various idiosyncratic forms."[15]

Released from the more traditional formality of her earlier work, she launched several series of new works with more organic and improvisatory approaches. These include the *In Situ, Breed, Relict, Fen, Targhee, American Fork, Surprise Creek,* and *Archive* series, each distinct from the next, ranging widely in scale, materials, and conception (*Breed No. 14, Fen No. 1,* and *Surprise Creek No. 1*). Taking the lead from the formal qualities of feathers, lines traced on the landscape by animal trails, and the synesthetic impressions evoked by particular experiences within specific landscapes, Dal Poggetto created works distinctly her own. Always working "according to impulse," she sought to "participate in all the energies" of a

---

14   Sandra Dal Poggetto, quoted in Mark Stevens, "Tensions, Paradoxes and Impurities: The Truth of the Matter," *In Situ: New Paintings by Sandra Dal Poggetto* (Billings: Yellowstone Art Museum, 2002), 6

15   Mark Stevens, "Tensions, Paradoxes and Impurities," *In Situ*, 6.

landscape. She began to call the marks she made in these works "condensations" of the experiences that resonate through her full sensorium – sounds, smells, textural impressions, the tiniest of visual details, an uncanny sense of the vastness of geologic time – while immersed in a High Plains landscape. "Somehow, it's all in there," she says. "Big space and things close at hand."[16]

When Sandra Dal Poggetto calls these abstract marks she makes on canvas and paper "condensations," one is reminded of the poet Lorine Niedecker, another artist who spoke deeply out of a particular place. The watery environment around Blackhawk Island, Wisconsin, was Niedecker's lifelong home, and yet she maintained unbreakable ties with cutting-edge artists in the larger world – Louis Zukofsky in Brooklyn Heights, Cid Corman in Japan, and Basil Bunting in Northumbria. Of the discipline of making poems, Niedecker wrote, "No layoff/ from this/condensery." This urge to condense arises in both artists not because of some art-world imperative, but because both seek to embody a deeper reality. Just as Dal Poggetto insists on geologic time as an inescapable dimension of landscape, Niedecker reminds us, "In every part of every living thing/ is stuff that once was rock."[17] Critic and poet Douglas Crase has called this strain in American arts the "evolutional sublime." In an essay on Niedecker, he expands on the notion:

> When I think of the [Walt] Whitman who found he incorporates gneiss, the [Gertrude] Stein who says anybody is as their land and air is, the [Wallace] Stevens who locates mythology in stone out of our fields or from under our mountains, then I have to admit that the sublimest American poetry has always read to me as if it would rather restore .. . a wealth that is wild outside the human voice.[18]

While Dal Poggetto's marks concentrate the richness of experience, her recent works are her most expansive to date. In particular,

---

16   Sandra Dal Poggetto, conversation with the author, Helena, MT, September 4, 2019; Sandra Dal Poggetto, "Hidden in the Wide Open," BBCW, 2014

17   Lorine Niedecker, "Lake Superior," *Lorine Niedecker: Collected Works*, ed. Jenny Penberthy (Berkeley: University of California Press, 2002), 232

18   Douglas Crase, "Niedecker and the Evolutional Sublime," *Lake Superior* (Seattle/New York: Wave Books, 2013), 28

her *American Fork paintings* – both in physical scale and through the import of their content – stand as the apotheosis of her ongoing exploration. In paintings as large as nine feet square (*American Fork No. 15*, 2016–2017), Dal Poggetto stretches far beyond the limitations of the "picture window" of classical landscape painting. Perhaps that traditional format reminds her too much of the sheet of glass that descended to separate her, seemingly irrevocably, from her beloved Sonoma landscape. Her first *American Fork* works still used a traditional horizontal/vertical grid, but soon she found another organizing principle.

In a 2014 conversation with Mark Stevens (her greatest interpreter) at the University of Montana, she speaks of rotation as this principle, taking into account the 360-degree horizon line and the movement of the heavens. "That is a very different awareness of landscape," she adds, "and I find it very exciting." She calls this "radial" composition. Again, seeking to construct her works in keeping with the spirit of the landscape, she notes, "You find radial composition all over the landscape. You find it in plant structures, in marine life – I am surrounded by fossils up on the East Front. That brings in another dimension, of time and of scope." Mark Stevens affirmed, "It is quite mysterious how you get that sense of scale and 360 in what is actually a two-dimensional work." He went on to say that the experience of viewing these paintings involves a "surrounding kind of feeling." These expanded landscapes, crafted out of oil, soft pastel, charcoal, and buckskin danglers, are populated by Dal Poggetto's "condensed little nodes," her "quick little sharp notes" that suggest but do not describe.[19]

If there is any artist whose work most resonates with Dal Poggetto with regard to the *American Fork* series, it is the American Cy Twombly, who spent the bulk of his adult life in Italy. This may seem an unlikely pairing. Twombly's paintings, in Dal Poggetto's words, represent a new form of history painting. She says, "Yes, Twombly is an influence: his evocation of deep physical space – the Mediterranean land and sea – and historical/mythological time with the combination of graphic media and oil paint marks, both abstract

---

19   Sandra Dal Poggetto and Mark Stevens, "Primal Colors: A Conversation," Montana Museum of Art & Culture, University of Montana, 2014. Retrieved from: https://www.youtube.com/watch?v=JkkWk-ogQcs

and representational on the ground of the canvas. The dynamic of pencil and oil marks in an unspecified space is quite thrilling somehow. An activated space."[20]

Dal Poggetto's most recent painting, *Archive No. 1*, achieves a new direction in her work and reveals, as do the later *American Fork* paintings, a clear and felicitous connection to Twombly's use of space. After two decades, *Archive No. 1* brings the image back into Dal Poggetto's work, but within the radial composition she invented for the *American Fork* paintings. Here are all the images that were important in her 1990s work: the PBS P-Head (standing in for technological man, now more technological than ever), all manner of plant life, and fish and amphibians of various sorts. No longer anchored to a stable ground, this swirling, more-than-360-degree landscape makes it impossible to tell up from down, the living creature from the fossilized one. This painting might be seen as a chilling warning: Does the *Archive* title suggest that these relics are all that remain of a once-vibrant world? Or is this work a celebration of what Dal Poggetto calls the "at-onceness" of all things? Clearly, we can stand before this vast painting and let its ambiguities wash over us, challenging us to contemplate a question its creator once asked during an interview: "Are we, as a species, destined to become fossils ourselves?"[21]

In his influential essay, "The Symbol of the Archaic," the great Kentucky polymath Guy Davenport argues that in early European modernism many artists – Picasso, Brancusi, Ezra Pound, H.D. (Hilda Doolittle), and James Joyce foremost among them – participated in a "renaissance of the archaic." Through their embrace of the art of other cultures and eras, from Cycladic sculpture to the cave paintings of Lascaux, ancient Chinese lyrics to the fragments of Heraclitus, Greek myth to the "color and robustness of the Etruscans," these artists sought to restore, in Davenport's words, the freshness of springtime cultures. He asserts, "[T]he impulse to recover beginnings and primal energies grew out of a feeling that man in his alienation was drifting tragically away from what he had first made as poetry and design and as understanding of the world." After the horrors of trench warfare and mechanized death in World War

---

20   Sandra Dal Poggetto, note to the author, February 7, 2020.

21   Sandra Dal Poggetto, conversation with the author, Helena, MT, November 3, 2021.

I, many moderns sought new vitality and meaning wherever they could find them.[22]

Like those early modernists, and in the face of fresh disasters (man-made climate change, accelerating species extinction, the wholesale annihilation of ecosystems), Sandra Dal Poggetto is intent on recovering primal energies. Through the rigor of her art, she seeks to offer new ways of perceiving, and being with, this actual physical world we share. Her project has little to do with cultural artifacts. Instead, it aims to recover that wonderfully intimate connection with the natural world she experienced as a child. Though, at first glance, some may find her abstract art difficult to understand, in fact these tender, expansive, unsettlingly gorgeous works create a poetic space – both spiritual and political – that can help us to live more fully. As Douglas Crase says, they "restore . . . a wealth that is wild outside the human voice."

---

22   Guy Davenport, "The Symbol of the Archaic," *The Geography of the Imagination* (San Francisco: North Point Press, 1981), 20, 28.

Richard Swanson

Organic Memory, Cockleburs, & Barbed Wire

Originally published in Rick Newby, *Richard Swanson: Material Witness, Sculpture 1994-1998* (Cheyenne, WY: Fine Arts Gallery, Laramie County Community College, 1999).

In an old biscuit factory in Helena, Montana's warehouse district, Richard Swanson fills his spacious studio with the materials that entice him. Often, he has no clear plan for these materials, and it is only out of working with them that forms and rhythms and textures – sculptures – emerge. For the most part, the materials are not those traditional to sculpture, but instead items commonly found, as Swanson says, in "fabric, hardware, and feed stores, ranches, lumber yards, millworks, and ravines": mattress ticking, window screen, baling twine, straw, peat moss, branches of Rocky Mountain maple, the "porcupine eggs" of cockleburs, barbed wire.

Swanson admits an affinity with the sculptors critic Robert Pincus-Witten has dubbed "post-Minimalist," artists like Jackie Winsor and Eva Hesse, whose emotionally charged works combine, as do his, "repetitive elements with non-traditional materials and organic forms." And like the post-Minimalist Martin Puryear, another sculptor he admires greatly, Swanson is imbued with a craft aesthetic and ethic, an almost spiritual need to lavish tremendous effort and care – the mark of the human hand – in the crafting of each of his sculptures.

Like the post-Minimalist sculptors, Swanson rejects the purist approach of Minimalists like Donald Judd and Carl Andre. The Minimalist aesthetic demands that artworks be made of neutral, "pure" materials such as wood, stone, and steel; be emptied of all reference to nature, emotion, or the hand of the artist; and have no effects, connotations, or references beyond those intended – and manipulated – by the artist. Swanson – unlike the Minimalists and very much in the tradition of the post-Minimalists – makes his works out of "impure" materials that often draw attention to themselves by their associations with specific uses or contexts (barbed wire, mattress ticking, cockleburs). And his sculptures are very clearly constructed – crafted – by human hands. They are one-of-a-kind objects, radiating energy, emotion, presence.

Further, Swanson wants his works to have multiple meanings, as many as there are viewers, and he delights in the connotations his workaday materials suggest to those who encounter his art. His *Balance and Bounty*, for example – ten top-like works each over eight feet high and formed of open-mesh steel fencing tightly packed with straw – suggested many things to passersby during the year they cavorted across a grassy hillside west of Drummond, Montana: giant plumb bobs, pirouetting human figures, an eccentric way of making bales.

This fascination with alternate, even contradictory, narratives, with abstraction that verges on story, may have something to do with Swanson's early training in psychobiology. The future sculptor began his career as a memory researcher, striving to understand – on a cellular level – how the human brain stores, organizes, and brings to consciousness the rich textures and forms of lived experience. Now Swanson finds himself exploring in sculpture what he terms "organic memory," not the literal memories of a midwestern farm boy or of an artist (and walker) who lives amidst the sere hillsides and pine forests of the semi-arid West, but the patterns, images, and forms that emerge out of his unconscious as he works with wire screen and peat moss, translucent nylon and canola seed, shimmering coils of galvanized barbed wire.

Many of Swanson's works partake of "vesselness." They literally contain something (as in *zipher* where each suspended section of wire screen is taut with its load of peat moss, "practically gravid," as Swanson says, "like a guppy belly ready to give birth – so full"), or they imply containment (as in *rebirbur* where the assemblage of cockleburs suggests, within its elegant, somber circle, imprisonment or a harrowing rite of fertility).

This urge to make vessels – and his craft aesthetic – comes naturally to Swanson for, despite his scientific training, he has spent more than two decades working in clay, as a studio potter and ceramic sculptor. It was only in the early 1990s that Swanson – creatively restless – turned to new materials, not abandoning clay, but exploring a parallel universe where he could more fully realize his organic memories. He returned to school in pursuit of a second master's degree, this time not in science, but in the fine arts.

Always a craftsman fascinated with the vessel, and with the human body (his voluptuous sculptural teapots take on the rounded forms of bodies in union, whether in dance or coition; see "The Arts of Slipcasting and Jitterbugging: Richard Swanson's Dancing Teapots" elsewhere in this volume), Swanson discovered in the first of his new sculptures, especially those made of cloth and stuffed with sawdust or straw, a "friendly quality," a softness that clay, always rigid after it is fired, could not match. Transporting these works, he said, was like "moving an invalid mother or a friend who's been injured." While not replicating the human form, many of these new sculptures have abstracted body parts (as *pelican* does the vertebrae) or bodily qualities (the intimate, torso-like heft of stuffed pieces like *prairie kelp*).

Swanson's sculptures grew increasingly animated. Often suspended from ceilings (*prairie kelp, v'vesa,* and *pelican*) or walls (*zipher*) with dark flexible line, they either implied movement or actually moved. Gravity, notes Swanson, became "my collaborator," and many of his works appeared to soar, hover, or totter skyward. Given this suggested movement, Swanson's works called out for interaction. At an opening, friends improvised a kind of May pole dance while holding onto the free ends of one of his sculptures. Not in the least nonplused, he found himself encouraging dancers to play with certain works, and soon he was collaborating full-tilt with the Montana Transport Company, a band of dancers co-directed by Amy Ragsdale and Karen Kaufman and headquartered at the University of Montana-Missoula.

Between 1994 and 1997, Swanson and Montana Transport Company created five separate works. Three were presented on the stage, and some featured Swanson works that existed first as sculptures and then were customized for performance (reinforced to bear the weight of moving dancers). Two were site-specific. The first, *Building Bridges,* included six wooden units suspended from the structure of a pedestrian bridge; in performance, as six dancers moved with Swanson's sculptures, two percussionists pounded out improvisatory rhythms on the bridge's steel frame. The second (and most recent) site-specific collaboration is *Balance and Bounty,* the herd of gyrating tops outside Drummond, Montana, where over the course of a year, in seasonal sessions, Montana Transport Company dancers were able to, in the words of dancer Renata Godfrey, "trudge & jump & hop & meander & run & run & run" in response to the sculptures.

Videographer Geoffrey Pepos of Missoula videotaped each dance session, and a video – to be co-edited by Pepos, choreographer Ragsdale, and sculptor Swanson – will be the ultimate outcome of the project. During their year on the landscape, Swanson's giant tops – he calls them "rebaled straw" – held up well. Scorched by sun and wind, drenched in rain- and hailstorms, blanketed by blizzards, stolen by vandals, and rubbed up against by cattle, they came off the hillside a little worn, but intact, after the autumn 1997 shoot.

In certain of his sculptures, Swanson has moved away from his softer materials, shaping works out of aluminum tubing, sheet metal, and barbed wire. The aluminum tubing and sheet metal pieces (like *syringia*) share an animation and lightness of spirit with softer works like *prairie kelp* and *v'vesa*, but Swanson's sculptures constructed of barbed wire – among them *radio, argonaut, sonar,* and *dervish* – while as formally elegant as any of his work (he calls them "drawings in air"), bring a darker tonality, a hint of threat and danger, to his oeuvre. Not unlike *rebirbur,* his work made of cockleburs, they fascinate and repel.

Richard Swanson does not know where his explorations of "organic memory" will lead him next. Perhaps, after the success of *Balance and Bounty,* he will place more large-scale works on the Montana landscape, and he and the Montana Transport Company are already talking about another collaboration. In his studio, Richard Swanson gathers new materials (his latest work, *argentina*, is constructed of sisal rope wrapped in copper wire), and he experiments, tests, plays, always seeking to create out of the common something extraordinary – and hauntingly familiar.

The Beauty of Decay
Joseph Baráz

Originally published in Rick Newby, *Joseph Baráz: Paintings &* *Sculpture, 1990–2011* (Helena, MT: JFG Temporary/Zadig, LLC, 2011).

> *Those works created from solitude and from pure and authentic creative impulses – where the worries of competition, acclaim and social promotion do not interfere – are, because of these very facts, more precious.*
>
> – Jean Dubuffet

In a high-ceilinged garage attached to a Victorian brick carriage house hidden away in a leafy neighborhood somewhere in the western United States, one might – if one is lucky – stumble upon a vast and unruly archive of stone, lead, wood, and plaster works of art. Created by Hungarian-born, Helena, Montana-based artist Joseph Baráz, these sculptures seem relics of a sensibility shaped by many cultures and eras; they feel timeless and yet profoundly of this historical moment.

Among Baráz's works, you will find a few classically inclined figures, but most are powerfully roughhewn expressions, partaking of a strain in late modern sculpture and painting that blends acute attention to materials and textures with a conscious rejection of refinement in favor of something more elemental, almost folkloric. One of Baráz's favorite words is "humble," and his works, small scale (for the most part) and highly tactile, achieve their humility without giving up an almost spiritual intensity.

Growing up in the 1950s in the beautiful Baroque city of Eger, Hungary, Baráz first encountered the visual arts in the gallery of the Istvan Dobo Castle Museum, where he saw 15th through 19th century works by French, Italian, German, Austrian, and Hungarian masters. And on the streets of Eger, he lived among fine examples of Baroque architecture, whose voluptuousness and textural richness would impact his own work.

But it was not until Baráz moved to Budapest, to enroll in a school for acrobats, that he had his first unforgettable encounter with a work of art. In Budapest's Szépművészeti Múzeum (Museum of Fine Arts), known for its significant Egyptian collection, he came upon an Egyptian bronze seated cat, dating from the 3rd century B.C. and scarcely six inches tall. The cat radiated a genuinely "mystic quality" (the "sensation of the work, despite its small size, was so powerful"). The experience prompted him to ask, "How does one create such a work?" And for the intervening nearly forty years, he has constantly sought to match the quality of spiritual presence embodied in that small, elegant object.

The Szépművészeti Múzeum also introduced the budding artist to the stele form. Stone or wood slabs, stelae are found in many cultures. Historically, they were intended to honor the dead, mark important boundaries, or commemorate military encounters. Works like the museum's *Stela of Sehotep-ib*, Middle Kingdom (Twelfth Dynasty, ca. 1800 B.C.), bear more than a glancing similarity – both in material (limestone) and size – to recent Baráz works like *Four Dots*, 2011; *Face with yellow*, 2002; and *Face with red*, 2002.

Born in 1952, the year before Stalin's death and four years before the Hungarian Revolution of 1956, Joseph Baráz grew up rebellious in a closed society. As a prodigious young acrobat, he found an outlet for anarchic energies, working with family circuses for several years. In 1972, he and his wife Agnes crossed the border into Germany, determined to start a new life in the West. They eventually departed the European continent for the New World, settling in 1976 in San Francisco. Always determined to be an artist as free as possible from all strictures, whether state or market driven, Baráz found work as a builder, swiftly developing his skills in carpentry, stonemasonry, and as an intuitive engineer.

Despite a physically demanding day job, Baráz obsessively made art, working in multiple media, but with an emphasis on sculpture. Equally obsessively, he immersed himself in the art of his time and place, discovering among the Bay Area artists who surrounded him kindred passions for expressive figuration and earthy abstraction. He was especially drawn to the works of sculptors Peter Voulkos and Stephen De Staebler, both of whom he met at Artworks Foundry in Berkeley, where all three artists were casting in bronze. During these years, both in San Francisco and later in the California wine country town of Sonoma, he would explore larger-scale sculpture in steel and bronze before settling for his current favorite materials, stone, lead, wood, and plaster.

Exceptionally literate and gifted with a quicksilver mind, Baráz ranged over world art history, drawing sustenance from such diverse sources as the American, German, and Italian Neo-Expressionists of the 1980s, especially Georg Baselitz, Julian Schnabel, Enzo Cucchi, and Anselm Kieffer; German modern master Joseph Beuys; American painter and sculptor Cy Twombly (see his *For the best painter,* created July 5, 2011, the day of Twombly's death); the Baroque sculptor and architect Borromini; Italian stonecutting traditions; the purity of Cycladic sculpture; and – always – classical Egyptian art.

Renaissance architecture, too, significantly influenced Baráz's approach. In his reading, augmented by a year spent in Italy in the 1980s, he found himself drawn to the rustication employed by such architects as Donato Bramante and, especially, the Mannerist Giulio Romano. Architectural historian Joseph Connors defines rustication as the "countrified way of laying stones, each particular stone retaining some of the individuality it had when hewn from the quarry." Connors goes on to note, "In the Renaissance, rustic roughness was recognized as having artistic possibilities." In Florence's Palazzo Medici, for example, "rustication and smoothed brick," blended vertically, "demonstrate the idea of a mixture between the natural and the artificial." Giulio Romano, notes Connors, was known for his "grotesquely big and uneven rough keystones," an extreme rebellion against classical perfection that matches Baráz's love for the supercharged tension between rough and refined.

During the course of his 40-year career, Baráz has produced many series, several of which are ongoing. Of singular importance is the group of touch-welcoming stone works he calls *Spiritual Tools,* inspired in part by Joseph Beuys' small objects ("societal talismans," in the words of critic Christopher French). Baráz's tools are true talismans, meant to initiate us to the mysteries, to soothe our shattered nerves. The most beautifully crafted of all Baráz's works, his *Spiritual Tools* possess the kind of mystic presence Baráz first felt when encountering that six-inch-tall Egyptian bronze cat.

In working with wood, Baráz often achieves a literally rough-hewn expression, using axes and hatchets to shape his human heads and torsos. But in 2010, he began a series of abstract works, roughly geometric, that combine white oil paints, plaster, and occasional iron or steel additions. These works, reminiscent of the sculpture of Brancusi or the late three-dimensional works of Cy Twombly, stand among Baráz's most compelling sculptures, monuments to a dream of modernist purity.

Another of Baráz's series honors the Book, as an irreplaceable repository of cultural richness. Baráz was not a reader until, in his teens, he met his wife, Agnes, and she introduced him to fine literature, lending him books and leading him to a love of poetry, fiction, and by extension, narrative film. In works like *Three Volumes* and *First Edition*, he has created monuments both to bookishness and to specific cultural moments and expressions. *Three Volumes* (with its weeping white paint and wood encased in lead) features a few lines in Hungarian from a poem by Baráz (in English, the lines read: "This book is about nothing/Mute and loud/Sitting on the throne of the eye"). Part of a new series of books with massive limestone pages, *First Edition* alludes to the indestructibility – and fragility – of the Book as an embodiment of the human spirit. Baráz's stele-like volumes have a presence both grief-laden and warmly evocative of the solace books can afford, as Austrian poet Ingeborg Bachmann has written, "in more intensely helping people live."

Just as Baráz browses through books, he browses through the physical world, always in search of materials to rescue and reuse. To glean, to forage, to scavenge: in the modern tradition, there is an important lineage of artists who have been drawn, even compelled, to reuse found materials. Think of Marcel Duchamp and his *Fountain* (urinal) of 1917, of the Cubists and their fragments of newspaper, of Kurt Schwitters and his collaged universe of Merz, of the Italian movement Arte Povera and its emphasis on nontraditional materials, of Louise Nevelson and her massive sculptures made of scavenged wood, of Robert Rauschenberg's *Combines*. The terms *bricolage* and *assemblage* sum up this impulse: to gather from the environment existing materials and create from them imaginative and convincing works of art.

For Joseph Baráz, the search for found materials is almost as important as the found materials themselves, and the provenance or origin of a found object can lend power and meaning to any given work, separate from – in addition to – his own manipulations. Wallpaper from an abandoned miner's shack in the Rocky Mountains, a fragment of worked marble from a twelfth-century Spanish monastery, a chunk of Ponderosa pine from a log split for Baráz household firewood: all are grist for Baráz's mill. Whether he finds his pieces of stone in the shallows of San Francisco Bay, along the Brooklyn waterfront, or on the slopes of Mount Helena, the character of each stone – its history, texture, color, shape – leads him to his subject, just as much as any inspiration that may strike him exterior to the stone.

Most of the stone for Baráz's recent series of stelae (a series to which he has devoted much of his creative energy in recent years) came from a New Jersey stone yard, when the artist spent some years in the early 21st century working in New York City. These discarded Indiana limestone slabs, approximately one foot square, proved perfect for Baráz's purposes, perhaps reminding him of the Egyptian stelae he encountered as a boy. Devoid of any significant history, the tablets called for Baráz to paint them as if they were canvas or board. As Baráz points out, painting on stone sculpture has a long and distinguished history. The Greeks and Romans polychromed their marble figures; in the 19th century, echoing the Greeks, Jean-Léon Gérôme used tinted wax to add color to his figures; and most recently, between 1981 and 1987, Brice Marden created his thirty-two *Paintings on Marble* on the Greek island of Hydra, painting with oil on locally found marble fragments.

Commenting on Baráz's stelae featured in a 2002 one-man exhibition in New Jersey, critic Tony Sienzant wrote, "The slabs . . . appear as fossil artifacts from an archaeological dig with his delicately etched . . . forms seeming to be the result of natural geological processes and the crude edges of the rock recalling excavated stones from antiquity." Before painting his stelae, Baráz incises, carves, and even, in Sienzant's phrase, "whacks into them with an axe." Working with tremendous energy and focus, he then paints on the stone, with oil or occasionally acrylic, images from his personal iconography: faces, flowers, torsos, landscapes.

Always speaking from a sensibility steeped in many traditions, these rusticated works are totems for our time, fetishes that emanate power, sometimes disquieting, often strangely (and wonderfully) reassuring. They are humble, and in their humility, they express, in Baráz's words, the "beauty of decay," of infinite (and intimate) cycles of birth, death, and rebirth. One could echo, in speaking of the art of Joseph Baráz, the German sculptor Wilhelm Lehmbruck (1881–1919): "Every work of art must carry with it a trace of the first days of creation – the smell of the earth, one might say. Something animal." And something truly human.

Abstracted from the Earth
The Art of Barry Hood

Originally published in Rick Newby & Brandon Reintjes, *Barry Hood: Flow* (Helena, MT: Holter Museum of Art, 2010).

From the beginning of his immersion in glass, Montana artist Barry Hood has focused his energies on depicting, echoing, articulating, and interpreting natural images, forms, and forces. Grounded in the Montana landscape, Hood is drawn to simplicity and purity, to vast spaces, states of water, fragments of plants.

Glass, Hood admits, can be overwhelmingly seductive: the flowing shapes, the gorgeous colors, the luminosity of the medium itself. And yet many of Hood's works have little of the traditional "beauty" associated with glass objects. They are not refined, smooth, or instantly eye-dazzling. Instead, they remind the viewer of the results of transformative natural processes, of volcanic rock or ice riven by sun and frozen again. They resemble the remains of something as yet undiscovered. And as manmade objects, they suggest an affinity with Japanese, and particularly Zen, aesthetics, in which spontaneity, earthiness, apparent rusticity, imperfection, even "corrosion and contamination" are found in works that are spiritually rich and that embody a quiet beauty, in Leonard Koren's words, "of the inconspicuous and overlooked aspects of nature."[1]

As a youth, Hood spent three years in Japan, and he was profoundly influenced by the artfully arranged relationships between the manmade and the natural – the vastly "different visual order"[2] – he encountered in Japanese temples and gardens. As curator Brandon Reintjes notes, Hood was also influenced by the Montana tradition of ceramic modernism embodied by Rudy Autio, his teacher at the University of Montana, and Peter Voulkos. In addition to abstract expressionism, both Autio and Voulkos were profoundly impacted by their encounters with Japanese ceramic tradition, particularly in the person of Shoji Hamada, who led a workshop at Montana's Archie Bray Foundation for the Ceramic Arts in 1952. Rudy Autio

1   Leonard Koren, *Wabi-Sabi: for Artists, Designers, Poets & Philosophers* (Berkeley: Stone Bridge Press, 1994), 22.

2   All quotations by Barry Hood, unless otherwise acknowledged, are drawn from a series of interviews with the author, Helena, Montana, 2003, 2007, and 2010.

later asserted, "Shoji Hamada, more than any other person, gave me an insight into what clay was about."[3] Autio then transmitted this sense of Japanese aesthetics, leavened by postwar American anxieties and energies, to a young Barry Hood.

Despite the direct influence of Rudy Autio, it is another Montana ceramic artist whose work has most inspired, and most closely resembles, that of Barry Hood. During his years in Montana's Flathead/Glacier region, Hood came to know and admire ceramist David Shaner, a former director of the Archie Bray Foundation and longtime resident of Big Fork on Flathead Lake's northeastern shore. Shaner, who fought passionately for the preservation of western wilderness, once wrote, "The evolution of forms in nature have always intrigued me – the weathering action of rocks . . . the smoothness of textures, and the subtleties of colors."[4] In a monograph devoted to Shaner's lifetime of work, the authors note, "Shaner represented nature directly in his sculptural works with his 'landscape plates' and the slabs he painted with leaves, reeds and grasses."[5]

Like Shaner, Barry Hood has found the natural world to be an inexhaustible – and the most important – source of subject matter. Hood's *Studies for Extinction,* with their imbedded "leaves, stems and grasses," echo the elegant simplicity of Shaner's plates, casseroles, and other pottery forms of the 1960s and 70s. And Hood's *Harts,* like Shaner's *Cirques* of the 1990s, his "most organic and complex forms," move beyond mimesis into an extraordinary expression, even embodiment, of natural processes.[6]

Just as important as Asian aesthetic principles or the work of other artists to Hood's work (and life) has been his experience of the Montana landscape. He grew up in a military family, and although the Hood family was continually moving, Montana was always home. His great-grandfather, George McCone, had been a Pony Express rider and prominent pioneer at Glendive in eastern Montana, bringing the first cattle herd into the county and serving as a state senator.

---

3   Rudy Autio, interview by Chere Jiusto and Rick Newby, Missoula, MT, November 3, 1998, Archie Bray Foundation Archives, Helena, MT.

4   David Shaner, quoted in *Following the Rhythms of Life: The Ceramic Art of David Shaner,* ed. Peter Held (Tempe: Arizona State University Art Museum, 2008), 45.

5   Ibid., 46–47.

6   Ibid., 50.

Often visiting cousins in Glendive, Hood was fascinated by the endless prairies of the "Big Open," and he would later say, "Some people feel [eastern Montana] is desolate; it's very flat and rolling country, with the predominant element being the sky. I'd go up to the hills or down to the river, overwhelmed with the expanse of the sky, the sacredness of it. . . . it was imbedded in me." This sense of spaciousness echoed Hood's experience of open space in Japanese architecture, painting, and gardens. He noted, "They [the Japanese] are so cramped in, physically; but it's part of their religious impulse that they find ways to transcend it."[7] This sense, in Hood's words, of a "nothingness that is something" – both Japanese and Montanan – has informed his work ever since.

Barry Hood has been a glass artist since 1974. In the early years, while he made his home in Whitefish, Montana, he worked primarily with etched glass, creating elegant large-scale commissions for public buildings and private homes. Even then, his subdued palette – his "airbrushing without color" – and his subject matter (shining mountains, surging trout streams, aspen groves) suggested a sensibility more attuned to the quieter rhythms of nature than to the high drama, even gaudiness, of much glass art. Hood achieved considerable recognition with his etched panels, and they have been featured in *Glass Art, Glass Artist, Sunset Magazine,* and *Southwest Art,* as well as the book, *Etched Glass: Techniques and Design* (Hand Books Press, 1998).

Despite his evident success, Hood turned his energies in the late 1990s to exploring new bodies of work that have taken him far from the precision and control of his etched glass. Not only was Hood eager to move from the appearance of spontaneity to a real spontaneity, he sought also to move from depictions of the natural world – the etched landscapes of his windows and doors – to the creation of glass objects that were, as in Zen tradition, "only slightly abstracted from the earth." He wanted to acknowledge, as directly as possible, the "beautiful gifts" the natural world has given him over

---

7   Michael Major, "The spaciousness of glass. . . the art of Barry Hood," *Glass Artist,* No. 4 (August/September 1995), 50.

decades spent among Montana's rivers, mountains, and prairies.

In 1998, at Pilchuck Glass School, Hood tried something new. He found a downed tree, hollowed out a section, and poured molten glass into the log. Unlike a traditional mold, where the material is impervious to temperatures upwards of 2,200 degrees, the wood burned. As the glass moved toward a solid state, it continued to interact with the burning wood, a process that was impossible to control (and hence all the more exciting because it was wholly spontaneous). The shifting of the glass within the log created an impossible-to-replicate texture: ridged and pitted, bubbled and bumped: the product of a burning tree's heart. These *Harts,* as Hood calls them, remain central to his artistic enterprise; they are "as good as it gets."

Since 2005, in addition to the ongoing work on his *Harts,* Hood has elaborated a series of sand castings. For these *Studies for Extinction,* he creates simple molds (arches and rectangles) in specially formulated sand, places botanical specimens (sheafs of wheat, aspen leaves, pinecones, and twigs) in the forms, and then pours 2,300-degree glass into the molds. The molten glass vaporizes the specimens, and Hood is left with glass panels etched, not by the human hand, but with "vestiges of carbon." Like his *Harts,* these *Studies* are true collaborations, products of a genuine yoking of the human and the non-human. There is something haunting about these shadowy images. They are not representations of things; they are the things themselves, immolated. They draw us in, through their evident fragility. They are totems or talismans, quiet celebrations of a vanishing earth.

"I'm not interested in something that's simply pretty," Hood reiterates. While Hood's etched glass had always been without color – he achieved the effects he wanted through subtle gradations of shading – with his recent work, he finds himself drawn, not to a rainbow of colors, but to color nevertheless. Using dyes and natural earth pigments, Hood achieves colors of a simplicity and elegance congruent with the rugged shapes and surface textures of the works themselves.

Barry Hood's *Harts,* his *Studies for Extinction,* and his *Poems for the Blind* (which incorporate Sufi poems inscribed in Braille) represent spectacular leaps of faith, a willingness to relinquish control in favor of improvisations that owe their success as much to the character of organic materials and the nature of fire as to the artist's design. Like the great Japanese potter Shoji Hamada, Barry Hood "works more in Grace, than in one's own power,"[8] and by so doing, he has created his finest, his most powerful and spiritually resonant, works to date.

---

8 Shoji Hamada, quoted in Soetsu Yanagi, *The Unknown Craftsman: A Japanese Insight into Beauty* (New York: Kodansha, 1972), 224.

Acknowledgments

First, I offer my deep thanks to my publisher, Aaron Parrett, PhD, executive director of Drumlummon Institute and a singular force in Montana arts. Together with that of the amazing Drumlummon board of directors, present and past, Aaron's support for my work in writing, editing, and publishing has been essential and inspiriting.

Thank you to my cherished friend Melissa Kwasny for her lovely foreword, and to Chere Jiusto for her superb work on our joint essay on the origins of the Archie Bray Foundation. I'm exceedingly grateful to the two designers – Geoffrey Wyatt and Eric Heidle – who did such fine work on this book. I thank, too, my writing community: Melissa and Chere, Bill Borneman, Krys Holmes, Matt Pavelich, Aaron Parrett, Roger Dunsmore, Jenni Fallein, Max Milton, Martha Kohl, Brandon Reintjes, Scott Hibbard, Sandra Dal Poggetto, Paul S. Piper, Caroline Patterson, Tom Harpole, Phil Cohea, Mark Gibbons, Niki Whearty, Randall LeCocq, Ken Egan, Tami Haaland, Patrica Vettel-Becker, Kirby Lambert, Jennifer Bottomly-O'looney, Marc Brenman, Patty Dean, Zachary Winestine, Joanne Pawlowski, David Axelrod, Drew Livesay, Mandy Smoker, Andrew Guschausky, Janet Henderson, Debra Magpie Earling, Robert Stubblefield, Paul Zarzyski, Bob Durden, Michele Corriel, Craig Lancaster, Russell Rowland, Allen Morris Jones, O. Alan Weltzien, and Gordon McConnell. A special thanks to Peter Rutledge Koch, Susan Filter, and Robert Bringhurst, who encouraged my peculiar passion for the histories of bookishness and modernism in Montana culture. Thanks too to Jim Todd and Henry Hunt, who first led me to the study of art history.

My heartfelt thanks to the periodical and book editors who published many of these essays, introductions, prefaces, and reviews. They include Harry Dennis and Ron Kuchta, *American Ceramics*; Lois Moran and Beverly Sanders, *American Craft*; Janet Mansfield, *Ceramics: Art and Perception*, Australia; Emmanuel Cooper, *Ceramic Review*, UK; Shwu-chun Huang, *Hsiung Shih* magazine, Taipei; Kostas Tarkassis, *Kerameiki Techni*, Athens; Marilyn Lysohir, *[high ground]* magazine; Glenn Harper, *Sculpture*; Jim Rains, *North Country Review*; Randy Provence and Austin Boyd, *Kinesis*; Robert Wrigley, Bill Turner, and Steven Christenson, *CutBank*; Lowell Uda and Phil Cohea, *Scratchgravel Hills*; Marianne Keddington, *Oregon Historical Quarterly*; Martha Kohl and Molly Holz, *Montana The Magazine of Western History*; Suzanne Hunger, *Writing Montana: Literature Under the Big Sky*; Chris Cauble, *The New Montana Story: An Anthology*; Lee Rostad, *Food of Gods and Starvelings: The Selected Poems of Grace Stone Coates*; Alexandra Swaney, *Notes for a Novel: The Selected Poems of Frieda Fligelman*; Bill Borneman and Scott Mainwaring, *Splendid on a Large Scale: The Writings of Hans Peter Gyllembourg Koch, Montana Territory, 1869–1874*; Marvin Sweet, *The Yixing Effect: Echoes of the Chinese Scholar*; Aaron Parrett, *On the Chinese Wall: New & Selected Poems, 1966–2018*, by Roger Dunsmore; Caroline Patterson, *We Proceeded On*; and Charles Finn, Stacy Miller, and Corey Oglesby, *High Desert Journal*.

I would also like to thank the museum and gallery professionals who commissioned a number of these essays for exhibition catalogs. These include Peter Held, Mary Evellyne Sorrell, Brandon Reintjes, Liz Gans, Marcia Eidel, and Yvonne Seng, Holter Museum of Art; Ben Mitchell, Yellowstone Art Museum; Peter Held, Ceramic Research Center, Arizona State University Art Museum; Matt West, Fine Arts Gallery, Laramie County Community College; Maggie Mudd, University Galleries, University of Montana, Missoula; Madeline Mallee, University of South Australia Art Museum; J. Scott Patnode, Jundt Art Museum, Gonzaga University; Emily Galusha, Northern Clay Center; Laura Millin and Stephen Glueckert, Missoula Art Museum; Peter and Turkey Stremmel, Stremmel Gallery; William Lieberman, Zolla/Lieberman Gallery; John Natsoulas, John Natsoulas Gallery; Valerie Serpa and Kirk Robertson; Churchill Arts Council; Holly Hanessian, National Council on Education for the Ceramic Arts; Joe Freeman Gans, JFG Temporary; and Amy Ruffo and Lena Vigna, John Michael Kohler Arts Center.

Thanks are due, too, to those folks at cultural institutions who commissioned talks on a variety of subjects. They are Donna Forbes, Gordon McConnell, Adrea Sukin, Jet Holubek, and Ben Mitchell, Yellowstone Art Museum; Ralph Beer, Carroll College; Susan Filter and Peter Koch, Colophon Club of San Francisco; Dr. William Farr and the Honorable Pat Williams, O'Connor Center for the Rocky Mountain West; and Audrey Cameron, University of Montana–Helena.

Finally, and above all, I acknowledge my beloved wife and most important collaborator, Elizabeth Antony Gans, for her abiding love, her brilliant insights, and her unexampled patience over the past nearly thirty-five years. It has been a marvelous journey.

Note: I've provided full publications credits in a headnote to each piece in this book.

Contributors

Chere Jiusto studied Fine Arts at the University of Montana and then moved to Helena to work as a Resident Artist at the Archie Bray Foundation for the Ceramic Arts. Her interest in historic places and the arts took her into a 40-year career in public interpretation and historic preservation throughout Montana. She served with the Montana Historical Society as the Curator of History for permanent exhibits on state history, then oversaw the state's National Register of Historic Places program. From there, she took on the role of Executive Director of Preserve Montana, a role she held for over 20 years.

An accomplished historian and writer, Ms. Jiusto co-wrote the essay "'A Beautiful Spirit': Origins of the Archie Bray Foundation for the Ceramic Arts" in 2001 with author Rick Newby, and she co-authored the book *Hand-Raised: The Barns of Montana* with Christine Brown, which received a 2012 High Plains Book Award. In 2017 Chere received a Montana Governor's Award for the Humanities, and in 2023 her outstanding contributions in the field were honored by a Montana State Historic Preservation Award. She lives in Helena with her journalist husband Jim Robbins and has recently retired, returning to her artistic roots and working in her home studio while still exploring the past and writing about the rich heritage of Montana.

Melissa Kwasny is the author of seven books of poetry, most recently *Where Outside the Body is the Soul Today* (Pacific Northwest Poetry Series, University of Washington Press) and the forthcoming *The Cloud Path* (Milkweed Editions 2024), as well as a collection of essays *Earth Recitals: Essays on Image and Vision*. Her first full-length nonfiction book, *Putting on the Dog: The Animal Origins of What We Wear*, explores the cultural, labor, and environmental histories of clothing materials provided by animals. She is also the editor of two anthologies: *I Go to the Ruined Place: Contemporary Poets in Defense of Global Human Rights* and *Toward the Open Field: Poets on the Art of Poetry 1800–1950*. She was Montana Poet Laureate from 2019–2021, a position she shared with M. L. Smoker.

Born in Kalispell, Montana, and educated at the University of Montana, **Rick Newby** is a poet, cultural journalist, independent scholar, and editor. Rick is the editor or co-editor of the anthologies *Writing Montana: Literature Under the Big Sky* (with Suzanne Hunger); *An Ornery Bunch: Tales and Anecdotes Collected by the W.P.A. Montana Writers' Project* (with Megan Hiller, Alexandra Swaney, and Elaine Peterson); and *The New Montana Story.* He is also editor of *Food of Gods and Starvelings: The Selected Poems of Grace Stone Coates* (with Lee Rostad); *Notes for a Novel: The Selected Poems of Frieda Fligelman* (with Alexandra Swaney); and Roger Dunsmore's *On the Chinese Wall: New & Selected Poems, 1966–2018.*

In the field of western studies, Rick is the editor of *On Flatwillow Creek: The Story of Montana's N Bar Ranch* by Linda Grosskopf; *The Rocky Mountain Region,* The Greenwood Encyclopedia of American Regional Cultures; *A Most Desperate Situation: Frontier Adventures of a Young Scout, 1858–1864,* by Walter Cooper (illustrations by Charles M. Russell); *In Poetic Silence: The Floral Paintings of Joseph Henry Sharp,* by Thomas Minckler; and *The Whole Country was . . . "One Robe": The Little Shell Tribe's America,* by Nicholas C. P. Vrooman.

Rick writes regularly about modern and contemporary art, and his essays on ceramic artists, painters, sculptors, and photographers have appeared in national and international journals and in numerous exhibition catalogs. Rick's most recent book on a visual artist is the monograph *Theodore Waddell – My Montana: Paintings & Sculpture, 1959–2016,* which received the High Plains Book Award, Art/Photography, 2018.

Rick's books of poetry include *A Radiant Map of the World* (recipient of the Montana Arts Council's 1981 First Book Award); *The Man in the Green Loden Overcoat,* with artist Jack Jasper (1983); *Old Friends Walking in the Mountains,* etchings by Doug Turman (1994); *The Suburb of Long Suffering* (2002); and *Sketches Begun in My Studio on a Sunday Afternoon and Completed the Following Day Near the Noon Hour on the Lower Slopes of the Rocky Mountains* (2008). As a poet, Rick has collaborated with printmakers, painters, sculptors, photographers, ceramic artists, videographers, performance artists, other poets, and jazz and classical musicians.

A past member of the Montana Arts Council and the Board

of Directors of the Montana Center for the Book, Rick served from 2006–2017 as the executive director of Drumlummon Institute and editor of the online arts journal *Drumlummon Views*. In 2009, Rick received the Montana Governor's Award for the Humanities, and in 2016, he received the Montana Governor's Award for the Arts.

Rick makes his home in Helena, Montana, and San Francisco with his wife Liz Gans.